CORPORATE FINANCE

A VALUATION APPROACH

McGraw-Hill Series in Finance

Archer and Kerr: Readings and Cases in Corporate Finance
Ball and Kothari: Financial Statement Analysis
Beaver and Parker: Risk Management: Problems and Solutions
Benninga and Sarig: Corporate Finance: A Valuation Approach
Bergfield: California Real Estate Law
Blake: Financial Market Analysis
Bowlin, Martin and Scott: Guide to Financial Analysis
Brealey and Myers: Principles of Corporate Finance
Brealey, Myers and Marcus: Fundamentals of Corporate Finance
Chew: The New Corporate Finance
Coates: Investment Strategy
Cottle, Murray and Block: Security Analysis
Doherty: Corporate Risk Management: A Financial Exposition
Dubofsky: Options and Financial Futures: Valuation and Uses
Edmister: Financial Institutions: Markets and Management
Edwards and Ma: Futures and Options
Farrell: Portfolio Management: Theory and Application
Francis: Investments: Analysis and Management
Francis: Management of Investments
Garbade: Securities Markets
Gibson: Option Valuation: Analyzing and Pricing Standardized Option Contracts
Hayes and Hubbard: Investment Banking
Heck: The McGraw-Hill Finance Literature Index
Ibbotson and Brinson: Investments Markets: Gaining the Performance Edge
James and Smith: Studies in Financial Institutions: Commercial Banks
Jarrow: Modelling Fixed Income Securities and Interest Rate Options
Johnson: Financial Institutions and Markets: A Global Perspective
Kau and Sirmans: Real Estate
Kester and Luehrman: Case Problems in International Finance
Kohn: Financial Institutions and Markets
Lang: Strategy for Personal Finance
Levi: International Finance: The Markets and Financial Management of Multinational Business
McLoughlin: Principles of Real Estate Law
Martin, Petty and Klock: Personal Financial Management
Peterson: Financial Management and Analysis
Riehl and Rodriguez: Foreign Exchange and Money Market
Robertson and Wrightsman: Financial Markets
Rothstein: The Handbook of Financial Futures
Schall and Haley: Introduction to Financial Management
Silverman: Corporate Real Estate Handbook
Sirmans: Real Estate Finance
Smith: The Modern Theory of Corporate Finance
Williams, Smith and Young: Risk Management and Insurance

CORPORATE FINANCE

A VALUATION APPROACH

Simon Z. Benninga
School of Business, Hebrew University, Jerusalem, Israel
Wharton School, University of Pennsylvania

Oded H. Sarig
Faculty of Management, Tel Aviv University, Israel
Wharton School, University of Pennsylvania

THE McGRAW-HILL COMPANIES, INC.

New York   St. Louis   San Francisco   Auckland   Bogotá   Caracas   Lisbon
London   Madrid   Mexico City   Milan   Montreal   New Delhi
San Juan   Singapore   Sydney   Tokyo   Toronto

McGraw-Hill
A Division of The McGraw·Hill Companies

To our families

CORPORATE FINANCE
A Valuation Approach

This book is printed on acid-free paper.

2 3 4 5 6 7 8 9 0   FGR   FGR   9 0 9 8 7

ISBN 0-07-005099-6

This book was printed in Times Roman by Ruttle, Shaw & Wetherill, Inc.
The editors were Michelle E. Cox and Judy Howarth;
the production supervisor was Kathryn Porzio.
The cover was designed by Joan Greenfield.
Project supervision was done by The Total Book.
Quebecor Printing/Fairfield was printer and binder.

Cover photograph by Reza Estakhrian/Tony Stone Images.

Library of Congress Cataloging-in-Publication Data

Benninga, Simon.
    Corporate finance : a valuation approach / Simon Benninga. Oded H.
Sarig.
        p.   cm. — (McGraw-Hill series in finance)
    Includes index.
    ISBN 0-07-005099-6
    1. Corporations—Valuation.   2. Corporations—Finance.   I. Sarig,
Oded H.   II. Title.   III. Series.
HG4028.V3B376   1997
    658.15—dc20   96-7925

International Edition

When ordering this title, use ISBN 0-07-114072-7.

ABOUT
THE AUTHORS

Simon Z. Benninga is currently associated with the School of Business at the Hebrew University of Jerusalem (where he chairs the finance group) and the Wharton School of the University of Pennsylvania. Professor Benninga has published in a wide range of finance and economics journals on topics including corporate finance, computational finance, and equilibrium models in micro and macro economics. He is the author of "Numerical Techniques in Finance," published by MIT Press in 1989, and the editor of the European Finance Review.

Oded H. Sarig is chair of the finance department at the Recanati School of Business Administration of Tel Aviv University. He is also associated with the Wharton School of the University of Pennsylvania. Professor Sarig has published in a wide range finance journals on topics including corporate finance, asset pricing, and equilibrium models in finance.

TEXT CREDITS

CONTENTS
IN BRIEF

CONTENTS

PREFACE

Almost every undergraduate and graduate program in finance has a corporate finance course that extensively uses case analysis. These courses focus on the use of financial tools in valuation. However, there is a serious lack of integrated textual material for these courses. In *Corporate Finance: A Valuation Approach* we aim to fill this gap.

Corporate Finance: A Valuation Approach is a self-contained, detailed description of the valuation process intended both for those who want to understand valuations and for those who plan to do valuations. Such an understanding can affect the handling of many aspects of the firm: the choice of strategic alliances, the selection among several possible lines of business, the combination of securities issued, and the design of compensation packages.

The materials in *Corporate Finance: A Valuation Approach* have been classroom-tested extensively and used successfully with both MBAs and undergraduates. We have used the book both to accompany case courses in corporate finance and as an independent text. Extensive introductory material and an accompanying instructor's manual make the book completely self-contained.

Corporate Finance: A Valuation Approach provides an integrated, comprehensive method of valuing assets, firms, and securities. We begin with a review of the financial and accounting techniques needed for the implementation of a full valuation. We proceed with a detailed discussion of the valuation process, leading the reader from the very first steps of building pro-forma financial statements, through the translation of these projections to values, to the division of firm value among the different security holders of the firm: shareholders, debt holders, and convertible security holders.

Our book integrates the three most important elements required for valuation:

1 *Consistent theoretical foundation to valuation.* We give students a unified, operational, and theoretically consistent approach to valuation. The primary emphasis of *Corporate Finance: A Valuation Approach* is the discounted cash-flow (DCF) approach to valuation, which incorporates modern capital structure theory and market-based cost of capital models. We also discuss multiple-based valuation as an alternative to DCF, relating multiples to the same theoretical foundations as DCF.

2 *Integrated structural approach to valuation.* A structural approach to valuation inculcates an invaluable discipline, leading the student to understand all aspects of the firm— operational and financial. In the integrated approach of this book, the marketing and operating aspects of the firm are translated into an integrated pro-forma statement (a subject rarely discussed in finance textbooks), the risk characteristics of the firm are embedded into the discount rate and the valuation multiples, and the financial contracts issued by the firm determine how value is divided among the various claimants.

3 *A series of consistent, worked-out applications.* At every juncture we provide the student and the instructor with examples which are true to life, thoroughly worked out, and reflective of the underlying theory:

- In Chapter 2 we use IBM financial statements to illustrate the relation between accounting statements and cash flows. The hypothetical case of Hacker Computers illustrates the basic principles of financial accounting and their relation to finance theory.
- Our Motel Case in Chapter 3 gives a preliminary example of cash budgeting and the valuation process. We build a cash-flow statement for a small business and use this cash-flow statement for valuation and for discussion of the effect of inflation and the use of multiples.
- In Chapter 4 we provide students with four easy-to-follow examples of pro-forma models. Each example illustrates a different aspect of the modeling techniques that make pro formas such a powerful tool.
- Our analysis of Acme Cleveland in Chapter 6 shows how to do a thorough financial statement analysis of a company and its industry.
- In Chapter 7 we show how J. M. Smucker Co. makes integrated use of techniques from three previous chapters. We construct a detailed pro-forma model which combines the formal aspects of pro-forma modeling (Chapter 4), an analysis of the firm's environment (Chapter 5), and a financial statement analysis (Chapter 6).
- In Chapter 9 we illustrate various methods of estimating the cost of capital using firms in the furniture industry as examples.
- In Chapter 10 we illustrate valuation by multiples using firms in the retail and airline industries.
- In Chapter 11 we illustrate the valuation of warrants using data from J. M. Smucker Co. and the valuation of convertible bonds using the Home Depot Inc. convertibles.
- Boeing is used to illustrate our calculation of debt securities value in Chapter 12.

ACKNOWLEDGMENTS

We have benefited from the comments of a superb set of academic reviewers: James Bicksler, Rutgers University; Michael Bond, Cleveland State University; Richard DeMong, University of Virginia; Michael Fishman, Northwestern University; Atul Gupta, Bentley College; Daniel Indro, Kent State University; Surendra Mansinghka, San Francisco State University; Hamid Mehran, Northwestern University; Mike Ryngaert, University of Florida; Louis Scott, University of Georgia; John Settle, Portland State University; Robert Tollen, The University of Texas at El Paso; and Ken Yook, St. Cloud State University.

We have used parts of this book in teaching classes at the Hebrew University of Jerusalem, Tel Aviv University, the Wharton School of the University of Pennsylvania, and the University of Frankfort. Many friends, students, and colleagues (these are often overlapping categories) have given us input, advice, and helpful comments. Among those to whom we owe a vote of thanks: Yakov Amihud, Rajat Bagrodia, Sasson Bar-Yosef, Eli Berkowitz, Roberta Coats, Theo Dagi, Tom Elletson, Arash Farin, John Ferrari, Mike Fink, Jamshed Ghandi, Tolga Habip, Nicholai, Hel, Yotaro Hongo, Shmuel Kandel, Doron Kliger, Michael Lau, Chris Leach, Kris Mack, Rob Mann, Rich McConnell, Dan Mingelgrin, Alex Mogel, Mary Grace Neviler, Roni Ofer, Susan Pass, Brett Patelsky, Megha Patodia, Barbara Pocalyko, Michael Pocalyko, Ariel Shenhar, Avi Shimoni, Dov Shmueli, Yael Shomron, Lawrence Singer, Harprit Singh, Bob Vicente, and Avi Wohl. Finally, we would like to thank the wonderful staff of McGraw-Hill who worked with us on this book.

Simon Z. Benninga
Oded H. Sarig

CHAPTER 1

FINANCIAL VALUATION TOOLS

OVERVIEW

Throughout this book we assume that you have mastered the use of the fundamental tools of financial analysis. To establish a common terminology used in subsequent chapters, we review these tools in this chapter. We examine the concepts of present value and net present value (NPV); discount factors and the term structure of interest rates, annuities, perpetuities, the Gordon formula, internal rates of return (IRR), risk-adjusted discount rates (RADR), the capital asset pricing model (CAPM), and beta; inflation, nominal and real interest rates, and the Fisher effect; and the law of one price and the principle of value additivity.

In this review we emphasize the valuation implications of financial tools. In particular, our starting point is the statement, from the perspective of a financial economist, that *the value of a security (or any other asset) is the value of the cash flows it will generate.* On the face of it, this definition of value seems almost to trivialize valuation problems: How difficult can it be to value *dollars*? Still, by now you probably know that a dollar is not a dollar is not a dollar—different dollars may have different characteristics, which means that the price investors are willing to pay *today* for dollars they expect to receive in the *future* depends on the characteristics of these dollars.

What distinguishes a dollar generated by a security from any other dollar? In other words, what are the characteristics that determine the value of a dollar that we expect a project to generate? Dollars differ by their:

- *Timing.* Dollars received early are worth more than dollars received later.
- *Risk.* Safer dollars are worth more than riskier dollars.

• *Purchasing power.* Dollars that can buy more goods are worth more than dollars that have lower purchasing power. That is, inflation matters.

• *Liquidity.* Dollars flowing out of liquid assets are worth more than dollars flowing out of assets that can be sold only at great expense or difficulty.

The technique for valuing cash-flow streams of differing characteristics is to assign to each cash flow a unit price—a price per dollar. The value of each component of a cash-flow stream is then this unit price times the number of dollars, and the value of the whole stream is the sum of the values of each of the components of the stream. The tools of financial economics basically help us to determine how many cents investors are willing to pay *today* for dollars of various characteristics. We review the treatment of differential timing, risk, purchasing power, and liquidity one at a time. To begin, we review the treatment of time (''the time value of money''). At this stage we abstract from the other issues by assuming that cash flows are riskless, of equal purchasing power, and perfectly liquid. We then consider:

• Risk and its effect on the prices of cash flows
• Changing purchasing power and its effect on the prices of cash flows
• Illiquidity and its effect on asset values relative to the values of otherwise identical but liquid assets

1.1   THE TIME VALUE OF MONEY

In this section we deal with the effect of time on the value of cash flows.[1] The idea is that while a dollar is a dollar is a dollar, a dollar received in the future has less value than a dollar received today. Thus, to value firms, their securities, or any other asset, we convert the future cash flows that these firms are expected to generate into equivalent amounts today, or into **present values.**

We denote cash flows by CF_t, where the subscript t denotes the time at which the cash flow is received or paid. To prevent confusion, we measure time (and all other variables used in this book) in units of years, with today as the time zero. Thus, a cash flow to be paid 6 months from today is denoted by $CF_{0.5}$ and a cash flow to be received 15 months from today is denoted by $CF_{1.25}$. CF_t denotes both cash payments and cash receipts: Cash receipts are positive flows, whereas cash payments are negative flows. For example, if you expect to *receive* $1,000 in 1 year, then $CF_1 = +1,000$; whereas if you expect to *pay* that sum in 1 year, then $CF_1 = -1,000$.

The present values of cash flows, which are the economic equivalent of cash flows in terms of *today's* dollars, are denoted by $PV(CF_t)$. We compute the present values of cash flows by attaching a per-dollar price to them—the **time-t discount**

---

[1]Throughout this book we calculate values by discounting *cash flows.* The derivation of cash flows in most corporate situations depends on understanding corporate financial statements. We discuss this topic in Chapter 2; this chapter also includes a review of basic financial accounting principles.

factors—denoted by **DF**$_t$**.** The present value of a future cash flow is the product of the price of a time-t dollar and the number of dollars to be paid:

$$PV(CF_t) = DF_t \cdot CF_t \tag{1.1}$$

For example, if investors are willing to pay $.80 *today* for each dollar to be paid in 3 years, then DF$_3$ = 0.80. Using DF$_3$, we can compute the amount that we are willing to pay today to receive *any amount* in 3 years: Say, if we expect in 3 years to receive a dividend of $150,000 from a stock, we value this dividend as

$$PV(CF_3 = \$150K) = .80 \cdot \$150K = \$120K$$

Assets typically generate multiple future cash flows—a *stream* of cash flows. The value of such an asset is the sum of the present values of each of the future cash flows, both inflows and outflows, that are associated with that asset. We convert each component of the cash-flow stream of the asset into an equivalent amount today by using the discount factor for the time of that cash flow. Adding these equivalent amounts gives the **net present value (NPV).** In notation, the NPV of an asset is calculated as

$$NPV = \sum_{t=0}^{T} DF_t \cdot CF_t \tag{1.2}$$

To illustrate the concept of NPV, consider the following situation. Suppose you have won a concession to broadcast the Super Bowl. The cost of the license is $150 million, to be paid immediately. In 3 months you will have to organize the cameras, crews, and so on, at a total cost of $360 million. In 4 months, when you receive the revenue from the commercials, you will collect $600 million. Someone who has not won the concession offers to buy your right for $60 million. Should you sell? (For the more ambitious person we can rephrase the question: "If you incorporate and go public, for what price would you sell shares in your firm?") To answer the question, you must first find the NPV of the concession. Looking at some market data, you find that the market price of a dollar in 3 months is $.90 and that the price of a dollar in 4 months is $.85.[2] Since you already know the future cash flows, you can now calculate the NPV of your concession (all figures in millions):

Time	CF		DF		PV(CF)
0.00	− 150	·	1.00	=	− 150
0.25	− 360	·	0.90	=	− 324
0.33	600	·	0.85	=	510
	Net present value				36

[2]As discussed below, the price of a dollar *today* is always 1. In other words, DF$_0$ = 1.

Thus, the NPV of the concession is $36 million. In your introductory finance course you have learned that an investment project should be accepted if and only if its NPV is positive. We can actually make a stronger statement about NPVs: *The NPV of an asset is the value you attach to the right to own the asset.* In our example you value the right to broadcast the Super Bowl at $36 million. If you sell this right, you will receive $60 million. Apparently, the other channel can generate a higher commercial revenue than you can! You are better off selling the concession for $60 million rather than running it by yourself. (Again, for the more ambitious entrepreneur, you should be willing to float shares in your franchise if the issue price exceeds $36 million divided by the number of shares.)

Where do discount factors come from? The price of a dollar today to be received in time t, DF_t, reflects the opportunity cost of funds invested today for t periods. Since for the present we are dealing with risk-free cash flows, we use the rate of return on risk-free investments to find the opportunity cost of risk-free funds. Denote the yield on a dollar invested in a risk-free instrument, such as a government bond, from today until time t by r_t.[3] Using r_t, which is called the **spot rate to time t,** we calculate the discount factor for time t as

$$DF_t = \frac{1}{(1 + r_t)^t} \tag{1.3}$$

For example, if the 1-year spot rate is 6 percent, then

$$DF_1 = \frac{1}{(1 + 6\%)^1} = \frac{1}{1.06} = 0.9434$$

and if the 2-year spot rate is 5 percent, then

$$DF_2 = \frac{1}{(1 + 5\%)^2} = \frac{1}{1.05^2} = 0.9070$$

The relation is true for maturities that are not necessarily whole years. For example, if the 15-month spot rate is 7 percent per annum, then

$$DF_{1.25} = \frac{1}{(1 + 7\%)^{1.25}} = \frac{1}{1.07^{1.25}} = 0.9189$$

Equation (1.3) gives a discount factor of 1.00 for time zero since $(1 + r_0)^0 = 1.0$ for all r_0. This is obvious since the price that we are willing to pay for a dollar

---

[3]An investment in government bonds is not literally risk free. Government bonds are only free of default risk since the government can always print money to pay back the bondholders. Holders of government bonds are subject to inflation risk—the risk that the purchasing power of the money they receive upon maturity will be different from the purchasing power of this money they projected when buying the bonds. Bondholders are also subject to a price risk in case they do not hold the bonds to maturity. We discuss these and other topics related to bond valuation in Chapter 11.

discount cash flows by using a nonflat term structure of interest rates, you have to discount *each cash flow separately* by using equation (1.3) to calculate discount factors for each cash flow. (See the box "A Small 'Bug' in the Standard Spreadsheet NPV Formula.")

If the actual or the approximate term structure of interest rates is flat, equation (1.4) simplifies to

$$\text{NPV} = \sum_{t=0}^{T} \text{CF}_t \cdot \frac{1}{(1 + r)^t} \tag{1.5}$$

The difference between equations (1.4) and (1.5) is that in equation (1.5) the spot rates of all dates are no longer indexed by time to maturity, since when the term structure is flat, spot rates to all maturities are equal. With this simplification, we can obtain formulas that give the values of simple cash-flow streams, which we discuss in the next section.

A SMALL "BUG" IN THE STANDARD SPREADSHEET NPV FORMULA

The first cell in the range to be discounted is the cash flow at the *end* of the current period (in this book, CF_1). The initial cash flow must be included as an *addition* to the formula (as shown).

Note that this is not true for the IRR (internal rates of return) formula; there the range must include all cash flows, from period 0 onward. The zero in the IRR formula is the starting point for the spreadsheet's algorithm for calculating the IRR. The precise value of this "guess" is not very important: Many guesses will lead to the same answer If the cash flows have two or more IRRs, they can usually be found by varying the guess.

Different spreadsheets have slightly different syntaxes for the IRR function. In Lotus and Quattro the function is written with the guess first, as @IRR (guess, cash flows). In Excel it is written as pictured here, with guess after the cash-flow range.

	B	C	D	E	F
4	year	cash flow			
5	0	−1000			
6	1	23			
7	2	124			
8	3	657			
9	4	550			
10	5	34			
11	6	234			
12					
13	interest	12.00%			
14	npv	74.41	<– =NPV(C13,C6..C11)+C5		
15	irr	14.29%	<– =IRR(C5..C11,0)		

1.2 SIMPLE FORMULAS

In many valuation problems we face a constant cash-flow stream that lasts for N periods, starting at the end of the first period. We call such a cash-flow stream an **annuity.** Examples of annuities include mortgage payments, car loan payments, and lease payments. For convenience, we think of each period as a year (hence, the name annuity), but the analysis can easily take into account monthly payments and quarterly payments. Since an annuity is comprised of *equal* periodic cash flows, we can take them out of the summation in equations (1.4) and (1.5). For a flat term structure this gives

$$\text{NPV} = \text{CF} \cdot \sum_{t=1}^{N} \frac{1}{(1 + r)^t} \tag{1.6}$$

This means that if we know the NPV of an annuity of $1 per payment ($\text{CF}_t = 1$, $t = 1, \ldots, N$), we can easily value *any* annuity of the same duration: We only have to multiply the known value of the $1 annuity by the number of dollars per period in the annuity we want to value. We refer to an annuity of $1 per period as a **standard annuity** and denote its value by **PVA.** The present value of a standard annuity—PVA—is a sum of a geometric progression.[5] Simplifying this expression, we obtain the present value of an annuity that lasts for N years if the term structure of interest rates is flat:

$$\text{PVA}(N, r) = \frac{1}{r} - \frac{1}{r} \cdot \frac{1}{(1 + r)^N} \tag{1.7}$$

For example, a 5-year standard annuity is worth 3.9927 if the spot rate for each of years 1–5 is 8 percent per annum. Using PVA(5, 8%), we can value a nonstandard 5-year annuity under an 8 percent interest. For example, the present value of a lease contract of $24,000 per year is obtained by multiplying PVA(5, 8%) = 3.9927 by 24,000 to get $95,825. (See the box "Calculation of Present Values of Annuities.")

From equation (1.6) we can obtain the value of a standard annuity lasting infinitely many periods, which is called a **perpetuity,** by allowing N in the formula to grow to infinity. This yields the present value of a standard perpetuity, **PVP,** as

$$\text{PVP}(r) = \frac{1}{r} \tag{1.8}$$

The value of a perpetuity is a specific case of a more general formula—**the Gordon formula.** The Gordon formula is very useful in valuations: Using the

---

[5]The first term in this progression—a_1—is $1/(1 + r)$ and the ratio of each term to the next term in the progression—q—is also $1/(1 + r)$. PVA is given by $a_1 \cdot (1 - q^N)/(1 - q)$, where N is the number of terms in the cash-flow stream being evaluated.

CALCULATION OF PRESENT VALUES
OF ANNUITIES

The PV(RATE, NPER, PMT) formula in Excel (and a similar function in Lotus) is used to calculate the present values of annuities of PMT dollars per period that last NPER periods at an interest rate of RATE. For example, PV(8%, 5, 1) gives the value of a standard annuity (i.e., $1 per period) that lasts 5 years at 8% interest (i.e., 3.9927). Similarly, PV(8%, 5, 24,000) gives the value of $95,825 for a 5-year annuity of $24,000 a year at 8 percent interest. (Note that the PV formula of Excel treats a positive PMT as an outflow, and thus returns a negative number when PMT > 0, and vice versa.)

formula, one can compute terminal values in cash-flow projections, appropriate earnings multiples, risk-adjusted discount rates, and more. The formula gives the present value of a constantly growing cash-flow stream under a flat term structure of interest rates. To illustrate its use, let P denote the market price of one share of stock, which we suppose equals the present value of all future dividends:

$$P = \sum_{i=1}^{\infty} \frac{D_t}{(1 + r)^t}$$

Here D_t denotes the expected dividend to be paid at time t and r denotes the discount rate.

Now suppose we assume that the dividends grow at a constant annual rate g. Under this assumption, and given the current level of dividends, D_0, we can rewrite the above equation as

$$P = \sum_{t=1}^{\infty} \frac{D_t}{(1 + r)^t} = \sum_{t=1}^{\infty} \frac{D_0(1 + g)^t}{(1 + r)^t}$$

Using the formula for the sum of a geometric series, we can write this last formula as

$$P = \frac{D_1}{r - g} \tag{1.9}$$

Note that next year's dividend, D_1, can be computed under the assumptions of the Gordon formula as $D_1 = D_0 \cdot (1 + g)$. Thus, we can rewrite the formula in terms of *this year's* dividends:

$$P = \frac{D_0(1 + g)}{r - g} \tag{1.10}$$

which is the Gordon formula.

The following is an illustration of one of the uses of the formula in valuation. Suppose, for example, you are valuing a stock. You have analyzed the firm's prospects; made specific profitability projections for the next, say, 3 years; and conclude that at the end of your projection period the firm will pay a dividend of $4 per share. Knowing that the firm will continue operating *beyond the projection period of 3 years,* you further project that in the long run dividends will grow at a 5 percent annual rate. Furthermore, suppose you think that the proper risk-adjusted discount rate for the shares is 10 percent. Using the Gordon formula, you can estimate the value of the stock *at the end of the 3-year projection period* by setting $D_0 = 4$, $g = 5\%$, and $r = 10\%$. This gives

$$P = \frac{D_0(1 + g)}{r - g} = \frac{4 \cdot (1.05)}{0.10 - 0.05} = 84$$

Another use of the Gordon formula turns the formula around and uses it to estimate the **risk-adjusted discount rate (RADR)** appropriate to a share from its market price.[6] Turning the Gordon formula around gives

$$r = \frac{D_0(1 + g)}{P} + g \qquad (1.11)$$

Thus, we can write the risk-adjusted **cost of equity** (i.e., the discount rate appropriate to discount shareholders' cash flows) as *the sum of the stock's expected dividend yield and the expected growth rate of the dividends.*

The following is an example of how you might use this version of the Gordon formula. Suppose a share of General Pills (GP) is currently selling for $53. GP has just paid a dividend of $8 per share. You believe that the dividend stream will grow, on average, by 6 percent per year. What is General Pill's cost of equity implied by its price and your projected dividend growth rate? To answer this question, we substitute into the Gordon formula and solve for the implied discount rate, r:

$$r = \frac{8 \cdot (1.06)}{53} + 0.06 = 0.22$$

So, General Pill's cost of equity is 22 percent.

The Gordon formula is simple but its simplicity is bought at a price of very strong assumptions that underlie its derivation. The Gordon formula assumes that the term structure of interest rates for *all* maturities is flat, or that the spot rate for 1 year equals the spot rate for year 2, 3, and so on. The Gordon formula also assumes that the growth rate of the cash flows is constant *forever.*

---

[6]We know we are cheating a bit here, since formally speaking we are still discussing *riskless* cash flows! But ... suppose we don't actually know the true growth rate of future dividends (because dividends are uncertain), but we let g denote the *expected growth of dividends.* Then the r we derive is quite properly the *risk-adjusted cost of equity.*

Despite its strong underlying assumptions, the Gordon formula is a very practical tool. In succeeding chapters we will use it to calculate terminal values in firm valuations where the assumptions of long-run constant growth rates and discount rates are plausible. We also use the formula to estimate costs of equity financing by employing the market price of the equity.

1.3 RISK ADJUSTMENTS

So far we have worked with certain cash flows and risk-free discount rates. This gives the following equation to use in calculating the value of an asset:

$$NPV = \sum_{t=0}^{T} \frac{CF_t}{(1 + r_t)^t}$$

Now we want to address the issue of how to accommodate uncertainty in valuing assets. When discussing uncertainty, we consider a situation where an action, such as the purchase of an asset, can lead to multiple outcomes, such as many possible returns on an investment.[7] The possible outcomes are mutually exclusive in that if one of the possible outcomes is realized, none of the other outcomes, which we considered possible at the outset, can also be realized. For example, you cannot realize a rate of return on your investment of 15 percent and *at the same time* realize a rate of return of 12 percent on the same investment, even though *when you bought the asset* you considered both rates of return possible. The possible outcomes are exhaustive in that one of the outcomes must be realized. For example, you must realize *some* rate of return on your investment.

Risk is a factor we have to take into account in valuing an asset. The "amount of risk" inherent in various investments affects their relative values. Nonetheless, the risk and the quality of investments are often unjustifiably mixed. It is useful to illustrate what we mean by *risk* with an example that makes clear that "a risky investment" and "a poor investment" are different concepts. Consider two assets that can both be bought for $10 at the beginning of the day and that will pay off at the end of the day. The first asset, asset A, will pay $9, whereas the second asset, asset B, will pay either $25 or $30. The cash flows of the two assets are presented below:

CASH FLOWS

Asset A	Asset B

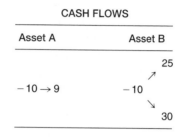

Clearly, the first asset is a poor investment prospect—you know *for sure* that by the end of the day you will have lost $1. It is similarly clear that the second asset is a good investment since at the end of the day you will have gained *at least* $15. So, the ranking of the assets in terms of their quality is clear. What about the ranking of the assets in terms of their risk? By now you must realize that the first asset is a *safe* investment, although a poor one, whereas the second asset is a *risky* investment, although a good one. Thus, *risk* and *value*, while related, are different concepts.

How do we describe uncertain prospects? We can enumerate all potential outcomes and their probabilities. This is what we typically do when building decision trees. Alternatively, we can describe the possible outcomes and their probabilities by using a formula, such as a statistical distribution function, to describe possible rates of return and their probabilities. Typically, we have a more modest goal than describing *all* possible outcomes and probabilities, and we describe uncertain prospects by using **summary statistics** that delineate certain properties of the risky outcome. The most common summary statistic that we use is the **mean, or average, or expected** outcome that depicts the central tendency of the distribution of possible outcomes. We denote the mean of an uncertain outcome x, or a **random variable** x, by either $E(x)$ or μ_x, and calculate it as

$$\mu_x = E(x) = \sum_{i=1}^{N} x_i \cdot p_i$$

where x_i denotes any of the N possible outcomes for x and p_i denotes the probability of each of the possible realizations of x.

A summary statistic that measures the dispersion of a random variable around its average is called the **variance** of the random variable and is denoted by σ_x^2. The variance is calculated by squaring the deviations from the mean before summing them, and thus converting negative deviations from the mean to positive numbers:

$$\sigma_x^2 = E[(x - \mu_x)^2] = \sum_{i=1}^{N} (x_i - \mu_x)^2 \cdot p_i$$

The variance is calculated by computing the average squared deviation. Thus, if the random variable of interest is returns on investments measured in percent per year, the variance of the return will be measured in units of percent squared per year squared, hardly an intuitive figure. Hence, we often use the square root of the variance of a random variable, or its **standard deviation,** $\sigma = \sqrt{\text{var}}$, to measure the dispersion of random variables using the same units of measurement with which we measure the original random variable.

Often we deal with more than one random variable. In this case, besides the properties of each of the variables, we would like to measure the extent to which these variables are correlated with each other. We use the **covariance (COV)** to measure the comovement of random variables. The covariance of random variables x and y, denoted by σ_{xy}, is calculated as

$$\sigma_{xy} = E[(x - \mu_x)(y - \mu_y)] = \sum_{i=1}^{N} (x_i - \mu_x)(y_i - \mu_y) \cdot p_i$$

The covariance of x and y will be positive if x tends to be *above* its mean whenever y is above its mean and will be negative if x tends to be *below* its mean whenever y is above its mean. Obviously, the covariance of x and y is the same as the covariance of y and x.

Finally, we can define the **correlation coefficient** as

$$\rho_{xy} = \frac{\sigma_{xy}}{\sigma_x \sigma_y}$$

The correlation coefficient is a measure of the *linear relation* between x and y. It is always between -1 and $+1$. If the correlation coefficient is $+1$ or -1, then the two distributions are **perfectly linearly correlated:**

$$x_i = a + by_i$$

$$\text{where } b > 0 \text{ if } \rho_{xy} = 1, \qquad b < 0 \text{ if } \rho_{xy} = -1$$

In the box ''Calculation of Means, Standard Deviations, Covariances, and Correlations'' we give an example of calculating some common summary statistics. As an exercise, graph the returns, year by year, to get a feeling for the meaning of the correlation coefficient.

Having defined all the terms that are necessary to review asset valuation under uncertainty, we can now turn to the discussion of this theory. When valuing assets under uncertainty, we cannot directly apply equation (1.4): The cash flows in each time period are no longer uniquely known—because the cash flows are uncertain, many realizations of the cash flows are possible at each date. We do, however, have *expectations* about these cash flows—their likely level and their risk. We use these expectations to convert equation (1.4) to a valuation formula that accommodates risk. There are two ways to take into account the risk in deriving the present values of risky cash flows:

The certainty-equivalent method. Adjust the *numerators* of present value calculations to reflect risk and then discount the resulting number by the *risk-free* discount rate. This is done by replacing the cash flows in equation (1.4) by their **certainty equivalents**—the *certain amounts* that we would be willing to accept *instead* of the risky cash flows. Since the certainty equivalent of a cash flow is already adjusted for the risk inherent in the flow, we discount certainty equivalents by using the risk-free discount rate.

Risk-adjusted discount rates. Adjust the *discount rates* to account for the risk

CALCULATION OF MEANS, STANDARD DEVIATIONS, COVARIANCES, AND CORRELATIONS

If you are unsure about calculating means, standard deviations, covariances, and correlations, see if you can replicate the following example (use a spreadsheet!).

Columns (1) and (2) give the returns on two stocks for the last 10 years. Calculate the mean and standard deviation of each stock's returns, assuming that the historical numbers are also the **distribution of next year's stock returns.**

Now calculate the difference between the mean return and each annual return. This should give you the numbers in columns (3) and (4). Multiplying these columns together times the probability (= 0.10) of each joint event should give you column (5).

Adding the entries in column (5) gives the *covariance* of the returns. Dividing this covariance by the product of the standard deviations gives the *correlation coefficient* of the returns.

	(1) Stock A	(2) Stock B	(3) R(A) − Mean	(4) R(B) − Mean	(5) Product * Probability
1	25.04%	6.08%	0.13901	−0.17466	−0.00243
2	21.86	32.55	0.10721	0.09004	0.00096
3	0.81	8.94	−0.10329	−0.14606	0.00151
4	7.65	−12.35	−0.03489	−0.35896	0.00125
5	22.43	34.88	0.11291	0.11334	0.00128
6	12.53	34.44	0.01391	0.10894	0.00015
7	33.55	9.68	0.22411	−0.13866	−0.00311
8	23.45	34.56	0.12311	0.11014	0.00135
9	−23.48	60.32	−0.34619	0.36774	−0.01273
10	−12.45	26.36	−0.23589	0.02814	−0.00066
Mean	11.14%	23.55%		Covariance	−0.0124
Sigma	18.15%	20.57%		Correlation	−0.3325

of cash flows. This is done by discounting the *expected* cash flows at a *risk-adjusted discount rate* that reflects the risk of the cash flows. In equation form we value assets under uncertainty by using the following equation:

$$\text{NPV} = \sum_{t=0}^{T} \frac{E(\text{CF}_t)}{(1 + r_t + \pi_t)^t} \tag{1.12}$$

where $E(\text{CF}_t)$ is the expected value of the cash flow at time t and π_t is the risk premium that is appropriate for the risk of CF_t. (The *risk premium* is the difference between the expected return of the asset and the risk-free rate: $\pi_i = E(r_i) - r_t$.) The sum of r_t and π_t is called the *risk-adjusted discount rate (RADR)*.

The second method is the one most commonly used. Here is an illustration of the method in an asset valuation context. We estimate that there is a 25 percent chance that an asset will pay $1,000 in 2 years and a 75 percent chance that it will pay $2,000. The 2-year spot rate is 3 percent *per year,* and we estimate that the risk of this cash flow should be compensated by an *annual* risk premium of 5 percent. What is the value of this asset?

The first step in analyzing this problem is to figure the expected cash flow in 2 years:

$$E(CF_2) = 1,000 \cdot 25\% + 2,000 \cdot 75\% = 250 + 1,500 = \$1,750$$

Something worth noting about the expected cash flow we have just calculated is that it is a cash flow that will never happen! The expected value measures the central tendency of the cash flows, in the sense that *deviations from the average add up to zero* (when weighted by the probabilities). But the actual expected cash flow in our example has zero probability of occurring.[8] Average values provide *some* information about the cash flows but are definitely not the whole picture.

Next we calculate the RADR as the sum of the pure time value of money, 3 percent; and the risk premium, 5 percent. The sum, 8 percent, is the RADR of the asset. Using this RADR, we find the value of the second-year expected cash flow as

$$PV(CF_2) = \frac{1,750}{(1 + 8\%)^2} = \frac{1,750}{1.1664} = \$1,500$$

Since the asset is expected to generate cash flows worth $1,500, the value of the asset is $1,500.

Where do risk premiums come from? The Capital Asset Pricing Model (CAPM) of Sharpe, Lintner, and Mossin is a theory of appropriate risk premiums. The CAPM pricing equation is part of the modern portfolio theory that prescribes well-diversified investment portfolios for investors who are interested in minimizing risk per unit of expected return. If investors hold diversified portfolios (in the formal derivation of the CAPM each investor holds the **market portfolio**—the portfolio that includes all the assets of the economy in proportion to their value), the risk of individual assets is measured *relative to the existing risk of the diversified portfolio*. It can be shown that the contribution of individual assets to the *total* risk of a portfolio is proportional to the *covariance* of the returns on this asset with the returns on the reference portfolio. It is, therefore, logical that the CAPM prescribes a risk premium that is proportional to this covariance.

The CAPM takes the reference portfolio to be the market portfolio. Since investors hold diversified portfolios, which are highly correlated with each other, we may use the CAPM as a good approximation for the risk-adjusted premium for investors with *any* diversified portfolio. The CAPM specifies that the risk premium commanded by any asset is proportional to the covariance of the returns on this asset with the returns on the market portfolio:

$$\pi_i \propto COV(r_i, r_m)$$

---

[8] Remember the statistician who drowned in a river whose *average* depth was 1 foot?

where π_i is the risk premium of asset i, r_i is the return on asset i, r_m is the return on the market portfolio, and "$\propto$" denotes "proportional to." Equivalently, we can write the CAPM formula for risk premiums as

$$\pi_i = k \cdot \text{COV}(r_i, r_m)$$

where k denotes the *price of risk per unit of covariance*. Since this relation holds for all assets, it also holds for the market portfolio. Using the market portfolio as a benchmark, we can calculate k:

$$\pi_m = k \cdot \text{COV}(r_m, r_m)$$

$$\Rightarrow \quad k = \frac{\pi_m}{\text{COV}(r_m, r_m)} = \frac{\pi_m}{\text{VAR}(r_m)}$$

where we replace $\text{COV}(r_m, r_m)$ with $\text{VAR}(r_m)$ because the covariance of a random variable with itself is the variance of this variable. Substituting the expression for k in the CAPM formula, we obtain

$$\pi_i = \frac{\pi_m}{\text{VAR}(r_m)} \cdot \text{COV}(r_i, r_m)$$

$$= \pi_m \cdot \frac{\text{COV}(r_i, r_m)}{\text{VAR}(r_m)}$$

We call the ratio of the covariance of the return of asset i with the return on the market portfolio to the variance of the return on the market portfolio the **beta** of the asset and denote it by β_i:

$$\beta_i = \frac{\text{COV}(r_i, r_m)}{\text{VAR}(r_m)} \tag{1.13}$$

Using β, we find that the CAPM equation simplifies to

$$\pi_i = \beta_i \cdot \pi_m \tag{1.14}$$

This means that the RADR of an asset has two components:

$$\text{RADR}_i = r_f + \beta_i \cdot \pi_M = r_f + \beta_i \cdot [E(r_M) - r_f]$$

the risk-free return (representing the time value of money), which is common to all asset returns, and a risk premium, which is asset specific.

Beta measures the contribution of an asset to the total risk of a well-diversified portfolio—the market portfolio—relative to the total risk of the portfolio. Thus, beta is a *relative* risk measure. It is easy to see that we can interpret the beta of an asset as a measure of risk relative to the risk of the market portfolio: A beta of 2 means that the asset is twice as risky as the market portfolio and should command twice the risk premium of the market portfolio; a beta of 0.5 means that the asset is one-half as risky as the market portfolio and should command one-half the risk premium of the market portfolio.

It is very important to remember that risk is measured relative to a diversified portfolio. Accordingly, beta is a measure of the extent to which the risk of an asset is **nondiversifiable.** The risk of an asset is diversifiable if it can be ''washed away'' by holding a diversified portfolio. Obviously, the part of the risk of the asset that is correlated with the return on the market portfolio cannot be diversified away even if we hold the most diversified portfolio possible—the market portfolio. That part of the risk of the asset that *cannot* be diversified away, the nondiversifiable or **systematic** risk, *is the only risk for which investors are compensated in the form of a risk premium.* The diversifiable risk of an asset is not compensated by a risk premium. This is because by appropriately structuring your portfolio, you can eliminate this risk. This doesn't mean, however, that a diversifiable risk doesn't affect asset values: The diversifiable risk of an asset can affect the *expected* cash flow of the asset—the numerator in the NPV formula under uncertainty![9]

Time Variations in Risk—The Case of Wild Wild Wildcatter

Note that in equation (1.12) we attached a time subscript to the risk premium of the asset valued. This is intended to highlight the fact that asset risk may change over time. If it does, you will have to use different risk premiums for different periods!

Consider, for example, The Wild Wild Wildcatter Co. (WWW), which is in the process of digging a new oil well. The digging process will last a year and will cost $80,000. At the end of the year WWW will have either a dry hole in the ground or a well producing 24,000 barrels a year forever. Oil is expected to be sold for $5 a barrel net of extraction costs. The following figure depicts the possible cash flows that WWW's well may produce:

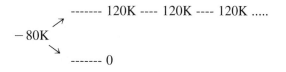

If WWW is successful in its exploration attempt, its cash flows, which are expected to be $120,000 a year, will be exposed to the regular risk to which other

---

[9]Recently, ideas about appropriate risk premiums of assets have relied on the *Arbitrage Pricing Theory (APT).* The APT describes what happens when asset returns are generated by multiple risk factors. Although the APT has some appealing properties, its application to the determination of the risk premiums of assets is more problematic and, consequently, is less frequently used in practice.

oil producers are exposed. WWW knows that the beta of the oil industry is 0.5 and also expects 0.5 to be the beta of its cash flows, *conditional on a successful exploration.* But in the first year WWW is exposed to an additional risk: WWW faces the risk of whether or not there *is* oil where the company is digging. WWW's experience, like that of other oil drillers, is that there is a 10 percent chance that the well will be wet. With a 90 percent probability, no oil will be found. *Does the difference in risk between the first year and subsequent years imply that a different risk premium should be used to discount the expected cash flows of different periods?*

Despite the inclination to say the opposite, the first year's risk premium in our example should be the same as for the following years. This is because the risk of finding oil *is not systematic.* WWW's success in finding oil is completely uncorrelated with the return to the market portfolio, indicating that WWW's *exploration* beta in the first year is zero. Thus, the first year's risk premium is the same as in all subsequent years! This is somewhat surprising: How can a highly uncertain cash flow not justify a higher risk premium? The solution to this conundrum lies in our focus on a *single* well. A single well indeed has a 90 percent chance of disappointing us. But, as knowledgeable investors, what if we hold a diversified portfolio that, among other shares, includes the shares of three other oil explorers besides WWW? Then, in fact, we are holding a portfolio of perhaps thousands of wells to be dug, each with a 10 percent chance of producing oil.

Notice in Figure 1.4 the probability distribution of the percentage of successful oil wells if we drill 1,000 wells, with each well having a 10 percent chance for success. Although each dig is a highly uncertain prospect with only a 10 percent chance of success, we see that the distribution of the percent of successful digs is much more certain. For example, there is over a 99 percent chance that between 8 and 12 percent of the 1,000 wells will produce oil! Thus, by holding a diversified portfolio, we replace a cash flow with 90 percent of being nil with an investment portfolio that with over a 99 percent probability will give us a cash flow that is roughly the expected cash flow in each well. Therefore, investors will not pay a risk premium for the risk of an *individual* well since this risk can be diversified by holding fractional ownership in *many* wells.

On the other hand, conditional on the success of WWW's exploration, the company's sales in year 2 and in subsequent years will be positively correlated with the return on the market portfolio. This is indicated by the expected beta of 0.5 in these years. Therefore, the discount rate for all years should be the same; we will assume it to be 8 percent.

How do we value the WWW project? Conditional on success in the exploration stage, the WWW well can be valued as a perpetuity of $120,000 at an RADR of 8 percent. Using the Gordon formula with $g = 0$, we find that the value of this cash flow *at the end of the exploration period* (i.e., at the end of the first year) is

$$\text{NPV}_{\text{success}} = \frac{120{,}000}{8\%} = \$1{,}500{,}000$$

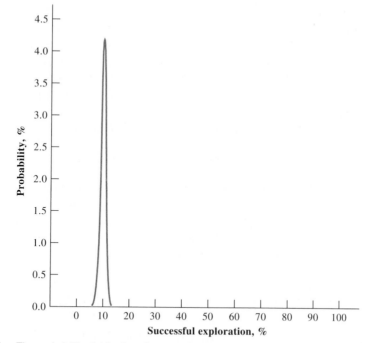

FIGURE 1.4   The probability distribution of successful drills for 1,000 oil wells.

Thus, at the end of the first year the well may have one of two values:

- A value of $1.5 million if WWW finds oil
- A value of $0 if the well is dry

To combine the two values, as the expected value at the end of the drilling period, we use the estimated probability of success. This is where the *diversified risk* enters the computation of values: While the risk of success is diversifiable, and so is not reflected in the RADR, it does affect the computation of the expected cash flows:

$$E(\text{CF}_1) = 1,500,000 \cdot 10\% + 0 \cdot 90\% = \$150,000$$

We have to discount this cash flow for the first year at 8 percent (recall, *no risk premium for the diversifiable exploration risk*) to obtain a value for the WWW project of

$$\text{NPV(WWW)} = -80,000 + \frac{150,000}{1 + 8\%} = \$58,889$$

Thus, it appears that, despite the small probability for success, a WWW oil well is a valuable investment opportunity.

1.4   INFLATION ADJUSTMENTS

So far in our discussion of the valuation of cash flows we implicitly assumed that investors are interested in cash flows per se. We know, however, that cash flows are only the means and that the end for investors is the consumption of goods and services of various types. The distinction between cash flows and what these cash flows can buy at different points in time leads to the next topic we discuss in this chapter—inflation and inflation adjustment.

What is inflation? **Inflation** is a change in the buying power of money. Thus, inflation is not a change in the *relative* prices of goods but, rather, a change in the price *level* of all goods. Although easy to define, inflation is hard to measure. This is because relative prices of goods and services change all the time and each of us consumes a unique combination of goods. Therefore, if you measure inflation by the change in the cost of your consumption basket, you may not learn much about the change in the cost of other peoples' consumption baskets. Moreover, since the relative prices of goods change all the time, how you allocate your income to different goods—that is, your consumption basket—also changes. So, in order to measure your own rate of inflation, you should use an ever-changing basket of goods! Still, since we deal with changes in an overall price level, various measures of inflation are likely to be similar in the long run. In our discussion, in this chapter and in others, we refer to inflation as measured by the U.S. Department of Labor Statistics or by similar government agencies around the world. These agencies typically use some average consumption basket to combine price changes of individual goods into a measure of the change in the price level—the inflation rate.

To illustrate the effect of inflation on valuation, assume that an average monthly consumption basket, which consists of 30 percent housing expenses, 25 percent food expenses, and so on, currently costs $2,000. The same basket will cost $2,100 next year. This implies an inflation rate of

$$i = \frac{2,100}{2,000} - 1 = 0.05 = 5\%$$

Now suppose a 1-year government bond yields 6 percent. Therefore, for every $1,000 worth of this bond that we buy today we will receive $1,060 the next year. The interest rate on this government bond is denominated in dollars and not in units of the consumption basket. These dollars ($1,000 today and $1,060 in 1 year) *have different buying power.* Therefore, the yield on the government bond is a **nominal interest rate.** Investors, however, care about the consumption power of their money, not its nominal value. In our example the $1,000 we invest in the bond today can buy 50 percent of a month's consumption. We don't expect the $1,060 to buy us 50% · 1.06 = 53% of a month's consumption 1 year from now because we anticipate that a monthly consumption basket will cost $2,100 in a year. Thus, in a year we expect to be able to buy only 1,060/2,100 = 0.505 = 50.5% of a monthly consumption basket. This implies that, *in terms of consumption, the real return* on our investment in the bond is 0.505/0.5 − 1 = 1%. More generally, investors convert nominal interest rates into **real interest rates** by adjusting nominal interest rates for the change in the buying power of money:

$$1 + r^{\text{real}} = \frac{1 + r^{\text{nominal}}}{1 + i} \qquad (1.15)$$

where r^{real} and r^{nominal} denote the real and the nominal interest rates, respectively. We can turn around this relation to derive the nominal interest rate from the real interest rate and expected inflation i as

$$1 + r^{\text{nominal}} = (1 + r^{\text{real}}) \cdot (1 + i)$$

$$\implies \qquad r^{\text{nominal}} = r^{\text{real}} + i + r^{\text{real}} \cdot i$$

This equation is called the **Fisher equation.**[10] The Fisher equation is often simplified by dropping the cross term, $r^{\text{real}} \cdot i$, since for low-inflation levels the product of the real interest rate and inflation is very small. This gives the *approximate* formula:

$$r^{\text{nominal}} \approx r^{\text{real}} + i \qquad (1.16)$$

In our example the 1-year real interest rate is

$$1 + r_1^{\text{real}} = \frac{1 + 6\%}{1 + 5\%} = 1.0095$$

$$\implies \qquad r_1^{\text{real}} = 0.95\%$$

or slightly less than 1 percent. The approximate formula gives

$$r_1^{\text{real}} = r_1^{\text{nominal}} - i = 6.0\% - 5.0\% = 1.0\%$$

Because market interest rates are nominal, measuring the real interest rate is a tricky business: In order to convert nominal rates to real rates, we must find some way to predict future inflation. Having projected the expected future inflation rate, we can use the Fisher equation to estimate real interest rates. As an illustration, consider Figure 1.5 from the *Economist Magazine,* which makes two assumptions:

• The nominal interest rate is the sum of the real interest rate and the expected inflation rate. For most of the countries represented in Figure 1.5, this is a good approximation.
• Instead of the expected inflation rate, which is very difficult to measure, the *Economist* uses the inflation rate of the preceding year. When the inflation rate is reasonably level, this is an acceptable compromise; however, it becomes more problematic in times of significant changes in the inflation rate.

[10]In honor of its discoverer, the famous American economist Irving Fisher (1867–1947).

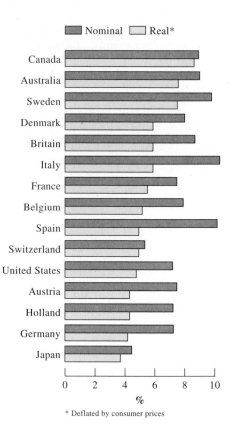

FIGURE 1.5   Ten-year real and nominal government bond yields. Real government bond yields are the nominal yield less expected inflation. Because expectations are hard to measure directly, the inflation rate used in the chart is the actual inflation in the preceding year. (*Sources:* J. P. Morgan; *Economist Magazine,* June 18, 1994, p. 123.)

How do we account for inflation in asset valuations? There are two *equivalent* ways to do this:

- Discounting *nominal* cash flows at *nominal* discount rates
- Discounting *real* cash flows at *real* discount rates

The key is to value assets in a consistent manner. In this context consistency means that when calculating values by using **nominal cash flows**—cash flows denominated in dollars that have different purchasing power—you should use nominal discount rates. On the other hand, if you use **real cash flows**—cash flows that are projected in dollars of *constant purchasing power* (e.g., constant unit prices, constant per-hour labor costs)—you should use real discount rates. *If you value assets by using cash flows and discount rates consistently, the values of the assets will be the same!* It is important to make sure that *all* figures are indeed on the same basis: All cash flows (including the terminal value!) and all discount rates (including those that determine the terminal value!) are either consistently nominal or consistently real.

Inflatable PC Co.—Discounting Cash Flows under Inflationary Circumstances

The following example illustrates how cash flows are discounted under inflation. Suppose the Inflatable PC Co. (IPC) sells 15,000 personal computers (PCs) a year for a price of $1,000 each. IPC perceives the PC market to have reached a steady state. This means that IPC projects that each company in the industry will maintain its current level of unit sales in the foreseeable future and that PC prices, like any other commodity, will rise at the rate of inflation. Now suppose inflation is projected to be 3 percent in the coming year and 4 percent in the following year. IPC has been offered a deal by PC-4-U (PCFU), a megaseller of PCs and IPC's only client, to pay $25 million now in return for 15,000 PCs to be delivered in each of the following two Christmas seasons. Should IPC accept the offer or wait and sell the PCs to PCFU each year at the prices that prevail in each Christmas season?

There are two issues involved in this decision. The first is the issue of a guaranteed versus an uncertain sale of 15,000 PCs; this is an important issue but will be ignored in our discussion of this example. We focus, instead, on the valuation issue of finding the present value of the projected sales to be replaced by the proposed contract. To simplify matters, we assume that all information is certain— sales figures, inflation projections, and price projections. This means that in order to discount the projected cash flows, we need to know the risk-free rate of return.

The yields on government bonds that appear in any financial publication are *nominal yields*. This is because the government promises a *nominal* payment upon maturity and not a payment in units of consumption. In this example we find that the 1-year spot rate is 4 percent (i.e., $r_1^{\text{nominal}} = 4\%$), whereas the 2-year spot rate is 4.5 percent (i.e., $r_2^{\text{nominal}} = 4.5\%$). As stated previously, we can approach the problem in two ways: Estimate the *nominal* cash flows and discount them at the *nominal* rate or estimate the *real* cash flows and discount them at the *real* discount rate. The two approaches are supposed to yield the same answer.

What are the projected nominal revenues? *Nominal revenues are calculated by multiplying unit sales by the nominal unit price, which is the current price plus an inflation adjustment*:

$$CF_1^{\text{nominal}} = 15{,}000 \cdot 1{,}000 \cdot (1 + 3\%) = \$15{,}450{,}000$$

$$CF_2^{\text{nominal}} = 15{,}000 \cdot 1{,}000 \cdot (1 + 3\%) \cdot (1 + 4\%) = \$16{,}068{,}000$$

Using the nominal spot rates, we find that the present value of the projected sales in the next 2 years is

$$PV(\text{sales}) = \frac{15{,}450{,}000}{(1 + 4\%)} + \frac{16{,}068{,}000}{(1 + 4.5\%)^2} = \$29{,}569{,}719$$

Now we redo the valuation by using *real* cash flows and *real* discount rates. The *real* revenue figures are easy to find: They are just 15,000 units times the *current,* that is, the inflation-*unadjusted* price of a unit or $15 million per year. To find the real discount rate, we have to *adjust the observed nominal rates for expected inflation.* For the first year this is a straightforward calculation:

$$1 + r_1^{real} = \frac{1 + 4\%}{1 + 3\%} = 1.00971$$

$$\Rightarrow \qquad r_1^{real} = 0.971\%$$

The computation of the real discount rate for the second year is slightly more complicated since we need to take into account inflation rates that are expected to change between year 1 and year 2:

$$(1 + r_2^{real})^2 = \frac{(1 + 4.5\%)^2}{(1 + 3\%) \cdot (1 + 4\%)} = 1.019441$$

$$\Rightarrow \qquad r_2^{real} = 0.967\%$$

Note that although the nominal spot rates for 1 year and for 2 years are different, *the real rates are virtually the same.* This example is a reflection of what is called the **Fisher hypothesis.** The Fisher hypothesis postulates that since real interest rates are determined by the real conditions in the economy while inflation is a monetary phenomenon, real interest rates and inflation are independent of each other. For example, if inflation expectations increase by 1 percent, nominal interest rates will increase by 1 percent, whereas real interest rates will stay at their original level. Some economic analysis suggests that, in the short run, inflation and real interest rates may not be independent of each other as the Fisher hypothesis postulates. Still, the common view is that in the long run inflation is a monetary phenomenon, which is separate from the real conditions of the economy. Since valuation problems are usually of the long-run type, throughout this book we adopt the Fisher hypothesis as the framework within which inflation is treated in valuing assets.

With the real cash flows and real spot rates calculated, we find the NPV of the expected sales to be

$$PV(sales) = \frac{15,000,000}{1 + 0.971\%} + \frac{15,000,000}{(1 + 0.967\%)^2} = \$29,569,805$$

which, except for rounding errors, is the same answer we obtained by discounting nominal cash flows. Should IPC, then, accept PCFU's offer? Clearly, the answer is "no," since the $25 million offered is less than the present value of future anticipated sales.

The IPC example illustrates an important point in choosing between a nominal and a real valuation: In both cases we have to estimate future inflation! When using nominal discount rates, we have to estimate inflation in order to predict nominal cash flows, such as the inflation-adjusted price of the good; whereas, when using real cash flows, we have to estimate inflation in order to convert the observed nominal interest rates to real interest rates.

The adjustment of discount rates for expected changes in the purchasing power of money was discussed in terms of *risk-free cash flows* and *risk-free discount rates*. This is indeed all the adjustment necessary for inflation, even for RADRs for risky cash flows. The reason is that risk premiums, of the market portfolio or of individual securities, are the same for both *nominal* and *real* RADRs. Intuitively, this is because changes in the purchasing power of money equally affect risk-adjusted returns and risk-free returns so that the *difference* between RADRs and risk-free rates is independent of inflation.[11] Using the notation of the preceding section, we can expect π^{real} and $\pi^{nominal}$ to be approximately the same. In practical terms this means that once we have adjusted the risk-free rate (or the cash flows) for inflation, the risk adjustment that we discussed in the preceding section equally applies to the computation of *nominal* RADRs and *real* RADRs.

1.5 LIQUIDITY ADJUSTMENTS

Throughout the book our discussions and illustrations pertain to valuations of publicly traded assets. Nonetheless, the same principles of valuation can be (and in practice are) applied to privately held firms. In such valuations we may need an adjustment of the values obtained by applying the methods described in the book. In this section we discuss these adjustments so that in the remainder of the book we can deal exclusively with liquid assets.

All the valuation techniques discussed in this book are based on *market prices*—of time, risk, and inflation—to value projected cash flows of securities. This means that an application of these techniques yields appropriate values for *publicly traded* assets—values of securities issued by publicly held companies or assets held by publicly traded companies. When we value securities or assets of *privately held* firms, we should first determine what the value is that must be estimated. If we need to estimate values of securities or assets of a firm in the event that the firm goes public (e.g., to price an IPO or an acquisition by a public company), then a straightforward application of the methods described in the book will provide the required answer. If, on the other hand, we need to estimate prices for *private placements* of securities, then we will have to discount the values of the securities if they were publicly traded in order to estimate their value as less liquid, privately held securities. Such an adjustment reflects the difficulty (i.e., the cost) of *realizing* the value of the projected cash flows.

Although the need to reduce the value of an asset to reflect its lower liquidity

---

[11]Strictly speaking, this is true only for low levels of inflation since we ignore the cross product of inflation and the real risk premium.

is self-evident, there are few guidelines on how either to measure liquidity or to price liquidity. Empirical studies of liquidity effects examine differences between prices of restricted and unrestricted shares or the discounts on privately placed blocks of shares relative to market trades. These studies document discounts ranging from a few percentage points to as high as 50 percent. U.S. court decisions and tax rulings often use a one-third discount for privately held securities relative to values of identical but liquid securities.

Since the empirical evidence on actual discounts indicates little about the *determinants* of the discounts, it is difficult to interpret and apply these average discounts to valuations of privately held firms. One possible approach to adjusting the values of liquid assets for illiquidity is to deduct *the estimated cost of going public.* The intuition underlying this approach is that the costs of going public must be incurred in order to attain the value of the liquid assets.

Using the cost of going public as the basis for figuring the discounts for illiquidity, we have the following *properties* for liquidity discounts:

• The cost of going public is a smaller fraction of the issue size for large issues than for small ones. Thus, the *percentage* liquidity discounts are smaller for large firms than for small firms.

• Underwriting fees are typically smaller for well-established firms than for newly formed firms. Thus, liquidity discounts of established firms are smaller than the liquidity discounts of recently established firms.

• Underwriting fees are typically larger for the flotation of complex securities than for the flotation of simple ''plain vanilla'' securities. Thus, the liquidity discounts of firms with complex capital structures are larger than those of firms with simple capital structures.

Although measuring the liquidity discount by the cost of going public appears to be a reasonable approach, keep in mind that privately held firms are *firms whose owners have opted to remain private.* This means that the values of such privately held firms *exceed their values as public enterprises less the cost of going public.* (On the other hand, since liquidity is valuable, the values of privately held firms cannot exceed their values as public companies.) The article in the box ''Cash-Flow Valuations Cannot Explain Everything'' shows that not all valuations are explained strictly by cash flows. The article, taken from the *Economist Magazine* of January 21, 1995, suggests that liquidity may affect the stock price.

1.6 ARBITRAGE AND RELATIVE ASSET PRICES

The valuation techniques discussed in Sections 1.1 through 1.5 are based on discounting expected cash flows at the opportunity cost of similar funds. An alternative approach to valuing certain cash flows is based on a simple comparison of cash flows and prices. This method is based on the **law of one price,** which says that, in equilibrium, two identical cash flows must have the same price. If this law is violated, then two shares of IBM (International Business Machines), for example,

---

CASH-FLOW VALUATIONS CANNOT
EXPLAIN EVERYTHING

Splitting headache

Children learn early on that the size of a pie does not depend on the number of slices that it is divided into. But when they grow up to be chief financial officers, they appear to follow a different rule: the more cuts, the better. In a bid to boost their share prices, corporations are increasingly turning to stock splits—transactions in which a firm issues two or more shares of stock in exchange for each share that is already outstanding. About 160 of the firms on the New York Stock Exchange performed such splits last year. At first glance, these deals ought to have no effect on a firm's overall market value—a single $100 share should simply become two $50 shares. Surprisingly, however, the pie often does get bigger.

Financial theorists have been aware of this phenomenon for some time, but have disagreed about what is behind it. Many academics believe that stock splits represent a subtle form of communicating with the market. If a management team believes the shares of its firm are undervalued, it can signal this to potential investors by performing a stock split. The fact that such splits are often followed by improved earnings announcements seems to support this thesis.

An alternative explanation, offered by many corporate financiers and traders, is that stock splits are designed to boost liquidity. Shares are traded more heavily, they argue, when priced within a certain range. Thus by splitting them when they rise above this range, a firm can enhance the liquidity of its shares, making them more attractive to investors.

Until recently, finance gurus were not able to come up with a convincing test of these competing explanations. But a clever new study by two financial economists, Chris Muscarella of Penn State University and Michael Vetsuypens of Southern Methodist University, may offer some insights.

Messrs Muscarella and Vetsuypens examined the performance of American Depository Receipts (ADRs). These are securities issued to American investors by American banks, and are backed by the underlying shares of foreign firms. In many cases, these firms choose to split their ADR shares without splitting their underlying stock.

Because these splits affect only the American market, and not the company's primary market, they should not be motivated by managers' desire to signal a firm's true value. Yet the authors find that, on average, the price of ADRs rises anyway after a stock split. Because no signaling motive exists, they argue, this positive market reaction must result from improved liquidity.

Despite this evidence, many financial economists still believe signaling plays a role. Suppose, for example, that managers wish to keep their shares trading in a certain range, for whatever reason. When the price gets too high, they may try to lower it by splitting the shares—but only if they expect it to keep rising (i.e., if it is undervalued). In these cases, a split in the ADR market could still result from management's inside information, and canny investors would respond by buying more ADRs. Settling the debate conclusively will require yet more research. Chief financial officers, meanwhile, will continue trying to divide and conquer.

---

that differ only in their serial number can trade for two different prices! But obviously, if this were the case, someone would buy the ''cheap'' share and sell the ''expensive'' share short, making some money now and offsetting all future dividends paid by IBM on the share sold short by the dividends received on the share held long. Moreover, even if selling shares short is not possible or is costly, no one would be willing to buy the expensive IBM share if the same future cash flows can be obtained by buying the cheap IBM share. If everyone does either thing, the price of the expensive share would fall and the price of the cheap share would rise. Thus, the law of one price is a minimum condition for an equilibrium to exist.

The law of one price means that if we can match the cash flows being valued with a cash flow or a combination of cash flows that are publicly traded, the value of the cash flow in which we are interested is simply the value of the matching traded cash-flow combination. We trivially use this principle when valuing our portfolio of, say, 100 shares of IBM and 200 shares of GM (General Motors) by multiplying the price of *other* IBM shares that were recently traded on an exchange by 100 and adding to this number 200 times the price of *other* shares of GM that were recently traded. But this simple idea also has strong implications in the study of both the effect of leverage on firm value and derivative securities, such as options. These implications are discussed in the relevant chapters (Chapters 8 and 12).

Implicit in the preceding example of employing the law of one price is another principle that we often employ in valuation—the **principle of value additivity.** This principle states that the value of a bundle of several assets is the sum of the separate values of the assets. To illustrate how this principle is used, consider a firm that, besides its operating assets, has liquid investment assets that are kept as a liquidity reserve. The principle of value additivity indicates that we can separately value the operating side of the firm and its liquid assets and can obtain the value of the firm as a whole by simply adding these separate values. Similarly, a firm that operates in several related lines of business can be valued by summing the separate values of each of the lines of the business. In particular, it is important to note that, by valuing each business line separately, we do not leave out the effect of synergies on the value of the whole firm: The value of these synergies is reflected in the cash flows of the separate units and the cash flows of the headquarters! The principle of value additivity, therefore, simplifies valuations by allowing us to break complicated cash-flow streams into components that are simple to understand.

SUMMARY

In this chapter we reviewed the basic valuation tools of finance. All of these techniques use market prices to value expected cash flows by finding the price of money that corresponds to the characteristics of the dollars valued—time, risk, purchasing power, and liquidity. These prices are then multiplied by the expected cash flows to derive asset or security values. In this chapter we reviewed these tools, as well as some simple formulas that apply to special cases of interest in valuation. These techniques will be used in subsequent chapters to value firms and their securities. The tools covered in this chapter are:

- *NPV.* The net present value of a stream of cash flows is

$$
\mathrm{NPV} = \mathrm{CF}_0 + \sum_{t=1}^{N} \frac{\mathrm{CF}_t}{(1 + r)^t}
$$

where CF_t is the cash flow at time t (CF_0 is the cash flow at time zero, and is negative for most assets, since it is often the cost of acquiring the asset). The discount rate r has to be appropriate to the riskiness of the cash flows CF_1, CF_2, ... Moreover, if the cash flows are nominal, then r is the nominal RADR, and if they are real (i.e., of constant purchasing power), then r should be a real discount rate.

• *Adjustment of discount rates to the term structure.* In principle each discount rate in the NPV equation should be appropriate not only to the riskiness of the cash flow, but also to the *date* at which the cash flow is expected. To do this, we match discount rates to the *term structure of interest rates* so that the NPV equation becomes

$$NPV = CF_0 + \sum_{t=1}^{N} \frac{CF_t}{(1 + r_t)^t}$$

• *Calculating the RADR for equity cash flows from the Gordon dividend model.* Assuming that the constant dividend growth is at annual rate g, assuming that the price of the firm's stock today is P, and assuming that the current dividend is D_0, we find that this model gives the RADR for equity cash flows as

$$r = \frac{D_0(1 + g)}{P} + g$$

• *Calculating the RADR for an asset using the Capital Asset Pricing Model (CAPM).* The CAPM postulates that the RADR for asset i (such as a stock, a portfolio of stocks, bonds, or any financial asset) is given by

$$RADR_i = r_f + \beta_i \cdot [E(r_M) - r_f] = r_f + \frac{COV(r_i, r_M)}{VAR(r_M)} \cdot [E(r_M) - r_f]$$

where r_f is the appropriate risk-free rate of interest and $E(r_m)$ is the expected rate of return on the market.

• *Inflation adjustments.* We must pay careful attention in differentiating between *nominal* cash flows and cash flows that have been adjusted for changes in the purchasing power of money (*constant dollar* or *real* cash flows). We discount nominal cash flows at nominal discount rates and discount real cash flows at real discount rates. The Fisher equation gives the relation between these two discount rates:

$$1 + r^{\text{nominal}} = (1 + r^{\text{real}}) \cdot (1 + \text{expected inflation})$$

EXERCISES

1.1 Use a spreadsheet to calculate the NPV (net present value) and the IRR (internal rate of return) of the following cash flows, when the discount rates are 2, 6, 10, and 14 percent.

Year-end	CF$_1$	CF$_2$	CF$_3$
1	−100	1000	10
2	20	−20	20
3	40	−30	30
4	60	−40	40
5	80	−50	50
6	0	−60	−50
7	0	−70	−40
8	−100	−80	−30
9	—	−90	−20
10	—	−100	−10

Plot the NPVs of the projects against the discount rates. Can you estimate the IRRs of the projects from the plots? What do the plots suggest about the relation between rates of return and project values?

1.2 A well-known case[12] concerns General Foods Corporation (GF). At the beginning of 1968 GF had just paid a dividend of $2.20 per share, and its stock price was $73.50. Given the dividend history of the company for the last 10 years, use the Gordon formula to estimate its cost of equity:

Year-end	Dividend
1958	1.00
1959	1.15
1960	1.30
1961	1.40
1962	1.60
1963	1.80
1964	2.00
1965	2.00
1966	2.10
1967	2.20

1.3 Your analysis of the XYZ Corp. suggests that XYZ's shareholders have an 80 percent chance of receiving a cash flow of $1 million at the end of next year. After this payment XYZ will cease to exist. On the other hand, there is a 20 percent chance that XYZ will be out of business by the end of the year. If XYZ fails, its shareholders will receive no cash flow at all. Your analysis further suggests that XYZ's stock beta is 0.5, the 1-year risk-free rate is 6 percent, and the risk premium for a unit beta is 8 percent. Ignoring taxes, what should be the value of XYZ today?

1.4 You also follow the OPQ Corp., a corporation engaged in the development of biodegradable clothes—clothes that self-destruct after being worn 3 times. Neither the technical feasibility nor customer acceptance is assured—there is only an 80 percent chance of success. Conditional on success, OPQ's shareholders will receive an expected cash flow of $600,000 at the end of each year, starting at the end of year 2 and lasting

---

[12]This exercise is based on "The Super Project" [in W. E. Fruhan, Jr., W. C. Kester, S. P. Mason, T. R. Piper, and R. S. Ruback (eds.), *Case Problems in Finance,* 10th ed., published by Irwin, 1994].

forever. On the other hand, there is a 20 percent chance that OPQ will be out of business by the end of the year. If OPQ fails, its shareholders will receive no cash. Your analysis further suggests that, *conditional on success,* the annual risk premium appropriate for OPQ's cash flows will be 3 percent. You also find that the perpetual risk-free rate is 5 percent per year. Ignoring taxes, what should be the value of OPQ's shares today? What is the difference between OPQ and XYZ in the preceding question?

1.5 The following table describes the per-share dividends paid by the ABC Corp. ABC pays dividends once a year on December 31. Assume that ABC's dividends are tax exempt:

Year	Dividend paid	Year-end CPI
1989	1.30	120
1990	1.35	122
1991	1.40	126
1992	1.50	129
1993	1.60	133
1994	1.65	132

a Assume that ABC Corp.'s shares sold for $30 immediately after the 1994 dividend was paid and that shareholders base their expectations regarding the *long-run* dividend payments of ABC's stock on this dividend history. What is the *real* cost of ABC's equity implied by its share price on January 1, 1995?

b Assume now that on January 1, 1995, investors expected the future annual inflation rate to be 4 percent *forever,* what would be the corresponding *nominal* annual growth rate implied by ABC's recent stock price? Answer this question in *two* ways: (*i*) Use the *real* RADR computed in part **a** and the *current* expected inflation rate, and (*ii*) use the *nominal* growth rate implied by the nominal dividend history of ABC and the Gordon formula to infer the nominal RADR consistent with ABC's current price. Why is there a difference?

1.6 The XYZ Corp. has just paid a dividend of $4 per share. You, a wily investor, believe that this dividend, paid annually, will grow by 20 percent per year for the next 5 years. After 5 years you think that the dividend growth will slow down to 8 percent per year, a dividend growth rate that you are convinced XYZ will maintain forever. You own XYZ stock, which is currently selling for $63 per share. What is the RADR implied by this stock price? (*Note:* This exercise requires a modification of the Gordon formula.)

USING FINANCIAL REPORTING INFORMATION

OVERVIEW

The purpose of this chapter is twofold:

* The first section of the chapter presents an overview of the balance sheet and the income statement. The emphasis is on how these traditional accounting statements relate to the derivation of the firm's free cash flow (FCF). This is a very important topic since all the valuation methods of this book depend on deriving cash flows.
* The remainder of the chapter presents a brief overview of financial accounting, using the example of a fictitious company, Hacker Computers. Depending on your knowledge of accounting, you may choose to skip this part of the chapter.

Accounting plays an extremely significant role in valuation: It is the language in which financial performance is written and the framework within which any valuation takes place. Accounting also plays a dual role in valuations. First, by using accounting numbers, we try to understand *historical* financial performance. That is, by using our understanding of the accounting language, we attempt to uncover the economic events that have led to the accounting reports of the firm being valued. The second use is to help us write, in a consistent manner, the economic events that we *project* for the firm. In this application we employ accounting techniques that will ensure that our projections are *complete* and *internally consistent*.

In the second part of this chapter, we will examine how economic events affect financial statements. This will help you to read historical accounting statements and to project economic performance in the form of pro-forma statements, which are the basis of most valuations. But projecting pro-forma financial statements is *not* our ultimate goal in an analysis of firm prospects: We are interested in cash-flow projection. Therefore, in the first part of our discussion of accounting we emphasize the relation between accounting statements and the various cash flows used in valuations.

This chapter does not contain a thorough review of financial accounting. Rather, we focus on those aspects of financial statements and reporting that are of most interest to financial analysts. Be aware that although our final results fit the standard accounting framework, some of our methods are nontraditional. We, after all, are mainly interested in the accounting framework for the insights that we can derive from it for finance. Generally speaking, accounting techniques are more useful in describing the *operating aspects* of firms, such as sales, costs, and assets employed, than in describing the *financial aspects* of firms. For instance, accountants explicitly record only *interest* as a cost of capital, whereas the capital gain portion (e.g., on a convertible bond) is typically never recorded as a cost of capital. Therefore, we use accounting techniques to describe the operating aspects of the firm and non-accounting tools to describe the financial aspects of the firm.

2.1   THE STRUCTURE OF THE BALANCE SHEET AND INCOME STATEMENT

The Balance Sheet

The two main accounting constructs are the **balance sheet** and the **income statement.** The balance sheet is a double-sided listing of the **assets** of a business (the left-hand side) and the **financing** of these assets (the right-hand side) at a given point in time (year-end, quarter-end, etc.).[1] While most accountants use ''assets'' to describe the left-hand side of the balance sheet, the nomenclature for the right-hand side is more varied. It is often called ''**liabilities**'' and sometimes termed ''**liabilities and owners' equity.**'' For brevity we shall usually prefer the former, although we shall not always be consistent in this usage.

The firm's income statement gives periodic (e.g., quarterly and annual) reports of the profits or losses of the firm over the period. The balance sheet is a *cumulative* statement showing the cumulative effect of the firm's actions up to a point in time, whereas the income statement is a report of the *flow of earnings* during a given period.

---

[1]Accountants, contrary to the opinion of some, are not necessarily *two faced*. But they are always *two sided.* Everything in accounting has to be written down twice. If you can figure out how to implement this rule, the rest is easy.

Exhibit 2.1

Balance Sheet

Assets	Liabilities and owners' equity

Current Assets—this category includes all the firm's *short-term* assets:
  Cash—money the firm has in the bank.
  Marketable Securities—securities held by the firm in lieu of cash; usually at their market value.
  Accounts Receivable—customers' unpaid bills to the firm. If some of these bills are expected never to be collected, they are subtracted from the accounts receivable as an "allowance for doubtful accounts."
  Inventories—either parts on hand, work in progress, or finished products, as yet unsold.
	Current Liabilities—all the firm's *short-term* obligations:
	  Accounts Payable—unpaid bills to suppliers.
	  Accrued Taxes—unpaid taxes (usually due in the short term).
	  Current Portion of Long-Term Debt—that part of the firm's long-term debt principal that has to be paid off in the next fiscal year.
	  Short-Term Borrowing—includes all borrowing that, in principle, has to be repaid within a year (revolving credits, overdrafts, etc.).

Fixed Assets
  Leased Property and Equipment—if the firm has long-term leases, the property and equipment leased *may* appear on the balance sheet as if it were actually owned by the firm.
  Plant, Property, and Equipment—these assets are listed at their cost of acquisition, minus the loss of value due to aging ("depreciation"). Depreciation schedules differ for various classes of assets, and are intended to allocate the cost of assets to the years in which the assets are in use.
  Land
Goodwill—if assets have been acquired at more than their market value, the excess is listed here (see the example later in this chapter).
	Long-Term Liabilities
	  Obligations under Leases—this is the debt equivalent of the firm's long-term leases that appear on the asset side of the balance sheet as "Leased Property and Equipment."
	  Long-Term Debt—borrowing by the firm that is to be repaid over a number of years. Includes bonds sold by the firm to the public as well as privately placed debt such as bank loans.
	Preferred Stock
	Equity—all investment in the firm made by its owners plus undistributed accumulated earnings. Equity is usually separated into:
	  Stock Value—the original amount paid for the capital stock of the firm.
	  Retained Earnings—those *profits after taxes* not paid out as dividends to shareholders.

Total Assets—The sum of the items in this column.	Total Liabilities and Owners' Equity—The sum of the items in this column.

Here we sketch a typical balance sheet and then an income statement, giving a short description of each of their items.

The items in the balance sheet (see Exhibit 2.1), both on the Assets side and on the Liabilities side, are organized in the order of their liquidity—from the most liquid item to the least liquid item. Accountants call "current" all items that are expected to be converted into cash within a year.[2] As you will see in subsequent chapters, when we project future financial performance in pro-forma financial statements, we will often find it useful to stray slightly from the traditional form of the balance sheet and income statement. In pro formas we will often prefer to classify items according to their economic nature—operational or financial. For example, in our pro-forma analysis of the firm, we will often lump together all the firm's debts (Current Portion of Long-Term Debt, Short-Term Borrowing, Obligations under Leases, and Long-Term Debt) into one item. This simplifies the economic and valuation analysis of the firm.

The Income Statement

The income statement provides information about the operating performance of the firm over a given time period. In much of this chapter we will stress that income statements *don't* provide full information about the amount of *cash* that accrues in the firm. The purpose of the income statement is to provide a measure of the *true economic performance* of the firm. If this sounds a bit philosophical, it is! But it's a worthy—and often informative—aim. We will show how one goes from a balance sheet and an income statement to a statement about the firm's cash flows.

Exhibit 2.2 illustrates a typical income statement.

Exhibit 2.2

Income Statement

Sales—the periodic (annual, quarterly, etc.) sales of the company.

Cost of Goods Sold (COGS)—the cost of making the goods sold in the period.

Selling, General, and Administrative Expenses (SG&A)—all other periodic operating expenses.

Interest—the periodic cost of money loaned to the firm either directly (bonds, loans, etc.) or indirectly (e.g., implied interest in lease contracts).

Profits before Taxes

Taxes—the allowance for taxes to be paid on the period's earnings. Some of the taxes are recorded as a current expense but will be paid only in the very distant future (if ever . . .). These are called "deferred taxes" and appear in the balance sheet as a long-term liability.

Profits after Taxes

Dividends—the cash paid to the shareholders of the firm. This is usually separated between dividends paid to the preferred shareholders and to the common shareholders.

Retained Earnings—these earnings are added to the accumulated earnings of the firm to yield the end-of-period balance of Retained Earnings in the balance sheet.

---

[2]The exception to this rule is when the business cycle of the firm lasts for more than a year. For example, a property developer building a condominium apartment building can list the apartments as current assets—inventory—even when their construction lasts more than a year. This is because the *business cycle* for this contractor lasts more than a year.

Accountants usually include depreciation charges as part of the cost of goods sold (COGS) and selling, general, and administrative expenses (SG&A). For analytical purposes it is more useful to show these charges separately on the income statement. Depreciation—the accountant's way of allocating the cost of fixed assets to years in which the assets are used—is treated completely differently in valuation: When calculating cash flows, we deduct the cost of the assets at the time in which the actual payment for the assets is made. Nonetheless, we want to keep tab of the depreciation charge, as it affects periodic tax payments. Separating the depreciation charge in the income statement helps us to make the necessary adjustments.

The Cash-Flow Statement

Cash flows are derived from the income statement and from *changes* in the balance sheet. In this book we are primarily interested in the Free Cash Flow (FCF), a concept that defines the *amount of cash that the firm can distribute to security holders.* There are two principal techniques to calculate the FCF—the **indirect method** and the **direct method.**

The *indirect method* of calculating cash flows starts with the firm's Profits after Taxes and makes appropriate adjustments to arrive at a number that shows how much *cash* the firm has taken in over the period. The adjustments that have to be made to the Profit After Taxes are of two types—operational adjustments and financial adjustments.

Operational Adjustments   These adjustments are made to present the results of the business activity of the firm on a *cash basis*:

• *Adjustments for changes in Net Working Capital (ΔNWC).* These adjustments are made because not all the sales are made in cash and because not all the firm's expenses are paid out in cash. The term and notation are somewhat misleading: Not all the firm's working capital items are operationally related; since we are interested in cash derived from the ongoing *business activity* of the firm, we ignore all other current items in our ΔNWC adjustment. Cash and marketable securities are the best example of working capital items that we *exclude* from our definition of ΔNWC, as they are the firm's stock of excess liquidity.[3] Another working capital item that we exclude from the adjustment is Notes Payable or Short-Term Borrowing: Since our aim in the FCF statement is to calculate the cash available to the firm from its *business* activities, we exclude from the FCF statement any cash flows relating to the firm's *financing* activities—short term or long term.

---

[3]The only exception we make is when cash is necessary for the actual operations of the firm (such as in the case of a supermarket chain that needs a certain amount of cash balances on hand in order to conduct its business).

- *Adjustments for investment in new Fixed Assets.* When investment in these assets is necessary for the ongoing business activity of the firm, it cannot be used to pay security holders and thus must be deducted to calculate the FCF.
- *Adjustments for depreciation and other noncash expenses.* Although depreciation is an expense for tax and financial reporting purposes (thus lowering Profits before Taxes, and hence Profits after Taxes—PAT), it is by itself not a *cash expense.* In the FCF statement we thus add the depreciation back into the PAT. The remaining effect of depreciation and other noncash expenses on the FCF is the *tax savings* they entail.

Financial Adjustments   These are adjustments for financial items included in the PAT. Since FCF is a concept that relates to the ongoing business (as opposed to financial) activities of the firm, we want to neutralize financial items when converting the PAT into FCF. Thus, for example, although the PAT includes Interest as an expense, we will *add back* the after-tax interest expenses to obtain the FCF. The adjustment of PAT for financial charges allows us to decompose the valuation of a firm into:

- The valuation of the *business side* of the firm by discounting the FCF;
- The valuation of the *financial side* of the firm (using financial techniques that are not necessarily compatible with accounting principles).

The concept of FCF is of cash flows that are generated by the *business activities* of the firm and are available (i.e., ''free'') for distribution to *all* suppliers of capital, such as equity holders, bondholders, convertible holders, and preferred stockholders. The calculation of accounting earnings (PAT), on the other hand, is done from the point of view of *shareholders,* which is only one group of capital suppliers. Hence, the financial adjustments.[4] The financial aspects of the firm, however, are not ignored: As you will see in Chapter 3, the financial aspects of the firm are treated separately by using techniques that can accommodate the contingent nature of financial cash flows.

Exhibits 2.3 and 2.4 illustrate the direct and the indirect methods of converting accounting earnings into FCFs. The indirect approach converts the PAT to FCF while the direct approach converts each item in the income statement to cash basis.

---

[4]In fact, accounting earnings are not even the shareholders' earnings since contingent financial costs, such as the cost of options to convert into or to buy shares, are not recorded.

Exhibit 2.5

Financial Cash-Flow Statement

Periodic payments	Interest Preferred dividend Regular dividend And so on	These periodic payments to the capital suppliers of the firm are *after tax*! (The free cash flows (FCFs) from which we pay these financial flows are also *after-tax* cash flows!)

Capital market transactions	Retirement of securities:
	  Debt retirement
	  Preferred stock retirement
	  Share repurchase
	  And so on
	New financing:
	  New bank loans
	  New bond flotation
	  Stock sale
	  Exercise of warrants
	  And so on
		These sums represent cash paid when old securities are retired or represent cash received when new securities are floated (privately or publicly).

Change in Cash	= FCF − financial cash flows	

Thus, the bottom line of the cash-flow statement is the *closing link* of the three accounting statements of financial performance:

- The income statement's bottom line—Retained Earnings—feeds into the closing balance sheet as the increase in Accumulated Retained Earnings.
- The income statement and the beginning and closing balance sheets are the basis for the computation of the cash-flow statements.
- The last line of the cash-flow statement—Change in Cash (and Cash Equivalents)—feeds back into the end-of-period balance sheet's Cash account.

The cross-reference of the three accounting statements means that we can use accounting methods to ensure that models of projected financial performance are internally consistent. This method of building integrated pro-forma financial statements is discussed in Chapters 4 through 7.

Calculating Free Cash Flows from "Consolidated Statement of Cash Flows"—An Example

The statement of cash flows included in the firm's financial statements gives all the items necessary to calculate the firm's FCF.[5] However, because this statement

---

[5]The firm's Income Statement and its Cash-Flow Statement are often the basis for predictions of its *future* FCFs. Note, however, that these statements reflect the *past* performance of the firm and are not, in themselves, necessarily predictive of *future* firm performance. In Chapters 4 through 6, we discuss how to predict future financial performance.

CONSOLIDATED STATEMENT OF CASH FLOWS
International Business Machines Corporation and Subsidiary Companies

(Dollars in millions)

For the year ended December 31:	1994	1993	1992
Cash flow from operating activities:			
Net earnings (loss)	$ 3,021	$ (8,101)	$ (4,965)
Adjustments to reconcile net earnings (loss) to cash			
provided from operating activities:			
Effect of changes in accounting principles	–	114	(1,900)
Effect of restructuring charges	(2,772)	5,230	8,312
Depreciation	4,197	4,710	4,793
Deferred income taxes	825	(1,335)	(3,356)
Amortization of software	2,098	1,951	1,466
(Gain) loss on disposition of investment assets	(11)	151	54
Other changes that provided (used) cash:			
Receivables	653	1,185	1,052
Inventories	1,518	583	704
Other assets	187	1,865	110
Accounts payable	305	359	(311)
Other liabilities	1,772	1,615	315
Net cash provided from operating activities	11,793	8,327	6,274
Cash flow from investing activities:			
Payments for plant, rental machines and other property	(3,078)	(3,154)	(4,751)
Proceeds from disposition of plant, rental machines			
and other property	900	793	633
Investment in software	(1,361)	(1,507)	(1,752)
Purchases of marketable securities and other investments	(3,866)	(2,721)	(3,284)
Proceeds from marketable securities and other investments	2,476	2,387	3,276
Proceeds from the sale of Federal Systems Company	1,503	–	–
Net cash used in investing activities	(3,426)	(4,202)	(5,878)
Cash flow from financing activities:			
Proceeds from new debt	5,335	11,794	10,045
Payments to settle debt	(9,445)	(8,741)	(10,735)
Short-term borrowings less than 90 days–net	(1,948)	(5,247)	4,199
Preferred stock transactions–net	(10)	1,091	–
Common stock transactions–net	318	122	(90)
Cash dividends paid	(662)	(933)	(2,765)
Net cash (used in) provided from financing activities	(6,412)	(1,914)	654
Effect of exchange rate changes on cash and			
cash equivalents	106	(796)	(549)
Net change in cash and cash equivalents	2,061	1,415	501
Cash and cash equivalents at January 1	5,861	4,446	3,945
Cash and cash equivalents at December 31	$ 7,922	$ 5,861	$ 4,446

FIGURE 2.1   IBM's 1994 annual report: consolidated statement of cash flows.

includes cash flows that derive from both financial and business activities, some changes must be made to the accounting statement of cash flows in order to calculate the firm's FCF.

We illustrate these changes by using the Consolidated Statement of Cash Flows included in IBM's 1994 Annual Report (see Figure 2.1).

The adjustments that we make to this statement to get the FCF for 1994 are illustrated in Exhibit 2.6. For ease of reference and comparison, this exhibit follows the format of IBM's consolidated statement of cash flows.

Exhibit 2.6

Adjustments to the IBM Consolidated Statement of Cash Flows
(To Get IBM's free cash flow in 1994)

Cash Flow from Operating Activities, in $ millions		
Net Earnings	$ 3,021	
Effect of changes in accounting principles	—	Where changes in accounting principles cause changes in earnings without any cash effects, these should be added back.[6]
Effect of restructuring charges	(2,772)	In 1992 and 1993 IBM charged its earnings with restructuring expenses. This is the cash effect of these charges in 1994 (even though for this year there were no restructuring charges).
Depreciation	4,197	This is a noncash charge to earnings that must be added back to get the cash flows.
Deferred Income Taxes	825	The increase in Deferred Income Taxes in the balance sheet; this reflects primarily timing differences in depreciation charges reported to shareholders and to the tax authorities. IBM paid $825 million less in taxes in 1994 than the tax expense reported in the income statement. Thus, we adjust the reported earnings to reflect only the *cash* portion.
Amortization of software	2,098	Another kind of depreciation with the same treatment.
(Gain) loss on disposition of investment assets	(11)	The 1994 profits include a gain of $11 million from sales of investment assets. This gain is not part of the *operating*

[6]For example, in 1993 IBM reduced its profits by $114 million to comply with an accounting regulation dealing with health benefits for employees on disability. Since this accounting change had no *cash implications,* the 1993 cash flow for IBM adds $114 million back to the Net Earnings.

Exhibit 2.6 *continued*

Adjustments to the IBM Consolidated Statement of Cash Flows
(To Get IBM's free cash flow in 1994)

Cash Flow from Operating Activities, in $ millions

(Gain) loss on disposition of investment assets *continued*		cash flows, and therefore is deducted from the earnings when the earnings are converted to cash flows. IBM includes this $11 million in the cash-flow statement as part of "Proceeds from marketable securities and other investments." We *don't* include these proceeds in the computation of the Free Cash Flow: This is a *financial* cash flow (resulting from the management of IBM's excess cash) and not a part of the firm's normal business activities.
Other changes that provided (used) cash:		These adjustments are part of ΔNWC—changes in net working capital. In 1994 IBM decreased its Accounts Receivable and Inventories and increased its Accounts Payable. These changes in net working capital were a substantial source of cash for IBM in 1994.
Accounts Receivable	$ 653	
Inventories	1,518	
Other assets	187	
Accounts Payable	305	
Other liabilities	1,172	

Cash Flow from Financing Activities, in $ millions

This section of the Consolidated Statement of Cash Flows of IBM includes only *financing* cash flows—net cash raised from new debt issues, preferred stock, common stock, and dividend payments. *None of these items is part of the Free Cash Flow (FCF),* which is intended to reflect the cash available to the firm from its business activities. However, IBM's Profits after Taxes (PAT) with which we start the statement, do include financing items—interest income and interest expense. Since the FCF is an *operating cash-flow* concept, we have to adjust for the financial items that were included in IBM's PAT.

Deduct after-tax interest income = 1,377 · (1.00 − 0.41)	$ (812)	To adjust the profits for financial items included in PAT, we deduct the after-tax interest income and add back the after-tax interest expenses included in PAT. (From the notes to the financial statements, IBM's effective tax rate in 1994 is 41 percent.)
Add back after-tax interest expense = 1,227 · (1.00 − 0.41)	724	
Effect of exchange rate changes on cash and cash equivalents	0	In 1994 the dollar value of IBM's non-dollar cash reserves grew by $106 million because of exchange rate changes. Because this change is neither generated by IBM operations nor an investment in long-term bsiness assets, it is not part of the FCF.

Net Cash Provided from Operating Activities	$11,705	We have called this construct "Cash Flow from Operations."

Exhibit 2.6 *continued*

Adjustments to the IBM Consolidated Statement of Cash Flows
(To Get IBM's free cash flow in 1994)

Cash Flow from Investing Activities, in $ millions

Payments for plant, rental machines, and other property	$(3,078)	IBM uses part of the cash flows generated by its operating activities to purchase long-term assets needed for its business. The Free Cash Flow (FCF) is the cash generated by the firm's business activities, which can be distributed to its security holders. The cash invested in Fixed Assets needed for the business cannot (by definition) be part of the FCF.
Proceeds from disposition of plant, rental machines, and other property	900	
Investment in software	(1,361)	
Purchases of marketable securities and other investments	0	IBM bought $3,866 million of securities during the year. Since this is a *financial flow,* this item is *not* part of the FCF.
Proceeds from marketable securities and other investments	0	IBM sold $2,476 million of its investment portfolio during the year, but—as in the previous item—this financial flow is not part of the FCF.
Proceeds from the sale of Federal Systems Company	0	The sale of this IBM subsidiary provided $1,503 million in cash. We would include this as part of the FCF if this sale of a subsidiary were part of IBM's normal business activities. If, for example, IBM had *acquired* a subsidiary (which would then contribute to its future cash flows), we would include the cost of this acquisition in the FCF calculation. For the prediction of *future* cash flows, disposition of subsidiaries should be included only if it is part of the firm's *recurring* business activities.

Investment Activities Included in the FCF	$(3,539)	The sum of the first three items in this section.

Free Cash Flow	11,705	Cash Flow from Operations
	(3,539)	Investment activities
	$ 8,166	Free Cash Flow

HACKER COMPUTERS
Balance Sheet
January 2, 1994

Assets		Liabilities and owners' equity	
Cash	$ 7,000	Equity	$10,000
Inventory	3,000		
Total	$10,000	Total	$10,000

Notice that while Hacker signed a binding contract to rent a store, the cost of this rental has not as yet been incurred, and therefore is left unrecorded: Accountants record only transactions that *have taken place* (whether settled immediately—cash transactions—or to be settled later—credit transactions). In this case the actual renting of the store had not as yet taken place, so its cost is not recorded.

January 3, 1994   Hacker assembles his first two computers. He uses $600 of parts to do this. The computers are put in the store window, along with a sign announcing their price—$1,000 each. The computers are still Hacker's inventory, but they are definitely in a different shape from raw materials. Let's show these computers in the inventory:

HACKER COMPUTERS
Balance Sheet
January 3, 1994

Assets		Liabilities and owners' equity	
Cash	$ 7,000	Equity	$10,000
Inventory			
Parts	2,400		
Finished Goods	600		
Total	$10,000	Total	$10,000

Although J. Random was very happy with the fact that he finally had two computers to sell, he realized that he had not as yet made any profit (or indeed, any sales!). Being conservative, J. Random Hacker didn't write the computers in the inventory at their selling price. Rather, he recorded the inventory in his books at cost. (Under the same *conservatism principle,* inventory values are adjusted downward when their market price falls below their cost.)

January 5, 1994   He sells a computer! How will we write this up on the balance sheet?[7] The changes to the asset side are clear:

HACKER COMPUTERS
Balance Sheet
January 5, 1994

Assets		Liabilities and owners' equity	
Cash	$7,000 + 1,000	Equity	$10,000
Inventory			
Parts	2,400		
Finished Goods	600 − 300		
Total	$10,700	Total	$10,000

Notice that the Total Assets figure is different from the Total Liabilities figure. This puts the balance sheet out of balance! The $700 difference in the two sides is clearly the profit on the computer that was sold. This profit belongs to Hacker, the business's owner, and we add it under the Equity category. In the process we change the way to record the initial investment of $10,000 that Hacker made in the business:

HACKER COMPUTERS
Balance Sheet
January 5, 1994

Assets		Liabilities and owners' equity	
Cash	$ 8,000	Equity	
Inventory		Initial Stock	$10,000
Parts	2,400	Retained Earnings	700
Finished Goods	300		
Total	$10,700	Total	$10,700

This entry restores the balance.

---

[7]Accountants record transactions in *journal entries,* transferring them afterward to the balance sheet or the income statement. We believe that it is conceptually clearer to show you that all transactions can be directly recorded in the balance sheet.

Now that you have the idea, let's speed up the process a little bit:

January 6–30, 1994   The following events happened:

- Hacker buys $3,000 of parts, paying cash.
- He makes 15 more computers, each with $300 of parts.
- He sells 10 of these computers, for $1,000 each, all in cash.

As an exercise, try to record each of these transactions separately in Hacker's balance sheet and arrive at the following January 30, 1994, balance sheet:

HACKER COMPUTERS
Balance Sheet
January 30, 1994

Assets		Liabilities and owners' equity	
Cash	$15,000	Equity	
Inventory		Initial Stock	$10,000
Parts	900	Retained Earnings	7,700
Finished Goods	1,800		
Total	$17,700	Total	$17,700

January 31, 1994   Hacker's accountant suggests that they prepare an income statement for the month, just to give Random an idea of how well he did in his first month of business. The accountant prepares a statement that ignores taxes:

HACKER COMPUTERS
Income Statement
January 1994

Sales (11 computers, $1,000 each)	$11,000
Costs of Goods Sold (COGS) (11 computers, $300 each)	(3,300)
Selling, General, and Administrative (SG&A) (rent)	(600)
Profits before Taxes	7,100

Hacker was astounded that "rent" appeared as an item on the income statement since he had not as yet paid the rent (the rent for January was due on February 2). The accountant explained that in the accounting method known as **accrual-basis accounting** both the balance sheet and the income statement should reflect all known and predictable expenses and revenue items for which the obligation (or right) was created during the accounting period. This means that in accrual-basis accounting items appear on the balance sheet and the income statement even though they have not as yet been received (if they are income) or have not as yet been paid (expenses). "It all makes sense," the accountant explained to Hacker, "if you consider that we are trying to give a true sense of what the business has really earned."[8]

He further explained that putting an as yet unpaid bill on the profit and loss statement would require putting that same item on the balance sheet as a Current Liability. Thus, the balance sheet would look like the following statement:

HACKER COMPUTERS
Balance Sheet
January 31, 1994

Assets		Liabilities and owners' equity	
Cash	$15,000	Rent Payable	$ 600
Inventory		Equity	
Parts	900	Initial Stock	10,000
Finished Goods	1,800	Retained Earnings	7,100
Total	$17,700	Total	$17,700

Finally, the accountant prepared a **cash flow statement** for Hacker. This statement shows the actual cash inflows of a business over a given time period.[9]

HACKER COMPUTERS
Cash-Flow Statement
January 31, 1994

Sales	$11,000
Parts	(6,000)
Cash flow	$ 5,000

[8]Remember that the income statement is supposed to show the *true economic profits* of the company. For example, the rent, even though it is as yet unpaid, should show up in any reckoning of these profits.

[9]Of all the cash-flow statements we will show in this book, the one that follows is the most primitive since Hacker has actually done very little.

Another way to find the cash flow is by using the indirect method—adjusting the earnings for the period for noncash items (see Exhibit 2.8).

Exhibit 2.8

HACKER COMPUTERS
Cash-Flow Statement
January 31, 1994

Profits	$ 7,100		
Increase in noncash Current Assets (CA)		2,700	An increase in current assets (ΔCA) is cash paid by the firm.
Increase in *nondebt* Current Liabilities (CL)		(600)	An increase in Current Liabilities (ΔCL) reflects accrual expenses that have not as yet been paid.
Net increase in *operating* working capital	(2,100)		The net cost of short-term assets; ΔCA − ΔCL.
Cash flow	$ 5,000		

February 1–28, 1994   In this month:

• Hacker buys $20,000 more in parts. The parts shop owner is so impressed with his business acumen that she lets him have until March 1, 1994, to pay for the parts.

• Hacker produces 30 more computers, 15 of which he sells during the course of the month. One of the purchasers, who buys 10 computers, promises to pay by mid-March. The other 5 computers are sold for cash. Because of market pressures, the price of the computers drops to $800 per unit.

• J. Random pays the rent of $600 for January.

These activities allow us to introduce some new concepts.

Consider the $20,000 in parts. How should we report these? On the Asset side of the balance sheet the parts inventory clearly went up by $20,000. However, since Hacker didn't pay for the parts in cash, there is no counterbalancing asset entry. Instead, we create an entry on the Liabilities side of the balance sheet, which indicates that Hacker bought something using short-term trade credit. We call this **Accounts Payable (A/P).** An account payable in effect represents a short-term loan that the firm has received from its suppliers. Usually, the suppliers expect to be repaid within several months. After this transaction the balance sheet now looks like the following statement:

HACKER COMPUTERS
Balance Sheet
February 28, 1994

Assets		Liabilities and owners' equity	
Cash	$15,000	Rent Payable	$ 600
Inventory		Accounts Payable	20,000
Parts	20,900	Equity	
Finished Goods	1,800	Initial Stock	10,000
		Retained Earnings	7,100
Total	$37,700	Total	$37,700

What about the computers that Hacker makes and sells? First of all, Hacker makes 30 more computers, which means that $9,000 of parts became finished goods. There is no problem recording the 5 computers that Hacker sold for $4,000 in cash. These 5 computers represent $1,500 of finished goods, $4,000 of cash, and $2,500 of retained earnings. Recording these transactions gives the following balance sheet:

HACKER COMPUTERS
Balance Sheet
February 28, 1994

Assets		Liabilities and owners' equity	
Cash	$15,000 + 4,000	Rent Payable	$ 600
Inventory		Accounts Payable	20,000
Parts	20,900 − 9,000	Equity	
Finished Goods	1,800 + 9,000 − 1,500	Initial Stock	10,000
		Retained Earnings	7,100 + 2,500
Total	$40,200	Total	$40,200

But what about the 10 computers that Hacker sells on credit? These computers represent $3,000 of finished goods. Hacker sells them for $8,000, but he doesn't get any cash for them. Instead, he bills the customer, giving her until the next month to pay. Assuming that the customer will pay Hacker, we write the *expected receipts* from this bill as **Accounts Receivable (A/R).** This is an asset. We can think of an account receivable as a customer's IOU; assuming that the customer's credit is good, this IOU has value, and therefore should be recorded with the Assets on the balance sheet. The balance sheet now looks like the following statement:

HACKER COMPUTERS
Balance Sheet
February 28, 1994

Assets		Liabilities and owners' equity	
Cash	$19,000	Rent Payable	$ 600
Accounts Receivable	8,000	Accounts Payable	20,000
Inventory		Equity	
Parts	11,900	Initial Stock	10,000
Finished Goods	9,300 − 3,000	Retained Earnings	9,600 + 5,000
Total	$45,200	Total	$45,200

Notice that we record the profits from this sale, even though we have not as yet collected the money (in a little while we will note that, even though the money is not in hand, we also have to pay taxes on these sales).

Finally, we have to record the rent payment for January in the balance sheet. Since by this time it's the end of February, Hacker actually *owes* another month's rent, which he has not as yet paid. We will record the payment of the rent, plus the fact that by the end of the month, Hacker owes more rent:

HACKER COMPUTERS
Balance Sheet
February 28, 1994

Assets		Liabilities and owners' equity	
Cash	$19,000 − 600	Rent Payable	$600 − 600 + 600
Accounts Receivable	8,000	Accounts Payable	20,000
Inventory		Equity	
Parts	11,900	Initial Stock	10,000
Finished Goods	6,300	Retained Earnings	14,600 − 600
Total	$44,600	Total	$44,600

March 1–30, 1994   This is a momentous month for Hacker Computers. On the basis of a strong balance sheet and great expectations of profitability, J. Random Hacker decides to buy the store in which the business is located. On March 1 he buys the store for $120,000, paying $10,000 in cash and financing the remainder with a mortgage from his local bank. The mortgage works as follows: Each month for the next 110 months Hacker Computers Inc. will pay $1,000 of the mortgage

principal and 1 percent interest on the outstanding principal.[10] This is the way the balance sheet looks after Hacker Computers Inc. buys the store. (*Note:* When Hacker buys the store, he also pays off the remaining rent.)

HACKER COMPUTERS
Balance Sheet
March 1, 1994

Assets		Liabilities and owners' equity	
Cash	$18,400 − 10,000 − 600	Rent Payable	$600 − 600
Accounts Receivable	8,000	Accounts Payable	20,000
Inventory		Mortgage	110,000
Parts	11,900		
Finished Goods	6,300		
Property, Plant, and Equipment (PP&E)	120,000	Equity	
		Initial Stock	10,000
		Retained Earnings	14,000
Total	$154,000	Total	$154,000

By *writing down everything twice,* accountants are able simultaneously to keep track of what's in the business and how it has been paid for. On the other hand, we can already tell that accounting numbers may mean something different from what they appear to mean. Take the total equity of $24,000 in the above balance sheet, for example. Note that it doesn't correspond to the amount of cash that the firm has on hand. Students often think that a firm's equity accounts represent some kind of safe deposit box with money in it. "Let's finance that new investment out of equity" is a line we often hear in class. In fact, the Equity really represents only the mathematical difference between the firm's Total Assets ($154,000 in the above balance sheet) and the money that the firm owes its creditors (in the example at this point: $20,000 to its suppliers and $110,000 to the bank). Of all the items on the balance sheet, Equity is the most metaphysical.

The other notable events of March 1–30, 1994, are the following:

• Hacker sells 45 more computers for $800 each. The cost of materials is unchanged, so these computers cost $300 a piece to produce. Thirty of the computers are sold for cash, and the rest are credit sales, with the balance due next month.

• Hacker purchases $30,000 worth of parts, paying $12,000 in cash, with the balance due by the end of April. Of these parts, $21,000 are made into computers.

• Hacker pays off the Accounts Payable from last month ($20,000).

• Hacker collects all of last month's Accounts Receivable ($8,000).

---

[10]Most mortgages are considerably more complicated and involve equal payments of interest and principal. We are keeping the story simple in the interest of clarity.

Recording these events on the balance sheet gives the statement in Exhibit 2.9.

Exhibit 2.9

HACKER COMPUTERS
Balance Sheet
March 30, 1994

Assets		Liabilities and owners' equity	
Cash	$ 7,800		
Accounts Receivable	12,000	Accounts Payable	$ 18,000
Inventory		Mortgage	110,000
Parts	20,900		
Finished Goods	13,800		
Property, Plant, and Equipment	120,000	Equity	
(PP&E)		Initial Stock	10,000
		Retained Earnings	36,500
Total	$174,500	Total	$174,500

March 31, 1994

• Hacker makes his first mortgage payment. In addition to the principal repayment of $1,000, he pays an interest of $1,100 (1 percent per month on the outstanding mortgage balance).

• He also decides to pay himself a salary; up to now he has not taken a cent out of the business, living instead on his mother's social security. In view of the great success of Hacker Computers, Hacker decides to pay himself $1,500 per month salary, starting with March.

• He notes the depreciation of the property on the balance sheet. The store is to be depreciated over 40 years, which works out to $250 ($= \$120,000/(40 \cdot 12)$) per month.

What is **depreciation**? Accountants view depreciation as a way of allocating the cost of a fixed asset—an asset expected to serve the firm for more than a year—to the years in which it produces goods or services. In principle, this allocation should be proportional to the use of the asset. Finance professors tend to view depreciation as a *legal fiction* that reduces a firm's tax obligations. Below we will see that Hacker's tax rate is 40%; the reduction in taxes resulting from one month's depreciation is therefore: *tax-rate · depreciation* $= 40\% \cdot \$250 = \$100$. This **depreciation tax shield** plays an important role in cash-flow calculations, which we will return to in Chapters 4 through 7.

After accounting for the sales of this month, we see that the balance sheet looks like the following statement (see Exhibit 2.10):

Exhibit 2.10

HACKER COMPUTERS
Balance Sheet
March 31, 1994

Assets		Liabilities and owners' equity	
Cash	$ 4,200	Accounts Payable	$ 18,000
Accounts Receivable	12,000		
Inventory		Mortgage	109,000
Parts	20,900		
Finished Goods	13,800		
Property, Plant, and Equipment (PP&E)		Equity	
		Initial Stock	10,000
At Cost	120,000	Retained Earnings	33,650
Accumulated Depreciation	(250)		
Net	119,750		
Total	$170,650	Total	$170,650

Notice how we have recorded the newest activities:

• All the payments in cash came out of the Cash accounts on the Assets side of the balance sheet.

• On the Liabilities side of the balance sheet, we have recorded the decrease in the mortgage principal against the mortgage itself. Interest and salary were recorded as decreases in retained earnings.

• The depreciation is recorded on the Assets side of the balance sheet as a *decrease* in the asset value; on the Liabilities side of the balance sheet the depreciation is recorded as a cost that reduces Retained Earnings.

Hacker's accountant informs him that Hacker Computers will have to pay a 40 percent income tax on all profits. Since Retained Earnings have gone up (before taking into account these taxes) by $33,650, the expected tax bill of $13,460 is recorded on the balance sheet as a Current Liability. Notice that these **Taxes Payable** reduce the Retained Earnings. Writing the whole balance sheet neatly, we obtain Exhibit 2.11.

Exhibit 2.11

HACKER COMPUTERS
Balance Sheet
March 31, 1994

Assets		Liabilities and owners' equity	
Current Assets		Current Liabilities	
Cash	$ 4,200	Accounts Payable	$ 18,000
Accounts Receivable	12,000	Taxes Payable	13,460
Inventory		Mortgage	109,000
Parts	20,900		
Finished Goods	13,800		
Fixed Assets		Equity	
Property, Plant, and Equipment		Initial Stock	10,000
(PP&E)		Retained Earnings	20,190
At Cost	120,000		
Depreciation	(250)		
Net Property	119,750		
Total	$170,650	Total	$170,650

Another thing happens on March 31: Hacker asks his accountant to show him an *income statement* for the quarter. This is how Hacker Computers' Income Statement looks (see Exhibit 2.12).

Exhibit 2.12

HACKER COMPUTERS
Income Statement
January 1–March 31, 1994

Sales	$59,000	In accrual-basis accounting sales are recorded whether paid for in cash or under credit terms. In Hacker's case 71 computers were sold—11 for $1,000 each and 60 for $800 each (of which 15 have not as yet been paid for).
Cost of Goods Sold (COGS)		The costs of making the computers sellable.
Parts 21,300	(22,800)	This also includes provisions for *expected* expenses associated with the goods sold, such
Salary 1,500		as expected warranty expenses. In Hacker's case COGS include parts worth $300 for each computer and Hacker's salary.[11]
Gross Profit	36,200	
Selling, General, and Administrative Expenses (SG&A)		Expenses incurred, but not necessarily paid for, in making Hacker's business function.
Rent 1,200	(1,450)	
Depreciation 250		
Operating Income	34,750	
Interest Expense	(1,100)	One month's mortgage interest.
Income before Taxes	33,650	
Taxes	(13,460)	Hacker Computers' tax rate is 40 percent. Since these taxes have not as yet been paid, they appear as a Current Liability on the balance sheet.
Net Income	20,190	
Dividends	(0)	Hacker has not actually paid any dividends (but we have put this line in for completeness).
Retained Earnings	$20,190	This line is the net income less any dividends paid.

[11]Hacker, an efficient business person, actually holds *two* positions: He works on the assembly of the computers and is a salesperson. In principle, his salary should, therefore, be divided between COGS (the assembly portion) and SG&A (reflecting his job in sales). Moreover, the COGS portion should be partially allocated to the yet unsold but assembled computers—Hacker's inventory. For the sake of simplicity we keep it all in COGS.

Notice the following factors:

• The cost of parts and finished inventory doesn't necessarily reduce the periodical profits. Only the cost of those parts that actually go into the computers sold is entered on the income statement. Not coincidentally, these are the same parts that totally "disappeared" from the balance sheet.

• In the income statement we ignore the difference between sales made in cash and those made on credit (i.e., those sales that get recorded as Accounts Receivable). Because Hacker uses accrual-basis accounting, we also ignore the distinction between parts paid for in cash and those acquired on credit (i.e., Accounts Payable).

• Even though Hacker has not as yet paid any income taxes, we take them into account in the income statement. We also list them in the balance sheet as Taxes Payable. The Taxes Payable are a little like Accounts Payable and, in fact, we put them in the same category (Current Liabilities) as the Accounts Payable.

• Finally, note that *every item on the income statement has already been listed on the balance sheet.* This means that, if the firm pays no dividends, the last line of the income statement (which records the additions to Retained Earnings) must correspond to the change in the equity account over the period.

Note that there is a difference between *Taxes Payable* and *Deferred Taxes.* Taxes Payable refer to taxes that the firm has not as yet paid but that it is obligated to pay. A good example is Hacker's quarterly taxes: At the end of March Hacker knows the exact sum that he will have to pay in taxes (based on first-quarter earnings) in mid-April. Deferred Taxes, on the other hand, refer to taxes for which there is no *current* obligation to pay but which we know the firm will be obliged to pay in the future. Deferred Taxes correspond to differences between tax expenses reported to shareholders and those reported to the IRS (Internal Revenue Service). Such differences arise when the financial reports to shareholders use different accounting methods, such as the depreciation method, from the tax returns.

Hacker's accountant also makes up a *cash-flow statement.* The accountant wants to "crank" the numbers as quickly as possible. Therefore, he starts from the net income figure that he has already calculated in the income statement and adjusts it to reflect all payments that have not as yet been recorded as accrued expenses, revenues that have not as yet been collected, and noncash expenses. Using the *indirect method,* he produces Exhibit 2.13.

Exhibit 2.13

HACKER COMPUTERS
Free Cash Flows
January 1–March 31, 1994

Profit after Taxes	$ 20,190	
Depreciation	250	Depreciation is a *noncash* expense, and therefore is added back to calculate the cash flow.
Increase in Accounts Receivable (A/R)	(12,000)	The increase in A/R represents sales that have not as yet been collected, and therefore have not as yet produced a cash inflow.
Increase in Inventories	(34,700)	The increase in Inventory has not been recognized as part of Cost of Goods Sold (COGS) but was *fully paid for,* and therefore is deducted from the cash flow.
Increase in Accounts Payable (A/P)	18,000	The increase in A/P represents costs that have not as yet been paid for, and therefore is added back to the cash flow.
Increase in Taxes Payable	13,460	Like the increase in A/P, these are taxes that have not as yet been paid.
After-Tax Interest Expense	660	We want to evaluate the *operating* side of the business and its *financial* side separately. The interest payment is a *financial* expense, and therefore is added back so that we can calculate the *operating* cash flows.
Cash from Operations (CFO)	5,860	
New Property, at Cost	(120,000)	Some cash from operations must be used to buy the assets, such as equipment and plant, that will allow the firm to generate *future* income. This is cash that cannot be freely used, for example, to pay dividends, to buy back shares, and to repay loans, and therefore is deducted from the CFO to arrive at the *free* cash flow.
Free Cash Flow (FCF)	$(114,140)	This is the cash that the firm can distribute to any and all of its suppliers of capital, for example, shareholders, debt holders, and warrant holders.

Shortcuts can be confusing. After going through all this trouble to generate the cash-flow statement in the simplest way, the accountant finds Hacker baffled by the numbers. The only choice the accountant has is to redo the statement explaining each entry's logic. To do this, he *converts Hacker's accrual income statement to cash basis* using the *direct method* (see Exhibit 2.14).

Exhibit 2.14

HACKER COMPUTERS
Cash-Flow Statement
January 1–March 31, 1994
(The direct method)

Collections			Credit sales are recorded as income but do not generate a cash inflow. Thus, to adjust Sales to cash basis, we deduct the increase in A/R.
Sales	$ 59,000		
− Increase in Accounts Receivable (A/R)	(12,000)	$ 47,000	
Operating Expenditures			Inventory, while not a cost of the computers sold, was paid for, and thus is included in expenditures. Expenses not as yet paid—A/P—do not represent a cash outflow. Depreciation is not a cash expense, and thus is added back.
Cost of Goods Sold (COGS)	22,800		
Selling, General, and Administrative Expenses (SG&A)	1,450		
+ Increase in Inventory	34,700		
− Increase in Accounts Payable (A/P)	(18,000)		
− Depreciation	(250)	(40,700)	
Cash Operating Taxes			The difference between taxes on Operating Income and the increase in Taxes Payable is the *tax shield on interest,* which is not cash generated by the firm's operations.
Tax on operating income (@ 40%)	13,900		
− Increase in Taxes Payable	(13,460)	(440)	
Cash from Operations (CFO)		5,860	
Net Increase in Plant, Property, and Equipment (PP&E)		(120,000)	
Free Cash Flow (FCF)		$(114,140)	

As the detailed computation of cash flows amply illustrates, *accrual earnings are not cash flows.* While both FCFs and Earnings measure the performance of the firm over the fiscal year (or other period), the accounting measure—earnings—and the finance/economic measure—cash flows—are different. Since the difference in the timing of the receipt or payment of cash flows is very significant in determining the economic value of a firm, *cash flows* are used in most valuations. It is important to remember, however, that earnings and cash flows are intimately related to each other. This is clearly illustrated by the indirect method of calculating cash flows, where the cash flows of Hacker are derived by adjusting the Profit after Taxes of the period.

We use the relation between accounting measures of performance and financial/ economic measures of performance in valuations and other corporate decisions: We project financial performance by using *accounting* principles and convert these accounting projections to cash flows (using either the direct or indirect method) so that financial/economic methods of valuation can be applied. The underlying principles of such modeling are explained in Chapter 4 and the details are provided in Chapters 5 through 7. As an exercise, try to build a worksheet that will use the beginning balance sheet of Hacker, the ending balance sheet, and the income statement to derive the cash-flow statement by using the *direct method.*

After the technical aspects of calculating cash flows are well understood, we can then consider the *meaning* of these numbers. Hacker's **Cash from Operations (CFO)** indicates that the sales of computers during the quarter led to a net inflow of money to the firm. On the other hand, because Hacker has bought fixed assets to continue its meteoric expansion, Hacker has a negative FCF. Negative FCFs must be financed by raising **additional capital** from outside sources, whereas positive FCFs may be used to serve any of the firm's security holders. Neither the positive CFO nor the negative FCF by itself implies a value judgment:

• CFO may be positive because the firm succeeds in postponing certain payments, such as taxes and payments to suppliers. ("The road to hell is paved with unpaid bills.")

• The FCF may be negative because the firm is purchasing assets that will later produce substantial income.

Note that we have been judicious about which Current Liabilities and which Current Assets we have taken into account in our cash-flow statement. For example, we have *not included the increase in cash in the cash flow* since this increase is the *result* of the activities of the firm and can be distributed—now or later—to the owners of the firm. Second, although in the case at hand we adjust for the changes in all of Hacker's Current Liabilities in the cash-flow statement, this doesn't always need to be so. In particular, when Current Liabilities include bank loans and other *financing* items that are not directly related to operations, they are excluded from the cash-flow calculations. This is because in our valuation we separate the valuation of the *operating* side of the firm from the valuation of the *financial aspects* of the firm (such as the effect of leverage on the value of the firm). There is no hard-and-fast rule about which items to include: The principle is to include only those items that are directly related to production and sales. (For the same reason, in the indirect method, we add back the after-tax cost of interest to the Profits after Taxes.)

The calculation of the FCFs, which reflects the *operating* side of the business, is complemented by the *financing* side of the business. Using the cash-flow identity—*cash inflows minus cash outflows equal the change in cash balances*—we can check our calculation of the FCFs by finding the **net financing flows** for the same period. If we have done our calculations correctly, this should give us the change in the balance sheet Cash item:

HACKER COMPUTERS
Explaining the Change in Cash Balances
January 1–March 31, 1994

Free Cash Flow (FCF)	$(114,140)
Net new Debt (mortgage)	109,000
Net new Equity	10,000
Net-of-Tax Interest	(660)
Dividend	0
Change in Cash	$ 4,200

When you build a model of the firm in a spreadsheet (the technique is fully discussed in Chapter 4), this result is a very useful tool. It helps us, as modelers of financial performance, to verify that our model is internally consistent. This is simply achieved by plugging back the change in cash into the projected end-of-period balance sheet. Now *the balance sheet must balance*! If it doesn't balance, we have to check some of the formulas we used to model the firm's operations.

April–June 1994   In April, after all these exciting accounting events, J. Random Hacker places his first advertisement in a computer magazine. He advertises his computers by mail and opens an 800 telephone number. The response is astonishing. Here is a summary (financial only—numbers themselves cannot possibly capture the excitement of these months) of Hacker Computers' major events for these months:

• Hacker sells $600,000 worth of computers. Most of these are sold on the telephone and paid for with credit cards. Credit card companies charge Hacker a 4 percent collection charge. At the end of the period Hacker has $200,000 of charges that are still outstanding, and he has collected $384,000 ($400,000 minus the 4 percent collection charge) from the remaining charges.

- Hacker buys $230,000 of parts. By the end of the quarter, one-half of these parts have been paid for, and payment for the other half ($115,000) is due in mid-July. Some $220,000 of these parts have been turned into a finished inventory; the computers sold include parts whose cost was $194,000.[12]
- Hacker pays off all the Accounts Payable (and collects all the Accounts Receivable) on the balance sheet at the *beginning* of the period.
- Hacker pays the $13,460 taxes on its first-quarter income.
- Hacker incurs sales costs (all paid in cash) of:

HACKER COMPUTERS
Sales Costs
April–June 1994

Advertising costs	$15,000
Telephone	2,300
Packing materials	3,000
Shipping and insurance	12,700
Salaries and wages	
J. Random	4,500
Other[13]	3,000
Total sales costs	$40,500

- Hacker had paid his mortgage during these months. Total payments were $6,240, which included $3,000 in principal, and $3,240 in interest charges ($1,090 for April, $1,080 for May, and $1,070 for June).

The income statement for the quarter appears in Exhibit 2.15.

---

[12]We are fudging an important issue here—inventory accounting. What happens if it costs $300 to produce some computers and (due to changes in parts prices) only $280 to produce other computers? When we sell a computer from the inventory of finished goods, which cost do we ascribe to it? There are two main methods to assign costs—*FIFO* (first-in, first-out), and *LIFO* (last-in, first-out). These methods can produce different profits! (Cash flows, however, will be the same.) Note that we finessed this issue in the first quarter's numbers by making sure that each computer costs the same $300 to make. In this quarter—and for the rest of this year—we simply state the number related to costs of goods sold, without relating to how it was calculated.

[13]Hacker's mother was answering the telephone and taking orders. Hacker had taken her out to dinner a couple of times to show her how grateful he was, but she had refused any cash payments (as a devoted mother, she was willing to do anything to help her little boy succeed). A couple of high school students— incipient nerds, all—had been hired to pack up the computers and occasionally to help put them together. These students were paid the minimum wage.

Exhibit 2.15

HACKER COMPUTERS
Income Statement
April–June 1994

Sales	$ 600,000	This includes *all* sales, whether or not collected.
Cost of Goods Sold (COGS)		
Parts 194,000		
Depreciation 750	(194,750)	Depreciation on the store for 3 months.
Selling, General, and Administrative Expenses (SG&A)		
Sales costs	(40,500)	
Collection costs	(24,000)	Includes all collection costs, whether or not paid.[14]
Operating Profit	340,750	
Interest	(3,240)	Mortgage interest for 3 months.
Profits before Taxes	337,510	
Taxes (@40%)	(135,004)	
Profits after Taxes	202,506	
Dividends	0	
Retained Earnings	$ 202,506	

The retained earnings of the current period are added to the Accumulated Retained Earnings for prior periods to obtain the closing balance of the Retained Earnings (in the end-of-period balance sheet). When modeling the financial performance of a firm, we use this relation between the income statement for the period and the change in the equity accounts of successive balance sheets to tie together the model of the income statement to the model of the balance sheet: We *compute* the end-of-period Retained Earnings figure of the balance sheet as the beginning-of-period Retained Earnings plus the change in Retained Earnings for the period—the last line of the income statement for the period.

Hacker's final balance sheet for the quarter is given in Exhibit 2.16.

---

[14]Remember that Hacker Computers' accountants use the *accrual method*: Even expenses that have not as yet been paid for in cash (or revenues that have not as yet been collected) are reported on the profit and loss statement. One of the functions of a *cash-flow statement* is to translate all these accrued items into cash-basis equivalents.

Exhibit 2.16

HACKER COMPUTERS
Balance Sheet as of June 30, 1994

Assets		Liabilities and owners' equity	
Current Assets		Current Liabilities	
Cash	$207,000	Accounts Payable	$115,000
Accounts Receivable	200,000	Taxes Payable	135,004
Inventory		Deferred collection costs	8,000
Parts	30,900		
Finished Goods	39,800		
Total Current Assets	477,700	Total Current Liabilities	258,004
Fixed Assets		Mortgage	106,000
Plant, Property, and Equipment (PP&E)		Equity	
Cost	120,000	Initial Stock	10,000
Accumulated Depreciation	(1,000)	Retained Earnings	222,696
	119,000		
Total	$596,700	Total	$596,700

Hacker felt quite smug on seeing these numbers. In just 6 short months he had built up a business from nothing! Now the business was earning over $200,000 a quarter (let's see,—on an annual basis that would be $800,000!; and if we took into account the phenomenal growth rate, . . .).

And then there was the balance sheet! J. Random remembered how the first balance sheet had shown Total Assets of just $10,000. And now here he was, the sole owner of a business whose balance sheet topped *half a million dollars*!

But alas, there was a fly in the ointment! And, as in so many of these cases, it was left to the hapless accountant to point out to J. Random the fact that he might be headed for a **cash crunch.** The accountant's reasoning was that by mid-July Hacker Computers' expected cash position would look like the following statement (see Exhibit 2.17).

Exhibit 2.17

HACKER COMPUTERS
Predicted Cash Balance, Mid-July 1994
Current Date: June 30, 1994

Initial Cash	$ 207,000
Payments: Accounts Payable	(115,000)
Payments: Taxes Payable	(135,004)
Receipts: Accounts Receivables, net of collection costs	192,000
Ending Cash	$ 148,996

Now this net cash position would barely enable Hacker Computers to continue its meteoric growth. For example, Hacker wanted to purchase $400,000 of parts at the beginning of July and to flood the computer magazines with advertisements for his new "Random Cube" series of computers. The expected cash position makes such expenditures problematic.

This is an example, although greatly simplified, of **cash budgeting.** Its starting point is the current cash balance, its entries are the various expected cash flows, and its bottom line is end-of-period cash balances one or several periods ahead. A full cash budget requires the projection of sales and expenses and is, in fact, a pro-forma cash-flow statement derived from pro-forma income statements and balance sheets. The technique of generating pro-forma statements is discussed in Chapters 4 through 7. At this point our objective is to introduce the notion that accounting statements are useful tools not only in describing the economic *history* of a business, but also in predicting its *future* financial performance.

Bringing in a New Partner

The accountant initially suggested that Hacker slow down the growth of the business. This would enable Hacker to build up more cash and to make a safer, more orderly expansion of the business. Hacker was quite unwilling to do this. He believed that the Random Cube was a real revolution in computing, which could sweep the market. Now was not the time to slow down the business; rather, it was the time to be more aggressive and to catch the competition unawares.

The accountant's next suggestion was that Hacker bring in a new partner. "Get some more equity in the business," he said, "and in the process perhaps you can find a partner whose skills match yours. You're strong on the computing end, but you need to put your house in order. Find someone who can help to run the business *and* who will put money into it." This sounded like a good idea to Hacker. It was getting a little difficult to deal with the suppliers, customers, banks, and accountants, and at the same time to concentrate on putting together high-quality computers. He could use a little help, and—as the accountant had convinced him—if the help had money, all the better.

Within weeks of this discussion, the accountant had introduced Hacker to Joyce Numerate. Joyce was a hard-working, wealthy heiress. After getting her MBA she had held several jobs at major local firms, but she was looking for a business of her own. Joyce's skills were a good match for those of J. Random: She was an expert in accounting and inventory systems and a good manager of people.

Random and Joyce hit it off immediately. They consulted with their accountant as well as with a well-known academic expert, who had written a book on valuing closely held companies, on the valuation. Estimates of the value of Hacker Computers' equity ranged from $300,000 to $1 million. The problem in estimating the value was that Hacker Computers had very few tangible assets. Most of the value in the business was related to J. Random Hacker's skills.

After intense but friendly negotiations, Joyce bought a 36 percent stake in Hacker

Computers (now renamed Hacker International) for $300,000. The manner in which this was done follows.

The company issued 5,625 new shares to Joyce.[15] These shares had a **par value** of $1. Since Joyce paid $300,000 for these shares, the remainder ($294,375) was listed on the balance sheet as **excess paid over par**.[16] This arrangement gave Joyce $5,625/(10,000 + 5,625) = 36\%$ of the shares of the firm. Note that this arrangement implies an equity value of $300,000/0.36 = \$833,333.33$ for Hacker Computers' equity *after the share issue,* or $533,333.33 for J. Random's shares.

Joyce would become the Chief Financial Officer of Hacker International, with a monthly salary of $2,000. J. Random's salary was also raised to $2,000 per month.

After the transaction the balance sheet of the newly renamed Hacker International was as follows (see Exhibit 2.18).

Exhibit 2.18

HACKER INTERNATIONAL
Balance Sheet
June 30, 1994

Assets		Liabilities and owners' equity	
Current Assets		Current Liabilities	
Cash	$507,000	Accounts Payable	$115,000
Accounts Receivable	200,000	Taxes Payable	135,004
Inventory		Deferred Collection Costs	8,000
Parts	30,900		
Finished Goods	39,800		
Total Current Assets	777,700	Total Current Liabilities	258,004
Fixed Assets		Liabilities (mortgage)	106,000
Plant, Property, and Equipment (PP&E)		Equity	
		Initial Stock (15,625	15,625
Cost	120,000	shares $1 par)	
Accumulated Depreciation	(1,000)	Excess Paid Over Par	294,375
	119,000	Retained Earnings	222,696
Total	$896,700	Total	$896,700

[15]Recall that the initial investment of $10,000 was recorded as 10,000 shares with a par value of $1 each.

[16]A share certificate has a nominal (and totally meaningless!) value assigned to it for accounting purposes. The original shares in Hacker Computers Inc. had a par value of $1; thus, J. R. Hacker's initial $10,000 investment in the firm was divided into 10,000 shares. When new shares are issued and investors pay *more* than their par value for the shares, the difference is called *excess paid over par*. This is often listed separately in the owner's equity section of the balance sheet.

The huge **cash cushion** of the new firm would enable it to withstand any reasonable market fluctuations without affecting its growth.

July–September 1994   In a moment we will discuss the financial events of this quarter. But first we discuss its main event.

It was not long before Joyce identified one of the main bottlenecks at Hacker International. "We need a production facility," she said. "We can't continue to operate in the back of a storefront on Nerd Street. We can also use someone to take over the actual production of computers so that you, J.R., can be freed up for general management and research."

Joyce started to scout around. Within weeks she had located Leroy Cheng of Cheng Enterprises. Cheng had a small production facility, where he did subcontracting and manufacturing for some bigger electronics and defense contractors in the area. He wanted to cash out of his business, but he was willing to continue as a salaried employee.

In many ways Cheng seemed an ideal fit: Cheng Enterprises had the facilities for producing the computers from the components that Hacker International bought from its suppliers. Cheng Enterprises also had space for packing up these computers and even had a small loading dock. Up to now Hacker had been carrying his finished computers out the door to the waiting delivery truck. (The neighbors were starting to complain about the constant traffic jams on Nerd Street.)

The Balance sheet of Cheng Enterprises follows (see Exhibit 2.19).

Exhibit 2.19

CHENG ENTERPRISES
Balance Sheet
June 30, 1994

Assets		Liabilities and owners' equity	
Cash	$ 6,322	Customer Advances	$ 5,000
Inventories	15,000	Taxes Payable	5,678
Accounts Receivable	23,000		
Property, Plant and Equipment (PP&E)		Mortgage	45,000
Building			
Cost	60,000		
Accumulated Depreciation	15,000		
	45,000		
Equipment		Equity	
Cost	80,000	Stock	1,000
Accumulated Depreciation	75,000	Retained Earnings	37,644
	5,000		
Total	$94,322	Total	$94,322

Joyce had spoken to a number of appraisers who had assured her that Cheng's building could be reappraised at $300,000, and that this value could be depreciated using straight-line depreciation over 20 years ($3,750 per quarter). The equipment owned by Cheng Enterprises would be fully depreciated in two more quarters (i.e., there would be a $2,500 depreciation charge in each of the next two quarters). The balance sheet of Cheng Enterprises included the remainder of a small mortgage that Leroy Cheng had originally taken out to buy his building. The bank holding this mortgage had since gone bankrupt, and the Reconstruction Finance Corporation, a federal agency currently holding the bank's assets, demanded that the mortgage be paid off immediately if the ownership of the company changed.

Joyce, J. Random, and Leroy hammered out the details of the deal as follows:

• Hacker International would purchase all the assets and take over all the liabilities of Cheng Enterprises for $600,000. This amount included the Current Liabilities (totaling $10,678) and the $45,000 mortgage, which Hacker agreed to pay off. Cheng would be paid the remainder ($600,000 − $10,678 − $45,000 = $544,322). Of this amount, Cheng would get $144,322 in cash. The remaining $400,000 would be financed by a note from Hacker International to Leroy Cheng. The note would be paid off in 20 equal quarterly installments of $20,000. The outstanding principal would bear 4 percent interest quarterly. Hacker International would have the option of paying off any outstanding principal early (its cash flow permitting), without penalty.

• Leroy Cheng agreed to stay with Hacker International for the next 6 years (until his retirement) for a salary of $4,000 per month. All of Cheng's five employees would likewise stay on.

Hacker was perplexed by the accounting for this purchase. In his nerdish way he assumed that when one bought out another company, one simply added its balance sheet to one's own balance sheet, item by item. But how could one justify paying $600,000 for a company whose whole Balance Sheet added up to only $94,322?

Joyce had a simple explanation: "Rewrite Cheng's balance sheet," she said, "to take into account the current value of its assets, making sure that the total is $600,000." Here is the way she did this (see Exhibit 2.20).

Exhibit 2.20

CHENG ENTERPRISES
Balance Sheet
June 30, 1994
Restated

Assets		Liabilities and owners' equity	
Cash	$ 6,322	Customer Advances	$ 5,000
Inventories	15,000	Taxes Payable	5,678
Accounts Receivable	23,000		
Property, Plant and Equipment (PP&E)		Mortgage	45,000
Building			
Cost	300,000		
Accumulated Depreciation	0		
	300,000		
Equipment		Equity	544,322
Cost	5,000		
Accumulated Depreciation	0		
	5,000		
Goodwill	250,678		
Total	$600,000	Total	$600,000

The Goodwill item, Joyce explained, was essentially a way of accounting for the value of acquiring Leroy Cheng and his production expertise. Although this looks like ''creative accounting'' (and it *is,* in fact, creative), there is a sound economic rationale behind the restatement: The balance sheet essentially reflects only historic numbers, and therefore it may fail to reflect current market value. In a case like the Cheng acquisition, where more is being paid for the company than its balance sheet value, we want to show *why* the surplus is being paid. We do this by restating the various asset items to show their current market value. Thus, for example, we wrote up Cheng's building from its historic (and depreciated) cost to its current market value.

After restating all assets based on their market values, we may be left with an increment that we cannot explain in terms of physical assets. This increment, which represents the value of buying an ongoing concern with a viable production technology, qualified people, and a market (as opposed to a ''dead'' collection of assets), is called *goodwill.*

The way the combination of Cheng Enterprises and Hacker International is accounted for—by restating asset values based on their market values on the day the deal is struck—is the way a business combination is accounted for under the **purchase method.** Under the **pooling-of-interest method** no goodwill is recorded and the accounts *are* indeed simply added up. Under the purchase method the adding up is done after restating the value of the assets and recording the value of the goodwill (if any). The default method of accounting for business combinations is the purchase method, and the pooling-of-interest method may be applied only if certain criteria are met.

Now Joyce added the Asset side of the Balance Sheet for Cheng Enterprises to Hacker International's Assets, making the appropriate adjustments for the payments (see Exhibit 2.21).

Exhibit 2.21

HACKER INTERNATIONAL
Assets after Buyout of Cheng Enterprises
June 30, 1994

	Current Assets	
Cash	$ 507,000	Hacker's cash
	+ 6,322	Add Cheng's cash
	− 144,322	Subtract sum paid to Cheng
	− 45,000	Subtract payment of Cheng's mortgage
	= 324,000	
Accounts Receivable (A/R)	200,000	Hacker's A/R
	+ 23,000	Add A/R from Cheng's balance sheet
	= 223,000	
Inventory		
Parts	30,900	Hacker's parts
	+ 15,000	Add Cheng's inventory (assumed to be parts)
	= 45,900	
Finished Goods	39,800	Hacker's finished goods
Total Current Assets	632,700	
Property		
Cost	120,000	Hacker's store
	+ 300,000	Add Cheng's property (revalued)
	= 420,000	
Accumulated Depreciation	(1,000)	Hacker's accumulated depreciation
	419,000	Depreciation of Cheng's property starts anew
Equipment		
Cost	5,000	From Cheng's balance sheet
Accumulated Depreciation	0	
	5,000	
Goodwill	250,678	From Cheng's balance sheet
Total	$1,307,378	

The Liability side of Hacker's balance sheet received similar treatment (see Exhibit 2.22). The new Hacker International balance sheet was impressive!

Exhibit 2.22

HACKER INTERNATIONAL
Liabilities and Owners' Equity after Buyout of Cheng Enterprises
June 30, 1994

Current Liabilities		
Accounts Payable (A/P)	$ 115,000	Cheng has no A/P.
Taxes Payable	135,004	
	+5,678	Hacker will pay Cheng Enterprises's taxes.
	=140,682	
Deferred Collection Costs	8,000	From Hacker's balance sheet.
Customer Advances	5,000	Hacker agrees to pay these off, when due.
Total Current Liabilities	$ 268,682	
Note to Cheng	400,000	Represents Hacker's debt to Leroy Cheng.
Mortgage	106,000	Only Hacker's mortgage; Cheng's mortgage was paid off by Hacker.
Equity		
Shares ($1 par each)	15,625	These items come only from Hacker's balance
Excess Paid over Par	294,375	sheet since the acquisition of Cheng is
Retained Earnings	222,696	accounted for as a purchase.
	532,696	
Total	$1,307,378	

As we explained before, the accounting method described here is called *purchase* accounting. Under *pooling-of-interest* accounting there is no restatement of the cost of the assets and no goodwill is created. Try to work out the postacquisition balance sheet of Hacker International under the pooling-of-interest method.

July–September 1994 (continued)   These were momentous months for Hacker International:

• Sales for the quarter were $3,468,322. The Random Cube series was an enormous success, offering a fully integrated system for less than the prices quoted by any of Hacker's competitors.
• Hacker purchased new parts for $1,322,880. Of these parts $850,433 ended up in the new computers. Another $253,451 became finished inventory.

The purchase of parts at different prices creates a problem: How do we value the parts inventory at the end of the fiscal period—using the prices of the initially purchased parts or the latest prices? This is the problem of **inventory valuation.**

This problem has a twin issue: How do we figure the cost of the units that were sold? Given the purchases and other manufacturing expenses incurred in the period, the decision to assign a certain fraction of these costs to the units in the end-of-year inventory means that the remaining costs are the cost of the units sold during the period—the COGS of the period. There are several methods of calculating inventory values. The extreme methods in terms of assigning values to inventories are called *FIFO* for first in-first out and *LIFO* for last in-first out. More simply stated, under FIFO inventories are *assumed* to be the last units bought, whereas under LIFO they are *assumed* to be the first units bought.[17] When prices change, such as in an inflationary environment, the two methods will generate different inventory values and, as a result, generate different periodical income. FIFO tends to cause the value of the inventory in the balance sheet to be closer to its current replacement value. LIFO tends to cause profits in the income statement to be closer to their current levels. Thus, if we are interested in understanding the current *profitability* of the firm so that we can better predict its future profitability, LIFO accounting will provide us with more meaningful numbers to use. FIFO accounting will provide better information on the value of the firm when we consider *liquidating* its assets.

• Hacker paid off all the Accounts Payable for the previous quarter. Of the new parts purchased, $650,000 were purchased in cash, with the rest of the payments coming due in October.

• By the end of the quarter, all the Accounts Receivable for the previous quarter had been paid off, with the exception of $9,322, which proved to be uncollectible and had to be written off altogether. Hacker had to pay all $8,000 of the deferred collection costs on the old Accounts Receivable.

• Of the new sales of this quarter, $2,850,489 were paid off by the end of the quarter, leaving end-of-quarter Accounts Receivable of $617,833. Because of their impressive volume, collection costs and payments to credit card companies had fallen to 3.5 percent of sales.

• Hacker spent $5,000 on maintenance for its buildings and equipment. This was taken off as an expense on the Profit and Loss Statement.

Accountants distinguish between two types of cash payments for **fixed assets—betterment** and **maintenance.** As the name suggests, betterment costs are those payments that extend the life of the fixed asset, reduce operating costs, improve product quality, and the like. Maintenance costs do none of the above: They simply assure that the fixed asset continues to operate as it should. Betterment expenses are **capitalized**: They are added to the cost of the asset.[18] Maintenance costs are **expensed**: They are deducted from the income for the period.

---

[17]The assumption used in determining the *value* of inventories is *independent* of the true flow of the units in inventory. Most inventory management systems probably make sure that the first units shipped in are those that are the first to be shipped out. Still, for *pricing* purposes we may work with LIFO as it often better captures the true profit of the firm.

[18]This is sometimes done in a peculiar way: When betterment expenses increase the useful life of a fixed asset, they are deducted from accumulated depreciation.

• Hacker International purchased (for cash) packaging and other equipment for $82,000. This equipment was put on the Balance Sheet and would depreciate over 6 years on the following schedule (depreciation would be taken on a quarterly basis):

Year	Percent (%)
1	20.00
2	32.00
5	19.20
4	11.52
5	11.52
6	5.76

Other expenses for the quarter were:

Salaries		
J. R. Hacker	$ 6,000	
Joyce Numerate	6,000	
Leroy Cheng	12,000	
Other salaries	22,500	
Total Salaries		$ 46,500
Advertising		33,458
Maintenance		5,000
Shipping, Packing, and Insurance		33,000
Total		$117,958

To develop a new balance sheet and profit and loss statement for this quarter, Joyce prepared a large spreadsheet, showing each of the items separately as direct adjustments to balance sheet categories. We leave this as a homework exercise (Problem 2.1).

SUMMARY

Most of the financial numbers we see in corporate finance have been prepared by accountants or are based on accounting concepts. It follows that a good understanding of financial statements is absolutely essential for most valuation exercises: Good understanding of accounting allows us both to comprehend the economic events underlying the accounting statements of prior years and to model expected financial performance in an integrated and consistent manner.

In this chapter we covered two main issues. First, we discussed how the traditional accounting statements—the income statement and the balance sheet—are related to a key construct in valuation—the free cash flow (FCF). Second, using the example of Hacker Computers, we illustrated the reflection of certain economic events in the financial statements.

The FCF of a firm is the cash flow that can be distributed to any and all the firm's suppliers of capital, such as debt holders, equity holders, and preferred stockholders. (Obviously, if the FCF is negative, then this is the sum that needs to be *raised* from the firm's suppliers of capital.) The FCF is an operating concept: It relates to the firm's *business activities* and not to its *financial activities*: The FCF equals the cash that the firm's sales have generated less the funds needed to be invested in the business to sustain such sales. The financial decisions of the firm are essentially decisions on *how to allocate the FCF*: for example, which fraction of the FCF should be used to serve debt holders (in interest or in redemption of principal), which fraction should be paid out as dividends (preferred or regular), and which fraction should be used to buy back shares.

FCF can be derived from the standard accounting reports, properly manipulated. The accounting statement of financial performance—the Income Statement—differs from the FCF computation since it is done on an *accrual basis* and from the point of view of shareholders only (i.e., not from the perspective of *all* suppliers of capital). The adjustment of income statements in order to calculate FCFs:

- Excludes noncash items that are accrued in the current accounting statements (e.g., sales on credit)
- Adds cash items that are not accrued in the current accounting statements (e.g., Inventory purchases)
- Deducts payments for fixed assets that under standard accounting practices are capitalized (i.e., written as Fixed Assets in the balance sheet)
- Adds back depreciation charges, which are not cash flows but, rather, are the way that accountants ''flow'' the cost of fixed assets into the income statements.

The calculation of FCF in the manner previously described is called the direct method of figuring cash flows. The method directly adjusts each component in the income statement to its *cash-basis* equivalent. For example, sales are adjusted to collections by accounting for the activity in the Accounts Receivable—uncollected client bills—throughout the period. An alternative method, the indirect method, begins with the result of the income statement—Profits after Taxes (PAT)—and adjusts these profits for the same noncash items accounted for in the direct method. The indirect method, which begins with the accounting measure of performance—PAT, makes one more adjustment to calculate FCF: To convert PATs, which are profits computed from the *shareholders'* point of view, to FCFs, which are cash flows that can serve *all* the security holders, we also need to *add back the after-tax interest expense* in the income statement. In fact, Interest Expenses are a *use* of FCF—part of the payments to debt holders. (Debt holders also receive principal repayment and, when the debt is convertible, they receive capital gains on the conversion option.)

The uses of the FCF reflect the financial decisions of the firm, such as dividend and interest payments and issuance or redemption of securities. The difference between the FCF that the business generates and the financial uses of these cash flows is the excess cash accumulated in the firm. Hence, the change in the cash balances of the firm between the end of two consecutive accounting periods is the FCF less the financial uses of cash in the period. Thus, we have the following relations among the different accounting and economic measures of financial performance:

- PAT less dividends paid in the period give the change in Retained Earnings between two consecutive balance sheets.
- Changes in noncash net working capital items, Fixed Assets, and Accumulated Depreciation between two consecutive balance sheets allow us to convert PAT to FCF—the cash generated by the business that is free to be distributed to any security holder.
- Changes in Liabilities and Owners' Equity between two consecutive balance sheets indicate how FCFs have been used (according to the firm's financial policies).
- Changes in FCFs less the financial flows give the change in the cash balances of the firm between two consecutive balance sheets.

We have left the story of Hacker International hanging in midair. Our purpose in developing this story was to show you how a firm's financial statements—its balance sheet, income statement, and cash-flow statement—are related.

In succeeding chapters we shall build pro-forma models with which we can predict how a firm's financial statements will look in the future. These pro-forma statements will combine the accounting framework with our expectations about the way the firm's sales and costs will develop. We shall use these pro-forma statements to provide a framework within which we can do valuation.

EXERCISES

2.1 Starting with the Hacker International balance sheet after the buyout of Cheng Enterprises on July 1, 1994, calculate the Hacker International balance sheet on September 30, 1994, and the Hacker International profit and loss statement and cash-flow statement for the third quarter of 1994. Calculate this by entering all the events for Hacker that are listed in the chapter for the period of July 1 through September 30.

2.2 To reexamine some of the differences between cash flows and earnings, consider the case of NEW and OLD. NEW and OLD are two almost identical producers of a widget: Both use the same production technology (which has not changed for years and is not expected to change in the future), both sell equal quantities of the same product to the same clients for the same price, and all their operating expenses are the same. The only difference between the two producers is that NEW bought the machine used in the production of the widget last year, whereas OLD bought the same machines 8 years ago. Assume that inflation averaged 5 percent per year over the last 8 years and that these machines are depreciated on a straight-line basis to a zero salvage value over a period of 10 years. Ignoring taxes, which company do you expect will have higher earnings this year? Which had higher cash flows? Why?

2.3 Consider the following pro-forma statements:

Year-End Balance Sheet

Year	0	1
Assets		
Cash	$ 100	$ 90
Other current assets	150	153
Fixed assets		
At cost	1,000	1,150
Accumulated depreciation	300	415
Liabilities		
Nondebt current liabilities	70	75
Debt (short and long term)	???	???
Equity		
Stock	400	400
Retained earnings	???	163
Profit and Loss for Year		
Sales	1,000	1,050
COGS (excluding depreciation)	(700)	(730)
Depreciation expense	(100)	(115)
Interest	(30)	(30)
Profit before Taxes	170	175
Taxes (@ 40%)	(68)	(70)
Profit after Taxes (PAT)	102	105
Dividend	(40)	(42)
Retained earnings	62	63

Try your skills as an accounting detective:
a What was the Debt outstanding at the end of year 1?
b What were the Retained Earnings in the balance sheet at the end of year 0?
c What was the Cash generated by the operations of the firm in year 1?
d What was the Free Cash Flow of the firm in year 1?

VALUATION: PROCESSES AND PRINCIPLES

OVERVIEW

In the preceding chapters we reviewed the mechanics of discounting and the basics of accounting. At this point we assume that you know:

- How to derive the cash from operations (CFO) and the free cash flow (FCF) from a set of accounting statements
- How to adjust for the effects of inflation on cash flows received or paid at different points in time
- How to account for the effects of risk and inflation on discount rates.

Now it is time to give you an idea of where we are going. Throughout this book we follow a well-defined process of projecting the firm's performance and translating these projections to the firm and security values. However, you can easily get lost in the detailed description of the different stages of a valuation, and since there are many trees in the process we describe, you may easily lose sight of the forest. To help you see the big picture, in this chapter we will try to present an overview of the valuation process. We will describe the process and the principles of valuation, and provide a simple valuation example.

Before we begin, a word of warning: The potential users of financial information are many and varied. They include credit granters, equity investors, management, potential acquirers, auditors, and competitors. Each of these users may be interested in different nuances of information, which means that the mode of analysis that is suitable for one user of information may not be suitable for another. We try to cover valuation techniques and valuation-related topics that are useful in many settings. Thus, we discuss and illustrate generic valuation tools and techniques. In practice, however, each application of these techniques is likely to be different and to reflect the specific objectives of the particular analysis in which you are involved. The ability to tailor generic tools to your specific needs is a skill you will develop with experience.

3.1   THE VALUATION PROCESS

Having warned you that we can deal at best in generalities in this chapter, let's take a look at the typical valuation process. Such a process involves both the *collection* and the *evaluation* of information in order to derive values for corporate securities. The ultimate goal of our information gathering and model building is the *translation of our expectations about the firm and its environment into projections of financial performance for the firm* and *the translation of the projected financial performance into values*—of the firm as a whole and of the securities it has issued.

Most valuation processes have five stages, which are discussed in the following subsections.

Stage 1—Study the Corporate Environment

Almost invariably, we begin by looking at the environment in which the firm operates. This includes both information about the firm's future sales prospects and a study of the mechanics of the firm's operations:

- Are industry sales expected to rise or fall?
- Is the firm's market share expected to expand or contract?
- Are industry prices expected to increase or decrease?

These are only a few of the many questions that need to be answered before we can proceed to the next stage.

The study of the firm's environment begins with a study of the economy. Various industries tend to perform differently in different stages of the economic cycle. For example, basic industries perform well when the economy gets out of a recession, cosmetic goods sell well in economic downturns, and interest-sensitive industries such as banks and insurers do especially poorly when the economy enters a recession. Thus, to the extent that economic activity can be predicted, an understanding of the future course of the economy is useful information in analyzing industries and firms.

When the firm we value does business abroad or has foreign competitors (which means virtually every firm we look at), such an analysis requires understanding the world economy as well as the domestic economy. At a first glance it is hard to see why, for example, a U.S. widget manufacturer that does no business in Europe should care about the European economy. On a second consideration, however, we can visualize a situation in which poor economic conditions in Europe might induce

European competitors to dump European widgets in the United States. This will lower the margins for the U.S. widget manufacturer! Therefore, a complete valuation of this U.S. widget manufacturer should take into account the economic conditions in Europe despite the fact that this firm has no direct dealings with Europe.

After analyzing the macroeconomic conditions, we proceed with an analysis of the industry in which the firm operates. The objective of the analysis of the industry and the positioning of the firm we value within its industry is to obtain *sales projections* for the firm. Obviously, the industry analysis should incorporate our projections of macroeconomic conditions. For example, depending on macroeconomic conditions, we may expect an energetic demand for personal computers or a stale demand for ski vacations. Beyond the macroconditions, in our analysis of an industry we consider *current and potential competition* in the industry, *relative advantages* (and disadvantages!) of the major players in the industry, and the demand for and the prices of the products of the firm and its competitors. Moreover, we want to think about the industry that we analyze relative to industries that sell substitute products. These factors allow us to project *growth in the industry's sales, changes in the firm's market share,* and the product of the two—*growth in the firm's sales.*

Stage 2—Construct a Model of Expected Financial Performance

Using our understanding of the firm's environment, we proceed with a detailed analysis of the firm's operating and financial prospects, which we express in the form of **pro-forma financial statements.** These pro-forma statements include, among other things, projections of the cash flows that the firm's security holders will receive. Just as important, they are part of a structural model of the firm's accounting statements from which the cash flows are derived.

Building a pro-forma model of the firm is an important disciplinary exercise. It forces you, the analyst, to be specific about how you think the firm works. In the process you usually learn a lot about what you know and (sometimes more important!) about what you don't know.

As discussed in the next few chapters, much of our analysis is related to sales projections. It is hard to overemphasize the importance of accurately predicting the firm's sales. Nonetheless, the next step is no less important: We proceed by converting the marketing view of the firm—the sales projections—into full-blown projections of financial performance. In doing so, we consider how well the firm will manage the business of producing and selling the goods. We do this typically by analyzing the way that the firm has managed its business *in the past* by using various **financial ratios** and other statistical tools. But, obviously, this is only part of the picture: Our projections of *future* financial performance should not be confined to an analysis of *past* relations. Firms and industries change, and such changes—to the extent that we can predict them—should be incorporated into our projection of future financial performance. For example, we cannot ignore changes in personal computer technology when projecting the financial performance of IBM. Obviously, current technology is not entirely reflected in IBM's *past* operations. This means that an analysis of ratios in IBM's *historical* financial statements may not reveal the *expected* relations among the components of IBM's *future* financial performance (such as the *expected* relation of Cost of Goods Sold (COGS) to Sales). But it is precisely the *projected* relations that we need in order to project financial performance based on our sales projections. Although predicting technological changes and their effects on financial performance may be difficult, we should consider at the very least what the technological changes that are underway imply for future financial ratios and financial performance.

The end result of our analysis of the firm's projected efficiency is a set of proforma financial statements that reflect our expectations regarding the firm's marketing, operating, and financial prospects.

As we will show in Chapter 4, the pro-forma financial statements provide an *integrated structural view of the firm*:

• The pro-forma sales projections reflect our view of the firm's marketing prospects.
• The pro-forma income statements reflect our view of the firm's efficiency.
• The pro-forma balance sheets reflect our view of the firm's financial policies and technology.

Together, these three factors allow us to project the firm's cash flows and their components. In particular, we can project both the free cash flows (FCFs) that the firm will be able to use to service *all* suppliers of capital—debt, equity, and convertible securities—as well as the cash flows that each of the security holders can expect to receive—debt holders' interest and principal repayment, shareholders' dividends or share repurchases, and so on.

Stage 3—Convert the Projected Financial Performance to Values

Once we have built a pro-forma model of the firm and derived the projected cashflow streams to the various security holders in the firm, we can value these securities: The present values of these cash flows, which are calculated by using a discount rate that reflects the risks of the cash flows, are the values of the securities that the firm has issued.

The projection of the financial performance of the firm, via the pro-forma statements, is carried a few years forward.[1] Thus, by using the pro-forma statements, we can directly project cash flows for these few years. But the firm doesn't cease to exist after the projection horizon merely because we make no further financial projections. Thus, we need to take into account the firm's ability to

---

[1]As described in the following chapters, the horizon for the financial projections depends on the extent to which we have reliable information about the firm—the less specific information we have about the firm, the shorter the period will be for which we project financial performance.

generate cash flows beyond the horizon for which we project specific financial performance. This is done by including in the cash-flow projection a **terminal value** as *the last cash flow.* This terminal value reflects our inability to project financial performance ad infinitum, yet allows us to capture the value of cash flows beyond the projection horizon.

There are many types of cash flows, each of which should be discounted at a rate reflecting its own risk. Here are some examples of projected cash flows that we can value:

1 The *free cash flow (FCF)* of the firm is the cash flow available to *all* security holders in the firm (such as debt, equity, and convertible securities) before any financing adjustments. The risk-adjusted discount rate (RADR) for this cash-flow stream is a subject of much discussion in finance; we will postpone a full discussion of this question until Chapter 8. In anticipation of Chapter 8, the following are two possibilities for estimating the RADR with which to discount the firm's FCF:

a Estimate the RADR of the FCF as the sum of the risk-free rate of interest and a risk premium that reflects the risk of the firm's *assets.* For example, under the capital asset pricing model (CAPM) the risk premium equals the beta of the assets (β^{assets} or β^a) multiplied by the risk premium of an asset with a unit beta (such as the market portfolio).

b Estimate the RADR of the FCF as a weighted average of the firm's cost of equity and cost of debt. In finance jargon this is usually called the **weighted average cost of capital (WACC).** In many cases the WACC will be equal to, or approximately equal to, the cost of equity in an otherwise identical firm that uses no financial leverage (i.e., uses no debt financing). The reasons that this might happen involve a complex interaction among taxation effects, the cost of equity, and the market value of the firm's debt (again, we will discuss these issues in Chapter 8). When the WACC is equal to the cost of equity in an otherwise identical but unlevered firm, the amount of debt that the firm has (its *leverage*) has no effect on the firm's value.

Discounting the FCFs at the WACC or at a RADR reflecting the risk of assets gives us *the value of the firm as a whole*—the value of the firm's assets. This value equals the sum of the values of *all* the securities that the firm has issued, such as debt, equity, preferred stock, and convertible bonds. In finance jargon this is usually called the **value of the firm.**

Once the value of the whole firm is estimated, we can value the securities that the firm has issued. The process of first finding the value of the pie—the whole firm—and then slicing it and allocating pieces to the different security holders reflects the fact that the securities that firms issue are **derivative securities.** Derivative securities are securities the value of which is *derived from the value of the assets generating their cash flows*—the **underlying assets.** In the case of a firm the *underlying assets* are the operating assets of the firm and the *derivative assets* are the securities that the firm has issued.

2 **Expected dividends** are cash paid out to shareholders.[2] The RADR for this cash flow is the **cost of equity,** which reflects the *shareholder's risk.* A terminal value for shareholders' cash-flow streams is the expected value of equity on the last projection date, possibly estimated by using the Gordon formula—the last projected dividend payment divided by the difference between the RADR of the equity and the projected long-run growth in dividends. The cost of equity of a levered firm, again the topic of much discussion in finance, is discussed in Chapter 8; in Chapter 9 we give examples of the actual computation of the cost of equity. You can estimate the RADR of the equity—the cost of equity capital— in one of the following ways:

   a By using a model of risk and return trade-off, you can estimate the risk of the equity and the appropriate premium. For example, under the CAPM you can estimate the beta of the equity (β^{equity} or β^e) from historical returns and use the CAPM relation between beta and expected returns in order to estimate the RADR of the equity.

   b By projecting the next dividend payment, D_1, and the long-run growth in dividends, g, you can invert the observed price of a stock, P, by using the Gordon formula to estimate the market's required rate of return from the stock:

$$\text{RADR}^{equity} = \frac{D_1}{P} + g$$

   c By averaging the historical rate of return of the equity under the assumption that the historical risk of the equity equals the current risk of the equity, you can use the historical returns as an estimate of the current required RADR.

   The value obtained by discounting the shareholders' projected cash flows— dividends and capital gain—at the shareholders' RADR is the *value of the shares.*

3 **Expected interest payments and repayments of principal** are the cash-flow streams paid out to holders of the firm's debt. The discount rate applied to this stream of payments is the firm's *cost of debt.* The cost of debt reflects current market conditions, primarily the term structure of interest rates, as well as the risk of the firm's debt, primarily the risk of default. The RADR for debt—the cost of debt—is often different from the *coupon rate* on the firm's debt. Less obvious but equally true is the fact that the *expected* cash flows to the debt holders are different from the *promised* cash flows to the debt holders—the promised coupons and par values. This is because, although the debt holders will never receive more than they were promised in the debt contract (the **indenture**), they might receive less: If the firm defaults on its debt, the debt holder will receive less than full payment of coupons and par values. These

---

[2]Expected dividends also include expected share repurchases, which are largely *dividend substitutes.* A fuller discussion of the shareholders' cash flows is provided in Chapter 13.

issues and the valuation of debt securities—the present value of expected debt holders' cash flows at the cost of debt—are discussed in Chapter 11.

Stage 4—Alternative Techniques

In the preceding description of stage 3 of a typical valuation we emphasized the discounting of projected cash flows as the estimated values of the firm and of the securities it has issued. There are, however, alternative valuation mechanisms that convert projected financial performance to firm and security values. In this book we will explore two valuation techniques:

1 The approach we prefer (and which we have previously outlined) is to use an RADR to discount the cash flows. This approach has the most support in the academic finance profession. Deriving an RADR is not simple. It involves:
   a Estimating the firm's basic business risk
   b Adjusting this business risk for financial risk factors
2 An often used alternative to discounting cash flows is to use **multiples,** such as **price/earnings (P/E)** and **market to book (M/B),** in order to convert the projected financial performance to values. In general terms, we value firms using multiples by finding the average multiples—P/E, M/B, and others—in the industry and then by *applying the average industry multiple to the projected performance of the firm we value.* For example, suppose:
   a You find that the average P/E ratio in the industry is 10 and that the average M/B ratio is 2
   b Your pro-forma statements include a projection of next year's earnings of $25 million and next year's book value of equity of $95 million
   You combine the *observed ratios* with the *projected performance* to derive two value estimates:
   c *Based on projected earnings,* you estimate the value of the firm as

$$\$25 \text{ million} \cdot 10 = \$250 \text{ million}$$

   d *Based on projected book value,* you estimate the value of the firm as

$$\$95 \text{ million} \cdot 2 = \$190 \text{ million}$$

As will be discussed in Chapter 10, the use of multiples is more problematic than the use of discounted cash flows. Based on the preceding simple example, you can see some of the problems with multiples:

• Multiple-based valuations are largely based on the projected performance in the *next* year, which means that they fail to consider fully longer-term trends and overemphasize current conditions.
• Multiple-based valuations fail to reflect *all* the determinants of values such as risk and financial leverage while they overly rely on accounting principles to reflect

correctly economic values. Implicit in the use of multiples is the fact that *everything that is not explicitly considered is equal in all firms in the industry.* Sometimes this is a reasonable assumption, whereas in many cases it is not tenable.

Nonetheless, no analysis is complete without at least looking for *confirming evidence* in the form of valuation by multiples. At the very least you should understand and be able to explain why the discounted cash flow (DCF)-based value that you estimate for the firm differs from multiple-based values.

Stage 5—Consider the Implications of the Estimated Values

Once we have estimated the value of the firm or of the securities it has issued, we can consider the implications of our estimates. Obviously, the implications depend on the context in which these estimations were done. For example:

• For a valuation done to determine whether a proposed acquisition of a firm will create value for the acquiring firm (e.g., in an M&A group of an investment bank) the relevant comparison is of the value of the firm to be acquired with the price required.

• For a valuation done as part of a strategic planning process (e.g., whether or not to pursue a proposed course of action) the question is whether or not the proposed investment yields a positive NPV. Alternatively, when choosing among mutually exclusive strategic options, the relevant question is which option has the highest NPV.

• For the choice of investment portfolios the relevant comparison is of the price of the security considered for the portfolio, such as stock, bond, and convertibles, with the estimated value of the security.

In many investment decisions the valuation of individual firms and securities is only one component in the investment selection process. Once the prospects of individual securities are estimated, we often turn to the question of *how best to combine individual securities into portfolios.* Modern portfolio theory details how portfolios can be formed in order to minimize risk given a desired level of expected return. This theory is the basis of the CAPM, one of our working tools in estimating RADRs. In this book we devote little attention to the question of portfolio formation. The theory and practice of forming portfolios, **portfolio theory,** is the subject of courses and books on investments.

The valuation process previously described ensures a consistent translation of information that we gather into values that correctly reflect our information and expectations. The "hard wiring" of the process yields a mechanically consistent conversion of our projections. A less disciplined process of valuation can take *slightly* inaccurate information and expectations and convert them into *extremely* inaccurate values. By carefully designing the valuation process to adhere to economic principles, we eliminate the added noise that can be introduced by less formal valuation processes. This, however, is not the only benefit of this valuation process. By following a formal valuation process, we are forced to consider *all* the aspects of the business. We cannot, for example, neglect to consider the risks of the firm because this is a key determinant of the appropriate discount rate. Furthermore, knowing how information is going to be used in the valuation process is useful when we consider what information should be collected in order to value the firm.

The hard wiring of the valuation process is not the only thing that we should do. We can also use information that is difficult to incorporate into the firm's value but is still valuable to have. One type of information is observable and can be used to check our conclusions—information about what the firm's *insiders* think of the value of their firm relative to its market price. Insiders are privy to more information than we as outsiders can collect about the prospects of the firm. Thus, it is useful to know what *insiders* believe is the value of their firm. For example, suppose we conclude that the market price of the shares is higher than the value of shares. In other words, our analysis indicates that the market overvalues the firm. It would be surprising to learn that the firm's insiders *buy* shares of their firm in the market because such buying indicates that *they* think that, at the prevailing market price, the shares of their company are a good buy! If we do observe insider purchases of shares, perhaps we should rethink our model. (Or, perhaps, after rethinking our model, we will conclude that the insiders are wrong! It has been known to happen.)

3.2   SEQUENTIAL VALUATION VERSUS DIRECT VALUATION

In the preceding section we described various cash flows that can be discounted to obtain the firm's values. In particular, we suggested that FCFs can be discounted (at the cost of capital of the *assets*) to estimate the firm's value and that shareholders' cash flows can be discounted (at the *shareholders'* cost of capital) to estimate the value of the equity. Discounting the firm's FCFs to estimate a value for the firm as a whole may be appropriate if we consider purchasing a division of a firm or a whole firm. In other cases, however, we do not require an estimate of the value of the firm as a whole; rather, we require the value of one or more of the various securities that the firm has issued. This might be the case, for example, if we are managing a stock portfolio and consider the purchase of a certain stock, or if we are planning to obtain control over a firm by making a tender offer for its stock. As we implicitly described in the preceding section, there are two ways to estimate the value of the securities of the firm:

• We can start by determining the value of the whole firm, subsequently dividing this value among the holders of the firm's various securities. We begin the process of allocating pieces of the whole "pie" to the different claimants by analyzing the risk of the most senior claim—the firm's debt—and valuing the debt holders' claim. We do this both for traded debt, such as bonds and commercial paper, and for nontraded debt, such as bank loans. Whatever is left of the pie after we figure the share of the debt holders is shared by the firm's less senior claim holders. As explained in Chapter 12, if the firm has issued **convertible securities,** such as **warrants** or **convertible bonds,** we value these convertible securities by using a different technique from discounting expected cash flows at an RADR. This technique requires that when convertible securities exist, we value them first—*before* we value the firm's equity. Finally, the value of the equity claim is calculated as the residual value—the value of the whole firm less the value of the debt and convertible securities. We refer to this process of estimating security values as the **sequential valuation process.**

• Alternatively, we can value each of the pieces of the pie separately. In this process the specific cash flows of each class of security holders are projected and discounted at the security's RADR—a discount rate that reflects the security's own risk. For example, we can project the cash flows that the shareholders will receive, which equal the firm's FCFs minus the payments to all claim holders who have seniority over the shareholders, and discount these cash flows at the shareholders'discount rate to estimate directly the value of the firm's equity. We refer to this process of estimating security values as the **direct valuation process.**

Although both the sequential and the direct processes should ultimately yield the same values for each of the firm's securities, we will often find that in practice one of the two procedures is easier to implement than the other. In addition, finance being an imperfect discipline, it is not uncommon to find that in practice the approximations that we make along the way cause these two procedures to give different answers!

In our experience it is frequently much simpler to value securities sequentially rather than directly. Here are three cases where sequential valuation is simpler than direct valuation:

• To value equity directly, we discount the equity holders' cash flows at the *equity* cost of capital. To find the RADR of the equity, which reflects the risk of the equity, we must know the *financial leverage* of the firm—the ratio of the total firm value to the value of the equity. But in order to find the financial leverage, we need to know the value of the firm and its equity, which is the reason for determining the discount rate in the first place! To be sure, the simultaneity problem we encounter here—the need to know both the value of the equity to estimate the cost of capital of the equity and the cost of capital of the equity to estimate the value of the equity—can be solved. But it is much simpler to find these values sequentially.

• To value equity directly, we need to subtract from the firm's FCFs the projected cash flows to be paid to the debt holders. Many firms use **floating-rate debt,** on which interest is reset periodically according to market conditions. For example, a firm may borrow at LIBOR + 2%, which means that its borrowing costs vary as the LIBOR (London Inter-Bank Offer Rate) changes over time. Because the coupon rate is repeatedly adjusted to roughly the market rate, the *value* of floating-rate debt rarely differs by much from par value. The interest charges on such debt, however, may vary considerably over time and are hard to predict. How then do we determine what interest charges to include in the pro-forma statements of distant years? Clearly, it is much simpler to deduct the value of the floating-rate debt from the value of the whole firm to estimate the value of the equity sequentially.

• Many corporations issue stock options to their top employees. The idea is that such options, called *warrants,* align the interests of top management with those of the shareholders. The valuation of warrants, and of other convertible securities, is discussed in Chapter 12. At this point we only need to know that the theory of option valuation indicates that when the firm has issued convertible securities, we no longer can value the firm's equity by simply discounting shareholders' expected cash flows at a single RADR. Moreover, valuation of convertible securities requires the value of the whole firm.

The preceding examples suggest that, even though the sequential valuation process and the direct valuation process when consistently applied yield the same values for the securities of the firm, the sequential valuation process is often simpler to apply. We can summarize the sequential valuation process by using the following table:

Analysis	Result
Analysis of economy and industry	Projection of sales
Analysis of firm	Projection of costs
Analysis of firm risk	Estimation of WACC Firm valuation
Analysis of debt risk	Debt valuation
Analysis of convertible securities	Valuation of convertible securities Valuation of stock

3.3   SOME GENERAL VALUATION RULES

In the remaining chapters we will gradually build a detailed valuation framework. Although at this point we cannot as yet relate to many elements of this valuation framework in detail, we can state some general rules of valuation. These rules, although almost self-evident, are often forgotten in the rush to value the hottest target.

Value Cash-Flow Streams

Ultimately, investors are interested in the amount of disposable income that they receive from an investment, whether a company or a savings account. Since firms cannot pay out more cash than they have available, this means that we should value the cash-flow streams produced by the firm and that are ultimately received by investors.

There are many alternatives to valuing cash-flow streams. Primarily these alternatives are based on accounting measures, such as price/earnings ratios and market/book ratios. For many special cases these alternative measures of value correspond to cash-flow valuation. Often they can be used as a way of double-checking your cash-flow valuation. But the ultimate measure of financial value should be the discounted value of the cash-flow streams produced by the company.

Nonetheless, one frequently finds value estimates that are based on other measures of value. Most common among the substitutes for **discounted cash-flow (DCF)** valuations are valuations based on the firm's earnings. Earnings, however, are not cash flows. Earnings are an *accounting* measure of performance that are defined according to accounting principles such as **matching** and **conservatism.** As you have seen in Chapter 2, the application of accounting principles often requires the allocation of certain costs and revenues to various accounting periods, *allocations that are independent of the true time of payment.* For example, although the purchase of a fixed asset occurs at a given point in time, accountants use depreciation to *allocate* the cost of the asset over the many years in which the asset is in use. But these allocations, although based on some ''sensible'' criteria, are arbitrary: They have *nothing* to do with the true flow of funds. As a result, the value of an asset that is calculated based on accounting earnings may be unjustifiably affected by these arbitrary allocations.

To see what may go wrong with valuations that are based on accounting earnings, consider two identical firms, the Accelerators Inc. (AI) and the Straightliners PLC (SP). Both AI and SP have a single identical machine, which costs $30 thousand, has a working life of 3 years, and has no salvage value. This machine can print 2,500 calendars per year. Each calendar sells for $16 and materials used in the production of one calendar cost $8. In order to simplify the example, we assume that neither firm pays taxes.[3]

Suppose now that you want to value AI and SP by using an ''appropriate'' *P/E ratio.* Toward that end, you calculate the average P/E ratio for all other firms in the industry and find it to be 10.[4] Then you examine the financial statements of AI and SP. You notice that while SP uses a straight-line depreciation schedule, AI uses an accelerated depreciation schedule—the **sum-of-year-digits** depreciation schedule. Thus, SP has an annual depreciation charge against earnings of $30,000/3 = $10,000, whereas AI has a depreciation charge of $30,000 · 3/(1 + 2 + 3) = $15,000 in the first year, $30,000 · 2/6 = $10,000 in the second year, and the remaining $5,000 in the machine's last year. The first-year earnings of AI and SP are:

	AI	SP
Sales	$ 40,000	$ 40,000
Materials	(20,000)	(20,000)
Depreciation	(15,000)	(10,000)
Profits	$ 5,000	$ 10,000

[3]If this is not enough, we also assume that both firms have no debt—only equity—in their capital structure. Having assumed away taxes, this additional assumption is small potatoes.

[4]This P/E ratio is an illustration of what we call *famous rules of thumb in finance.* A few of these rules are:

Whenever in doubt as to what is the right P/E to use, use 10.
If you don't know the RADR, use 10 percent.
The answer to almost any troublesome finance question should include the word ''risk.''
When in doubt, blame the accountants.

Applying the industry's P/E ratio, you find that AI's value is $50 thousand, one-half the $100 thousand value that you estimate for SP. This is astonishing since we know that both firms have the same equipment and do the same business. This difference only exists because AI's accountants *chose* a different depreciation schedule from that of SP's accountants!

An obvious fix to this problem is to correct for the difference in reported earnings that is due to the difference between the depreciation schedules that these firms use before we derive and compare values. The problem with this adjustment idea is that our example is misleading in its simplicity—the simplicity here misleads us into thinking that we can always undo the accounting tricks that firms play on us. Unfortunately, financial statements are neither that simple nor that clear. Undoing the accounting decisions of firms is often a very tricky business. At best we can arrive at ''guesstimates'' as to what depreciation charges would have been under different depreciation schedules.

The best solution to the particular problem raised in the preceding example is to offset depreciation charges altogether. In other words, use cash flows rather than accounting earnings. This is because *cash flows are not affected by arbitrary accounting allocations,* such as depreciation, tax allowances, and inventory valuation.

P/E ratios present another problem that was neatly swept under the rug in the previous example. When using cash flows, we can find the price of money to be paid in (almost) any future date by looking at the yield of a bond maturing on that date. How do we find the price of earnings? Or, what is the ''appropriate'' P/E? The problem is that, unlike cash flows of different dates that are traded in financial markets, there is no market in which earnings are traded. Earnings are a measure of the ongoing profitability of a business. They are often informative about the state of the business. But earnings cannot be *sold.* The only cash that the firm produces is contained in its cash flows, and these cash flows are ultimately valued in market prices.

We often circumvent our problem of not knowing what an appropriate P/E ratio is by looking for average P/Es of similar firms as an indicator of what P/E to apply to the earnings of the firm that we value. Typically, the average P/E doesn't correspond to the P/E of *any* of the comparable firms. Rather, P/Es are typically spread over a wide range. This in itself indicates that we can learn little from the P/E of one company about the appropriate P/E with which to value another company.

Make Sure to Deal Consistently with Inflation

Of the characteristics of cash flows mentioned in Chapter 1—timing, risk, purchasing power, and liquidity—inflation is the element that is most often neglected in valuations. When you project pro-forma financial statements, ask yourself: Do my cash-flow projections properly differentiate between an increased *volume* of business and a *change in the prices* of the product? In other words, can you identify your projected cash flows as *nominal cash flows* or as *real cash flows*? If not, you are on the wrong track.

It doesn't make much difference—in principle, at least—whether you project and discount nominal cash flows or real cash flows, as long as you are consistent. This is because, when you are ready to discount the cash flows, you can discount them at nominal or real discount rates, respectively. The point is that you have to know whether your projected cash flows are nominal or real in order to be able to match a discount rate to them. Discounting nominal cash flows at a real rate or real cash flows at a nominal rate yields incorrect NPV and security valuations. Although simple in theory, this principle is often tricky to apply. It is easy, for example, to neglect to consider the effect of inflation on sale prices (and consider only real sales growth), yet later calculate tax payments after deducting depreciation charges that are based on the *nominal* cost of the fixed assets.

It is frequently simpler to value consistently on a nominal basis: Observed discount rates are often nominal and tax computation usually reflects nominal values only. Nonetheless, there is no better way to project cash flows and discount them: Use either nominal values or real values, whichever you feel more comfortable with. So long as you carefully consider the effect of inflation on cash flows and discount rates, you are home safe.

Identify the Recipient(s) of Cash-Flow Streams

Firms produce many different kinds of cash-flow streams. **Equity investors** receive dividends as long as they hold their shares in the firm; when they sell these shares, they receive the market value of their shares. **Bondholders** receive a stream of interest payments and repayments of principal. Holders of **convertible bonds** receive interest payments until maturity or conversion, whichever occurs first; then they receive either the par value of the bond—if they chose not to convert—or the equity holders' cash flows—if they convert. Holders of **preferred stock** get a fixed stream of dividends and a liquidating payment in bankruptcy. The reason we care about who receives what is that it helps us to assess the risk characteristics of the cash flows, which is important because of the next principle:

Match the Discount Rate to the Characteristics of the Cash-Flow Stream

The RADR that is appropriate for discounting a given set of cash flows can depend not only on the risk of these cash flows, but also on the timing, purchasing power, and liquidity of the cash flows. Implementing this principle is tricky, and we postpone a fuller discussion of the problems involved to Chapters 8 and 9.

Carefully Take into Account the Timing of Cash Flows

The discounting equations presented in most finance textbooks assume that the cash flows being discounted are *year-end* cash flows. In contrast, most of the cash flows we discount when valuing projects, firms, or securities—for example, sales,

COGS, investments, and taxes—are *cash flows that are paid and received through-out the year.* To discount these cash flows as if they were year-end cash flows would be inappropriate: Although some operating cash flows will be paid at the end of the year, some of these flows will be paid as early as tomorrow! This means that *operating cash flows should be discounted as midyear cash flows* rather than as end-of-year cash flows.[5] In particular, cash flows projected for the first year should be discounted only for *half* a year rather than a full year, the cash flows projected for the second year should be discounted for *one and a half* years only rather than for 2 years, and the like. Expressed in an equation form, the correct discount rule for operating cash flows is

$$NPV = \sum_{t=1}^{N} \frac{E(CF_t)}{(1 + RADR_t)^{t - 1/2}} + CF_0$$

If the term structure of the RADR appropriate for the cash flow is flat, this equation will simplify to

$$NPV = (1 + RADR)^{1/2} \cdot \sum_{t=1}^{N} \frac{E(CF_t)}{(1 + RADR)^{t}} + CF_0$$

This simplification is very useful when using a spreadsheet: Spreadsheets assume that all cash flows are year-end cash flows, which means that present values calculated by using these spreadsheets should be adjusted. The preceding formula shows how to adjust the spreadsheet computation: Calculate the present value of the cash flows of year 1 through N by using the spreadsheet equation, multiply this present value by $(1 + RADR)^{1/2}$, and add the cash flow of the first year (which doesn't need to be discounted).

Double-Check Your Valuation

Valuation is never a sure thing: There are too many guesstimates involved in predicting cash flows and in calculating discount rates for us to be totally sure of the value that we calculate for a company and its component securities. One way to double-check your work is to use several methods of calculating the values. For example:

• Calculate discount rates by using several different methods—the Gordon model and CAPM, for example, for the cost of equity.
• Use a multiple method (e.g., P/E) alongside a more full-blown cash-flow discounting method.

The purpose of using several methods is *to check whether you are in the ballpark.* By the time you finish a valuation, you should feel comfortable with the

---

[5]This is only an approximation: An exact calculation of the average discount time is not exactly midyear. But the approximation is a good one.

value range that you calculate. If you have succeeded in doing this, you are on the right track.

3.4   THE COUNTRY MOTEL—CASE STUDY

We will emphasize some of the points discussed in the preceding sections by looking at a case study. The purpose of the case is to illustrate:

• The calculation of cash flows of different types for a small business: monthly FCFs and monthly equity cash flows.
• The relation of different versions of the cash flow—the cash flow as derived from a spreadsheet version of the firm's checkbook and the cash flow as derived from the firm's accounting statements.
• A very simple calculation of the value of a business. We want to show you how to differentiate between the *value of the business as a whole* and *the value of the equity of the business.*
• A simple example of cash management. Although this is not the main purpose of this case study, it is a pleasant by-product of the analysis.

The Case

The date is January 1, 1991. Exactly 1 year ago you and your spouse purchased a small (25-unit) country motel for $400,000. The motel is located in an area that gets both summer and winter tourism. Besides yourselves, you employ two local college students, who help you to clean up and take turns at the desk.

Each of the college students earns about $1,000 per month. You and your spouse together draw $4,000 per month from the business as a salary. Additional salary costs are social security (8 percent of salaries) and $300 per month for your medical insurance (the students are insured through their college). Thus, total monthly salary costs are $6,780.

Although monthly occupancy rates vary, you have decided to use an average monthly occupancy rate of 71 percent in your cash-flow projections.

Your room rates vary by occupancy (they also vary by season, but for simplicity you have decided not to include this in your initial cash-flow projections). All rooms can accommodate couples. Your policy has been not to charge extra for children. Current rates are:

Average room rates	
Single occupancy	$45
Double occupancy	$55

Typically, about 60 percent of your guests are couples (with or without children). You have calculated that the marginal cost per paying guest is about $5 per night (this includes laundry and the wear-and-tear on towels and sheets).

Taxes   There is an 8 percent state sales tax and a 3 percent local hotel tax. Both taxes are added onto the guests' bills, collected by the innkeeper, and paid to the state or the city on the 15th of each month for the whole of the previous month. In addition, you pay city property taxes in March (the city's fiscal year is April to March); last year these taxes were $23,310. To comply with an Environmental Protection Agency ruling, the city has to build a new water treatment plant this year; thus, there has been a discussion of a considerable rise in taxes to pay for the plant. In your cash-flow statement you assume that property taxes for the coming year will be $30,000.

Other Large Expenses   You have hired a local company on a retainer ($300 per month) to do small maintenance and upkeep. At the start of the winter season you do necessary major maintenance and major repairs. Last year these were:

Roof and gutters	$ 2,500
Painting	$10,000
Other maintenance	$ 5,500

This year you anticipate that repairs of this type will recur, and that there will be an expense of $18,000 in October.

Utilities   The city charges you a flat rate of $500 per month for water. Electricity, used for both heating and cooling the rooms, costs about $800 per month.

Insurance   A comprehensive insurance policy will cost you $32,000 this year; half of this is due in January, with the remainder payable at the beginning of July.

Mortgage   You have a $300,000, 11 percent, 20-year mortgage. The interest rate is fixed, and payments are made monthly (the monthly interest rate = 11/12%).

Additional Assumptions and Facts

1   The hotel tax due January 15, 1991, on December 1990 billings is $5,500.
2   Your ending bank balance for December 1990 was $3,456.
3   The motel is a sole proprietorship. You pay taxes only at the personal income tax rate. Last year (your first year of operation) the motel lost money, and your accountant has assured you that you owe no income taxes (state or federal) for the 1990 tax year. (In our calculations we assume that there is no tax-loss carry forward to the current year.) This year you anticipate a profit, and she has advised you to make quarterly estimated tax payments of $3,000 (federal income tax) and $500 (state income tax). These payments are due in January, April, July, and October. In the following analysis we assume that the federal tax is 28 percent and the state tax is 3.2 percent (both flat rates).

4 For tax purposes you are allowed straight-line depreciation over 20 years, so the annual depreciation is $20,000.

5 All property and sales taxes are deductible for income tax purposes; the state income tax is deductible for the federal tax, but the federal tax is not deductible for state income taxes.

A Cash-Flow Spreadsheet

We start by modeling the expected monthly cash flows of the motel (Exhibit 3.1). The top left-hand section of the spreadsheet contains the projection parameters: the occupancy rates, the percentage of single versus double occupancies, the marginal cost of each guest, etc.

Exhibit 3.1

Motel Cash Flows on a Monthly Basis

	Percent	Rate	January	February	March	April	May	June	July	August	September	October	November	December
Double occupancy	60%	$55.00												
Single occupancy	40%	$45.00												
Occupancy rate (percent)	71%													
Marginal cost per guest/night	$5.00													
Rooms	25													
Hotel taxes	11%													
December taxes payable	5,500													
Days in month			31	28	31	30	31	30	31	31	30	31	30	31
Initial cash balance			3,456	-5,773	3,823	-13,694	-5,373	6,911	18,232	11,516	23,700	35,021	26,305	37,627
Inflows														
Billings			28,063	25,347	28,063	27,158	28,063	27,158	28,063	28,063	27,158	28,063	27,158	28,063
Hotel taxes on billings			3,087	2,788	3,087	2,987	3,087	2,987	3,087	3,087	2,987	3,087	2,987	3,087
Total Inflows			31,150	28,135	31,150	30,145	31,150	30,145	31,150	31,150	30,145	31,150	30,145	31,150
Outflows														
Personnel costs			6,780	6,780	6,780	6,780	6,780	6,780	6,780	6,780	6,780	6,780	6,780	6,780
Hotel taxes			5,500	3,087	2,788	3,087	2,987	3,087	2,987	3,087	3,087	2,987	3,087	2,987
Federal taxes			2,500			2,500			2,500			2,500		
State taxes			500			500			500			500		
Property tax					30,000									
Marginal costs, guests			4,402	3,976	4,402	4,260	4,402	4,260	4,402	4,402	4,260	4,402	4,260	4,402
Insurance			16,000						16,000					
Utilities			1,300	1,300	1,300	1,300	1,300	1,300	1,300	1,300	1,300	1,300	1,300	1,300
Maintenance			300	300	300	300	300	300	300	300	300	18,300	300	300
Total Outflow, before Mortgage			37,282	15,443	45,570	18,727	15,769	15,727	34,769	15,869	15,727	36,769	15,727	15,769
Mortgage														
Beginning principal			295,625	295,238	294,848	294,454	294,057	293,656	293,251	292,843	292,431	292,015	291,595	291,171
Monthly payment			3,097	3,097	3,097	3,097	3,097	3,097	3,097	3,097	3,097	3,097	3,097	3,097
Interest			2,710	2,706	2,703	2,699	2,696	2,692	2,688	2,684	2,681	2,677	2,673	2,669
Principal			387	390	394	397	401	405	408	412	416	420	424	427
Total Outflow			40,379	18,539	48,667	21,823	18,866	18,823	37,866	18,965	18,823	39,866	18,823	18,866
Cash flow to owners			-9,229	9,596	-17,517	8,321	12,284	11,321	-6,716	12,184	11,321	-8,716	11,321	12,284
Ending cash balance			-5,773	3,823	-13,694	-5,373	6,911	18,232	11,516	23,700	35,021	26,305	37,627	49,910
Total Cash Flow			46,454											

The logic of the spreadsheet is very simple, as shown in Exhibit 3.2:

Exhibit 3.2

Item	Method
Estimate *monthly inflow of cash.*	Use occupancy rates, percentages of double versus single occupancy, and projected room rates. Add in hotel taxes.
Estimate monthly cash costs to get *total outflow of cash.*	Includes salaries, taxes, other expenses, and mortgage payments.[6]
Estimate *monthly cash flow.*	This is the *total inflows* minus *total outflows* of cash during the month. Equivalently, this is the beginning of the month cash balance minus the end of the month balance.
Estimate *ending cash balance for month.*	Equals cash balance at the beginning of the month minus monthly cash flow. The ending cash balance for the current month becomes the beginning cash balance for the next month.

Here are two examples which illustrate the computations in Exhibit 3.1:

- Billings in month (t) are the product of:
    number of days in month
    number of rooms
    occupancy rate
    average room rate
- Mortgage interest expense in month (t) equals:
    Mortgage principal outstanding at the beginning of the month times the monthly mortgage interest rate (11/12%)

The cash-flow projection spreadsheet is really a simple exercise in **cash management** (sometimes called **short-term asset and liability management**). It is difficult to exaggerate the importance of such an exercise in practical corporate finance. Depending on the size of the business and the complexity of the problems that the firm faces, you may want to do a cash management model on a monthly, weekly, or even daily basis.

The motel's cash flow in a single month equals the difference between the month's inflow and outflow. Thus, for example, to derive the cash flow for January, we have:

January inflow	$ 31,150
January outflow	(40,379)
January cash flow	$ − 9,229

[6]The mortgage payment schedule involves a separate set of calculations. We leave this as an exercise.

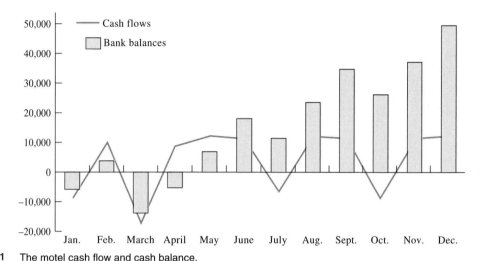

FIGURE 3.1   The motel cash flow and cash balance.

The *cash balance* at the end of the month is the sum of the month's initial cash balance plus the month's cash flow:

January initial cash balance	$ 3,456
January cash flow	−9,229
January ending cash balance	$−5,773

Not surprisingly, the difficult months for the cash flow are those with heavy one-time payments—taxes, insurance, and repairs.[7] Note from the spreadsheet (Exhibit 3.1) that there are several months when the motel is projected to have a negative cash balance. (See also Figure 3.1, which shows the motel's cash flow and cash balance.) In the exercises for this chapter we ask you to relate to the financing costs of these negative cash balances.

Projecting the Pro-Forma Profit and Loss Statement

The preceding cash-flow spreadsheet can be used to derive the pro-forma (i.e., expected) Profit and Loss Statement for the end of the year. This Profit and Loss Statement treats the motel as if it were an independent business. (As you will show in the exercises for this chapter, the pro-forma tax return of the owners at the end of the year looks somewhat different.) We can use this pro-forma Profit and Loss Statement to calculate the FCF of the motel (see Exhibit 3.3).

[7]In the exercises for this chapter we ask you to consider the cost of financing the negative cash flows for these months. In Exhibit 3.1 we have assumed that the interest paid on positive cash balances is zero and that there is no cost of financing negative cash balances.

Exhibit 3.3
Pro-Forma Profit and Loss Statement

Total cash inflow	$366,762
Expenses	
Personnel	81,360
Other expenses	121,030
Mortgage interest	32,278
Taxes	
Property taxes	30,000
Hotel taxes	38,759
Depreciation	20,000
Total expenses	323,427
Profit before taxes	43,335
State tax (3.2%)	1,387
Federal tax (28%)	11,746
Profit after taxes	$ 30,203

Note: Addition of columns may not agree because of rounding.

The Profit and Loss Statement treats the salaries of the owners as an expense. This is justified, for if the owners did not work in the motel themselves, they would have to hire someone to do it. Assuming that $4,000 per month is a market wage for this kind of work, the equity cash flows that we have calculated are correct. Moreover, the calculation of the motel's cash flows should also deduct the owners' wage: This wage is theirs in their capacity as *workers* of the motel, not as the motel's owners.

Adding the monthly cash flows to owners, as displayed in Exhibit 3.1, gives anticipated annual equity cash flows of $46,454. We can do an alternative calculation of these cash flows from the pro-forma Profit and Loss Statement:

Profit after taxes	$30,203
Add back depreciation	20,000
Less mortgage principal payments	4,881
Cash flow to equity owners	$45,322

These two cash flows are different, but they can be easily reconciled by noting that the estimated taxes paid by the owners underpay the state taxes and slightly overpay the federal taxes, compared to the provision for these taxes in the pro-forma Profit and Loss Statement:

Reconciling Exhibit 3.1 with Exhibit 3.3	
Total of monthly cash flows	$46,454
Difference in taxes	
State taxes	−613
Federal taxes	1,746
Net	$45,321

Whose Cash Flows Are These?

Remember that one of our principles was: "Identify the recipients of the cash flows." If you look closely at the cash flows that we have calculated so far you will see that they are **equity cash flows:** We have taken out the payments to the debt holders of the motel (i.e., the mortgage payments). The FCFs generated by the motel—the cash that can be used to pay *all* security holders—are larger than the equity cash flows. We can calculate the motel's FCFs in two ways:

Free Cash Flows The indirect method	
Profit after taxes	$30,203
Add back depreciation	20,000
Add back after-tax interest	22,496
Free cash flow	$72,699

Note that the effective tax rate is 30.304 percent. This takes into account the tax deductibility of the state income tax. Thus:

$$\text{effective tax rate} = 28\% + (1 - 28\%) \cdot 3.2\% = 30.304\%$$

We can also calculate the FCF directly, from the individual items (see Exhibit 3.4).

Exhibit 3.4

Free Cash Flows
The direct method

Total cash inflow	$366,762	
Total expenses	(291,149)	includes depreciation, excludes interest
Net	75,613	
Taxes on above	(22,914)	at effective tax rate of 30.304%
Net	52,699	
Add back depreciation	20,000	
Free Cash Flow	$ 72,699	

If you want to value the *equity* of the hotel by discounting the *equity holders'* cash flows at the *equity* RADR, then the cash flows to equity (calculated from either the pro-forma Profit and Loss Statement or the spreadsheet after the adjustments for taxes) are precisely the cash flows that you need. If you want to value the motel as a whole, independent of the split of its current financing between debt and equity, then you need the FCF. Moreover, if you value the motel's equity in a sequential process, you also should begin with the FCF, value the motel as a whole unit, and then divide the debt and the value of the equity. This is the course we will take in the next subsection.

Calculating the Value of the Motel

To calculate the value of the motel, we have to make lots of bold assumptions (this is why cowardly students don't go into finance!):

- The projected annual cash flows will recur in each of the next 10 years.
- The motel has a real, pretax, residual value at the end of 10 years that is equal to the price paid for it ($400,000).
- All the projected cash-flow numbers assume that there is no change in prices. Thus, except for the *nominal* depreciation cash flows, we have implicitly projected cash flows of constant purchasing power—*real* cash flows. This means that the cash flows can be divided into a real and a nominal component:

Annual expected real cash flow from operations	66,639
Annual expected nominal cash flow—depreciation tax shield	6,061

- The real RADR that is applicable to all risky cash flows is 20 percent and the real RADR that is applicable to risk-free cash flows is 7 percent.[8] The annual expected inflation rate over the next 10 years is 3 percent per year. This means that the *nominal discount rates* corresponding to the above real rates of interest are

$$\text{RADR}^{\text{nominal}} = (1 + 20\%) \cdot (1 + 3\%) - 1 = 23.6\%$$

and for the risk-free rate

$$r_f^{\text{nominal}} = (1 + 7\%) \cdot (1 + 3\%) - 1 = 10.21\%$$

Note that neither the $\text{RADR}^{\text{nominal}}$ nor the r_f^{nominal} equals the yield on the motel's mortgage. This is because the mortgage is somewhat risky but not as risky as the motel itself. Thus, it is compensated by a yield exceeding the risk-free rate, yet (as a senior secured claim) lower than the RADR of the motel. We discuss these issues in Chapters 9 and 11.

- The depreciation tax shield is nominally risk free.

Now we are ready to do some calculations. The value of the motel today can be represented as

$$\begin{aligned} &\text{PV(real nondepreciation CFs @20\%)} \\ &+ \text{PV(nominal depreciation tax-shields @10.21\%)} \\ &+ \text{PV(nominal, after-tax residual @23.60\%)} \end{aligned}$$

The first two items can be easily calculated:

$$\text{PV(real nondepreciation CFs)} = (1 + 20\%)^{1/2} \cdot \sum_{i=1}^{10} \frac{66,639}{1.20^i} = 306,045$$

$$\text{PV(nominal depreciation tax shields)} = (1 + 10.21\%)^{1/2} \cdot \sum_{i=1}^{10} \frac{6,061}{1.1021^i}$$
$$= 38,745$$

Two things are worth noting about the previous computations of present values:

- The motel's operating cash flows are *real*—they are expected to change with changes in the purchasing power of money—whereas the depreciation tax savings are *nominal*—they have a fixed dollar value that is independent of what a dollar can buy. Accordingly, we value the operating cash flows by using the *real* RADR and the depreciation tax shields by using the *nominal* r_f.

---

[8]Where do we get these numbers? For this you will have to wait until Chapters 8 and 9. For now we ask you to accept the fact that these numbers are correct.

• Both cash flows being valued are *operating* cash flows, which means that they *accrue throughout the year*. Hence, we value these annual flows by using *mid-year* discounting (rather than year-end discounting).

In order to calculate the present value of the motel's residual value, we have to do some preliminary calculations. First of all, we assume that the motel's *nominal residual value* at the end of 10 years will be its current value inflated over 10 years: $400,000 \cdot (1.03)^{10} = 537,567$. On the other hand, since the model is being depreciated at 20,000 per year, its *book value* (i.e., cost less accumulated depreciation) in 10 years will be:

Initial cost of motel	$ 400,000
Accumulated depreciation[9]	(220,000)
Motel book value at the end of year 10	$ 180,000

Selling the motel for $537,567 will thus create a substantial taxable **capital gain** for the owners. Our calculations will have to take into account the tax payments on this capital gain:

Motel nominal market value, year 10	$ 537,567
Book value, year 10	(180,000)
Capital gain	357,567
Capital gains tax (30.304%)	(108,357)
Net	$ 429,210

This is an example of an important practical rule: *Every cash flow has an associated tax implication.* To take this point one step further, even zero cash flows may have tax implications: Suppose you think that after 10 years the residual value of the hotel is zero; then the owners of the hotel will have a *capital loss* on their hotel that may entail a tax refund or tax savings! Thus, whenever you consider a cash flow, look for all the associated tax payments.[10]

---

[9]Note that at the point in time at which we are doing these calculations, the motel has already been depreciated for 1 year. Thus, in 10 years the accumulated depreciation will be $11 \cdot 20,000$.

[10]There is another way to do the cash-flow calculation associated with the motel's residual value. Assume that the *full value* of the motel is taxed at the average rate, and that the motel's book value generates a *tax shield*. Then the cash flow is given by

$$\text{Residual cash flow} = (1 - 0.30304) \cdot 537,567 + 0.30304 \cdot 180,000 = 429,210$$

We can now calculate the present value of the motel's terminal value. In this case we have chosen not to use midyear discounting.[11]

$$PV(\text{nominal, after-tax residual}) = \frac{429,210}{1.2360^{10}} = 51,580$$

The market value of the motel is given by the sum of these three items:

$$\text{Motel market value} = 306,045 + 38,745 + 51,580 = 396,370$$

The Motel's Equity Value

We have decided that the value of the motel today is $396,370. How much of this is equity? This is a simple calculation since

$$\text{Value of motel} = \text{value of equity} + \text{value of debt}$$

Since the current value of the mortgage is $295,625, the value of the equity is given by $396,370 − $295,625 = $100,745.

Double Checking

As already mentioned, valuation is not really a science: It's more of an art! You need to double-check some of your calculations. Here are a couple of simple double checks:

- A 50-room motel in your area has just been sold for $900,000. If the value of motels is proportional to the number of rooms, this gives an estimated value for your motel of $450,000. This is acceptably close to the value of the motel that we have estimated (396,370). The difference in values may indicate that small motels are worth less proportionally than large motels, possibly because of operating economies to scale. (See Exercise 3.3 at the end of this chapter.)
- Shares of a publicly traded motel chain are selling for a price/earnings (P/E) ratio of 4. Applying this ratio to our earnings estimate of $30,203 gives an estimated market value of the equity of your motel of $120,812. Unlike the previous benchmark this value estimate should be compared to the estimated value of your motel's *equity*. Although this is different from the value that we calculated previously ($100,745), it is—considering the "fuzzinesss" of our projections—"in the ballpark."

---

[11]The interpretation of the terminal value will determine whether or not we choose to use midyear discounting: If the terminal value stands for the discounted value of all the cash flows beyond the horizon period, we should use midyear discounting. If, as in the case of the example here, the terminal value is intended to stand for the sale of the motel at the *end* of year 10, we should not use midyear discounting.

In Chapter 10 we discuss such comparisons in detail. It is important, however, to emphasize even at this early stage that the second comparison is a lot more problematic than the first one. The first comparison is of the values of *whole* firms. As such it is independent of the leverage of the firms. The second comparison, on the other hand, is of the *equities* of two firms. For the second comparison to make sense we must verify that the leverage of the two firms is the same.

SUMMARY

In this chapter we gave a bird's-eye view of the valuation process and discussed some useful rules to follow. The valuation process that we described includes the following steps:

• An analysis of the firm's environment that begins with the largest setting—macroeconomic conditions—and proceeds with a detailed analysis of the industry and the position of the firm within it. The end result of this stage is the sales projections for the firm that reflect your understanding of the firm's marketing prospects. We discuss this stage of the analysis in Chapter 5.

• A conversion of the marketing view of the firm into complete projections of financial performance. This is achieved by a detailed study of the way that the firm is operated and is expressed as a set of pro-forma financial statements. This part of the process is discussed in Chapter 6 and is illustrated in Chapter 7.

• Next, the projected financial performance is converted into a value estimate by discounting the cash flows that the firm is expected to generate and an expected terminal value. The estimated discount rate should reflect the characteristics of the discounted cash flows, such as timing, risk, purchasing power (inflation), and liquidity. The estimation of the cost of capital is discussed in Chapters 8 and 9.

• The pro-forma statements can be used to obtain the value estimates that are not based on discounted cash flows. Alternative valuation methods base value estimates on a comparison of the projected financial performance of the firm to the financial performance of similar firms that are publicly traded. This is done by using price multiples—prices scaled by performance measures—such as the P/E ratio. Multiple-based valuations are discussed in Chapter 10.

• Finally, but not the least important, is the decision stage: What do we make of the estimated value? Depending on the context, the next step might be a strategic decision of the firm—to invest in a project, to expand into a market, to sell a division, or to make an acquisition decision—such as to propose a merger, to tender for shares, or to render a portfolio decision—for example, to add a stock to the portfolio or to sell a bond from a portfolio.

In the valuation process we first estimate the value of the *whole firm* and only subsequently divide this value among the various security holders of the firm. In particular, the value of the firm's equity is estimated as a residual—the estimated value of the firm less the estimated value of the more senior securities. We call this valuation process *sequential.* An alternative process is to estimate *directly* the equity holders' cash flows, the RADR appropriate for these cash flows, and the value of the equity as the discounted equity cash flows at the cost of capital of the equity. Carefully executed, the direct valuation method yields the same value estimate as the sequential valuation method. However, the direct valuation method often presents problems that are difficult to deal with—equity holders' cash flows that are difficult to project when the interest rate of the debt is floating; discount rates that are difficult to estimate without first knowing the leverage of the firm (which means you know the answer to your question before you begin analyzing it!); and valuation when the firm has issued convertible securities (such as employee options), the analysis of which requires an estimate of the value of the whole firm. Hence, we prefer the sequential valuation method, which avoids many of these problems.

The sequential valuation method is composed of the following steps:

• An analysis of the economy and the industry that yields the Sales projection
• An analysis of the firm aimed at converting the Sales projection to complete pro-forma financial statements
• An analysis of the risk of the firm's FCF to estimate the firm's cost of capital
• A valuation of the *whole* firm by discounting the projected FCF at the firm's cost of capital; this is the value of the "whole pie" shared by all the security holders of the firm
• An analysis of the risk of the firm's debt to estimate a risk-adjusted yield to maturity that is appropriate for this debt; this risk-adjusted yield to maturity is used to value the firm's debt—the most senior claim on the value of the whole pie. (This issue is discussed in Chapter 11.)
• A valuation of the firm's convertible securities based on the remaining value— the whole value of the firm less the value allocated to the debt holders. (The valuation of convertible securities issued by firms is the topic of Chapter 12.)
• A valuation of the firm's equity as the residual claim

Throughout the book we follow the logic of the sequential valuation method. The process and logic of the direct valuation method, however, is very close to those of the sequential method. The parallels between the methods and the tangential yet nontrivial issue of dividend policy are discussed in Chapter 13.

EXERCISES

The following exercises relate to the motel case discussed in the chapter.

3.1 What would be the motel's mortgage payments if the mortgage terms had initially been 8 percent annually on a monthly basis (= 2/3% per month) and a 10-year mortgage maturity.

3.2 Build a spreadsheet for Exhibit 3.2. Show how the following affect the *total annual equity cash flow* and *pro-forma Profit and Loss Statement* from the motel: a decrease in the marginal cost per guest from $5 to $3 per night and a 10 percent across-the-board increase in room rates.

3.3 a Using the spreadsheet that you built in Exercise 3.2, perform a sensitivity analysis on the *total cash flow* while varying the number of rooms from 25 to 50. Note that your sensitivity analysis assumes that labor costs are fixed (i.e., the same personnel can operate a 25-room motel and a 50-room motel). Is this reasonable?

   b Use your spreadsheet to do a sensitivity analysis on the *value* of 25- to 50-room motels; use the costs of capital given in the chapter. Was the 50-room motel mentioned in the chapter underpriced?

3.4 The spreadsheet you built in Exercise 3.2 has one major problem: It doesn't explain how the negative bank balances of the motel are financed. Revise the spreadsheet to incorporate the following assumptions: The motel has a credit arrangement with its local bank. Under the credit arrangement the owners can borrow (i.e., finance negative bank balances) at a rate of 2/3 percent per month and the same bank pays the motel owners 0.6 percent per month on positive bank balances.

3.5 Assume that on their tax returns the motel's owners report all expenses reported on the pro-forma Profit and Loss Statement *except for their own salaries, social security, and medical insurance*. Generate a pro-forma end-of-year tax return for the owners.

BUILDING PRO-FORMA FINANCIAL STATEMENTS

OVERVIEW

In this chapter you will learn how to build a **pro-forma** model of the firm. A pro forma is a *prediction* of how the firm's financial statements—its balance sheets, its income statements, and its cash-flow statements—will look in succeeding years. The importance of such predictions is difficult to exaggerate. A list of uses for pro-forma statements includes the following:

• Pro formas can be used for *valuation* of the firm's securities. As explained in Chapter 3, we value the firm and its securities by discounting the firm's future expected cash flows. Pro formas are used to predict these cash flows. Furthermore, by changing the assumptions of our pro-forma models, we can see how these cash flows might vary under alternative scenarios—that is, do a **sensitivity analysis.**

• Pro formas can be used for the evaluation of the *credit worthiness of firms.* A lender is interested primarily in the ability of the firm to generate enough cash to meet the schedule of the interest and the principal payments of the loan. Pro-forma statements can be used not only to predict the amount of cash that the firm will generate in the future, but also to examine its ability to meet its debt service obligations.

• Pro formas are an excellent *financial planning tool.* By modeling the firm's future operating and financial environment, we can do tax planning, anticipate financing needs or excessive cash accumulation, and simulate the effects that various decisions will have on the firm and its security holders.

• Pro formas can be used to judge the value of *strategic decisions.* By explicitly enumerating the effects of strategic decisions, such as product introduction or the sale of a division, we can quantify the extent to which they increase shareholder value and compare it to the cost of the strategic change. Moreover, the valuation process itself, which requires a detailed analysis of the impact of strategic decisions on cash flows and risks, is beneficial in that it is a disciplinary mechanism imposing on planners a careful consideration of *all* the effects of a strategic decision.

Basically, the pro forma is an integrated model of the firm's financial statements incorporating our views of the firm's efficiency in producing and selling its product. By intelligently parameterizing the model, we can use pro formas to predict the firm's financial performance in the coming years. In doing so, we use accounting conventions to assure that our model is internally consistent. For example, we make sure that the income statement and the balance sheet are properly linked, that the cash-flow statement properly reflects the income statement and changes in the balance sheet, and that the balance sheet always balances. In other words, we use accounting tools and techniques to ensure accurate financial predictions. By using pro formas, we can predict the financing that the firm will need under various assumptions about growth, operating ratios, and financing ratios, and how sensitive the firm is to changes in its business and financial environment.

Of course, it is always important when projecting and modeling financial performance to keep a proper sense of proportion. Pro formas should not be taken any more seriously (and perhaps less!) than the average quality of the inputs and thought that went into designing them. The process we describe in this chapter helps us to keep the accuracy of the financial projections as high as the accuracy of its inputs. The process of building pro-forma models, by its detailed and structured nature, helps to guard against negligence in explicitly considering all the aspects germane to financial performance.

In this chapter we will discuss the process of building financial models through the use of a series of simple pro-forma statements. The statements differ in the complexity of the models used and in the basic financing assumptions. The various pro formas have a lot in common, however. The financial statements we build in this chapter are **sales-driven pro formas**.[1] This means that, as much as reasonably possible, we assume that the various items in the balance sheet and the income statement depend directly on the sales of the firm. Thus, for example, we will usually assume that the Costs of Goods Sold (COGS) are directly related to Sales. Or, to take a more radical example, we will often assume that the firm's Fixed Assets depend directly on Sales. Sales-driven pro formas implicitly assume that, *in the long run,* all the productive assets of the firm are related to Sales (although the relation doesn't need to be linear).

Many of the simplifying assumptions that we use in illustrating pro-forma building can be easily changed, whereas changing others may require a great deal of sophistication and complication. In succeeding chapters we will explore how these advanced (and complicated) tools and relations can best be introduced into pro-forma models. Since corporate finance is a messy subject prone to many errors, you may want to weigh the costs of improving a pro-forma model by making it

---

[1] A word about notation: We capitalize all references to specific items in the firm's financial statements. Thus, "Sales" (with a capital "S") refers to a line on the income statement, whereas "sales" does not.

more precise as opposed to the benefits of leaving the model simplistic and some-what inexact.[2]

We will build our models by using spreadsheets. This format allows us to specify the interactions among items in the balance sheet, the income statement, and the cash-flow statement through formulas that relate spreadsheet cells. Because the spreadsheet is such a natural way of looking at the firm's financial statements, it is easy to see the consequences of changes in the operating parameters of the firm through simple manipulation of cell entries or cell relations.

Spreadsheets help in another way: In pro-forma models items are often mutually dependent. For example, the Interest paid by the firm may depend on the firm's Debt, and this Debt may, in turn, depend on the amount of financing that the firm needs, which may depend on the Interest that the firm pays. This creates a problem since in projecting future financial performance we have to find several variables *simultaneously*. Resolving such simultaneous relations (''circularities'' in spread-sheet jargon) is easily done on any spreadsheet program. In Lotus and Quattro, for example, you will see a CIRC indicator at the bottom of the screen when the program senses that two or more cells are mutually dependent. In these programs a few presses on the RECALC button (F9) usually suffices to solve the system (you know it is solved when the numbers on the screen stop changing). In Excel you have to specify **Tools|Options|Calculation** when you bring up the spreadsheet and then put an **x** in the box for **Iteration;** this will cause Excel to recalculate automatically until a solution is reached. Solving mutual dependencies in this way in a spreadsheet is much simpler than solving them as a system of simultaneous relations.

4.1   THE SIMPLEST PRO-FORMA MODEL

We start with a very simple model (model 1) that illustrates many of the basic structural features of a pro-forma financial statement. The balance sheet in model 1 looks like this:

Current Assets	Current Liabilities
Fixed Assets	Debt
	Stock
	Retained Earnings

Both the ''Stock'' and the ''Retained Earnings'' cells are part of the firm's equity and we collectively refer to them as Equity. Stock represents the initial Equity capital (par value plus Additional Paid-in Capital). This very simple balance sheet is coupled to an equally simple income statement:

---

[2]As one of our friends puts it, ''It is better to be approximately right than precisely wrong.''

Sales
Cost of Goods Sold (COGS)
Interest
Profits before Tax
Taxes
Profits after Tax (PAT)
Dividends
Addition to Retained Earnings

To get a spreadsheet pro-forma model to generate numerical output, we have to model and quantify both the way that the firm works and its sales environment. The spreadsheet framework means, of course, that these relations can be easily modified in order to examine the effects of proposed strategic decisions or to do sensitivity analysis. Here are the relations that we assume for our first and simplest model, whose output is shown in Exhibit 4.1:

1 Sales grow at a constant annual rate (the example in Exhibit 4.1 shows 7 percent per year). In subsequent equations we denote this growth by SALES_GROWTH.

2 Fixed Assets needed to support the projected level of sales are 70 percent of Sales. We denote this ratio by FA_SALES.

3 There is no depreciation of Fixed Assets. (This assumption is made here for illustrative simplicity; in succeeding models we will introduce depreciation.)

4 Current Assets (such as accounts receivable and inventories) are 15 percent of Sales and Current Liabilities (such as accounts payable) are 7 percent of Sales. We denote these ratios by CA_SALES and CL_SALES, respectively.

Note the *hidden assumption* behind the relations built into model 1: Current Assets and Current Liabilities are assumed to contain only *sales-related* items. Thus, Current Assets could contain Inventories or Accounts Receivable, but not Marketable Securities since the purchase of marketable securities is a *financial* decision that has nothing to do with projected sales levels. In most cases the Current Assets as defined here would also not include Cash. Of course, Cash may be related to Sales (e.g., cash held in the registers of a retailer). In such cases the *operating portion* of the Cash should be included in Current Assets and the *excess* cash—cash that may be distributed as dividends without affecting the normal operations of the firm—should *not* be part of the Current Assets that are tied to Sales in the pro-forma model.[3] Equivalently, Current Liabilities, in our pro-forma model, don't contain Short-Term Debt or the Current Portion of Long-Term Debt. This is because these are *financial* liabilities, not *operating* liabilities, and as such they are not

---

[3]This is easier said than done: How can *outside analysts* know how to split Cash into *operating* and *financial* portions? Sometimes this is possible: Cash used to buy Marketable Securities is almost always excess cash and not part of the normal operations of the firm.

directly related to Sales. Implicitly, then, we have *redefined* Current Assets and Current Liabilities to include only the *operating* elements of both. In model 4 (below) we return to this point by showing how to model balances of Cash and Marketable Securities—Current Assets that are not directly related to Sales.

5 Costs of Goods Sold—COGS—are 70 percent of Sales. We denote this ratio by COGS_SALES.
6 The firm pays INTEREST of 10 percent on its Debt.
7 The firm pays out 60 percent of its Profit after Tax as Dividends. We denote this ratio by DIVIDEND_PAYOUT.
8 The effective tax rate, denoted by TAX_RATE, is 53 percent.
9 The firm doesn't sell any more Equity. Financial needs are met by long-term borrowing—simply called Debt in this and in succeeding models. Excess funds are used to pay back Debt.

In modeling terms assumption 9 means that long-term Debt is a ''plug'': This is defined as follows:

$$\text{Debt} = \text{Total Assets} - \text{Current Liabilities} - \text{Stock} - \text{Retained Earnings}$$

Note that by modeling the relation of Debt to the firm activity in this way, we guarantee that Total Assets equal Total Liabilities. The plug allows us to ''close'' our pro-forma model of the firm: The dual-entry technique of accounting ensures that our model's components and relations are internally consistent.

One of the most useful things that you can ask about a firm is ''What is the plug?'' This question is both a modeling and a financial question! In modeling terms, the plug indicates how you, the modeler, assign the cash generated by the firm to the elements of the closing balance sheet. In financial terms, the answer to this question indicates how the firm ultimately finances its activities. For example, if you believe that the firm will use excess cash to pay down Debt, then you will choose Debt as the plug. Alternatively, if you think that excess cash will be simply accumulated (say, to be used later for share repurchases or dividends), then Cash will be your plug. *The model's plug is a reflection of the firm's financial policies.*

10 The initial balance sheet is given. Period 0 (in our case a period is equivalent to a year, but, depending on your planning horizon, it might be a quarter, a month, or perhaps even a week) is always the most recent period for which *actual* figures (as opposed to pro-forma projections) exist. Only a few of the year 0 numbers are actually needed for succeeding years. In model 1, because all asset figures are calculated based on the projected level of Sales and because Debt is a plug, we only need to know the Stock and the Retained Earnings of year 0 in order to calculate the balance sheets of succeeding years. In more sophisticated models we will also need to know something about year 0 Fixed Assets and Debt. In Exhibit 4.1 the year 0 balance sheet looks like the following statement:

Current Assets	150	Current Liabilities	70
		Debt	280
Fixed Assets	700	Equity:	
		Stock	400
		Accumulated Retained Earnings	100
Total Assets	850	Total Liabilities and Equity	850

The following is one example of how circularity enters model 1:

- Debt is a plug that equals the difference between Total Assets and Equity.
- Equity is the sum of Stock and Accumulated Retained Earnings.
- Accumulated Retained Earnings are last year's Accumulated Earnings plus this year's incremental Retained Earnings.
- This year's earnings are Operating Income minus Interest Expenses.
- This year's Interest Expense is the product of the interest rate times the amount of Debt—wherein lies the circularity.[4]

A spreadsheet program will indicate that the model's cells mutually depend on each other. This means that when you change one of the model's parameters, for example, SALES_GROWTH, values in many cells will change in a way that should be *simultaneously* solved. Repeatedly recalculating cell values causes the program to solve the simultaneously determined values by iterative calculation until convergence is achieved.

The equations for model 1 and all the succeeding models are merely spreadsheet representations of the basic accounting rules and the economic relations we project. Let's take a look at the equations for the balance sheet and income statement of model 1 in year *t*:

BALANCE SHEET EQUATIONS

```
Current Assets(t) = Sales(t) * CA_SALES
Fixed Assets(t) = Sales(t) * FA_SALES
Current Liabilities(t) = Sales(t) * CL_SALES
Debt(t) = Total Assets(t) - Current Liabilities(t) - Stock(t)
          - Accumulated Retained(t)
Stock(t) = Stock(t - 1)
Accumulated Retained(t) = Accumulated Retained(t - 1) + Retained(t)
```

---

[4]This assumes that all the current year's debt is raised at the beginning of the year. We could have the difference between the end-of-year Debt and the beginning-of-the-year Debt raised throughout the year. In this case Interest Expenses would be a function of the *average* amount of debt outstanding through the year—INTEREST * ((DEBT($t - 1$) + DEBT(t))/2)—a different form of circularity.

PROFIT AND LOSS EQUATIONS

```
Sales(t) = Sales(t − 1) * (1 + SALES_GROWTH)
Costs of Goods Sold(t) = Sales(t) * COGS_SALES
Interest(t) = Debt(t) * INTEREST
Profit before Tax(t) = Sales(t) − Costs of Goods Sold(t) − Interest(t)
Taxes(t) = Profit before Tax(t) * TAX_RATE
Profit after Tax(t) = Profit before Tax(t) − Taxes(t)
Dividends(t) = Profit after Tax(t) * DIVIDEND_PAYOUT
Retained(t) = Profit after Tax(t) − Dividends(t)
```

Exhibit 4.1 gives sample output for model 1.

Exhibit 4.1

Model 1

Sales growth	7%					
Initial Sales	1,000					
FA_Sales	70%					
CA_Sales	15%					
CL_Sales	7%					
COGS_Sales	70%					
Interest	10%					
Dividend payout	60%					
Tax rate	53%					
Year	0	1	2	3	4	5
		Profit and Loss				
Sales		1,070	1,145	1,225	1,311	1,403
Cost of Goods Sold		749	801	858	918	982
Interest		28	28	28	28	27
Profit before Tax		293	316	340	366	393
Taxes		155	167	180	194	209
Profit after Tax		138	148	160	172	185
Dividend		83	89	96	103	111
Retained Earnings		55	59	64	69	74
		Balance Sheet				
Current Assets	150	161	172	184	197	210
Fixed Assets	700	749	801	858	918	982
Total Assets	850	910	973	1,041	1,114	1,192
Current Liabilities	70	75	80	86	92	98
Debt	280	280	279	277	275	273
Equity						
Stock	400	400	400	400	400	400
Accumulated Retained	100	155	214	278	347	421
Total Liabilities	850	910	973	1,041	1,114	1,192

Note the structure of pro-forma models as reflected in the printout of model 1:

- Each year is a separate column in the worksheet.
- Each row is a separate entry in either the balance sheet or the income statement.

Using this structure, we first carefully build the economic and accounting relations among the entries of the first year's pro-forma statements via worksheet formulas. We then derive all future years' pro-forma statements by copying the first year's column as many times as necessary. If the first year is correctly modeled, all other years will also be correct.

One of the simplifying assumptions that we make in this model (and in other models of this chapter) is that the parameters of the model are *constant,* such as the constant annual growth rate and the constant relation between COGS and Sales. This is *not* necessarily a typical case: Often the projected performance parameters are expected to change over time. This added realism, however, is very simple to handle: Instead of referring in your worksheet model to a *fixed* parameter cell (such as B5 for the SALES_GROWTH parameter), you can refer to a *varying* parameter cell (such as B$5 for the SALES_GROWTH parameter of year 1 and C$5 for the SALES_GROWTH parameter of year 2). To illustrate such a model, we replicate model 1 with the parameter COGS_SALES changing from 70 percent to 60 percent in increments of 2 percent per year in Exhibit 4.2.

Finally, note that in model 1 we have deliberately left blank the profit and loss cells for year 0 in order to emphasize that these data are not needed for financial projections in this model. However, these data are necessary for more general financial models. Moreover, information about prior years' performance is typically extensively used since the analysis of *past* performance (which is described in Chapter 6) is the basis on which expectations for *future* financial performance are formed and modeled into pro-forma statements.

Exhibit 4.2
A Variant of Model 1 in Which Ratio of COGS to Sales Changes Annually

Sales growth	7%					
Initial Sales	1,000					
FA_Sales	70%					
CA_Sales	15%					
CL_Sales	7%					
COGS_Sales	70%	68%	66%	64%	62%	60%
Interest	10%					
Dividend payout	60%					
Tax rate	53%					

Exhibit 4.2 *continued*
A Variant of Model 1 in Which Ratio of COGS to Sales Changes Annually

Year	0	1	2	3	4	5
Profit and Loss						
Sales	1,000	1,090	1,188	1,295	1,412	1,539
Cost of Goods Sold		741	784	829	875	923
Interest		29	30	30	29	28
Profit before Tax		320	374	436	507	587
Taxes		169	198	231	269	311
Profit after Tax		150	176	205	238	276
Dividend		90	106	123	143	166
Retained Earnings		60	70	82	95	110
Balance Sheet						
Current Assets	150	164	178	194	212	231
Fixed Assets	700	763	832	907	988	1,077
Total Assets	850	927	1,010	1,101	1,200	1,308
Current Liabilities	70	76	83	91	99	108
Debt	280	290	296	298	293	282
Equity						
Stock	400	400	400	400	400	400
Accumulated Retained	100	160	230	313	408	518
Total Liabilities	850	927	1,010	1,101	1,200	1,308

4.2 DERIVING CASH FLOWS FROM PRO-FORMA STATEMENTS

From the income statement and the changes in balance sheet items over the fiscal year we can derive the cash flows of the year. This is true of both financial statements describing *past* performance and pro-forma statements describing *predicted* performance. Using the *indirect method* of calculating FCFs, we start with the net income of a year and adjust it for noncash charges, unpaid bills, and financial decisions (i.e., nonoperating decisions). It is easy to derive the firm's cash flows for the pro formas shown in Exhibit 4.1. We do this in Exhibit 4.3.

Exhibit 4.3
Deriving the Free Cash Flow for Model 1
The cash flows relate to the model in Exhibit 4.1 (with a constant ratio of COGS to Sales)

Year	0	1	2	3	4	5
Profit after Tax		138	148	160	172	185
Interest * (1 − tax)		13	13	13	13	13
Change in Net Working Capital		(6)	(6)	(6)	(7)	(7)
Cash Flow from Operations		145	155	166	178	190
New Fixed Assets		(49)	(52)	(56)	(60)	(64)
Free Cash Flow		96	103	110	118	126

The adjustments we make in Exhibit 4.3 to calculate the FCFs in model 1 reflect our assumption that *all* Current Assets and Liabilities are directly related to the firm's operations. Thus, when we subtract the change in Net Working Capital from Profit after Tax, we implicitly assume that the whole change is due to changes in such factors as Accounts Payable, Accounts Receivable, and Inventories. If, for example, nonoperating assets such as Cash and Marketable Securities are held by the firm and are included in the balance sheet as part of Current Assets, the change in Net Working Capital should *not* include the change in the value of these assets. We discuss the treatment of such assets or other financing-related cell entries by using the more advanced pro-forma models described later in the chapter.

4.3   SENSITIVITY ANALYSES WITH PRO-FORMA MODELS

So now that you have the pro-forma model, what can you do with it? Suppose you want to see how the growth rate of Sales affects the firm's FCFs. By extending the model to 15 years (Aren't those spreadsheet copy commands wonderful?), we can generate lots of output. In Figure 4.1 we graph the FCF for three possible future growth rates of Sales: 0, 5, and 15 percent.

The flat line in Figure 4.1 shows that in the no-growth scenario the firm has constant, flat FCF. When the growth rate of Sales increases to 5 percent, the FCF initially drops as additional investments in Fixed Assets are needed to support the projected growth, but it eventually catches up with, and exceeds, the FCF in the no-growth scenario. When the growth rate is 15 percent, this effect is exaggerated even more—a larger initial drop in FCF, followed by a rapidly growing FCF.

In Exhibit 4.4 we show the FCFs for the case of 15 percent growth. Comparing Exhibit 4.4 to Exhibit 4.2 illustrates what happens to cash flows when we change

FIGURE 4.1   The Free Cash Flow (FCF) as a function of growth. The graph shows the FCF for three different growth rates (0, 5, and 15 percent).

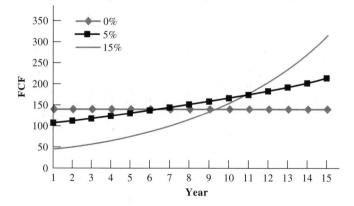

the growth rates. When the growth rate of Sales is higher, the firm's Cash Flow from Operations (CFO) is larger. However, with high growth, the firm needs more Fixed Assets, and these reduce the FCF below the levels attained with lower growth rates. Only in later years do we see the payoff from the higher Sales growth rate.

Exhibit 4.4

Model 1 Free Cash Flows When Sales Growth Equals 15 Percent

Year	0	1	2	3	4	5
Profit after Tax		146	167	192	220	252
Interest * (1 − tax)		16	19	23	27	32
Change in Net Working Capital		(12)	(14)	(16)	(18)	(21)
Cash Flow from Operations		150	173	199	228	263
New Fixed Assets		(105)	(121)	(139)	(160)	(184)
Free Cash Flow		45	52	60	69	79

At this point the trade-offs between the Sales growth and FCF seem clear. But there is more to the story. What about the firm's financing? Looking at Exhibit 4.4, we note that we have not taken into account the firm's financial flows—dividends, interest (*after tax!*), and changes in the amount of borrowing that is needed to support the firm's activity. (Remember that Debt is the plug of model 1.) Doing this, we show in Exhibit 4.5 why the firm needs Debt to pay for at least some of its increase in assets.

Exhibit 4.5

Accounting for the Increase in Debt When Sales Growth Equals 15 Percent

Year	0	1	2	3	4	5
Free Cash Flow		45	52	60	69	79
Minus:						
Dividend		(88)	(100)	(115)	(132)	(151)
Interest * (1 − tax)		(16)	(19)	(23)	(27)	(32)
Increase in Debt		59	68	78	90	104

So, we now have seen that when the Sales growth is high:

• Initial FCFs will be lower, but future FCFs will be higher
• Debt will increase, largely because the high Sales growth implies high expenditures on new Fixed Assets

In Figure 4.2 we do another sensitivity analysis: We graph the ratio of the firm's Debt to Equity for growth rates of 0, 5, and 15 percent.

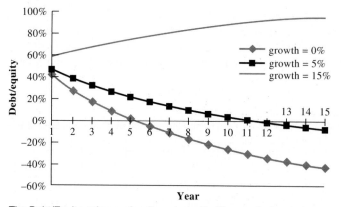

FIGURE 4.2   The Debt/Equity ratio as a function of growth. The graph shows the Debt/Equity ratio in model 1 for sales growth rates of 0, 5, and 15 percent.

Negative Debt?

Figure 4.2 illustrates what all modelers know: Sometimes the simplest, most plausible model produces entirely unexpected results. Consider, for example, the fact that the Debt/Equity curve for the 0 percent Sales growth in Figure 4.2 *goes below the x-axis.* How could this happen? The simple answer is that our model predicts a *negative debt.* Before even discussing this phenomenon, let's document it: Exhibit 4.6 shows the model output for 0 percent growth.

Now let's think like financial modelers and ask a few intelligent questions:

• *What is going on?* Exhibit 4.6 clearly shows that when the firm has low growth, the firm generates enough cash flows to pay off its whole debt. This happens in part because Total Assets don't grow.[5] Technically, since Debt is the plug in the model, after year 5 the plug becomes negative.

Exhibit 4.6

Model 1 Output for 0 Percent Growth

Sales growth	0%										
Initial sales	1000										
FA_Sales	70%										
CA_Sales	15%										
CL_Sales	7%										
COGS_Sales	70%										
Interest	10%										
Dividend payout	60%										
Tax rate	53%										

[5]Note that in this simple model the absence of depreciation means that in the no-growth case the firm spends no money on Fixed Assets. When we start to model depreciation, this no longer needs to be true—then the firm will need to *replace* Fixed Assets even when Sales growth is zero. This issue is discussed in Section 4.5.

Exhibit 4.6 *continued*

Model 1 Output for 0 Percent Growth

Year	0	1	2	3	4	5	6	7	8	9	10
					Profit and Loss						
Sales		1,000	1,000	1,000	1,000	1,000	1,000	1,000	1,000	1,000	1,000
Cost of Goods Sold		700	700	700	700	700	700	700	700	700	700
Interest		23	17	12	7	1	−5	−11	−17	−23	−29
Profit before Tax		277	283	288	293	299	305	311	317	323	329
Taxes		147	150	153	156	159	162	165	168	171	174
Profit after Tax		130	133	135	138	141	143	146	149	152	155
Dividend		78	80	81	83	84	86	88	89	91	93
Retained Earnings		52	53	54	55	56	57	58	60	61	62
					Balance Sheet						
Current Assets	150	150	150	150	150	150	150	150	150	150	150
Fixed Assets	700	700	700	700	700	700	700	700	700	700	700
Total Assets	850	850	850	850	850	850	850	850	850	850	850
Current Liabilities	70	70	70	70	70	70	70	70	70	70	70
Debt	280	228	175	121	65	9	−48	−106	−166	−227	−288
Equity											
Stock	400	400	400	400	400	400	400	400	400	400	400
Accumulated Retained	100	152	205	259	315	371	428	486	546	607	668
Total Liabilities	850	850	850	850	850	850	850	850	850	850	850
Year	0	1	2	3	4	5	6	7	8	9	10
Profit after Tax		130	133	135	138	141	143	146	149	152	155
Interest * (1 − tax)		11	8	6	3	0	−2	−5	−8	−11	−14
Change in Net Working Capital		0	0	0	0	0	0	0	0	0	0
Cash Flow from Operations		141	141	141	141	141	141	141	141	141	141
New Fixed Assets		0	0	0	0	0	0	0	0	0	0
Free Cash Flow		141	141	141	141	141	141	141	141	141	141

- *What does it mean?* Our model indicates that after year 5 all the firm's Debt has been paid off. In a more realistic model (and in the real world) the firm would now *build up cash.* But because the current version of our model doesn't allow the firm to build up cash, these cash reserves show up as a negative debt.
- *Is the model internally consistent?* Thankfully, the answer is "yes." When the model shows a positive debt, the firm pays interest, and this shows up in the income statement as an expense. When the model indicates a *negative debt* (which is equivalent to *positive* cash reserves), the interest shows up as a *negative expense,* which means it is actually treated as income. This makes sense: The cash buildup leads to interest income.[6]

---

[6]As currently set up, the firm is paid interest at its debt rate. Being more realistic, we might project the interest on cash reserves as lower than the interest charged on the firm's Debt.

• *Is the model aesthetic?* Nobody likes to see a balance sheet with a negative debt, even if it seems to make sense (once explained). Perhaps we should change the model by putting in a proviso that there can be no negative debt. We will leave this issue until model 4, later in this chapter.

4.4   A BASIC VALUATION EXERCISE

We can use our model to do a basic valuation exercise. Suppose we want to value the firm by discounting its FCFs for 5 years, plus some terminal value at the end of the fifth year. The resulting table might look something like Exhibit 4.7.

Exhibit 4.7

A Primitive Valuation Exercise
Assumes Sales growth equals 9 percent, discount rate equals 20 percent

Year	1	2	3	4	5
Free Cash Flow	83	91	99	108	118
Terminal value					1168
Total predicted cash flow	83	91	99	108	1286
Discounted	831				

Note: The *terminal value* is calculated as

$$\text{Terminal value, year 5} = \sum_{t=6}^{t=\infty} \frac{\text{cash flow}_t}{(1 + \text{discount rate})^{t-5}} = \frac{\text{cash flow}_5 \cdot (1 + \text{Sales growth})}{\text{discount rate} - \text{Sales growth}}$$

The discounted value calculated here assumes that the cash flows occur smoothly throughout the year. As discussed in Chapter 3, this is done by "grossing up" the annual present value by a one-half-year discount factor. In the preceding example the present value was calculated by

$$831 = (1.20)^{0.5} \left[\frac{83}{1.20} + \frac{91}{(1.20)^2} + \frac{99}{(1.20)^3} + \frac{108}{(1.20)^4} + \frac{1{,}286}{(1.20)^5} \right]$$

In Exhibit 4.7 we also show one way of estimating terminal values: We assume that the cash flows produced by the firm will grow forever *at a constant compound growth rate.* This means that the *terminal value* of the firm—the value at the end of the projection period—is given by the discounted value of all future firm cash flows. The terminal value formula in Exhibit 4.7 illustrates how to calculate this terminal value.[7]

By doing a sensitivity analysis on growth rates, we can derive the sensitivity of the firm's value to the projected rate of the Sales growth (see Figure 4.3).

---

[7]A word of warning: The calculation of the firm's value illustrated here is based on many quick and dirty assumptions about terminal values and discount rates. In succeeding chapters we will discuss these issues in much more detail. This example is a preliminary illustration of how pro-forma modeling techniques can be used to value firms.

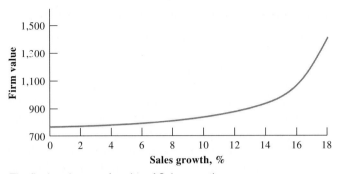

FIGURE 4.3   The firm's value as a function of Sales growth.

4.5 INTRODUCING DEPRECIATION INTO THE MODEL

One of the shortcomings of model 1 is its disregard of depreciation. In model 2 we correct this problem. The basic structure of model 2 is very similar to that of model 1. In model 2, however, we assume that in each year *t*, the Fixed Assets of Cost that appear in that year's balance sheet are depreciated at a 5 percent rate. Then this gives us the following equations:

```
Assets at Cost(t) = FA_SALES * Sales(t)
Depreciation Expense(t) = 5% * [Fixed Assets at Cost(t)
                          + Fixed Assets at Cost(t − 1)]/2
Accumulated Depreciation(t) = Accumulated Depreciation(t − 1)
                          + Depreciation Expense(t)
Net Fixed Assets(t) = Fixed Assets at Cost(t) − Accumulated Depreciation(t)
```

Looking carefully at these equations, you will see that we have assumed that the Fixed Assets *at Cost* are proportional to Sales. One alternative is to assume that *Net* Fixed Assets are a function of Sales. It all depends on the kind of firm that we are discussing. If the productive capability of assets is related to their *depreciated* value, then it is logical to assume that Net Fixed Assets are a function of Sales. This might be the case, for example, for airplanes, where aging airframes and engines require expensive overhauls that reduce the time that an airplane can spend in the air. If we are discussing a department store, on the other hand, it seems reasonable to assume that aging (and hence depreciation) has very little relation to the amount of Sales that can be extracted from the fixed assets. For such a case a more fitting assumption would be that Fixed Assets *at Cost* are a function of Sales. Another important case is one where a given level of Fixed Assets can support practically any variation in Sales. A telemarketing company might be a case in point. It all goes back to one of our basic points: *You cannot build a proper financial model of the firm unless you understand how it works!*

The economic assumptions underlying our model of depreciation are:

- Assets used by the firm in a given year are purchased throughout the year.
- The *Fixed Assets at Cost* are a function of Sales.
- Depreciation is straight line.
- In our model assets don't die! In our model we have made no provision for the cessation of depreciation deductions on assets that are fully depreciated. The normal life of a fixed asset includes three phrases: (1) The asset is on the firm's books and is being depreciated. (2) The asset is still on the books but it is not being depreciated; the reason is that it is already fully depreciated. (3) The asset is no longer active, and thus is removed from the books. It is difficult, to say the least, to model this in a simple spreadsheet model, and we have proceeded by using a much simpler depreciation method. In a more elaborate model this can be modeled by including an aging schedule of assets in the pro-forma model. (The Smucker valuation in Chapter 7 includes an example of Fixed Asset replacement.)

Exhibit 4.8 shows a sample output for this model. Note that, as in model 1, Debt is still the plug. Also note that while Depreciation is usually included in COGS or SG&A, we have chosen to break it out as a separate line item in the profit and loss statement.

Exhibit 4.8

Model 2

Sales growth	7%					
Initial Sales	1,000					
FA_Sales	90%					
CA_Sales	15%					
CL_Sales	7%					
COGS_Sales	70%					
Interest	10%					
Dividend payout	60%					
Tax rate	53%					
Depreciation rate	5%					
Year	0	1	2	3	4	5
Profit and Loss						
Sales	1,000	1,070	1,145	1,225	1,311	1,403
Cost of Goods Sold		749	801	858	918	982
Depreciation		47	50	53	57	61
Interest		26	23	20	16	13
Profit before Tax		249	271	294	320	347
Taxes		132	144	156	169	184
Profit after Tax		117	127	138	150	163
Dividend		70	76	83	90	98
Retained Earnings		47	51	55	60	65

Exhibit 4.8 *continued*

Model 2

Balance Sheet						
Current Assets	150	161	172	184	197	210
Fixed Assets						
At Cost	900	963	1,030	1,103	1,180	1,262
Accumulated Depreciation	300	347	396	450	507	568
Net Fixed Assets	600	616	634	653	673	694
Total Assets	750	777	806	837	870	905
Current Liabilities	70	75	80	86	92	98
Debt	280	255	228	198	165	128
Equity						
Stock	300	300	300	300	300	300
Accumulated Retained	100	147	198	253	313	378
Total Liabilities	750	777	806	837	870	905

4.6   MODELING THE FINANCING OF THE FIRM: THE TARGET DEBT-EQUITY RATIO

In the two models that we have exhibited thus far, all incremental financing came from the Debt. In model 3 we change this assumption. We assume that the firm chooses a target Debt/Equity ratio (denoted below by the variable TARGET_D_E(t) for year t), and that for each year new financing is chosen so that this target is met.

The relevant equations become:

```
Debt(t) = TARGET_D_E(t) * [Stock(t) + Accumulated Retained(t)]
Stock(t) = Total Assets(t) - Current Liabilities(t) - Debt(t)
          - Accumulated Retained(t)
```

Note that we have defined *Debt* in this case to exclude Current Liabilities. Although this is often done by financial analysts, depending on your modeling environment, you may want to change the definition of the Debt/Equity ratio to include also Current Liabilities. Also note that the introduction of a target Debt/Equity ratio means that the plug in model 3 combines both Debt and Equity, which are here measured by book and not market values.

Exhibit 4.9 shows some sample output for a firm with a very high growth rate. Over the next 5 years the firm wishes to reduce its Debt/Equity ratio from its year 0 level of 56 percent (Debt = 262; Equity = Stock + Retained Earnings = 468) to 40 percent.

Note the cash flows at the bottom of Exhibit 4.9: Even though the firm has very healthy CFOs, its FCFs are negative. This often happens in a high growth situation: The firm's growth requires investment in new assets, and this, in turn, leads the firm to require more financing. In Exhibit 4.9 this financing is supplied partially by Debt and partially by new Equity, in order to match the target Debt/Equity ratio.

Exhibit 4.9

Model 3

		0	1	2	3	4	5
Sales growth	23%						
Initial Sales	1,000						
FA_Sales (at cost)	95%						
CA_Sales	15%						
CL_Sales	7%						
COGS_Sales	70%						
Interest	10%						
Dividend payout	60%						
Tax rate	53%						
Depreciation rate	10%						
Year		0	1	2	3	4	5
		Profit and Loss					
Sales		1,000	1,230	1,513	1,861	2,289	2,815
Cost of Goods Sold			861	1,059	1,303	1,602	1,971
Depreciation			106	130	160	197	242
Interest			29	33	38	45	50
Profit before Tax			234	290	360	445	552
Taxes			124	154	191	236	292
Profit after Tax			110	137	169	209	259
Dividend			66	82	101	125	156
Retained Earnings			44	55	68	84	104
		Balance Sheet					
Current Assets		150	185	227	279	343	422
Fixed Assets							
At Cost		950	1,169	1,437	1,768	2,174	2,675
Accumulated Depreciation		300	406	536	696	894	1,136
Net Fixed Assets		650	763	901	1,071	1,281	1,539
Total Assets		800	947	1,128	1,350	1,624	1,961
Current Liabilities		70	86	106	130	160	197
Debt		262	287	331	384	447	504
Equity							
Stock		368	430	492	570	667	806
Accumulated Retained		100	144	199	266	350	454
Total Liabilities		800	947	1,128	1,350	1,624	1,961
Target Debt-Equity Ratio		56%	50%	48%	46%	44%	40%
Profit after Tax			110	137	169	209	259
Depreciation			106	130	160	197	242
Interest * (1 − tax)			13	16	18	21	24
Change in Net Working Capital			(18)	(23)	(28)	(34)	(42)
Cash Flow from Operations			211	260	319	393	483
New Fixed Assets			(219)	(269)	(331)	(407)	(500)
Free Cash Flow			(7)	(9)	(11)	(14)	(17)

4.7 NONOPERATING ASSETS AND LIQUID ASSETS

Often a firm builds up liquid assets—either Cash or Marketable Securities.[8] These assets are not directly needed, as are Inventory and Accounts Receivable, for example, for Sales, but instead they represent a store of value for the firm. Model 4 shows one scenario under which such assets can arise. In model 4, the firm raises incremental financing only with Debt. However, once raised, Debt cannot be repaid in the time horizon covered by the pro-forma model; this might happen, for example, if the firm's Debt is publicly traded and noncallable. This means that there can be situations in which the firm has too much financing: The firm has funds that can be used to pay off some of its liabilities, but it cannot do so.

This situation calls for a new asset, which we will call *Cash and Marketable Securities.* In the modeling sense Cash and Marketable Securities is only a new kind of plug. For an accountant it would be merely another kind of Current Asset. We list Cash and Marketable Securities separately because we want to differentiate it from the "Sales-based" Current Assets, which we have considered thus far. This differentiation is important both in a modeling sense and in an economic sense which will become clear when we discuss cash flows used in valuation.

Model 4 is really a version of model 2. The new definition of *Debt* is complicated because of the condition that the Debt cannot decrease from the previous year's level. In modeling terms this means that the Debt has to be defined with a conditional statement.[9] To show how to model such a situation, let's return to our (revised) basic balance sheet:

Cash and Marketable Securities	Current Liabilities
Current Assets	Debt
Fixed Assets	Stock
	Retained Earnings

Notice that we have deviated from the standard accounting terminology, in which Liquid Assets are also Current Assets. In our current terminology "Current Assets" refers only to those Current Assets that are directly related to Sales.

Remember our story: The firm cannot reduce its Debt, but it can increase the Debt. Therefore, we have to consider the following cases:

Case 1 Suppose we need to float more Debt than we had last period:

```
Current Assets(t) + Net Fixed Assets(t)
    - Current Liabilities(t) - Stock(t) - Accumulated Retained(t) > Debt(t-1)
```

---

[8]Remember our discussion of model 1? When the firm there had *low growth,* its Debt became negative. A more aesthetic modeling solution to this would have been to replace a *negative debt* by interest-bearing *Cash and Marketable Securities.*

[9]@IF(...) in Lotus and Quattro, =IF() in Excel.

In this case

```
Debt(t) = Current Assets(t) + Net Fixed Assets(t)
          − Current Liabilities(t) − Stock(t) − Accumulated Retained(t)
```

(i.e., for this case the Debt is just the standard plug of model 2).

Case 2   Suppose the preceding condition doesn't hold. Then we have the cash to repay some debt, but cannot. In this case:

```
Debt(t) = Debt(t − 1)
Cash and Marketable Securities(t) = Total Liabilities(t)
                                    − Current Assets(t) − Net Fixed Assets(t)
```

The definition of *Debt* says that we plug for Debt only when the current year's plug is larger than last year's Debt. If this is not so, there is no change in the Debt level, and Cash and Marketable Securities become a plug.

Model 4 is an important variation of a pro-forma model. Often firms build up assets that are inessential to their actual line of business. This can happen because, as in our discussion about model 4, the firm cannot pay off its Debts, or repurchase its Equity. It can also occur because the dividend payout is lower than it can feasibly be in anticipation of future share repurchases.

Exhibit 4.10 shows model 4 for a growth rate of 10 percent; you will notice that, given the parameters of this case, the firm builds up Cash and Marketable Securities. In Exhibit 4.11 we change the parameters of the model by raising the growth rate and the Dividend payout; Cash and Marketable Securities decline to zero, at which point the firm has to raise additional Debt financing. In both Exhibits 4.10 and 4.11 we have assumed that Cash and Marketable Securities bear interest at the rate of 9 percent. This interest appears as a separate line in the profit and loss statement and is, of course, taxable. Depending on the precise form of the liquid (or "nonworking") assets, you may want to change this assumption. Note that in Exhibits 4.10 and 4.11 the Fixed Assets of year 0 don't conform to the relations projected for years 1 through 5. In general, the initial balance sheet doesn't need to conform to the *projected* ratios for subsequent years.

Exhibit 4.10

Model 4 with Moderate Growth Rate and Low Dividend Payout

Sales growth	10%					
Initial Sales	1,000					
FA_Sales	95%					
CA_Sales	15%					
CL_Sales	7%					
COGS_Sales	70%					
Interest on Debt	10%					
Interest on Cash, Mkt. Securities	9%					
Dividend payout	40%					
Tax rate	53%					
Depreciation rate	10%					
Year	0	1	2	3	4	5
Profit and Loss						
Sales	1,000	1,100	1,210	1,331	1,464	1,611
Cost of Goods Sold		770	847	932	1,025	1,127
Depreciation		102	110	121	133	146
Debt Interest		40	40	40	40	40
Interest on Cash, Mkt. Securities		19	24	31	38	47
Profit before Tax		206	238	269	305	344
Taxes		109	126	143	161	182
Profit after Tax		97	112	127	143	161
Dividend		39	45	51	57	65
Retained Earnings		58	67	76	86	97
Balance Sheet						
Cash and Marketable Securities	100	207	270	343	425	517
Current Assets	150	165	182	200	220	242
Fixed Assets						
At Cost	1,000	1,045	1,150	1,264	1,391	1,530
Accumulated Depreciation	300	402	512	633	765	911
Net Fixed Assets	700	643	638	632	625	619
Total Assets	950	1,015	1,090	1,174	1,270	1,377
Current Liabilities	70	77	85	93	102	113
Debt	400	400	400	400	400	400
Equity						
Stock	380	380	380	380	380	380
Accumulated Retained	100	158	225	301	387	484
Total Liabilities	950	1,015	1,090	1,174	1,270	1,377

Note that the year 0 balance sheet ratios do not conform to the **predicted** ratios for subsequent years, since year 0 figures reflect the **current** state of the company.

Exhibit 4.11

Model 4 with Higher Growth Rate and Dividend Payout
The firm now needs Debt financing

Sales growth	16%					
Initial Sales	1,000					
FA_Sales	95%					
CA_Sales	15%					
CL_Sales	7%					
COGS_Sales	70%					
Interest on Debt	10%					
Interest on Cash, Mkt. Securities	9%					
Dividend payout	70%					
Tax rate	53%					
Depreciation rate	10%					
Year	0	1	2	3	4	5
		Profit and Loss				
Sales	1,000	1,160	1,346	1,561	1,811	2,100
Cost of Goods Sold		812	942	1,093	1,267	1,470
Depreciation		105	119	138	160	186
Debt Interest		40	40	40	41	46
Interest on Cash, Mkt. Securities		11	8	4	0	0
Profit before Tax		214	252	294	342	398
Taxes		113	134	156	181	211
Profit after Tax		100	119	138	161	187
Dividend		70	83	97	113	131
Retained Earnings		30	36	41	48	56
		Balance Sheet				
Cash and Marketable Securities	100	120	84	42	0	0
Current Assets	150	174	202	234	272	315
Fixed Assets						
At Cost	1,000	1,102	1,278	1,483	1,720	1,995
Accumulated Depreciation	300	405	524	662	822	1,008
Net Fixed Assets	700	697	754	821	898	987
Total Assets	950	991	1,040	1,096	1,169	1,302
Current Liabilities	70	81	94	109	127	147
Debt	400	400	400	400	407	464
Equity						
Stock	380	380	380	380	380	380
Accumulated Retained	100	130	166	207	255	312
Total Liabilities	950	991	1,040	1,096	1,169	1,302

How should we define the cash flow for model 4? As in previous cash-flow calculations, we want to make sure that the CFO doesn't include items deriving from the firm's financing (this is why in previous cash-flow calculations we *added back* interest after taxes). (See Exhibit 4.12.) Similarly, since the Cash and Marketable Securities (which reflect a *financial* decision) are not needed for operations, we *subtract* the interest earned on them from the Net Profit after Tax.

Exhibit 4.12

Model 4 Cash Flow

With parameters of Exhibit 4.10 (growth equals 10 percent; dividend payout = 40 percent)

Year	0	1	2	3	4	5
Profit after Tax		97	112	127	143	161
Depreciation		102	110	121	133	146
Debt Interest * (1 − tax)		19	19	19	19	19
Interest on Cash, Mkt. Sec. * (1 − tax)		(9)	(11)	(15)	(18)	(22)
Change in Net Working Capital		(8)	(9)	(10)	(11)	(12)
Cash Flow from Operations		201	220	242	266	293
New Fixed Assets		(45)	(105)	(115)	(126)	(139)
Free Cash Flow		156	115	127	140	154

SUMMARY

The subject of this chapter—pro-forma financial statements—is the backbone of any valuation, such as of firms, of projects, of securities, or of strategic decisions. Pro formas are models of projected financial performance. Using accounting principles, we make sure that pro-forma statements reflect our economic understanding of the firm in a way that is internally consistent. Additionally, since pro formas are built as *integrated* financial statements, that is, integrated income statements, balance sheets, and cash-flow statements, pro formas are a natural setting for sensitivity analyses and an examination of scenarios.

The pro-forma building technique discussed and illustrated in this chapter is based on Sales projections—Sales-driven pro formas. The implicit assumption is that, in the long run, the firm doesn't produce what it doesn't sell and cannot sell what it has not produced. Accordingly, almost all items in the pro formas that are predicted are predicted *relative to the projected level of operation—relative to projected Sales.* (The items that are *not* projected relative to projected Sales are those that are needed to ''close'' the model—to balance the projected balance sheets.)

Pro formas are typically structured in the ''worksheet format'' where each column is a separate accounting period—in valuations this is typically a year—and each row is a separate item (such as Sales, COGS, Depreciation, and Debt). This structure allows us to enumerate carefully the economic and accounting relations among the different items of the projected financial statements and then simply to copy these relations as far into the future as we want. The only remaining step in this case is to specify the model's parameters correctly for each of the projection periods.

Pro formas preserve the relations among accounting statements:

• The last line of the income statement—the addition to Retained Earnings—is the change in the Retained Earnings line in the balance sheet.

• The income statement and the changes in the balance sheet items are the basis for cash-flow statements.

On the other hand, since our objective in building pro formas is to be able to do an *economic* analysis of projected financial performance, we stressed in this chapter distinguishing between the *operating* aspects and the *financial* aspects of the firm. The operating aspects are naturally tied to the level of activity of the firm—to Sales. The financial aspects, on the other hand, are often a residual. In modeling terms we represent the financial aspects by a plug: The plug is the way that we allocate the residual financing of the firm—the excess cash (to be distributed or retained) or the required new financing—among Debt, Equity, Cash, or Marketable Securities. The plug is the modeling tool that allows us to close the model and to ensure that the projected balance sheets indeed balance.

It cannot be emphasized strongly enough that an intelligent pro forma depends on a skillful blend of modeling skills and knowledge of the business environment that you are modeling. Since each firm and every situation are unique, you should not take the models we have discussed in this chapter (and will discuss in other chapters of this book) to be immalleable casings from which you can pour accurate casts of any business situation. At best, they are starting points to be embellished upon and to be changed as circumstances demand.

At this stage in the book our models also have a few notable shortcomings. One of these is our failure to give more than a cursory modeling of the asset side of the firm. A better model of assets would explore in greater detail the construction of the firm's Fixed Assets and Current Assets. A depreciation schedule that takes into account the aging of the firm's assets and accelerated depreciation might well be added to the model. (This is not trivial and not always worth the effort, but an example in the Appendix to Chapter 7 illustrates how to incorporate accelerated depreciation into a pro-forma model.) Another shortcoming of the model (which is easily remedied; see the exercises to this chapter) is the assumption of constant growth rates. A more fundamental problem is the assumption that as many balance sheet items as possible are proportional to Sales.

In succeeding chapters we will show that all these problems can be solved. One word of warning: At some point you may find that your models grow so complex that although they are now extremely accurate, you no longer know from where the results came. At this point you may be reminded of the modeling motto of the U.S. Army: KISS = Keep it simple, stupid!

EXERCISES

4.1 Reproduce in spreadsheets models 1 through 4 discussed in this chapter. For each model, make a spreadsheet that includes a balance sheet, an income statement, and a cash-flow statement.

4.2 In model 2, show that if you assume that Net Fixed Assets are a function of Sales, you introduce another circularity caused by depreciation.

4.3 In model 2 (*before* the changes asked for in the previous exercise), change the model to show the effect of assuming that new Fixed Assets are purchased at the beginning of the year.

4.4 In model 2, assume that the Sales' growth rate changes from year to year (i.e., it is no longer a constant). Suppose the growth rate in any given year t is equal to twice the gross national product (GNP) growth, if the GNP grows by more than 3 percent, and otherwise is zero (you are selling a "Yuppie" product!). Plot the effect on the firm's Debt/Equity ratio of the following GNP growth scenario: year 1, GNP growth 4 percent; year 2, GNP growth 3.5 percent; year 3, GNP growth 1 percent; year 4, GNP growth 2 percent; and year 5, GNP growth 3.5 percent.

4.5 The following questions relate to model 3 of the chapter (the model in which the firm sets itself a series of Debt/Equity ratios). For each of the questions, try to answer the question intuitively first, and then use your model to see whether you are right. Then give an economic reason for the behavior of the model.

a If you increase the ratio of NWC/Sales in the model, what will happen to the amount of the firm's Debt in each of the years 1 through 5?

b If the firm's depreciation rate increases from 10 percent to 12 percent, what will be the effect on the firm's Free Cash Flows (FCFs)?

c In model 3 the firm has a target Debt/Assets ratio. Suppose instead it decided to maintain a *fixed amount of Debt* equal to the level of the initial Debt of 262 and to maintain the *amount of incremental retained earnings* at the same level as in model 3 (i.e., $\Delta R/E = 44$ in year 1, $\Delta R/E = 55$ in year 2, ...). What will happen to the dividends over the model period? Will they increase or decrease?

d Consider the case where the firm has a downturn in Sales in year 4 so that instead of projected Sales of 2,289, it has a projected year 4 Sales of 1,500. Assume that there are no other changes in either the model or the Sales projections. As currently programmed, what will happen to the Stock and the Debt in year 4 of model 3?

4.6 A firm has a revolving loan agreement with the bank that specifies that the firm can draw down a loan (up to a given size) but that subsequent cash must be applied to the loan to repay it. This means that you have *two plugs*: Cash balances in Assets and the Revolving Loan balances in Liabilities. Program this model.

ANALYZING THE FIRM'S ENVIRONMENT

OVERVIEW

In Chapters 5 and 6 we review the information needed to build an accurate pro-forma model of the firm. This information has two aspects:

• In order to project sales for the firm, you have to analyze the firm's operating environment and the firm's place within this environment. This is the topic of the current chapter.

• To convert the marketing view of the firm's prospects (expressed as sales projections) into full financial projections, you need to project the *efficiency* with which the firm will generate the projected sales. The analysis of the firm's efficiency is described in the following chapter. This analysis will show you how to model individual balance sheet and income statement items.

Combining the sales projections derived in this chapter with the projected operating efficiency, you will have the information that is necessary to build a complete pro-forma model of the firm.

The process of valuing a firm begins with a thorough analysis of its environment: You cannot predict the firm's sales, costs, or capital investments unless you understand the conditions under which the firm produces and sells its products. Accordingly, the study of the firm's environment typically is a "top-down" process: From your understanding of the broadest environment you can deduce the prospects of the firm's immediate environment. *The objective of the analysis of the firm's environment is to estimate the firm's sales in future years* by:

• *Projecting the sales of the industry as a whole.* This depends on the analyst's projections of macroeconomic conditions and the industry's characteristics.

• *Projecting the market share of the firm within the industry.* This depends on the analyst's evaluation of the industry's main players and their strengths and weaknesses.

A typical analysis of the firm's environment has three steps:

Step 1 Begin by considering the firm's macroeconomic environment—prospects for future employment, inflation, income, regulations, and taxes. This macroanalysis is often extended beyond national boundaries to take into account foreign competition, to project raw material prices when these are imported from other countries, or to project the foreign macroenvironment when the firm's products are exported.

Step 2 Once you understand the macroenvironment, analyze the prospects of the industry to which the firm belongs. In projecting industrywide sales, you should take into account how the industry is affected by the projected macroconditions. For example, a projected decline in economic activity—a recession—calls for a shift in consumer demand from luxury goods and high-quality brands to low-cost substitutes. Alternatively, in a period of high inflation you should reasonably expect the industry's sales to grow faster—in nominal terms—than if you expect low inflation.

Step 3 Once you understand both the macroenvironment and the overall industry prospects, you can consider the future of the firm you value. Suppose, for example, that you project poor economic conditions and a shift in consumer demand to low-cost brands. If the firm that you are analyzing is the industry's price leader, it will probably *increase* its market share as customers gravitate to this firm from high-quality, high-price competitors. Macroeconomic conditions do not necessarily affect all the firms of an industry equally!

Although, in principle, a full analysis of a firm includes all the stages just described, often the labor is divided: Some analysts specialize in macroanalysis—analyzing and predicting macroeconomic conditions—and some specialize in microanalysis—following specific industries and firms. In many investment banks these analyses are performed by different departments of the bank. Since our focus is on valuation issues, we take a user perspective in describing how macroeconomic analysis is done. Accordingly, in this chapter we describe how to read a macroanalysis rather than how to do one. We focus more on the microinterpretations of macroanalysis and, obviously, on microanalyses of industries and firms.

The chapter is organized according to the deductive process of projecting the sales prospects of a firm. We begin by describing how macroeconomic activity is analyzed, proceed with a discussion of industry's sales projection, and conclude with a discussion of the projection of the sales of individual firms. Clearly, the economic and marketing models and tools that are covered in a few semester-long courses cannot be fully described in one chapter. However, since we have a specific application in mind—using economic and marketing models to value projects, firms, and securities—in this chapter we give a bird's-eye view of these models, focusing on their application to the prediction of sales.

5.1　THE ANALYSIS OF MACROECONOMIC ACTIVITY

Economic activity varies over time. This suggests that it is worthwhile to measure and to try to predict changes in economic activity. Although the preceding sentence seems trivially true, this statement is not innocuous: We must consider how we *want* and *can* measure economic activity.

Measuring the Level of Economic Activity

The two most widely used aggregates of the level of macroeconomic activity are the **gross national product (GNP)** and the **gross domestic product (GDP)**:

• The *gross national product* is the value of all goods and services produced by using the resources *owned* by a nation. The GNP calculation doesn't distinguish between resources located in the country and resources owned by the citizens of the country that are physically located abroad. On the other hand, the GNP doesn't include the value of products produced locally by resources owned by foreigners.

• The *gross domestic product* measures the value of the products produced domestically, independent of who owns the resources used in the production.

In Figure 5.1 we plot the U.S. GNP and the GDP for 1970 through 1992 (in dollars of constant value—1987 dollars). Clearly, we see that the GNP and the GDP are highly correlated and, indeed, are virtually identical. Nonetheless, as their

FIGURE 5.1　The U.S. gross national product (GNP) versus the gross domestic product (GDP), 1971–1992, in constant (1987) dollars.

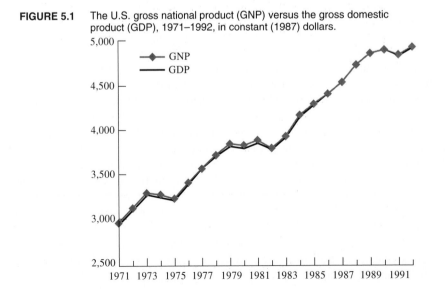

definitions suggest, the GNP is more related to the nation's *income* than the GDP. Thus, the GNP may be more useful than the GDP in predicting sales of consumption goods (such as books, air transportation, and cars), whereas the GDP, being more related to the nation's *production,* may be more useful in predicting the sales of intermediate products (such as personal computers, machinery, and raw materials). Today, the standard measurement of national economic activity is based on the GDP, which means that the GDP series are more readily available for international comparison and analysis. Thus, from now on we will primarily refer to the GDP while keeping in mind the high correlation between the two measures of activity.

Because no one person or entity knows the quantities and prices of *all* goods and services produced in any given period, the GDP is easier to define than to measure. In practice, the level of economic activity is only *estimated* so that we use *estimates* of activity to measure and predict the level of economic activity. In the United States the GDP is estimated by the Bureau of Economic Analysis, an agency of the U.S. Commerce Department. It is estimated on a quarterly basis, and the first estimate of a given quarter is published in the third week after the end of the quarter. Revised estimates are released in the following 2 months as more accurate information is collected and processed. This means that, as with all accounting figures, we know what really occurred—that is, the accurate national product of a given quarter—only after it actually happened.[1]

Despite the fact that the measurement of the level of economic activity can be done accurately only after the fact (and even then with a lag), for the purpose of decision making we would like to know roughly where the economy is now and where it is headed in a timely fashion. Toward that end, various government and private agencies report *indicators* of the level of economic activity. There are three types of economic indicators: **leading indicators, coincidental indicators,** and **lagging indicators.**

- *Leading economic indicators* are indicators that tend to rise and fall *ahead* of similar changes in the level of economic activity. Therefore, leading economic indicators are useful in predicting *future* trends in economic activity.
- *Coincidental economic indicators* tend to move *with* the level of economic activity. Therefore, the coincidental indicators are useful in assessing the *current state of the economy* even before the actual GDP figures are estimated.
- *Lagging indicators* lag the movement of economic activity. They are useful in assessing, after the fact, the relations between various economic statistics and the actual level of economic activity. (Such analysis can help us to formulate better models and indicators of economic activity.)

Ostensibly, for valuations (which are based on discounting *future* cash flows) the leading economic indicators are the most relevant indicators. There are quite a few intuitive statistics of macroeconomic activity that can be indicators of future trends of the economy. Each of these indicators, however, will have its own

---

[1]Even then, the figures are often corrected in subsequent months.

idiosyncratic behavior. A better way to estimate trends in the economy is to aggregate a few of these indicators; the Bureau of Economic Analysis of the Department of Commerce does this monthly: The Bureau publishes a monthly index that averages 11 series of leading indicators. The 11 components of the **index of leading economic indicators** are listed in Exhibit 5.1.

Exhibit 5.1

Components of the Index of Leading Economic Indicators

Average workweek of production workers in manufacturing

Initial claims for state unemployment insurance (inverted before inclusion in the index)[2]

New orders for consumer goods (adjusted for inflation)

Vendor performance—companies receiving slower deliveries from suppliers

Contracts and orders for plant and equipment (adjusted for inflation)

New private housing building permits issued

Change in manufacturers' unfilled orders (durable goods industries)

Change in sensitive materials prices

Stock prices (S&P 500 index)

Money supply (M2, adjusted for inflation)

Index of consumer expectations

The index of leading economic indicators leads the level of activity in the economy by about one-half year. By itself, this is bad news: It suggests that the index of leading economic indicators is useful in forecasting economic activity only in the short run—in the next 6 months. To compound the problem, monthly changes in the index of leading economic indicators, which are used to measure *changes* in the trend of economic activity, are typically less important than three or four consecutive changes in the same direction. Thus, only after observing several consecutive changes in the index can we conclude that a change in the *direction* of the economy is actually taking place. This further reduces the usefulness of the leading indicators in assessing future economic conditions.

Figure 5.2 shows quarterly percentage changes in the real GDP (annualized) and the percentage changes in the previous quarter's leading economic indicators (LEI). As you can see, there is a fair degree of correlation. Regressing the changes one on the other gives an $R^2 = 31\%$, which is respectable for regressions of this type; however, it is clear that the LEI do not, by themselves, fully predict changes in economic activity, even in the short run.

The inability to use empirical relations to predict long-run macroeconomic activity is a reflection of a theoretical gap in understanding and predicting long-run trends of economic activity. Although history shows that macroeconomic activity is cyclical, economists can only partially explain the phenomenon. For example, economists argue that the fact that it takes time to build factories (or

---

[2]An *increase* in this leading indicator component indicates a *decrease* in unemployment.

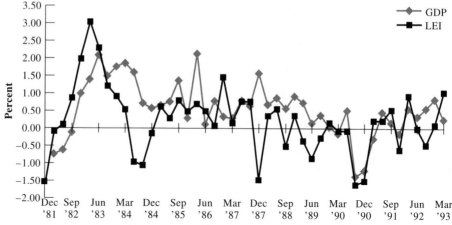

FIGURE 5.2   Real GDP changes versus changes in leading economic indicators.

more generally, to adjust the level of production) creates fluctuations in economic activity. Rigidities in employment contracts—the fact that it is difficult to adjust wages upward or downward in relation to economic conditions—and other long-term relations may exacerbate these fluctuations.

From the perspective of someone who tries to value a firm based on projected macroeconomic conditions, the fact that we do not fully understand why economic activity is cyclical means that it is difficult to predict business cycles and their duration from theoretically founded relations. Instead, we rely on statistical relations between leading indicators and the level of economic activity (which can only be measured after the fact!) to predict *short-run* fluctuations in macroeconomic activity. For example, history shows that a few consecutive increases in the index of leading economic indicators indicates an upturn in economic activity over the next half a year or thereabouts. In the long run, however, we typically assume that economic activity will be average—neither a recession nor a boom. This is the first time we encounter the problem of "blurriness": As we look further into the future, our vision becomes more and more hazy; we have a relatively clear view of the future only in the short run. You will face the same problem when projecting industry's characteristics and the firm's performance. Unfortunately, most of the value of firms and their securities is in their distant future, about which we have only a faint knowledge (at best . . .).

The predictions of various economists for the future economic trends are often surveyed and published. This is very useful information. Evidence suggests that the average prediction is a much better indicator of future economic conditions than any individual prediction. In essence, by averaging a few predictions, we get rid of the idiosyncrasies of each of the forecaster's opinions and obtain a more accurate prediction. Thus, when valuing a firm and its securities, we should preferably use consensus predictions, published monthly, for example, by Blue Chip Economic Indicators—a private firm.

The consensus predictions typically state projected economic growth over the next 2 years, as well as two other important statistics—projected unemployment and projected inflation rates. You can use all three projections in estimating projected industry and firm sales. Projected growth in the GDP and projected changes in unemployment can be used to project growth in unit sales—**real sales growth rates.** Projected inflation rates can be used to project changes in unit price, which when multiplied by the projected real growth rate will give the projected sales growth in *dollar* terms—**nominal sales growth rate.** In the following section we describe some ways of estimating these growth rates.

5.2 THE EFFECT OF MACROECONOMIC CONDITIONS ON INDUSTRIES

In the previous section we described how economists attempt to project future macroeconomic conditions. You deduce from these projections the likely effect of future macroconditions on the prospects of the industry that you analyze. To reemphasize, macroeconomic projections are typically of any accuracy only in the short run, which means that for long-run sales projections we have little choice but to assume average macroeconomic conditions.

We distinguish between two possible effects of macroeconomic conditions on industries: (1) the effect on the *level* of the industry's sales and (2) the effect on the *composition* of the sales. We start our discussion with an analysis of the dependence of the level of the industry's sales on macroconditions.

The Level of the Industry's Sales and Macroeconomic Conditions

The industry's sales and profits typically reflect macroeconomic conditions. Obviously, the *extent* to which an industry's performance reflects macroeconomic conditions depends on the industry. Some industries, such as food, health care, and other consumer staples, are less affected by changes in economic conditions. Sales of other industries, such as airlines or luxury consumption goods, critically depend on macroconditions: They rise when the economic conditions improve and decline when economic conditions deteriorate.

Figure 5.3 presents an example of an industry where sales are highly correlated with macroeconomic conditions: It depicts domestic car sales, in millions of cars per year, and annual changes in the GDP (adjusted for inflation). Evidently, when the economy flourishes, that is, when national income grows at a fast rate, sales of domestic cars increase, whereas when the economy is in a slump, that is, when national income hardly grows or even declines, car sales decline.

The high correlation of automobile sales and changes in the GDP is useful since you can use *published* projections of GDP growth rates to predict future car sales. If you think that macroconditions are a key determinant of the activity of an industry, you will be able to project the industry's (short-run!) sales based on projected macrogrowth rates. To do so, you:

• Estimate the relation between the sales of the industry and growth rates by using historical values

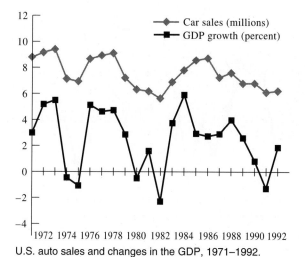

FIGURE 5.3   U.S. auto sales and changes in the GDP, 1971–1992.

• Forecast industry sales by applying the estimated relation to the forecasted growth rate

To illustrate, we can use the GDP and car sales to project next year's expected car sales based on GDP growth projections. We begin by regressing annual automobile sales on real annual changes in the GDP. Here is the regression output from a spreadsheet, which gives respectable results:[3]

Regression Output

Constant	6.75831076
Std Err of Y Est	0.77496101
R Squared	0.58287254
No. of Observations	22
Degrees of Freedom	20
X Coefficient(s) 0.375086374	
Std Err of Coef. 0.070951875	

Two parameters are estimated in this regression—an intercept and a slope coefficient. The intercept corresponds to the number of cars that are estimated to be sold when the nation's income doesn't change—for a 0 percent growth rate in the GDP, 6.76 million cars are sold on average. The slope coefficient suggests that for each 1 percent inflation-adjusted increase in the GDP 375,000 more cars will be sold. Figure 5.4 depicts the actual and fitted annual car sales.

---

[3]When estimating economic relations such as those illustrated in this chapter a ''respectable'' R^2 is anything in the range of 30 to 60 percent. Anything more than 60 percent is extraordinary. (One of our colleagues has a rule of thumb for regressions in finance: Any R^2 greater than 80 percent is bogus!—there simply aren't any economic relations that can be estimated with this degree of linearity.)

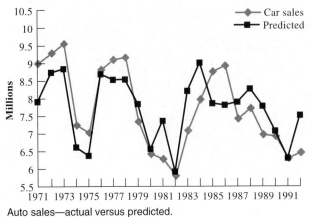

FIGURE 5.4   Auto sales—actual versus predicted.

Data Mining—Being Ex-Post Smart

How did we know that auto sales correlate well with *changes in the GDP*? The answer is that we didn't! Instead, we looked at the data in another way before determining that the same relation was meaningful both economically and statistically. Figure 5.5 shows the data as we first looked at them—the raw data depicted in the graph of annual automobile sales and the *level of the GDP* (in billions of 1987 dollars).

As you can see, the first attempt to correlate auto sales with a measure of economic activity did not go so well: The regression data on car sales versus the GDP doesn't work nearly as well as the previous model:

Regression Output

Constant	10.9560329
Std Err of Y Est	1.07732705
R Squared	0.19387164
No. of Observations	22
Degrees of Freedom	20
X Coefficient(s) −0.82009396	
Std Err of Coef. 0.373932812	

Having failed in this attempt, we reexamined the data and ended up with *changes in the GDP,* as opposed to the *level* of the GDP, as a measure of the economic activity that can explain the volume of car sales. Academic economists snidely refer to such a procedure as *data mining,* but it is done all the time.[4] Instead of sneering at data mining, we prefer to use it judiciously—by using economic reasoning to figure some potential determinants of an industry's activity and selecting

---

[4]We like to call it "playing with the data," which makes it sound as if you are having fun trying to figure out how things work.

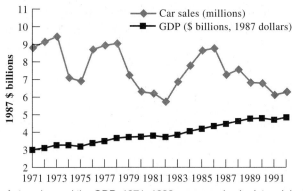

FIGURE 5.5   Auto sales and the GDP, 1971–1992—an exercise in data mining?

the statistical representation of the relation which fit the data best. Hopefully, the best-fitting relation will agree with economic intuition as well. In that case not only will you play with the data, but you may learn something from it too!

Adjusting for Inflation

When estimating the relation between the industry's sales and economic activity, you should use inflation-adjusted figures. Analyses based on current-dollar values—dollars of differing purchasing power—may lead to misleading or spurious results. The problem may arise whenever inflation affects both the dependent variable (such as dollar sales of an industry) and the explanatory variables (such as the GDP). The use of inflation-adjusted figures avoids spurious correlations and allows you to estimate the economically meaningful relations that determine economic activity.

When using inflation-adjusted figures in the analysis of possible relations between the industry's sales and macroeconomic activity, you have to make sure of the end results of your predictions. Specifically, after adjusting all historical figures to *current-year* dollars and relating one variable to another (e.g., using regression techniques), you end up predicting the industry's sales in terms of *current* dollars— dollars of the current year's purchasing power. To arrive at *current-dollar* sales for future years, you should adjust for the expected inflation rates. To illustrate the technique, let's go back to our regression example. In this example car sales figures don't need to be adjusted for inflation as they are in terms of the number of cars, but the GDP figures that we use are in *constant dollars*—dollars of 1987. Regressing the number of cars sold annually on the annual changes in the GDP, we estimated the following relation:

$$\text{Annual car sales} = 6.76\text{MM} + 0.375 \cdot \text{GDP growth } (\%) \qquad R^2 = 58.3\%$$

Suppose the consensus economic predictions are of a 2 percent growth rate for 1993. This means that, based on these projections and the estimated regression relation, we expect that 6.76MM + 0.375 · 2 = 7.51 million cars will be sold in 1993. To translate the expectation for sales of 7.5 million car sales to expected *dollar* sales, we use the average car price. For example, suppose the average car price for 1992 was $11,000. This implies that expected sales of 7.5 million cars is equivalent to a *1992-dollar* sales figure of $82.5 billion. However, we probably don't expect the average car price in 1993 to be the same as the average car price in 1992. Suppose inflation is projected to be 4 percent in 1993. We then may project an average 1993 car price of $11,000 · (1 + 4%) = $11,440 and *1993-dollar* sales of $86.6 billion next year. Obviously, you may think that 1993 car prices will change by more (or less) than the projected inflation rate. In this case you may project the domestic auto industry's sales in 1993 based also on your expected rate of car price changes.

Short-Run Effects of Macroconditions on Industries

Industry dependence on macroconditions is different in different stages of the business cycle. Figure 5.6 presents a typical business cycle and a corresponding cycle in stock prices. The figure depicts the fact that stock prices lead the economic activity. This is because stock values reflect the firm's *future* profitability so that an anticipated change in economic activity, which implies a corresponding change in profits, leads to a *current* change in stock prices. Historically, stock prices have led the economy by about one-half year and have been a most consistent leading economic indicator.

Three points of reference in the economic cycle are marked on the graph: Point 1 denotes the time at which the economy slows down or even enters a recession; point 2 denotes the time at which the economy begins recovering from a slowdown; and point 3 denotes the peak of economic activity. When the economy slows

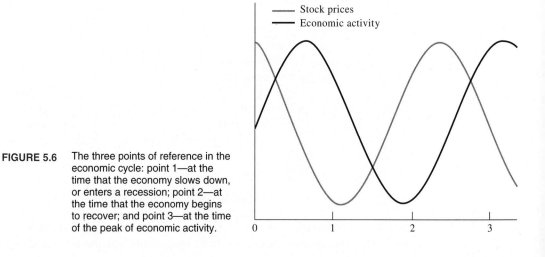

FIGURE 5.6   The three points of reference in the economic cycle: point 1—at the time that the economy slows down, or enters a recession; point 2—at the time that the economy begins to recover; and point 3—at the time of the peak of economic activity.

down, point 1 in the figure, most industries suffer in sales, and consequently profits decline. Some industries, however, do relatively well. These are typically consumer staples industries whose demand is fairly independent of macroeconomic conditions. For these industries the relatively small decline in revenues may be more than offset by lower labor and material costs that are typical of such recessionary periods. (It also turns out that cosmetic goods sell well when the economy turns south. Apparently, people like to look especially good when they are looking for employment.) When the economy begins to pick up momentum, point 2 in the figure, most industries' profit outlook improves and capital investment projects, which have been postponed in the down years, are reinstituted. As a result, capital goods tend to sell well in this period (and, accordingly, profits of manufacturers of capital goods are among the first to recoup when the economy gains momentum). For similar reasons, housing construction picks up so that housing supply product sales also pick up. When the economy is growing at full steam, point 3, all industries do well. The products that sell especially well are luxury goods that are the latest to join the party of increased sales following a downturn in the economy. When you consider macroconditions an estimating an industry's sales, these regularities may help to fine-tune industry's sales projections.

The Composition of the Industry's Sales and Macroeconomic Conditions

In the top-down approach to forecasting the firm's sales you proceed from the projection of the industry's sales to the projection of the firm's sales effectively by forecasting the firm's future market share. We discuss how market shares and the industry's sales are related and projected in the following sections. Prior to the discussion of market shares, however, we need to emphasize that market shares may also depend on macroeconomic conditions, even in industries where total industry demand is relatively independent of economic conditions (such as food and health care).

Firms choose differing marketing strategies, such as product characteristics, pricing, and placement. The different positioning of firms in the same industry implies that, depending on macroeconomic conditions, consumers switch from one brand to another to match the characteristics of their consumption to the desired consumption basket. In particular, when economic conditions are poor, consumers tend to switch from high-quality and high-cost brands to lower-quality and to lower-cost brands. For example, one of the phenomena of the early 1990s' recession was the flourishing of discount outlets, where lower-price substitutes for goods typically bought in department stores can be found, whereas department stores lost sales, some to the point of being forced into bankruptcy. Obviously, a reverse trend is typical of good economic times.

To illustrate this point, we plot in Figure 5.7 the ratio of the annual sales of K-Mart (discount stores) to those of Macy's and the GNP in the years 1988 through 1992. We see in the figure that when economic conditions worsen, as indicated by a decline in the GNP, the market share of K-Mart increases, whereas when eco-

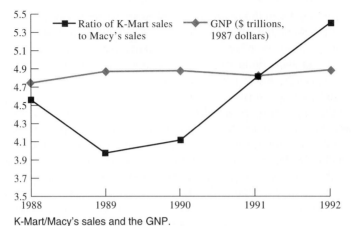

FIGURE 5.7 K-Mart/Macy's sales and the GNP.

nomic conditions improve, the market share of Macy's increases.[5] Although there are many other determinants of market shares, Figure 5.7 illustrates the fact that the positioning of the firm in the marketplace is a key determinant of the variation of its market share as macroeconomic conditions change.

The discussion and the example make it clear that in your projection of the industry's sales you should consider not only the effect of macroeconomic conditions on the *level* of sales but also on its *composition.* In particular, when the economy is expected to get into or remain in a slump, you should expect that producers of low-cost products will increase their market shares while producers of high-cost products will see their market shares decline. You should expect the reverse to happen when the economy flourishes.

5.3 PROJECTING LONG-RUN INDUSTRY SALES

The analysis of the dependence of industries on macroeconomic conditions is useful in forming expectations about the very short-run prospects of industries. This is mostly because macroeconomic conditions can be predicted, at least with any accuracy, only in the short run—at most 1 or 2 years forward. Lacking ability to predict reliably distant economic conditions, you should *assume that macroeconomic conditions will be average in the long run*—neither a slump nor high prosperity. The projection of long-run industry sales, therefore, depends only slightly on macroeconomic conditions. Rather, these projections depend mostly on the industry's fundamentals, which means that we need to understand these fundamentals in order to be able to predict the industry's sales. Since each industry has a different story, we cannot give a recipe ''The Best Way to Predict the

[5]What happened in 1991? Why did the GNP improve but K-Mart's sales relative to Macy's improved even more? Macy's filed for Chapter 11. If you are going to get in the prediction business, you will need to have an explanation for everything!

Industry's Sales.'' Instead, we present some general principles and tools that are useful in many projections.

Many predictions of an industry's sales begin by looking for historical patterns, that is, relating the annual industry sales, for example, to prior year sales, to the size of the economy (e.g., number of households), to the age profile of the population, and to the average wage. The first trick in such analyses is to try *to offset the effects of inflation on the variables examined*: The prediction of the industry's sales is more accurately done when separated into real terms—in terms of either the number of units sold in a year or dollars of constant purchasing power—and to an inflation adjustment. This is because predictions of the industry's sales are often driven by an analysis of the consumer demand, and the consumer demand, in the long run, is independent of the price level. The simplest way to see why this must be true is to consider what will happen to the consumer demand for goods and to the industry's sales if existing dollars were to be exchanged for ''new dollars,'' for example, at a rate of five new dollars for each one old dollar. Suddenly, all prices will increase fivefold—a 400 percent change in the price level. Since income and wealth will also suddenly increase fivefold, demand for goods *denominated in real units* will remain the same. The reported sales of all industries and firms, however, will suddenly ''jump'' by 400 percent, commensurate with the change in the price level. Clearly, this ''change'' in sales, which has no fundamental economic reason, is something we don't want to include in an analysis of patterns of sales. Moreover, when inflation affects both the dependent variable and the explanatory variable of a statistical analysis (such as regression analysis), failure to convert all numbers to dollars of equal purchasing power may cause the effects of inflation to mask fundamental economic-driven relations that truly explain sales. Thus, your best bet is to analyze the consumer demand for goods *only after adjusting for the effects of inflation.*

The adjustment of sales for the effect of inflation can be done to dollars of any purchasing power, to dollars of any year. However, since you probably will have the best intuition (and data) for dollars of *current* purchasing power—current dollars—it makes sense to convert all historical sales figures to equivalent sales in terms of *today's* dollars. The conversion of prior years' sales to current-dollar sales is done by using a price index, say, the **consumer price index (CPI)** and the following relation:

$$\text{Sales}_{\text{current dollars}} = \text{Sales}_{\text{original year's dollars}} \cdot \frac{\text{current CPI}}{\text{original year's CPI}}$$

Although the adjustment may seem small and of little importance for low levels of inflation, you have to keep in mind the type of sales analyses that we have in mind—analyses oriented to the prediction of *long-run* industry and firm's sales. This means that we are likely to analyze *long* histories of sales, to analyze *long-term* relations, and to project *long-term* sales prospects. For such long-term relations and predictions, *even under low levels of annual inflation,* the *accumulated* effect of inflation may be significant as even small annual inflation adjustments compound to substantial effects on sales. To illustrate the adjustment method and the magnitude of the effect of inflation, we use the sales figures of J. M. Smucker Inc., the largest U.S. producer of jams and jellies, that are analyzed in detail in Chapter 7. Exhibit 5.2 shows the conversion of Smucker's prior years' sales to constant dollar sales. We begin with the sales figures reported in Smucker's income statements, which are sales in dollars of changing purchasing power, and convert them to sales in terms of 1992 dollars by multiplying by the CPI ratios.

Exhibit 5.2

Adjusting Smucker's Sales for Inflation

Fiscal year (ending April 30)	Sales ($M)	Average CPI in year	Constant dollar sales (1992 $)
1986	262.80	108.57	333.07
1987	288.26	110.62	358.57
1988	314.25	115.18	375.41
1989	366.86	120.25	419.79
1990	422.36	126.12	460.80
1991	454.98	132.97	470.82
1992	483.47	137.60	483.47

Note: Smucker's financial year ends April 30. The CPI in each row of the table is the *average monthly CPI for the year ending April 30.*

The average annual inflation rate in the period was about 4 percent. Yet the accumulated effect on 1986 sales is 27 percent. More importantly, the annual growth rate of Smucker's sales, which judging by Smucker's income statements is 10.8 percent, is only 6.5 percent when the effect of inflation is neutralized. This is an important number to estimate and project, as it may critically affect the *projected* long-term growth rate of Smucker's sales. Obviously, if you use the 6.5 percent average annual growth rate to base the projected growth rate of Smucker, this can only serve as the base for projecting *real* growth rates. To obtain *current-dollar* sales projections, you should inflate the constant-dollar projected sales by the projected inflation rate.

A second trick in projecting industry sales is to "think at the margin": Rather than predict the *level* of the industry's sales, it is often simpler to think in terms of *changes* in the level of sales—or in the growth rate of sales. By doing so, you implicitly recognize an inherent inability to understand fully why the industry's sales levels are what they are. Consequently, you think about and try to predict possible *changes* in the industry's sales levels. In practical terms, this means that the focus of the analysis is on predicting *growth rates* of sales rather than on levels of sales: growth driven by technological changes, by changes in consumer tastes or income, and by changes in competition (within the industry and from substitute products). (Remember that growth can be negative!)

A conceptual tool that is often used in analyzing and predicting the industry's sales is the **product life-cycle model.** This model describes common stages in the life cycle of a consumer product. Figure 5.8 is a graphical presentation of the

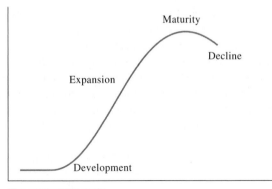

FIGURE 5.8   The product life cycle.

model: On the horizontal axis we plot time delineating the different stages in the life cycle of a product; on the vertical level we plot annual unit sales. The model describes four stages that are typical of consumer products.

• In the first stage the product is being developed and early versions of it are introduced. Consumers are not yet familiar with the product, so sales levels are typically low. The same is true of competition: Since at this stage only a few producers possess the necessary knowledge for production and distribution of the product, there is hardly any competition to consider.

• As the product and its potential gain recognition, the consumer demand increases and the industry enters a stage of rapid expansion. The initial producers of the product, capitalizing on their initial success and presence in an expanding market, generate large profits.

• The high profits of the initial producers attract additional firms to enter the market, which increases competition and reduces profits. Sales continue to expand, although at a much smaller pace, as the industry is now a mature one.

• As consumers become satiated with the product, some industries experience declining sales. Other industries continue to operate at existing levels without further expansion.

A case in point is any generation of personal computers (PCs) that you want to consider. Take, for instance, the 486 generation of IBM-compatible PCs. Soon after Intel's 486 processor became available, PC producers began manufacturing 486-based PCs. Initially, few producers had the necessary know-how, the 486 chip was expensive relative to the 386 chips, and few software vendors had programs that used the full capabilities of the new chip. Hence, few 486-based PCs were sold (relative to the total sales of PCs) and their prices and profit margins were higher than those of other PCs. As the 486 chip became the standard, its cost declined, more software became available, and clone chips were introduced, sales volume picked up substantially while prices and profit margins declined. Finally, Pentium-based machines began replacing the 486-based machines as the industry standard, which reduced the sales volume, prices, and margins of the 486-based PCs.

The example of the 486-based PCs illustrates both the usefulness of the product life-cycle model and its shortcoming. The product life-cycle model is a useful *starting point* for the analysis of the industry's sales. Knowing which stage of its life cycle the industry's product is in, we can reasonably accurately predict what will happen in future stages. The problem in implementing the model, however, is that *most industries are not single product industries.* Rather, most industries produce a multitude of products, the nature of which may change over time but not necessarily change the nature of the industry as a whole. The PC industry is a case in point. The product life-cycle theory may well describe the sales of any *generation* of PCs—the 8086, 286, 386, 486, or Pentium-based machines: Introduction, when few and expensive PCs use the newly introduced processor; rapid growth, when all PC producers introduce models that use the new processor; and maturity and eventual decline, when the processor is replaced by the next generation. Yet the PC industry as a whole merely changes the platform on which it builds the machines: While the machines become faster and more powerful, the nature of the business—designing, producing, marketing, and servicing the latest-generation PC at the lowest possible cost—remains essentially the same over many product generations.

Another example of a product life cycle is illustrated in Figure 5.9. This graph

FIGURE 5.9 The life cycles for dynamic random access memory (DRAM) chips of different sizes—the 1-megabit (mb) chip is on the declining portion of its life cycle; the 4-mb chip is at maturity; the 16-mb chip is in its expansion phase; and the 64-mb chip is still in its developmental stage. (*Source: The Economist,* August 26, 1995.)

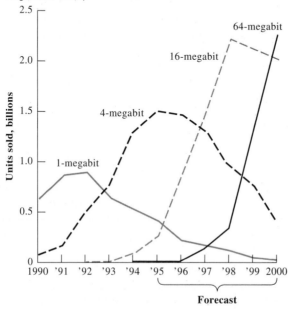

shows life cycles for dynamic random access memory (DRAM) chips of different sizes.

A similar example to that of the PC industry is the music business where the medium has changed from 45-rpm long-play records, to 33-rpm vinyl records, to audio cassettes, to CDs. Yet the business of producing and selling music has remained essentially the same, with the necessary technical adaptation. In some industries, such as the fashion industry, product cycles may be even faster than the prior two examples. Should we conclude that the fashion industry's sales will decline when the current mode will no longer be in vogue? Thus, when using the product life-cycle model, do so with care.

Despite its limitation, the product life-cycle model corresponds to an economically sound and empirically documented phenomena: When an industry generates high profits, it attracts new entrants; these new entrants cause prices and profit margins to decline. An opposite phenomenon occurs in industries where profit margins are too low: In such industries companies are being bought by competitors or get out of business via bankruptcies. (Recent examples of such consolidations driven by excess capacity and too low profits include the air transportation business, department stores, and the banking industry.) The consolidation of such industries reduces competition and restores profitability to normal levels. The two phenomena are, in fact, two facets of the same thing—**regression toward the mean.** In the context of predicting the industry's sales and profit margins regression toward the mean implies that, in the long run, the industry's profits tend to revert to normal levels—levels that are commensurate with the industry's risks. You should take into account this phenomenon in projecting long-term market shares and profit margins.

5.4 COMPETITION ANALYSIS AND THE PROJECTION OF THE FIRM'S SALES

Once you understand the prospects of the industry, it is fairly easy to translate these projections to projections about the prospects of the firm you value. This is because market shares of firms are typically slow to change. Therefore, knowing the current market share of the firm and the industry's projected sales allows you to obtain an initial estimate of the firm's sales potential:

Projected firm sales = projected industry sales · projected market share

Obviously, the current market share is only the starting point for the analysis: You should estimate *changes* in the market share that reflect your perception of the strong and weak points of the firm you value.

It will be presumptuous on our part to try to summarize a whole set of market-share theories and models in one section. Yet some things are worth stressing. First, as in the case of predicting the industry's sales, it is often simpler to think in terms of *changes* rather than in terms of *absolute values*. In the context of predicting the firm's sales, marginal thinking means that, based on the marketing strategy of the firm, you analyze and project *changes* in market shares. Changes in market shares are driven by recent and expected:

- Changes in consumer tastes
- Entry or exit of firms from the industry
- Relative strengths and weaknesses of firms in the industry
- Shifts in demand that are driven by economic conditions at large
- Marketing strategies of the firms in the industry

Marketing models of market shares can be grouped into those models that stress consumer attitudes toward products and those that stress sellers' efforts and characteristics. In the first type of models the emphasis is on modeling consumer choice and in the second the emphasis is on modeling marketing efforts and their effects. Consider, for example, a market-response model similar to the model presented in Kotler (1984).[6] In this model M_i denotes the marketing efforts of firm i and *market shares are assumed to be proportional to the firm's marketing efforts.* A little algebraic manipulation shows that the proportionality assumption implies that the market share of firm i, denoted by λ_i, equals

$$\lambda_i = \frac{M_i}{\sum_{j=1}^{N} M_j}$$

where N is the number of firms in the industry and ΣM_i denotes the sum of the marketing efforts of the firms in the industry. A variant of this model allows for marketing efforts that are of differing efficiency. Let κ_i denote the relative efficiency of the marketing efforts of firm i. Then the preceding market-share equation should be only slightly modified:

$$\lambda_i = \frac{\kappa_i \cdot M_i}{\sum_{j=1}^{N} \kappa_j \cdot M_j}$$

For the purpose of predicting *future* market shares, an important implication of this model (and of several variants of it) is that *the percentage change in a firm's market share is proportional to the percentage change in its marketing efforts*:

$$\frac{\Delta\lambda_i}{\lambda_i} \propto \frac{\Delta M_i}{M_i}$$

($\propto$ means "proportional to.") This observation has two important implications for the prediction of the firm's sales:

---

[6]P. Kotler, *Marketing Managements: Analysis, Planning, and Control,* 5th ed., Prentice-Hall, Englewood Cliffs, N.J., 1984.

- Recent changes in marketing efforts of firms imply similar imminent changes in market shares.
- To project future changes in market shares, we should project the marketing strategies of the firms in the industry, of both current players and the potential entrant.

The focus on changes in market shares reflects marginal analysis—the analysis that focuses on marginal effects rather than on predicting levels. It also is a practical way to reflect our prior analysis of the firm's environment, both econ-omywide and industry specific, in the projection of the firm's sales: There is an intuitive and simple relation among projected changes in market shares, projected growth of the industry, and projected changes in the sales of individual firms:

$$(1 + \text{growth of firm sales}) = (1 + \text{growth of industry sales})$$
$$\cdot (1 + \text{fractional change of market share})$$

For example, suppose you project that sales of the XYZ industry will grow at the fast rate of 20 percent next year. As a result of the fast growth rate of the industry, new firms (for which the factories are currently being built) will start producing next year. You estimate that this added competition and production capacity will reduce the market share of the firm you value from 8 percent to 7 percent. These two estimates jointly imply that you project that the sales of the firm next year will grow at the rate of 5 percent over this year's sales:

$$1 + \text{growth} = (1 + 20\%)\left[1 + \left(\frac{7\% - 8\%}{8\%}\right)\right] = 1 + 5\%$$

The starting point for many projections of the firm's sales is often an analysis of prior years' sales growth. Like the analysis of industry sales, it is desirable to separate growth into *unit* sales growth and changes in unit *price*. There are two reasons for this separation. First, prices and quantities often move in different directions. Accordingly, marketing strategies are designed to optimally exploit this trade-off.[7] This means that in order to predict the future sales of firms in a way that reflects the expected marketing strategies of the firm and its competitors, one must consider separately the two components of dollar sales. The second reason for the separation is that typically production costs are tied to *unit* sales, not to *dollar* sales. Therefore, to predict firm profitability better, we need to be able to measure volume in the same units that we use to estimate costs.

The need to estimate unit sales and price changes separately is problematic to outsiders who are evaluating firms, such as stock analysts and M&A specialists, who often are not privy to information about the firm's unit sales and unit prices. When such analysts look at prior years' sales and try to decompose them into unit

---

[7]Recall the four Ps of marketing strategy: *product, price, promotion,* and *place.*

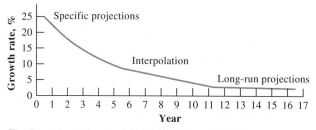

FIGURE 5.10   The three stages in growth projections.

sales growth and price changes, they must *estimate* the appropriate decomposition. One way to do this is to deflate reported sales, which are in terms of current dollars, by a price index. The preferred price index to use is the industry's price index. If no industry-specific index exists, a general price index, such as the CPI, will do. The example of adjusting Smucker's sales given in Section 5.3 is a case in point.

In predicting the firm's sales growth, we often use a **three-stage growth model.** In this model we make three types of growth projections for the short, medium, and long run. In the short run, given that we typically have a good understanding of the industry and the firm's relative position in the industry, we make specific projections on an annual basis. In the long run, given the tendency of industries' and firms' profits to regress toward the mean, we project that the firm's sales will grow at the long-run growth rate of the economy. In the intermediate run we interpolate between the latest specific projection we made for the short-run and the long-run growth prospects. Figure 5.10 describes a typical three-stage growth model. We see three distinct periods here:

- In the first 6 years we estimate specific growth rates that decline from 25 percent in the first year to 10 percent in the sixth year.
- After the first 12 years we estimate that the firm (and the industry) will enter a steady-state growth of 3 percent per annum.
- Between years 6 and 12 we interpolate the growth rates down from 10 percent to 3 percent at equal steps.

The three-stage model entails making specific growth projections in the first years, making long-run growth projections, *and specifying the periods to which these rates are applicable*; or in other words, specifying the transition years—from the short-run identifiable firm-specific prospects to the intermediate regression-toward-the-mean period to the long-run period.

SUMMARY

In this chapter we reviewed several models and techniques that are used to predict the industry's and the firm's sales. The overall approach of predicting the firm's sales is top-down:

- Begin with an analysis and prediction of macroeconomic conditions.
- Proceed with an analysis and prediction of the industry's prospects in the context of the expected macroconditions.
- Culminate with an analysis and prediction of firm-specific sales that reflect the projected industry's sales and composition.

The three levels of analysis are typically carried out by separate groups of people: The macroanalysis is typically the domain of macroeconomists, whereas analysts and corporate specialists focus on the industry-level and firm-specific parts of the process.

The macrolevel analysis is the most problematic part: We know that macroeconomic activity is cyclical, yet there is little theory to explain this cyclicality. Consequently, macroeconomists rely on empirical regularities and leading indicators of economic activity to predict trends in macroeconomic activity *in the short run*. In fact, since valuations require the prediction of the firm's performance over several years, specific macroeconomic predictions are useful only in the *very* short run—typically 1 to 2 years ahead. For longer prediction horizons we simply assume that macroeconomic activity will be average—neither a boom nor a bust.

In converting the short-run macropredictions into industry-specific predictions, we want to take into account the effects of these conditions on both the *level* of the industry's sales and its *composition*: Industries respond differently to changing macroconditions, and the within-industry composition of sales depends on macroconditions.

In the analysis of sales (as well as many other valuation-related issues) we prefer *to think at the margin*. In the context of analyzing and predicting industry and the firm's sales this means that we prefer to think of *changes* in sales—the *growth rates* of sales—instead of analyzing and predicting the *level* of sales. The underlying reasoning is that we cannot fully understand how industry sales are determined and we have a better chance to understand *changes* in consumer preferences, budgets, costs, and competition as determinants of *changes* in sales.

Another element in the analysis of growth rates of sales is the separation of growth into *real growth*—growth in unit sales—and *inflation effects*—the effect of changing the purchasing power of money on unit prices. Economic activity—consumer demand and producer supplies—primarily reflects *real* not *nominal* factors. Hence, to be able to analyze the industry's sales and its determinants meaningfully, we should think in real terms. We do so by translating prior years' figures into equivalent figures in terms of dollars of current purchasing power. For example, to translate sales of prior years to current-dollar equivalent sales, we can use the CPI and the following relation:

$$\text{Sales}_{\text{current dollars}} = \text{Sales}_{\text{original year's dollars}} \cdot \frac{\text{current CPI}}{\text{original year's CPI}}$$

To convert predictions of the *industry's* sales growth to consistent predictions of the *individual firm's* sales, we need to think of the firm's current and future *market shares.* We can project the firm's sales by directly projecting market shares and multiplying the projected market shares by the projected industry's sales or, once more, think at the margin: Relate the industry's sales growth to the firm's sales growth via projected *changes* in market shares:

$$(1 + \text{growth of firm sales}) = (1 + \text{growth of industry sales})$$
$$\cdot (1 + \text{fractional change of market share})$$

Market shares of mature industries are slow to change, especially in industries where brand loyalty is commonplace (such as food stuff and health products). This suggests that in mature industries the sales growth of individual firms are not expected to differ materially from the industry's expected growth rate. On the other hand, when market-share changes are expected, you can use marketing models of market shares to try to predict market-share changes. A common thread in several such models is the prediction that changes in market shares are proportional to changes in marketing efforts of the firms in the industry. This result can help to predict changes in market shares in particular short-run changes in shares that can be traced to recent changes in marketing efforts.

A common paradigm in which the firm's sales are projected is the *three-stage model.* In this model we make three types of growth:

• In the short run, given that we typically have a good understanding of the industry and the firm's relative position in the industry, we make specific projections on an annual basis.

• In the long run, given the tendency of the profits of industries and firms to regress toward the mean, we project that the firm's sales will grow at the long-run growth rate of the economy.

• In the intermediate run, we interpolate between the latest specific projection we made for the short-run and the long-run growth prospects.

The three-stage model entails making specific growth projections in the first years, making long-run growth projections, *and specifying the periods to which these rates are applicable*; or in other words, specifying the transition years—from the short-run identifiable firm-specific prospects to the intermediate regression-toward-the-means period to the long-run period.

EXERCISES

5.1 Consider the relation between annual car sales and the annual GDP growth estimated in the Section 5.2.

    a If you expect the relation to continue to hold and that GDP growth rates for 1997, 1998, and 1999 will be 2, 3, and 2 percent, respectively, how many cars do you expect the industry to sell in each of these years?

    b Suppose in 1996 the average car sold for $15,000 and inflation is expected to be 3 percent per year in each of the following 3 years. What are the expected dollar sales of the industry? What are the expected sales in dollars of constant value—say, of 1996?

c Suppose the market share of *foreign* car manufacturers is expected to increase in 1997 to 50 percent from the 40 percent share it was in 1996. What do you expect the *domestic* producers to sell in 1997?

5.2 Assume that the widget industry has only four manufacturers—A, B, C, and D—whose market shares in 1997 are 35, 30, 25, and 10 percent, respectively. Further, assume that marketing expenses are the only determinants of market shares.

a Suppose in 1998 manufacturer A plans to increase its marketing expenses by 20 percent and, following this change, B, C, and D will also increase their marketing expenses but only by 10 percent. What are the expected market shares of A, B, C, and D in 1996?

b Suppose the total industry's sales in 1997 ("the market") were $600 million and marketing expenses in 1997 were 5 percent of sales. Suppose now, instead of increasing its marketing expenses by 20 percent, A plans to reduce its unit prices by 2 percent in 1998. The other producers in the industry are not expected to lower their unit prices in response. What effect do you expect this change to have on the market shares of A, B, C, and D? (*Hint:* Think of the price reduction as another form of marketing expense, say, a coupon.)

5.3 Suppose you expect the sales of the ABC Co. to grow at the rates of 12, 9, and 7 percent in 1997, 1998, and 1999, respectively. You also expect that ABC's industry will be in a steady state with a constant long-term growth rate of 2 percent from the year 2001 and onward. If ABC's sales in 1996 were $240 million, what can you reasonably expect ABC's sales to be in the years 1997 through 2005?

CHAPTER **6**

ANALYZING THE FIRM'S OPERATIONS

OVERVIEW

The analysis of the macroenvironment of the firm yields Sales forecasts that reflect our view of the firm's environment and competitive position. To translate these Sales projections into full-blown projections of the financial performance of the firm, we need to forecast the efficiency with which the firm will be able to produce these Sales. These forecasts of efficiency, which are largely based on a ratio analysis of the firm, are the focus of this chapter. Implicit in the process of translating Sales projections into projected financial performance is the assumption that *financial performance is closely related to Sales.* In doing this, we implicitly assume that, in the long run, the firm's production of goods and services equals its Sales. Thus, in calculating the prospects of the firm, we ask how production costs are likely to be related to Sales; what capital investments will be needed to support the production of the units to be sold; and how much working capital will be required to maintain the projected Sales (= production) level.

The primary tool in this analysis is a thorough study of the firm's past performance, typically by using financial ratios. The objective of this analysis is to predict future financial ratios. Often a financial statement analysis, like any other statistical analysis, implicitly assumes that the relations observed in the past will also prevail in the future. For example, if in the past Accounts Receivables were 8 percent of annual Sales, we might expect them to be 8 percent of Sales in the future as well.[1] But obviously, with the aid of economic intuition and additional information about

---

[1] Why do we care about the ratio of Accounts Receivable to Sales? We would like to project the firm's Free Cash Flow (FCF) based on the sales projection. To do so, we need to know the working capital requirements that are commensurate with the projected Sales level, part of which is the Accounts Receivable.

the firm's operations, we can modify past relations to take into account projected changes. For example, if we know that the firm has changed its credit sales policy from "NET 30" (which means that bills must be paid in full within 30 days of purchase) to "NET 45," we should not assume that Accounts Receivable will continue to be 8 percent of Sales. Rather, we should project an increase in Accounts Receivable to $8\% \cdot (45/30) = 12\%$ of Sales. The projected ratio of 12 percent reflects both past experience and our knowledge of the changes that the firm has instituted.

The preceding example highlights another aspect of financial ratio analysis: The analysis of financial statements through ratios is largely the tool of analysts outside the firm—such as investors, investment bankers, and competitors. Insiders, by virtue of being privy to information that outsiders don't have (such as cost accounting reports), can often base their financial projections on the *true* relations among various variables. For example, whereas an analyst working in an investment bank may predict the Cost of Goods Sold (COGS) on the basis of its past relation to Sales, an analyst within the firm may ask the production manager what materials, labor, electricity, and other costs are per unit of production and use this information to predict COGS based on the Sales projection. However, the distinction between outsiders and insiders is not that clear-cut. Often the analysis of financial statements will raise questions that cannot be answered by the financial statement information alone. In these cases analysts typically discuss these questions with the firm's management, frequently obtaining information beyond that which is available in the financial statements. This information is eventually incorporated into the analysts' projections, which now reflect both financial statement information and additional inside information.

The goals of financial statement analysis, which are varied, reflect the analyst's objective. Financial statement information may be used by:

• Lenders to the firm, such as banks, bondholders, and insurance companies, that are interested in the credit worthiness of the firm
• Equity investors who are interested in deciding whether the firm's stock is a good buy or not
• Firms seeking acquisitions that try to determine whether the firm is a potential acquisition candidate—an acquisition that can generate synergies with the acquiring firm—and how much the firm is worth
• Tax examiners who try to identify tax returns more suspect than others
• Competitors who try to study the cost structure and technology of their competitors

The multiplicity of objectives means that we cannot have a generic financial statement analysis: *The financial analysis performed should fit the objective of the analyst.* We have a particular objective for our analysis—to predict the financial performance of the firm (expressed in terms of its FCF), based on our prediction of the firm's Sales. Thus, our analysis of financial statements should allow us to perform this task. Recall that the firm's FCF is derived in the following process:

Sales
- (COGS + SG&A)
- Increase in Net Working Capital = Increase in Accounts Receivable
               + Increase in Inventory
               - Increase in Accounts Payable

- Taxes actually paid in cash   = Taxes expense
               - Increase in Deferred Taxes
               - Increase in Taxes Payable

+ Depreciation   = Increase in Fixed Assets at cost
- Net capital expenditures

= Free Cash Flow

The computation of FCFs highlights the elements of the analysis that we would like to perform—that is, to relate the projected Sales with operating costs, the components of working capital, and capital requirements [Property, Plant, and Equipment (PP&E)]. In the following discussion we examine these relations in detail. Note that in the FCF calculation we lumped together the COGS and the Selling, General, and Administrative Expenses (SG&A). This is because for many companies we cannot separate the components of the cost.[2] For example, for many corporations we don't know how much of the depreciation expense was charged to the COGS and what portion was charged to the SG&A.[3] Since in relating costs to Sales we often exclude the depreciation charge, which reflects the somewhat arbitrary allocation of sunk costs to items sold, we should lump together the COGS and the SG&A expenses to avoid *arbitrarily* dividing the depreciation charge between the COGS and the SG&A.

The primary tool in financial statement analysis is the analysis of financial ratios. Financial ratios take two numbers from the financial statements and convert them into a ratio that has some economic meaning. Since with a typical financial statement, which includes well over 100 separate items, you can generate thousands of different ratios, before calculating any given ratio you should consider its potential relevance. Useful ratios are those for which we have good economic intuition—that is, ratios that we can interpret and hopefully project. In particular, *the form of the ratio may be of importance in simplifying interpretation.* For example, a ratio often used in analyzing the inventory requirements of the firm is the **inventory turnover** ratio, which is calculated by dividing the COGS by Inventory. A similar ratio—**inventory days**—is computed by dividing Inventory by (COGS/365), which is the ratio of inventory to an estimate of the cost of daily sales. The latter ratio can be interpreted in relation to the time that it takes to produce the good, season-

---

[2]Obviously, firm insiders, who are privy to more information than outside analysts, don't need to lump together these components since they know how to separate the cost components that outside investors observe only as a lump sum.

[3]In some cases we do know where depreciation charges appear. For example, a retailer's COGS, which include all the costs that make the goods sellable, don't include depreciation charges (such as depreciation of facilities and cash registers), since these are all part of SG&A expenses.

ality, and other economic factors. On the other hand, the inventory turnover ratio, which ostensibly has a simple relation to the inventory days ratio, is harder to interpret. Whenever possible we prefer to use ratios that have clear economic interpretation, even if other ratios exist that almost do the trick. But our economic intuition doesn't need to be yours: If a certain ratio that we use has no intuitive appeal to you while a slightly modified ratio does, you should use the ratio for which you can provide economic interpretation and not the one that we propose here.

Since ratios come in all shapes and sizes, various classifications of ratios have been proposed in the past. These classifications are based on the ratio's source of information (e.g., the balance sheet or the income statement ratios), nature (ratios of *flow* variables such as the COGS to Sales or *stock* variables such as Inventory to Total Assets), or economic relevance. Such a classification is only a tool in considering which ratios to use. No particular significance should be attached to this classification. Nonetheless, for the sake of completeness, and since our focus is on economic prediction, we present a representative classification of ratios:

- **Efficiency ratios,** such as inventory days, are used to measure the efficiency with which the firm conducts its business. These are the primary ratios that we will use in order to translate Sales projections into full projections of financial performance.
- **Profitability ratios,** such as the ratio of the firm's Gross Profit to Sales—the **Gross-Margin ratio,** as their name suggests, are ratios used to measure the profitability of the firm.
- **Valuation ratios,** such as the ratio of the stock price to earnings per share—the price/earnings (P/E) ratio, are ratios that describe the way that the market values the firm and the way that certain characteristics of the firm (such as Sales, Operating Profits, and book value) are related to the value of the firm.
- **Liquidity ratios,** such as the ratio of Current Assets to Current Liabilities—the **current ratio,** are used to examine the liquidity of the firm, which is the firm's ability to meet short-term cash outflow needs.
- **Leverage ratios,** such as the ratio of the firm's Long-Term Liabilities to Total Assets—the firm's **financial leverage,** are used to measure firm's long-term solvency, which is the firm's ability to meet its long-run debt service obligation.

Since our focus at this stage is on the translation of Sales projections to full proforma statements, we are mostly concerned with efficiency and profitability ratios. In later chapters we will use valuation ratios to convert the projected performance to values (Chapter 10) and liquidity and leverage ratios to asess the risk of the firm's debt (Chapter 11).

6.1   PRINCIPLES OF RATIO ANALYSIS

There are so many possible financial ratios that we can neither enumerate all of them nor describe all the ways in which they can be judged. Still there are some ways in which ratios are commonly analyzed. In this section we will describe the three primary methods of judging ratios.

Comparing Ratios Cross Sectionally

The first method of analyzing ratios is *comparing ratios cross sectionally.* A cross-sectional analysis of ratios involves the comparison of a given ratio in the firm that is being analyzed to the same ratio in other similar firms. The objective is to determine whether the ratio for the firm that we analyze is "too high" or "too low" relative to the norm. Implicitly, when doing a cross-sectional analysis, we take the norm to be the level of the ratio in similar firms. Obviously, for this assumption to make sense the firm that we analyze and the firms taken to represent the norm must indeed be similar: They should belong to the same industry, appeal to similar clienteles, and employ the same technology.[4] Since there are no two identical firms, you will have to decide what constitutes a comparable firm. The tighter your criteria are, the higher the similarity will be between the firm that is being analyzed and its comparison group, and the more meaningful the comparison will be. (In financial ratio analysis as well as in other analyses, the firms to which we compare the analyzed firm are often referred to as **comparables**.) The problem with similarity criteria that are *too* tight, however, is that they reduce the number of comparables quite fast. So, in selecting the appropriate similarity criteria, we have a trade-off between increasing the similarity and reducing the number of firms to which the analyzed firm can be compared.

Observing an abnormal ratio—a ratio that is higher or lower than the industry's average—doesn't need to be a cause for alarm: It may merely reflect the firm's unique policies. For example, suppose our market analysis suggests that the analyzed firm's marketing strategy is of high volume and low margins. We can verify this perception by using the *Gross-Margin ratio*—the ratio of Gross Profits to Sales. If our perception is correct, the firm's gross margin *should be* lower than the industry average. Thus, what is important is not that the firm's ratio differs from the industry's average ratio but, rather, why it does—What is the economic rationale for the observed cross-sectional differences of ratios? Understanding the economic rationale is required for accurate predictions of *future* ratios, which is our objective.

The Time Series of the Firm's Ratios

The problem of comparing ratios across firms is that no two firms are alike. Thus, we must carefully consider the reasons that the ratios of one firm differ from those of other firms. One way to rectify this issue is to use the firm itself to establish the norm for the different ratios by examining the *time series of the firm's ratios.* In this method we compare a ratio over time by examining its *trend.* The idea is that each firm's unique features determine its ratios so that by examining *trends* in ratios we can detect *changes* in the firm's operations.

Although comparing a firm to itself solves some difficulties with cross-industry comparisons, there are other problems of which you should be aware in comparing the ratios of the firm over time. First, firms change their production, marketing,

---

[4]In many industries the size of the firm, measured by either annual Sales or Total Assets, determines the efficiency with which the firm operates. When such *returns to scale* are important, we further try to assure that the comparison group and the firm being analyzed are of a similar size.

and financial policies. The examination of trends in financial ratios can reveal such changes. The problem is that in many cases intentional and unintentional changes lead to the same changes in the ratio that cannot be unraveled by outside analysts. For example, a decline in the firm's gross margin may indicate a change in marketing strategy—to a low-margin high-volume strategy, an increase in raw material prices, more competition in the firm's markets, a higher incidence of deficient products that are sold at a discount, or various other explanations. Because financial statements *summarize* many events, trends in financial ratios are not easy to interpret. Second, because financial reporting is done on an **historical-cost basis**—a basis that reflects the prices at the time that the different assets were bought or sold—inflation may cause spurious trends to creep into various ratios. For example, since the COGS of industrial firms includes the Depreciation of PP&E, and since these Depreciation charges may reflect the cost of the assets many years ago, inflation may cause the Gross-Margin ratio to ''improve'' over time: The sale price of the firm's product increases with inflation as do the marginal production costs (such as materials, labor, and electricity), but the part of the production costs that represents the use of PP&E—the Depreciation charges—remains constant. Thus, to the extent possible we should take into account the effects of inflation on ratios before comparing ratios of different years. Finally, the use of past ratios as the norm against which the current ratios of the firm are compared masks problems and strengths of the firm. For example, if the firm inefficiently manages its inventory, comparing the inventory period of this year to last year's ratios will not reveal the existence of a problem since the benchmark we use to begin with is too high. Thus, *a complete ratio analysis should include both a cross-sectional and a time-series comparison of ratios.*

The Economic Interpretation of Ratio Changes and Deviations

Comparing ratios across firms and over time helps us to detect deviations and changes. The economic interpretation of these deviations is the essence of a good analysis of financial statements. In other words, the financial ratios that we obtain for the firm should be compared to our economic understanding of the firm's environment, business, policies, and effectiveness. This is what differentiates a technically correct but uninformative financial statement analysis from an analysis that sheds light on the firm's operations and that, as a result, allows accurate predictions of its future financial performance. Since industries and firms are quite varied, it is impossible to give guidelines on how to interpret economically all ratios in all industries. In interpreting ratios, you should always think of the business of the firm that you analyze. Nonetheless, we illustrate some important economic interpretations of specific ratios that we discuss in the remainder of this chapter— ratios used to convert Sales predictions to full pro-forma statements.

Comparing Ratios on a Scale-Free Basis

Often a starting point in financial statement analysis is the restatement of the firm's and its comparables' financial statements on a scale-free basis: We restate all

the *economic* relation of operating costs to Sales, we must first remove from these costs the *allocated* part—the Depreciation charges. The difficulty with doing this is that we don't know how the Depreciation charges are split between the COGS and the SG&A. Thus, in our analysis of the relation between the costs and the Sales we work with the *sum of the COGS and the SG&A minus the periodic Depreciation charges.* We don't, however, completely neglect Depreciation charges. These charges are an important determinant of the tax payments that the firm incurs. We will return to Depreciation when we discuss the Capital Expenditures part of our analysis of the financial statements. Because Depreciation charges are closely related to the cost of PP&E, we analyze the two together.

The most common tool in analyzing the dependence of operating costs on Sales is to consider a ratio of the type:

$$\frac{COGS + SG\&A - Depreciation}{Sales}$$

When the Depreciation charges can be separated into their COGS and SG&A components, you may want to look at the ratios separately:

$$\frac{COGS - Depreciation\ allocated\ to\ COGS}{Sales}$$

and

$$\frac{SG\&A - Depreciation\ allocated\ to\ SG\&A}{Sales}$$

For example, when valuing a retailer, we know that all Depreciation charges are in SG&A costs so that the relation of the COGS to Sales can be examined by the ratio

$$\frac{COGS}{Sales}$$

Note that this ratio has a simple relation to the Gross-Margin ratio:

$$Gross\ Margin = \frac{Gross\ Profit}{Sales}$$

$$= \frac{Sales - COGS}{Sales}$$

$$= 1 - \frac{COGS}{Sales}$$

This relation suggests a potential problem with the use of the Gross-Margin ratio: In general, the COGS includes Depreciation charges, *which are unrelated to Sales.* Thus, unless you know how to divide the periodic Depreciation charges between the COGS and the SG&A, it is probably better to lump the COGS and the SG&A together so that we can deduct Depreciation charges from their sum.

AMT is an industrial firm. As such we cannot separate its Depreciation charges into their COGS and SG&A components (unless we obtain information beyond that which is included in the financial statements). Thus, we carry the analysis of both components of AMT's operating costs lumped together. Exhibit 6.3 presents this ratio for AMT and its comparables for the 5-year period of 1988 through 1992.

Suppose we use the historical ratio to predict future costs. A simple way to do this is to calculate the average ratio for AMT—93.6 percent—and to predict *future* production costs on the basis of the projected future sales as

$$\text{COGS} + \text{SG\&A} - \text{Depreciation} = 0.936 \cdot \text{projected Sales}$$

Thus, for example, if we project that in 1993 AMT will increase its Sales to $190 million, the preceding relation suggests that nondepreciation operating costs will be $0.936 \cdot 190 = \$177.8$ million. There are a few factors to consider before adopting this simple approach. First, note that AMT's costs are well above the costs of its comparables, which average to only 92.0 percent of Sales. We may want to inquire about the reason for the difference. (We suggest one possible explanation in the discussion that follows.) More important, you should think of whether the difference is permanent (e.g., because it represents differences in the

Exhibit 6.3

	Fiscal year				
	1992	1991	1990	1989	1988
	AMT				
Net Sales	$ 177,594	$ 183,940	$ 199,493	$ 191,034	$ 176,090
Cost of Goods Sold (COGS)	131,096	137,228	144,708	140,263	136,909
Selling, General, and Administrative Expenses (SG&A)	40,199	43,165	46,831	44,762	42,959
Depreciation Charges	7,418	7,278	7,214	7,084	10,716
Operating Costs to Sales	92.28%	94.11%	92.40%	93.15%	96.06%
	Comparables				
Net Sales	$1,974,764	$1,723,975	$1,716,462	$1,613,448	$1,334,784
COGS	1,515,131	1,325,843	1,320,963	1,218,876	1,007,642
SG&A	367,680	330,620	328,639	287,079	251,809
Depreciation Charges	60,256	56,944	55,834	52,477	25,086
Operating Costs to Sales	92.29%	92.78%	92.85%	90.09%	92.48%

firm's strategies) or transitory. Although we are hard pressed to explain a difference in the costs that lasts for 5 years as "transitory," if you are convinced that this is the case, then you should project that AMT's operating costs (as a function of Sales) will gradually move toward the industry norm. In this case you will produce a *schedule* of projected ratios that reflects this convergence. For example, you may project a ratio of 93.6 percent for 1993, 92.8 percent for 1994, and the industry norm—92.0 percent—thereafter.

A more promising avenue to pursue is to try to find an economic explanation for the difference. Again, consider Exhibit 6.3. Note that the ratio of operating costs to Sales, while fairly stable for the comparables, is quite volatile for AMT. In particular, AMT's ratio of costs to Sales is relatively low when AMT's Sales are relatively high and relatively high when AMT's Sales are relatively low. To see this, we present in Figure 6.1 a graph of AMT's ratio of the COGS plus the SG&A minus Depreciation on Sales—[COGS + SG&A − Depreciation]/Sales— as a function of the level of Sales.

Figure 6.1 suggests a possible explanation for the difference between AMT's costs and its competitors' costs. AMT is about one-half the size of its comparables. If production costs include a fixed component, the ratio of operating costs to Sales will be lower for large firms than for small firms: The larger the firm is, the more it sells; the larger the Sales are, the smaller the ratio of fixed costs to Sales is, which is part of the ratio of operating costs to Sales. Similarly, when we examine how the ratio varies over time, we should observe that it is low when Sales are high and high when Sales are low—something we observe in AMT's ratios (see Figure 6.1). In calculating a simple ratio of operating costs to Sales, we *implicitly assume that there are no fixed costs*. If we think that operating costs are partially fixed, we should explicitly take into account the fixed component.

To see how this can be done, we should discuss the economic relation of operating costs to Sales. Accountants typically distinguish between the COGS,

FIGURE 6.1   A graph of AMT's ratio of the Cost of Goods Sold (COGS) plus the Selling, General, and Administrative Expenses (SG&A) minus the Depreciation to Sales—[COGS + SG&A − Depreciation]/Sales— as a function of the level of Sales.

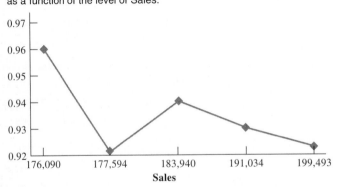

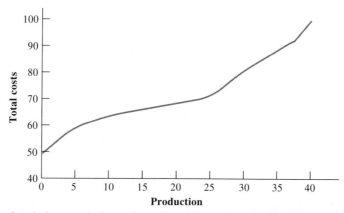

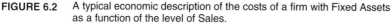

FIGURE 6.2   A typical economic description of the costs of a firm with Fixed Assets as a function of the level of Sales.

which are all the costs incurred in making the goods sellable and other operating costs such as marketing and administrative costs. Economists, and financial economists in particular, prefer to distinguish between **fixed costs (FC),** which are costs that don't change even when the Sales level changes, and **variable costs (VC),** which do change when Sales change. In Figure 6.2 we present a typical economic description of the costs of a firm with fixed costs. Figure 6.2 reflects the following economic assumptions:

- Fixed costs of production are incurred even if nothing is produced.
- Marginal (i.e., per-unit) production costs are initially high since small quantities are costly to produce.
- Marginal production costs initially decline as more is produced since now more economical lot sizes are produced.
- Eventually, marginal production costs increase since larger quantities stress the fixed resources of the firm (such as PP&E, managerial time, and distribution channels).

In practice, we often assume that *marginal costs,* at least in the range that we analyze and predict, don't change when the level of production changes. Thus, in practice, *we approximate the exact relation between costs and Sales by a linear function.* This approximation assumes that production costs—the sum of the COGS and the SG&A—have a fixed component—the fixed costs—and increase at a constant rate with Sales. Functionally, the relation is

$$COGS + SG\&A - Depreciation = FC + VC \cdot Sales$$

where FC is the fixed-cost component and VC is the variable-cost component. By using this relation, we can see the mathematical reason that the ratio of operating costs to Sales is inversely related to Sales when fixed costs are present:

$$\frac{\text{COGS} + \text{SG\&A} - \text{Depreciation}}{\text{Sales}} = \frac{\text{FC} + \text{VC} \cdot \text{Sales}}{\text{Sales}}$$

$$= \frac{\text{FC}}{\text{Sales}} + \text{VC}$$

which is small when Sales are high and large when Sales are low.

Whenever you believe that the firm's operating costs include a fixed component, it is advisable to try to *estimate the fixed and the variable component separately.* One way in which you can estimate these separate components is by using a **linear regression.** In a linear regression you estimate the (linear) relation between a **dependent variable** and variables that determine the dependent variable's value— the **independent variables** or **explanatory variables.** For the purpose of examining costs, you would like to estimate the following regression equation:

$$\text{COGS} + \text{SG\&A} - \text{Depreciation} = a_0 + a_1 \cdot \text{Sales}$$

a_0 in this regression equation represents the fixed operating costs and a_1 represents the variable costs per \$1 of Sales. (See box "Estimating a Linear Regression in a Spreadsheet.")

To illustrate the technique of separately estimating the FCs and VCs, we estimate the regression equation for AMT's costs as a function of its Sales (in \$ millions):

$$\text{COGS} + \text{SG\&A} - \text{Depreciation} = 30.23 + 0.773 \cdot \text{Sales}$$

ESTIMATING A LINEAR REGRESSION IN A SPREADSHEET

To estimate a linear regression in a spreadsheet, you must arrange the data in columns—one column for the dependent variable and adjacent columns for the independent variables. For example, to perform the regression of COGS + SG&A − Depreciation on Sales, we arranged the following column structure:

Sales	COGS + SG&A − Depreciation
177.594	163.877
183.940	173.115
199.493	184.325
191.034	177.941
176.090	169.152

By using the command sequence

```
Tools|Data Analysis|Regression  in Excel,
    or  /Data Regression  in Lotus
```

we specified the Sales column as the **x-variable** and the COGS + SG&A − Depreciation as the **y-variable** and obtain the regression output:

Regression Output

Constant	30.230
Std Err of Y Est	2.680
R Squared	0.913201
No. of Observations	5
Degrees of Freedom	3
X Coefficient(s)	0.772783
Std Err of Coef.	0.137553

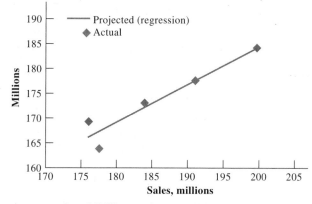

FIGURE 6.3   A presentation of AMT's actual costs and the estimated regression relation.

We measure both the costs and the Sales of AMT in millions of dollars per year. Thus, the intercept term of 30.23 means that we estimate the FCs of AMT as $30.23 million per year. The slope coefficient of 0.773 means that we estimate the marginal costs of AMT's product to be 77.3 percent of its selling price. The actual costs and the estimated regression relation are presented in Figure 6.3.

Once we have estimated the fixed and variable components of the operating costs, the projection of future costs based on the projected Sales level is straightforward:

$$\text{Projected \{COGS + SG\&A − Depreciation\}}$$

$$= FC^{Est.} + VC^{Est.} \cdot \text{projected Sales}$$

where $FC^{Est.}$ denotes the estimated fixed costs and $VC^{Est.}$ denotes the estimated variable costs. For example, if we project Sales of $190 million for AMT in 1993, we would project that its operating costs, net of depreciation, will be

$$\text{Projected operating costs} = 30.23 + 0.773 \cdot 190 = \$177.1 \text{ million}$$

Comparing this projection to the one that we obtained by simply dividing the operating costs by Sales—$177.8 million—we note that the difference in projected costs seems trivial. Remember, however, that AMT operates with a very low-profit margin. Thus, this small difference in projected costs translates into a very meaningful difference in profits. To illustrate, assume that AMT 1993 Depreciation charges will be slightly above its 1992 Depreciation charge, $7.5 million, and its 1993 tax rate will be similar to its 1992 rate—40 percent. The simple projection will then imply a net profit of

$$(190 − 177.8 − 7.5) \cdot (1 − 40\%) = \$2.82 \text{ million}$$

whereas the more detailed analysis and projection of costs will imply a net profit of

$$(190 - 177.1 - 7.5) \cdot (1 - 40\%) = \$3.24 \text{ million}$$

or a 15 percent difference.

Having projected the operating costs that are commensurate with the level of Sales that we project for the firm, we can project the firm's profit by projecting its Depreciation charges and its tax rate. We deal with Depreciation charges as part of our discussion of the projection of Capital Expenditures—the addition to PP&E that is needed to produce the projected Sales. Thus, we finish the discussion of the projection of the components of the income statement by discussing the projection of the firm's provision for tax.

Tax expenses are both easy and difficult to estimate: easy because the details of the tax code are well publicized and can be used to estimate the firm's tax liability; difficult because there are many tax breaks and special provisions that create a difference between the firm's effective tax rate and the statutory tax rate. Nonetheless, the financial statements of firms typically include a note that explains the difference between the firm's **effective tax rate**—the ratio of Income Tax Provision to Income before Interest or the average income tax rate on the firm's reported income—and the **statutory tax rate**—the tax rate on corporate income specified in the tax code. This note can help us to understand previous years' tax provisions and to predict future tax payments on projected earnings.

There are two types of differences between reported earnings and earnings that the tax code determines to be the **taxable income.** The first type of difference is a **timing difference:** a difference between the time that the tax code recognizes either an income or an expense item and the time at which the financial statements record this item. For example, tax authorities may allow an accelerated depreciation of fixed assets, whereas in the financial statements the firm uses a straight-line depreciation schedule for the same assets. This is a difference in recording the same expense since, eventually, both the tax authorities and the firm will fully depreciate the same asset cost. The second type of difference is a **permanent difference:** a difference between the way that the tax code measures income and the way that financial statements report income that never reverses itself. If the tax code limits the deductibility of certain expenses, for example, food and entertainment, then the financial statements will record the expense whereas the tax return will never show this expense. As a result, the income reported in the financial statements will be lower than the income reported on the firm's tax return.

The two types of differences between the financial statement income and the tax return income manifest themselves in our analysis and projection of tax expenses. Permanent differences affect the provision for taxes in the income statement—the **Tax Expense** reported in the firm's income statement, which is calculated as

$$(\text{projected income before taxes} - \text{permanent differences}) \cdot \text{tax rate}$$

where the tax rate is the sum of all tax rates—federal, state, and local. Timing differences, on the other hand, appear in the balance sheet as Deferred Taxes. These are tax obligations that are expected to be paid when the timing differences reverse themselves. In particular, the balance of Deferred Taxes of any fiscal year is

$$\text{Cumulative timing differences} \cdot \text{tax rate}$$

The tax *payment* for a given year equals the tax expense minus the increase in the Deferred Tax account. In addition, there can be a small delay in tax payments, reflected as either a current liability to be shortly paid—**Taxes Payable**—or as a current asset shortly to be received—**Tax Refund Due.**

The preceding discussion means that *when analyzing the tax accounts, your objective is to estimate three elements: the permanent differences that the firm will have between its taxable income and reported income, the timing differences, and the tax rate to which the firm will be subject.* As a first step in determining those elements, we calculate the ratio of

$$\text{Effective tax rate} = \frac{\text{Tax Expense}}{\text{Income before Taxes}}$$

We would like to compare this ratio to the **statutory tax rates**—the corporate income tax rates specified in the tax code—and to understand the difference. For AMT the ratio over the last 5 years is given in the following table:

	Fiscal year (in $ thousands)				
	1992	1991	1990	1989	1988
Income before tax	$ 6,544	$ 5,537	$ 6,893	$ 8,874	$(27,766)
Income taxes	2,925	2,465	3,830	3,720	(1,725)
Effective tax rate	44.70%	44.52%	55.56%	41.92%	6.21%

Note that, except for 1988 when AMT suffered a loss that was not wholly tax deductible, AMT's effective tax rate was always above the statutory federal corporate tax rate of 34 percent. Since timing differences affect only the balance sheet's tax-related items, the difference between the income statement's effective tax rate and the statutory tax rate reflects *permanent differences,* the origin of which we must understand to be able to predict future effective tax rates. The notes to the financial statements often explain the differences of the past. For example, a common explanation for permanent differences is the one provided by Smucker in its 1992 report as to why its provision for taxes in 1990, 1991, and 1992 were not the 34 percent statutory federal tax rate of these years:

	Fiscal year		
	1992	1991	1990
U.S. statutory tax rate	34.0%	34.0%	34.0%
State and local taxes	3.9%	3.9%	4.0%
Other	1.3%	1.8%	1.6%
Total	39.2%	39.7%	39.6%

Since state and local taxes are permanent differences, we should include them in our projection of future effective tax rates. In general, we project the firm's effective tax rate as the *projected* federal corporate tax rate plus all the projected permanent adjustments, such as *projected* state and local taxes. If we don't have specific knowledge of the nature of the ''other'' permanent differences that appear in the analyzed firm's footnote, we can estimate future differences of these types as an average of past permanent differences.

When analyzing the effective tax rates of firms, we must remember that tax regimes change frequently. Thus, we should consider at a time only the tax rates of a given regime. For example, in analyzing AMT's effective tax rates, we should not include data from before 1988—the year in which the Tax Reform Act of 1986 took full effect. Moreover, since tax changes are often long debated before implementation, projected tax rates should reflect your perception of the *future* statutory tax rates that the firm will face. For example, in 1993 the federal corporate tax rate was increased to 36 percent from the prevailing 34 percent. Anticipating passage of the corporate tax rate increase, the effective tax rate we project for AMT is its current effective tax rate of 44 percent adjusted upward by 2, or 46 percent.

The timing differences of the firm affect the time at which the tax expense provided for will actually be paid. Timing differences mostly pertain to differing depreciation charges, and thus are part of our discussion of capital investments.

6.4 THE ANALYSIS OF THE COMPONENTS OF WORKING CAPITAL

In the preceding section we discussed the projection of most income statement items (with the exception of Depreciation, which is related to Fixed Assets). Now we turn our attention to the projection of the balance sheet. Once we have projected balance sheet items, we will be able to convert the projected Net Income into projected FCFs. We separate the discussion of balance sheet projection into the projection of working capital items, which is dealt with in this section, and the projection of Fixed Assets and related items, which is considered in the next section.

Credit sales give rise to Accounts Receivable (A/R). In turn, the change in A/R determines the difference between Sales and collections. The amount of A/R that a firm has depends on its credit policy and on the fraction of its sales done on credit: The more credit that the firm gives its clients or the larger the fraction of the firm's Sales to credit customers, the larger the amount of A/R will be outstanding relative to Sales. Obviously, the firm's credit terms and the fraction of credit customers are related—the better the credit terms of the firm are, the larger will be the fraction of customers who choose to buy on credit.

The terms of sales are commonly quoted as "$x\%$, n, net m," which means that a client gets an $x\%$ discount if the bill is paid within n days after the sales date (i.e., payment within n days is considered as if it were a cash purchase); otherwise the billed amount—net—must be paid within m days of the sales. For example, "2, 10, net 30" means a 2 percent discount off the purchase price for payment within 10 days or full payment within 30 days.[7]

A ratio that we use in the analysis of the relation of A/R to Sales is the **average collection period.** The average collection period is the number of days of Sales that are represented by the year-end A/R and is calculated as the ratio of A/R to the average daily sales:

$$\text{Average collection period} = \frac{\text{Accounts Receivable at year-end}}{\text{annual Sales}/365}$$

As with any other ratio, the average collection period of the firm is compared to the collection period of its competitors and to the firm's ratio in the past. A more important comparison here is, given the economics of the business, the ratio that we might logically expect. Specifically, given that the A/R is determined by the firm's credit policy and by the fraction of credit sales, we want to compare this ratio to the *expected ratio, given the firm's credit policy and credit sales.* To illustrate, assume that the ABC Co. has annual sales of $12 million and that its year-end A/R is $400,000. This gives us average daily Sales of $12,000,000/365 = \$32,877$ and an average collection period of $400/(12,000/365)$ or **12.2 days.** On the face of it, this number may be in line with ABC's comparables' average collection period and with the previous experience of ABC itself. We would like to determine, however, whether this ratio makes economic sense. Toward that end, we collect information about ABC's terms of sales and credit experience. We learn that ABC's terms of sales are "net 30": All accounts must be settled at the billed price within 30 days. We further learn that 25 percent of the firm's Sales are due to credit customers; other customers pay cash at the time of purchase. Given that there is no cost for taking an extra day of credit provided that credit has been taken by a client, we can safely assume that credit clients take 30 days to pay their bills. This information allows us to calculate the *expected* average collection period as follows. If *all* customers were credit customers, the average collection period would

---

[7]Although the discount for cash purchases is small—2 percent in this example—keep in mind that it is for a very short period—20 days in our example. Compounding this loan interest to an annual basis shows that this is equivalent to an annual interest rate of $(1 + 2\%)^{(365/20)} - 1 = 43.5\%$. Thus, taking such a loan is not as inexpensive as it may seem at first.

be 30 days—the period that each credit client would take to pay the balance. Since only 25 percent of Sales are to credit customers, the expected collection period is 25 percent of 30 days, or 7.5 days. Now we have a problem: Although economic reasoning suggests that ABC's average collection period should be 7.5 days, it actually is much longer. Maybe some of ABC's receivables should be reclassified as a doubtful debt. A worse case could be where ABC is inflating Sales by recording sales to nonexistent clients whose "debt" never existed and will never be paid. As the example clearly illustrates, the ability to judge ratios against a benchmark based on economic considerations is very useful in understanding the current position.

Another factor that we should consider in examining the economics of the average collection period, as well as other ratios, is seasonality in the business being analyzed. Consider, for example, a typical retail store in which roughly 30 percent of annual retail sales are made in the month of December. Thus, if we calculate the average collection period for December assuming, as we do in the preceding formula, that sales are evenly spread throughout the year, we will miscalculate the expected average collection period. To illustrate this, continue with the example of the ABC Co., assuming now that it is a retailer. If all of ABC's clients were credit customers, then on December 31 all of its December clients (possibly except for those who bought on December 1) will still owe ABC money. Thus, ABC's A/R at the year-end will be 30 percent of its annual sales. The average collection period that we will calculate then will be

$$\text{Average collection period} = \frac{\text{A/R}}{\text{Sales}/365}$$

$$= \frac{30\% \cdot \text{Sales}}{\text{Sales}/365}$$

$$= 30\% \cdot 365 = 109.5 \text{ days}$$

Since only 25 percent of ABC's sales are to credit customers, we expect the average collection period to be $25\% \cdot 109.5 = 27.4$ days—quite different from the expected average collection period when we ignore the seasonality. Note that the expected collection period of 27.4 days applies only to December: For balance sheets of other months we expect a lower average collection period since sales in these months are relatively low. In general, the effect of seasonality in the business on estimated financial ratios depends on the month for which these ratios are estimated or, in other words, depends on when the fiscal year of the firm being analyzed ends.

Exhibit 6.4 depicts AMT's and its comparables' average collection period. The most notable aspect of the average collection period of AMT is that it is one-half its industry's standard: AMT's average collection period is about 1.5 months, whereas the industry seems to be granting credit for about 3 months. Moreover, the difference is not unique to 1992: The average collection periods of both AMT and its comparables are rather stable over the last 5 years. Given the nature of the industry—goods are sold to manufacturers and not to retail customers—it is safe to assume that close to 100 percent of the sales in the industry are to credit customers. Thus, the difference in the average collection period is probably due to different terms of credit sales that AMT and its competitors use. A full investigation of this issue should verify that this is indeed the case. More importantly, the *projected* average collection period should reflect our projection of the future policies of AMT: If we project AMT's credit policies to continue, then we will continue to use an average collection period of 45 days to project AMT's A/R. On the other hand, if we project that AMT's credit terms will have to change to meet the terms of its competitors, the *projected* average collection period should be 3 months.

Exhibit 6.4

	Fiscal year				
	1992	1991	1990	1989	1988
	AMT				
Net Sales	$ 177,594	183,940	199,493	191,034	176,090
Accounts Receivable (A/R)	$ 22,506	22,998	25,440	24,507	25,764
Average Collection Period	46.3	45.6	46.5	46.8	53.4
	Comparables				
Net Sales	$1,974,764	1,723,975	1,716,462	1,613,448	1,334,784
A/R	$ 621,265	582,438	444,807	417,211	385,057
Average Collection Period	114.8	123.3	94.6	94.4	105.3

Projecting Future Accounts Receivable

So far we have only analyzed AMT's *past* A/R, but, of course, our goal is the prediction of the *future* A/R based on our Sales projection. We can use the same ratio with which we analyze the *past* A/R to predict the future A/R, or, alternatively, we might combine facts about the historic collection period with additional information to make a prediction that *differs* from the historic firm average.

As an example, recall the ABC Co.: ABC had Sales of $12 million and an average collection period of 12.2 days. Suppose your analysis of the firm yields the following information:

• ABC has just announced an improvement in its credit terms from ''net 10'' to ''net 20.''

• As a result of the improvement in credit terms, you expect next year's Sales to increase to $18 million from this year's $12 million.

• You further expect that the fraction of sales to credit customers will double next year from this year's level.

This information can be used to predict next year's A/R. First, since the credit period granted to credit clients has doubled, *you expect next year's average col-*

lection period also to double—24.4 days instead of 12.2 days this year. Second, since you expect the fraction of credit sales to double, *the expected average collection period of next year is doubled again*—48.8 days instead of 24.4 days. Now, given the Sales projection, we can estimate the A/R of next year. This entails inverting the average collection period ratio:

$$\frac{\text{Projected A/R}}{18,000/365} = 48.8$$

$$\Rightarrow \quad \text{Projected A/R} = \frac{48.8}{365} \cdot 18,000 \approx \$2,400$$

Or, in general terms

$$\text{Projected A/R} = \frac{\text{projected average collection period}}{365} \cdot \text{projected Sales}$$

Thus, when ABC increases its sales, ABC must also increase its working capital by $\$(2.4 - 0.4)$ million. Obviously, to decide whether such a sales increase makes sense, ABC's management should compare the annual cost of maintaining this larger working capital base—the lost interest on the capital used to finance the credit to the customers—to the added profit resulting from the increased sales. Just as important, when building our pro-forma model for ABC, we should check whether the new credit terms are *sustainable, given the firm's desired debt/equity policies and other credit restrictions.*

Projecting Inventories

The next working capital component that we analyze is Inventories. Inventories are held for various reasons:

• Demand for the firm's product varies over time and inventories allow smooth production.
• Production takes time so that inventory in the form of partially completed products must exist.
• Buying raw materials in bulk is cheaper than purchasing and shipping small quantities, and therefore holding raw material inventories is costly but less than the buying of small quantities.

Thus, understanding the economics of the business, such as the length of production, the uncertainty of demand, and inventory ordering costs, is a crucial precondition to the analysis of the firm's inventory levels. Moreover, often it is important to analyze separately the components of inventory, such as raw materials, work in progress, and finished products, rather than their sum total in order to understand the inventory demands and policies of the firm. For example, a stable level of raw materials and work in progress and an increase in finished goods inventories may indicate that the firm is experiencing lower than normal levels of sales, and thus is having difficulties in selling its product. A decline in finished goods, on the other hand, may indicate the reverse. Although by themselves such changes in inventory levels may mean nothing, they should trigger questions, and additional information should be sought to explain these changes. This is because, typically, inventory levels reflect the way that the business is conducted in a particular industry, which in most cases doesn't change much from one fiscal year to the next. This means that inventory levels don't materially change without reason as well.

Two related ratios are often used to analyze inventory levels. The first—*inventory days*—is calculated by comparing the size of the inventory to the cost of sales on an average day:

$$\text{Inventory days} = \frac{\text{Inventory}}{\text{cost of daily sales}} = \frac{\text{Inventory}}{\text{COGS}/365}$$

A variant of this ratio that is sometimes used is calculating the ratio by using Sales instead of the COGS in the ratio. We prefer to use the COGS because calculating inventory days with Sales instead of the COGS confuses two factors that we prefer to consider separately. To see this, note that the difference between Sales and the COGS reflects the firm's gross margins, which differ from one firm to the next (e.g., due to different marketing strategies). Thus, when the ratio of inventory days is calculated with Sales instead of the COGS, the ratio of one firm may differ from the ratio of another firm because of either a true difference in inventory management or a difference in their gross margins. Because inventory days calculated with Sales reflects both inventory management policies and profit margins, we cannot use this ratio to compare the inventory management of firms, which is the objective of calculating this ratio in the first place. Thus, we prefer to calculate inventory days with the COGS.

A related ratio that is often used instead of inventory days is *inventory turnover*:

$$\text{Inventory turnover} = \frac{\text{COGS}}{\text{average Inventory}}$$

$$= \frac{\text{COGS}}{[\text{beginning Inventory} + \text{ending Inventory}]/2}$$

When the inventory doesn't change over the period, the inventory turnover is just the inverse of inventory days (with a scaling factor of 365). Thus, an analysis of one ratio is very similar to an analysis of the other.

There are two differences between the ratios that make us prefer to use the inventory days ratio over the inventory turnover ratio:

• First, in inventory days we use the ending inventory level, whereas in the inventory turnover we typically use the average inventory. Since the beginning level of inventories cannot reflect the knowledge of this year's Sales and the COGS, we believe that it is more reasonable to compare only the ending Inventory to the COGS of this year. Thus, if you use the inventory turnover ratio to analyze inventories, you will probably be better off by using the ending Inventory only in its calculation.

• Second, and more importantly, we find it easier to interpret inventory days than inventory turnover ratios. For example, we can compare inventory days either to the length of production in an industrial firm or to the frequency in which goods are ordered by a retailer facing four seasons.

The ability to consider the economics of the ratio is useful in interpreting its level and, perhaps more importantly, in projecting future inventory levels that reflect our perception of changes in the industry. Still, if you find the inventory turnover ratio easier to interpret than inventory days, the inventory turnover should be the ratio to use.

Note that in calculating inventory days or the inventory turnover, we have not excluded Depreciation from the COGS as we did when analyzing production costs. There are two reasons for this. First, for most firms we cannot, by using only financial statement information, show how much of the depreciation charge is included in the COGS and how much of it is included in the SG&A. Second, even if we can estimate the depreciation charges included in the COGS, we would still not know how much depreciation is included in the cost of the inventories. Thus, we include Depreciation charges in both the COGS and Inventories in our analysis of inventory levels. To the extent that the fraction of Depreciation charges in the COGS and Inventories are the same, there is no harm in including depreciation in both.

In Exhibit 6.5 we provide calculations for inventory days for AMT and its comparables. Note that for AMT we have information about some of the components of its inventory—Work in Progress and Finished Goods are reported sepa-

Exhibit 6.5

	Fiscal year				
	1992	1991	1990	1989	1988
		AMT			
Cost of Goods Sold (COGS)	$ 131,096	137,228	144,708	140,263	136,909
Work in Progress and Finished Goods	$ 17,354	21,970	25,987	25,986	23,056
Inventory days	48.3	58.4	65.5	67.6	61.5
Raw Materials and Supplies	$ 7,910	11,237	10,941	12,413	9,909
Inventory days	22.0	29.9	27.6	32.3	26.4
Inventories—Total	$ 25,264	33,207	36,928	38,399	32,965
Inventory days	70.3	88.3	93.1	99.9	87.9
		Comparables			
COGS	$1,515,131	1,325,843	1,320,963	1,218,876	1,007,642
Inventory	$ 399,497	427,227	442,822	443,569	370,260
Inventory days	96.2	117.6	122.4	132.8	134.1

rately from Raw Materials. We calculate in the table separate inventory days ratios for the components of the Inventory. This is useful in that we now can examine separately the efficiency with which AMT manages its inventory purchases— through Raw Materials' inventory days—and the way it manages its production— through Work in Progress and Finished Goods' inventory days. Unfortunately, detailed inventory information doesn't exist for all of AMT's comparables, so for them we calculate only the aggregate inventory days' ratios.

The inventory days ratios of AMT, for both the components and the total, decline considerably over the period 1988 through 1992. This is also true of AMT's competitors: Their inventory days, although higher than those of AMT, consistently decline from their 1988 level of 134 days to a much lower level of 96 days in 1992.[8]

AMT's improvement is evident in its management of its raw materials inventory, where inventory days declined from about 30 days to 22 days in 1992 as well as in its Work in Progress and Finished Goods inventory where inventory days declined from more than 60 days to 48 days in 1992.

The observed trend in inventory and production management at AMT and its comparables suggests that future inventory levels will not be as high as they were in the past. Thus, when projecting AMT's financial performance based on Sales projections, that is, when preparing pro-forma statements for AMT, it is more reasonable to project inventory days that reflect *current* practice than past practices. Given the preceding trends at AMT and its industry, an inventory days ratio of 70 is a more reasonable expectation for future inventory levels than the average inventory days ratios in the 1988 through 1992 period of 87.9 days.

We can project inventory levels by converting the projected level of the COGS to the projected level of inventory:

$$\text{Projected Inventory} = \frac{\text{projected inventory days}}{365} \cdot \text{projected COGS}$$

If COGS include no fixed costs, projected COGS will be based on Sales projections and on the ratio of the COGS to Sales. In this case we can substitute for projected COGS and get

$$\text{Projected Inventory} = \frac{\text{projected inventory days}}{365}$$
$$\cdot \text{projected} \left[\frac{\text{COGS}}{\text{Sales}} \right] \cdot \text{projected Sales}$$

[8]The improvement in the inventory days ratio may be a reflection of the streamlining of U.S. industry: Both production and inventory management improved in this period to make U.S. producers more competitive in the world arena against, for example, Japanese producers who use inventory and production methods such as ''Just in Time.'' On the other hand, the improvement in the ratio may just reflect a parallel improvement in U.S. economic conditions.

which can also be written as

$$\text{Projected Inventory} = \frac{\text{projected inventory days}}{365}$$
$$\cdot \, (1 - \text{projected Gross Margin}) \cdot \text{projected Sales}$$

For example, suppose we project AMT's 1993 Sales to be $190 million, its Gross Margin to be 26 percent, and its 1993 inventory to represent the cost of 70 days of sales (i.e., we expect AMT's 1993 inventory days ratio to be 70 days). This means that we expect AMT's inventory at the end of 1993 fiscal year to be

$$(70/365) \cdot (1 - 26\%) \cdot \$190,000 = \$26,964$$

The expectation of a $27 million inventory at the end of 1993 reflects our perception of AMT's production efficiency, through the projected Gross Margin; our perception of AMT's efficiency in managing its inventory, through the inventory days ratio; and our projection of AMT's marketing prospects, through the projected Sales level.[9]

Projecting Accounts Payable (A/P)

The last component of the operating items in working capital that we discuss is Accounts Payable (A/P). A/P is treated by accountants as a short-term loan. Although this view is partially correct, it ignores the fact that the A/P differs from other loans that the firm takes: Regular loans (such as bank loans, commercial paper, and bonds) represent a conscious financial decision to finance operations by a loan; the A/P, on the other hand, is typically incidental borrowing. The major decision leading to the creation of A/P is the purchase of products or services of a given vendor for their particular properties, such as quality, price, availability, and compatibility. The creation of a trade credit is typically a by-product—the preferred supplier happens to extend credit to customers. Thus, we consider the A/P largely as part of the *operating* side of the business, not part of the financial side of the business.

Obviously, the decision to rely on vendor financing is not always an operating decision: Reliance on vendor financing may reflect a conscious financial decision. When a firm decides to use vendor financing, one would observe an increase in A/P beyond the level that is justifiable by concurrent COGS and SG&A. It is worth mentioning that reliance on vendor financing is almost always a red flag for financial problems since vendor financing, although quoted in small numbers, is very costly (refer to footnote 7, page 179). Thus, the decision to use excessive vendor

---

[9]A technical note about modeling: When building a spreadsheet pro-forma model of the firm, we need only to relate the Inventory to the COGS (through the inventory days parameter). Assuming that the COGS is modeled as a proportion of Sales, the iterative spreadsheet solution will implement the substitutions outlined in the three last equations.

financing may indicate an acute financial shortfall or restricted access to other sources of funding. Typically, however (possibly because vendor financing is so costly and because terms of trade often allow corporations to pay bills with a considerable lag), the A/P merely represents incidental financing and should be analyzed as such.

The A/P is the flip side of A/R. Whereas A/R represents lending by the analyzed firm to its clients, the A/P is the result of the firm borrowing from its suppliers. Thus, it is not surprising that the analysis of the A/P resembles the analysis of the A/R. We should consider the period of credit typically awarded by the firm's suppliers, the fraction of the firm's purchases done on credit, and the effects of seasonality. Moreover, the ratio often used in the analysis of the A/P—the **average payable period**—is a variant of the average collection period used in the analysis of A/R:

$$\text{Average payable period} = \frac{\text{Accounts Payable}}{(\text{COGS} + \text{SG\&A} - \text{Depreciation})/365}$$

There are a few facts to note about the way that we calculate the ratio:

• We lump together the COGS and the SG&A. This is because we often don't know how to allocate the A/P to the COGS and the SG&A. If you have information allowing you to separate the A/P attributable to the COGS from the A/P attributable to the SG&A, you will be able to analyze separately the two components of the A/P, although you will probably learn little beyond that which you can learn by aggregating the expenditures and the A/P.

• We have deducted Depreciation from the sum of the COGS and the SG&A. The reason is that Depreciation charges are not cash expenditure, so there is no credit associated with them.

The average payable period of the firm, like any other ratio, can be compared to the industry average and to previous periods. To illustrate the ratio's computation, we calculate in Exhibit 6.6 the ratio for AMT and its comparables.

Exhibit 6.6

		Fiscal year			
	1992	1991	1990	1989	1988
AMT					
Accounts Payable (A/P)	$ 31,234	31,730	28,847	36,181	31,547
Cost of Goods Sold (COGS)	$ 131,096	137,228	144,708	140,263	136,909
Selling, General, and Administrative Expenses (SG&A)	$ 40,199	43,165	46,831	44,762	42,959
Depreciation Charges	$ 7,418	7,278	7,214	7,084	10,716
Average Payable Period	69.6	66.9	57.1	74.2	68.1

Exhibit 6.6 *continued*

	Fiscal year				
	1992	1991	1990	1989	1988
	Comparables				
A/P	$ 308,939	291,715	206,986	197,151	169,675
COGS	$1,515,131	1,325,843	1,320,963	1,218,876	1,007,642
SG&A	$ 367,680	330,620	328,639	287,079	251,809
Depreciation Charges	$ 60,256	56,944	55,834	52,477	25,086
Average Payable Period	$ 61.9	66.6	47.4	49.5	50.2

While the average payable period exhibits considerable variation, there is no apparent trend, for either AMT or its comparables. The average payable period of AMT appears to be larger than the average payable period of its comparables, but the difference is rather small. However, whereas AMT's average payable period of about 67 days is roughly in line with AMT's average collection period of 45 days, there is a large difference between its comparables' average payable period of 55 days and their average collection period of 106 days. Since both the clients and the suppliers of AMT and its comparables are large corporations, it is strange to see a very long average collection period and a very short average payable period. Thus, apparently AMT's current average payable period of about 67 days can predict better AMT's future A/P relative to sales projections.

To predict the future A/P, you can use the projected average payable period together with the projected COGS, SG&A, and Depreciation:

$$\text{Projected A/P} = (\text{projected average payable period}/365)$$
$$\cdot \text{ projected } \{COGS + SG\&A - Depreciation\}$$

For example, by using the regression estimates of AMT's cost components, FC and VC, we can estimate that if AMT's 1993 Sales are $190 million, the COGS + SG&A − Depreciation will be $177.1 million. By using the historical average payable period of 67 days as the projected average payable period, we can project that if AMT 1993 Sales are $190 million, its A/P will be

$$\text{Projected A/P} = (67/365) \cdot 177.1 = \$33 \text{ million}$$

Note that since the projected (COGS + SG&A − Depreciation) reflect the projected Sales as well as the estimated relation between operating costs and Sales, the projected A/P is effectively driven by our Sales projection. This is most easily seen when the equation relating operating costs and Sales is substituted into the equation for the projection of A/P:

$$\text{Projected A/P} = (67/365) \cdot (30.23 + 0.773 \cdot 190)$$

where \$190 million is the projected 1993 Sales.

Projecting Other Working Capital Items

The discussion of the relation of A/R, Inventory, and A/P to Sales doesn't cover all the items that can possibly be part of the working capital of a firm. Yet the preceding analysis should guide you in analyzing other components of working capital that may appear in some financial statements. The principles of the analysis should now be clear:

- Establish a pattern that relates the desired item to Sales.
- Try to separate fixed components from variable components.
- Try to exclude irrelevant components.
- Use a ratio that lends itself to economic interpretation.

6.5 THE ANALYSIS OF CAPITAL INVESTMENT REQUIREMENTS

The prediction of capital investments that are necessary to support projected sales is predicated upon an understanding of the relation between Sales and Fixed Assets—Plant, Property, and Equipment (PP&E). This is perhaps the most problematic component of FCFs to predict because, on the one hand, there doesn't need to be a simple (e.g., linear) relation between PP&E and Sales, and, on the other hand, this is typically the largest component of FCFs. The problem in relating PP&E to Sales is that PP&E provides the *capacity* to generate sales but the *utilization* of this capacity may change over time, making statistical inference about the relation of PP&E to Sales difficult without the knowledge of utilization rates. For example, an airline that has 50 planes with 150 seats in each can have an average booking of 20 or 80 percent of available seats, which allows quite a variation in Sales relative to existing capacity—PP&E. Yet because the valuation of a firm emphasizes *long-term* prospects, we often model capacity and Sales as being linearly related, implicitly thinking of utilization as being fixed. To put this another way, we believe that capital expenditures are taken only when increased sales justify increasing the capacity. Moreover, to the extent possible, obtaining information about the rate at which the *existing* capacity is utilized can greatly help in projecting capital investment needs, at least in the short run.

The first step in analyzing capital investment requirements is to determine how to measure capacity in the industry that you analyze. Capacity in different industries means different things. For example, for retailers capacity is often square footage of exhibition area, for an airline it may be the number of seats coupled with the number of gates or flights, and for a mail-order service it may be the number of envelope stuffing machines. The appropriate measure of capacity is important in that it indicates how to calculate meaningful ratios relating PP&E to Sales. PP&E

is reported in the financial statements at cost, accumulated depreciation, and net. For many businesses capacity doesn't deteriorate with the age of the asset. For example, a square foot of retail floor space typically generates the same level of sales independent of whether it is brand new or old, machines typically generate the same hourly output independent of age, and trucks carry the same payload independent of age. When the capacity is almost independent of the asset's age, the better way to measure the relation between the capacity and sales is by relating the *cost* of PP&E to Sales. When the capacity does deteriorate with the asset's age, it is better to relate the *net value of the fixed assets*—PP&E net of Accumulated Depreciation—to the level of sales. In our examples we assume that the capacity is independent of the PP&E's age and, accordingly, we relate the *cost* of PP&E to Sales.

A ratio that is often used in the analysis of the relation between Sales and PP&E is the ratio of **Sales to Fixed Assets:**

$$\text{Sales to Fixed Assets} = \frac{\text{Sales}}{\text{average PP\&E}}$$

$$= \frac{\text{Sales}}{[\text{PP\&E}(1/1) + \text{PP\&E}(12/31)]/2}$$

The use of the *average* PP&E instead of the year-end PP&E implicitly assumes that assets are bought throughout the year. If the sales of a given year are generated by assets in place at the beginning of the year instead of average assets (e.g., because the acquisition and the startup of fixed assets is a lengthy process), you can calculate the ratio by using only the PP&E of the *beginning* of the year. This implies that *next year's sales are constrained by the existing capacity*—the PP&E at the end of the current fiscal year.

Depreciator Inc.—A Simple Example

In the discussion of the analysis of PP&E we use the example of Depreciator Inc. (D):

	Fiscal year	
	1992	1993
Sales	$2,400	$3,000
Property, Plant, and Equipment (PP&E)		
Cost	6,000	6,900
Accumulated Depreciation	1,800	2,490

If sales in this industry are related to the *average* PP&E (e.g., if PP&E is trucks that are purchased evenly throughout the year and are put to use as soon as they are purchased), then the 1993 ratio of Sales to Fixed Assets should be calculated as

$$\frac{3,000}{(6,000 + 6,900)/2} = 0.465$$

On the other hand, if the industry is such that only assets in place can generate sales, then the 1993 ratio of Sales to Fixed Assets should be calculated as

$$\frac{3,000}{6,000} = 0.5$$

In addition, if the productive capacity of the fixed assets deteriorates with age, this deterioration can be captured by calculating the ratio of Sales to Net Fixed Assets:

$$\frac{3,000}{6,000 - 1,800} = 0.714$$

Note that in deducting the accumulated depreciation of the PP&E from their original cost, we implicitly assume that the accounting depreciation charges correctly depict the decline in the productive capacity of the PP&E, which is hardly a trivial assumption. This is an important point, for one of the ways that we analyze ratios is by comparing the ratios of one firm to the ratios of similar firms in its industry. To the extent that firms in the industry employ different depreciation schedules, which is possible since there is no natural or correct way to depreciate fixed assets, computing the ratio of Sales to Fixed Assets after Accumulated Depreciation has been deducted from the PP&E's cost makes comparison across the industry difficult. The computation of the ratio on a before-depreciation basis usually makes cross-sectional comparison simpler and more meaningful because it doesn't depend on the depreciation policies of the firms being compared.

Analyzing AMT's Fixed Assets

In Exhibit 6.7 we present the Sales to Fixed Assets ratio of AMT and its comparables when fixed assets are included both before and after depreciation.

Exhibit 6.7

	Fiscal year				
	1992	1991	1990	1989	1988
	AMT				
Net sales	$ 177,594	$ 183,940	$ 199,493	$ 191,034	$ 176,090
Property, Plant, and Equipment (PP&E) at Cost	141,032	139,682	138,875	134,651	131,930
Accumulated Depreciation	(103,970)	(100,106)	(95,140)	(88,936)	(85,864)
PP&E net	37,062	39,576	43,735	45,715	46,066
Sales to Gross Fixed Assets	1.26	1.32	1.44	1.42	1.33
Sales to Net Fixed Assets	4.79	4.65	4.56	4.18	3.82
	Comparables				
Net sales	$1,974,764	$1,723,975	$1,716,462	$1,613,448	$1,334,784
PP&E at Cost	1,017,564	1,087,579	1,030,743	940,578	872,645
Accumulated Depreciation	(649,962)	(706,563)	(672,237)	(617,122)	(571,879)
PP&E net	367,602	381,016	358,506	323,456	300,766
Sales to Gross Fixed Assets	1.94	1.59	1.67	1.72	1.53
Sales to Net Fixed Assets	5.37	4.52	4.79	4.99	4.44

The ratio of Sales to Gross Fixed Assets—fixed assets at original cost—averages 1.35 for AMT, whereas its comparables sell at a 25 percent higher rate of 1.69. This suggests that AMT's comparables utilize more of their productive capacity than does AMT, which in turn suggests that AMT may be able to expand its sales by as much as 25 percent without making additional investments. A similar picture emerges from the comparison of the Sales to Net Fixed Assets of AMT and of its comparables.

Note the difference between the changes over time of the Sales to Gross Fixed Assets and the Sales to Net Fixed Assets ratios for both AMT and its comparables: The ratio of Sales to Net Fixed Assets grows over time, whereas the ratio of Sales to Gross Fixed Assets, while varying over time, doesn't exhibit any time pattern. The most probable explanation for the difference in the ratios time pattern is that the productive capacity of AMT's assets and of its comparables doesn't deteriorate with age. Because the capacity hardly varies with age, sales don't depend on the *depreciated* value of the assets. Consequently, when we incorrectly relate Sales to Net Fixed Assets, the denominator is unjustifiably reduced over time as more depreciation is accumulated on the Fixed Assets, which creates an artificial trend in the ratio. This indicates that in order to project future PP&E needs of AMT, we should relate Sales to Gross Fixed Assets, not to Net Fixed Assets.

The fact that Accumulated Depreciation should not be considered in determining the relation between PP&E and the Sales that they can support doesn't mean that accumulated depreciation is a redundant piece of information. So far we have considered the *total* PP&E needs that are commensurate with the projected sales level. This analysis allows us to determine the capital investments that are necessary to *expand* the capacity to facilitate projected sales *growth*. This is, however, only part of the capital expenditures needed: Firms also buy PP&E to *maintain* the productive capacity. To estimate the capital expenditure that is required to maintain the productive capacity, we should estimate the age of the fixed assets of the firm and the life expectancy of the assets. The depreciation figures—annual Depreciation charges and Accumulated Depreciation—are useful in this task.

We use the annual Depreciation charge to estimate the average expected life of the firm's fixed assets. It is easy to see that the ratio of

$$\frac{\text{Cost of Fixed Assets}}{\text{Annual Depreciation charges}}$$

is an estimate of the **average expected life** of Fixed Assets.[10] Obviously, since land is not depreciated, if possible we exclude the cost of land from the cost of fixed assets before calculating the ratio. Sometimes the estimated useful life of fixed assets is reported in the first note to the financial statements of the firm—the note describing the accounting policies of the firm—and thus nullifying the need to calculate this ratio.

The next step is to calculate the average fraction of the expected life of the assets that has been exhausted. This can be done by calculating the ratio of accumulated depreciation to the cost of the assets:

$$\text{Fraction of expected life exhausted} = \frac{\text{Accumulated Depreciation}}{\text{Cost of Fixed Assets}}$$

The average remaining years of the firm's assets is easily calculated from these two numbers:

$$\text{Remaining years} = (1 - \text{fraction of expected life exhausted}) \cdot \text{average expected life}$$

In Exhibit 6.8 we present these calculations for AMT and its comparables.

The average useful life of AMT's Fixed Assets (net of Land), with the exception of 1988, is estimated to be slightly below 19 years. Moreover, the estimated average remaining life of its assets monotonically declines from 6 years in 1989 to 4.6 years in 1992. Since the total cost of PP&E hardly changes from 1989 to 1992, we may expect the remaining life of the Fixed Assets to decline by a year at a time.

---

[10]Strictly speaking, the interpretation of the ratio as the expected life of the fixed assets is true only when the firm uses a straight-line depreciation schedule. Under some conditions of homogeneous purchase of fixed assets, however, the ratio equals the average life expectancy of fixed assets under other depreciation schedules as well.

Exhibit 6.8

	Fiscal year				
	1992	1991	1990	1989	1988
AMT					
Property, Plant, and Equipment (PP&E)	$ 141,032	$ 139,682	$ 138,875	$134,651	$131,930
Land	2,712	2,840	2,858	2,996	2,978
PP&E–Land	138,320	136,842	136,017	131,655	128,952
Annual Depreciation	7,418	7,278	7,214	7,084	10,716
Average Useful Life	18.6	18.8	18.9	18.6	12.0
Accumulated Depreciation	103,970	100,106	95,140	88,936	85,864
Remaining Useful Life	4.6	5.0	5.7	6.0	4.0
Comparables					
PP&E	$1,017,564	$1,087,579	$1,030,743	$940,578	$872,645
Land	22,237	23,509	14,313	13,588	12,342
PP&E–Land	995,327	1,064,070	1,016,430	926,990	860,303
Annual Depreciation	60,256	56,944	55,834	52,477	25,086
Average Useful Life	16.5	18.7	18.2	17.7	34.3
Accumulated Depreciation	649,962	706,563	672,237	617,122	571,879
Remaining Useful Life	5.7	6.3	6.2	5.9	11.5

The actual decline is slightly less than one-half year in each fiscal year. This reflects the fact that although AMT doesn't *expand* the production capacity, it *replaces* the capacity that finishes its useful life. This can be verified from cash-flow statements of AMT, which show its actual expenditures on PP&E and the footnotes to the financial statements that provide details on asset acquisition and retirement. In fact, by using the historical statements of a firm, we can estimate the whole age structure of PP&E and employ this schedule to estimate the investments needed to replace retired assets.

In our analysis of financial statements in the previous sections we have ignored the effect of inflation on ratios. The reason is that the ratios that we have discussed compare cash flows of the same year. This means that inflation little affects the ratios considered in the previous sections. For example, in calculating the average collection period for 1992, we compare the Sales in 1992, which are denominated in 1992 dollars, to Accounts Receivable at the end of 1992, which are also denominated in 1992 dollars. This is not the case when fixed assets are concerned. This is because, typically, fixed assets are held for long periods so that their cost may reflect the value of dollars of many years ago. Even if inflation is running at a modest rate, the accumulation of low-inflation rates can materially affect estimated ratios that compare current dollars to the historical cost of fixed assets. It is a good idea, therefore, when calculating ratios that involve fixed assets to try to estimate their cost in terms of today's dollars. One way to do this is to use the estimated schedule of the ages of the fixed assets and to inflate their cost by a price index, such as the producer price index (PPI). Consider, again, the example of Depreciator Inc. Assuming that inflation in 1993 was 4 percent and that the new assets purchased in 1993 were evenly purchased throughout the year, we adjust the PP&E cost for 1993 inflation as shown in Exhibit 6.9.

Exhibit 6.9

DEPRECIATOR INC.
Inflation Adjustments to Equipment Costs

Property, Plant, and Equipment (PP&E) in 1993	6,900	
PP&E in 1992	6,000	
⇒ PP&E bought in 1993	900	
Adjusted cost of "old" assets		$6{,}000 \cdot (1 + 4\%) = 6{,}240$
Adjusted cost of assets bought in 1993		$900 \cdot (1 + 4\%/2) = 918$
Inflation-adjusted PP&E, 12/31/93 dollar		$6{,}240 + 918 = 7{,}158$

Obviously, as you have just seen in the case of AMT, a full adjustment of the historical cost of PP&E to current dollars is much more complicated when assets are both bought and retired each year. But the principle is the same. We discuss this issue in Chapter 7.

SUMMARY

In this chapter we discussed the financial ratio analysis of the firm. The objective of our analysis is the conversion of Sales projections into complete financial projections expressed as integrated pro-forma financial statements. We take an outsider's point of view: As outsiders we are not privy to information about the actual relation between sales and costs or investments, so we must use historical relations as reflected in the financial statements of prior years to *infer* these relations. Obviously, to the extent that other nonfinancial statement information is available, it also becomes part of our analysis.

The primary tool of outsiders analyzing a firm is the examination of financial ratios—ratios that take several numbers from the financial statements and combine them into an *economically meaningful relation*. The key words here, economically meaningful relations, should guide you in the selections of financial ratios from the hundreds of ratios you can use: *Use those ratios for which you have the best economic intuition.* The purpose of the analysis is to infer from past financial ratios (and other economic information) what *future* ratios will look like. The projected future ratios are the ratios that you will use to build pro-forma financial statements that convert your Sales projections into complete projections of financial statements. Only those ratios for which you have economic intuition and understanding can be predicted with any reliability!

To understand financial ratios, we need some benchmarks with which to compare the ratios of the firm being analyzed. Three types of benchmarks are often used—cross-industry average ratios, past ratios of the firm, and ratios driven by economic considerations. Each benchmark is based on some assumptions:

• Comparing the firm's ratios to the industry average implicitly assumes that firms in the industry are operated in similar ways, use similar technologies, appeal to similar clienteles, and employ similar marketing strategies.

• Comparing the firm's current ratios to those of prior years implicitly assumes that the firm's basic modes of operation have not changed; that is, the firm uses similar technologies, appeals to similar clienteles, employs similar marketing strategies, and so on, as it did in prior years.

• Comparing the firm's ratios to benchmarks based on the fundamentals of the business (such as comparing the average collection period to the firm's credit policy and the gross-margin ratio to the firm's pricing policies) is not based on assumed similarity to other firms or the stationarity of these ratios over time. Rather, this comparison requires the knowledge of the specific policies of the firm as well as some nonpolicy parameters (such as the percentage of clients who buy on credit).

The use of *accounting data* to analyze the efficiency with which the firm carries its business means that special attention should be paid to the *effects of inflation* on the ratios. Accounting statements are based on *historical costs*. Therefore, before comparing ratios over time or across firms, make sure that *all numbers are restated to equivalent constant purchasing-power basis.* This is particularly true of ratios that use balance sheet data, such as Fixed Assets, and Inventories; for these items the *cumulative* effect of inflation may be significant even when *annual* inflation rates are quite small.

In this chapter we considered ratios that are useful in converting Sales projections to forecasts of FCFs—ratios that relate costs to Sales and ratios that relate the *operating* items on the balance sheet to Sales. This fits the method of valuation that we recommend and follow in this book—the sequential valuation method: We first value the operating side of the business arriving at a value estimate for the *whole* firm and only subsequently *divide the whole-firm value among its security holders.* If you want to build a full-blown pro-forma financial statement of the firm or to value the firm's equity directly by projecting and discounting the cash flows of the *equity holders* (a subject discussed in Chapters 11–13), you will also need to project *financial ratios*—ratios that describe how the firm will be financed. You can find a discussion of these ratios as part of our discussion of the division of the value of the firm among its security holders in Chapters 11 and 12.

EXERCISES

6.1 You collect the following information from the financial statements of the XYZ Corporation: 1991 Sales, $120,000; Accounts Receivable as of 12/31/91, $3,000; and Allowance for Uncollected Funds as of 12/31/91, $200.

You know that the firm has increased the time that it allows its credit customers to pay their debt from 30 days to 45 days and that, as a result, it expects the fraction of credit sales (of total sales) to double and its sales in 1992 to be 10 percent higher than 1991 sales.

Given this information, calculate the expected Accounts Receivable on 12/31/92.

6.2 The following information is taken from the 1989 through 1991 financial statements of The Successful Retailer Inc. (TSR) and from management projections for 1992. (Note that retailing companies include Depreciation expenses in the SG&A.)

	1989	1990	1991	1992 (Projected)
Sales	$635,000	$590,550	$637,794	$688,818
Cost of Goods Sold (COGS)	444,500	413,385	446,446	?
Selling, General, and Administrative Expenses (SG&A)	133,350	124,016	133,937	144,652
Accounts Receivable	24,356	22,652	?	26,420
Accounts Payable	54,674	50,846	54,913	?
Prepaid Expenses	4,932	4,587	4,954	5,350
Inventory	156,575	145,615	157,264	169,846
Accumulated Depreciation	95,020	112,737	111,871	132,535

From the notes to the company's financial statements you learn that TSR has lost money for several years and, as a result, has a huge tax loss that is carried forward. In 1991 TSR sold a fully depreciated asset whose original cost was $20,000. No assets were sold or scrapped in either 1989 or 1990.

a What is TSR's expected collection period for the 1992 year-end?

b Estimate TSR's COGS for 1992.

c Estimate the Free Cash Flows (FCFs) for the company from 1989 through 1992.

6.3 Your friend has a stand at which she sells business magazines. The stand is located at the entrance to the NYSE. To understand better what she sells, she wants to get an MBA and plans to rent out the magazine stand during the 2-year period of her MBA studies.

You offer your help in determining the appropriate rent. You collect the following information: Sales in 1990 and 1991 were $100,000 and $120,000, respectively; the COGS were $78,000 and $92,000, respectively; and the 1992 sales are expected to be $140,000. There are no SG&A expenses in this business.

Based on this information, estimate 1992 gross profits. (*Hint:* Consider fixed costs.)

6.4 The SLS Co. had $100,000 sales in 1998. In 1999 SLS will give a 15 percent discount to its corporate clients who account for 80 percent of its annual sales. As a result, SLS expects unit sales to corporate clients to increase by 25 percent. If SLS's sales to individuals remain constant at 1998 levels, what will be SLS sales in 1999?

6.5 Consider the following financial information for ABC & Co.:

	1990	1991	1992	1993 (Projected)
Sales	$875,000	$910,000	$946,400	$1,003,184
Cost of Goods Sold (COGS)	682,500	709,800	738,192	
Selling, General, and Administrative Expenses (SG&A)	87,500	91,000	94,640	
Operating Profits	105,000	109,200	113,568	
Tax (35%)	36,750	38,220	39,749	
Net Profits	68,250	70,980	73,819	
Accounts Receivable	143,835	149,589	155,573	
Inventory	65,445	68,063	70,786	
Accounts Payable	84,144	87,510	91,010	
Property, Plant, and Equipment (PP&E) at Cost	325,000	346,000	367,840	
Accumulated Depreciation	100,000	?	127,500	

Some additional information is that the COGS includes depreciation expenses of $15,000, $17,000, and $18,500 in 1990, 1991, and 1992, respectively; and in 1991 ABC sold PP&E with an original cost of $10,000 and an Accumulated Depreciation of $9,200 for $8,000. No other PP&E was disposed of in the period 1990 through 1992.

a Estimate ABC's 1993 year-end Accounts Receivable, assuming that past relations continue to hold in 1993.

b What were ABC's collections from clients in 1992?

c ABC always collects its Accounts Receivable on time, and thus doesn't make an allowance for uncollected funds. Except for one major client, all Sales are on a cash basis. The major client's credit terms are ''net in 90 days.'' Calculate the *proportion* of ABC's total Sales that are made to this major client.

d What were ABC's Capital Expenditures in 1991?

e What was ABC's Accumulated Depreciation at the end of 1991?

f Calculate ABC's Free Cash Flow in 1992.

6.6 a The Only Variables Co. (OVC) has no fixed costs and its variable costs are proportional to sales. OVC operates in an industry where competition intensifies yearly. As a result, while sales in the industry are expected to grow at the phenomenal rate of 20 percent next year, OVC expects its market share in 1993 to be only a half of its 1992 market share. If OVC's Earnings before Interest and Taxes (EBIT) in 1992 was $100 million, what will be OVC's 1993 expected EBIT?

b SFC is in the same business as OVC but uses a different technology that entails some fixed costs. In 1992 OVC and SFC had the same sales and EBIT. SFC, like OVC, expects that its market share in 1993 will be half its 1992 level. Do you think that SFC's 1993 EBIT will be larger or smaller than those of OVC? Explain.

J. M. SMUCKER—
PROJECTING FINANCIAL
PERFORMANCE

OVERVIEW

In this chapter we illustrate the techniques described in the preceding chapters to model and project financial performance. We use data about J. M. Smucker Inc., the largest jam and jelly producer in the United States, to illustrate the different steps of this process. By using the Smucker data, we intend to give the exercise a real-world flavor rather than to draw conclusions about Smucker's value as an investment opportunity.

Most of the chapter is devoted to the building of a pro-forma model for Smucker. We have used only publicly available information. In many cases analysts have more information available (this would certainly be true if the valuation were part of a friendly takeover). Building a pro-forma model involves many compromises and trade-offs: We often have to choose between making our model more detailed or choosing a level of generality that allows us to get an overview of the company. We will be frank about these compromises so that you can get a feel for the modeler's dilemma.

Having built a model for Smucker, we proceed to value the company as if we know its cost of capital. This involves two more compromises:

• Since detailed models for calculating the cost of capital are given only in Chapters 8 and 9, we will make some arbitrary assumptions about Smucker in order to arrive at a cost of capital that is suitable for valuation.

• Part of the valuation involves the valuation of Smucker's warrants. In this chapter we use a very simple warrant valuation model in order to illustrate the main ideas. A detailed warrant valuation model is given in Chapter 12.

The chapter begins by describing Smucker's business and history. We proceed to predict Smucker's sales. Then we analyze Smucker's prior financial performance, as reflected in its financial statements, to arrive at projected ratios that are needed to convert sales projections to complete pro-forma statements. We combine the projected sales and financial ratios into integrated pro-forma statements for the following 5 years. Next we discuss the estimation of the terminal value for Smucker at the end of the 5-year projection period. Finally, we illustrate how the forecasted cash flows can be translated into values for the firm and its stock.

7.1 A SHORT DESCRIPTION OF SMUCKER

The J. M. Smucker Company, based in Orrville, Ohio, is the leading producer of jams, preserves, and jellies in the United States. The company was founded in 1897, and to this day the firm is actively managed by the Smucker family, which owns about 30 percent of the shares. Brand names of the company include Smucker's, Knudsen Family, Dickenson's, and Simply Fruit.

Smucker's hallmarks are its commitment to product quality and its conservative financial policies. The company has a negligible amount of debt in its capital structure.

Although over 90 percent of the company's 1992 sales were domestic, Smucker has made an increasing commitment to expanding its international sales. The company's main marketing efforts outside the United States are concentrated in the United Kingdom, Australia, and Canada.

7.2 SALES PROJECTION

Smucker sells food products both in the United States and abroad—Australia, Canada, and the United Kingdom. Since Smucker is an established brand name in the United States while it is still in the process of penetrating the international arena, we project Smucker's domestic and international sales separately. Although at the date of this analysis, the end of 1992, the company is expanding its international operations, these still constitute less than 10 percent of its total sales.

Smucker's products, jellies and jams, enjoy a relatively stable market. This is a mature industry where relatively few innovative products emerge. The stable demand is coupled with an established technology to produce jellies and jams. These two factors suggest that the prices of Smucker's products rise roughly at the rate of inflation. A food-industry analyst following Smucker would check this prediction by examining the actual prices of Smucker's products over time and by comparing them to the rate of inflation. Since this is just an illustrative example, we take this prediction as correct without further verifying its validity.

Under the assumption that the price of Smucker's goods appreciates at the rate of inflation we can estimate the *constant-dollar* sales of Smucker by adjusting the reported annual sales to changes in the consumer price index (CPI). This is not quite as accurate as knowing the actual tonnage of jellies and jams that are shipped each year, but it is a close enough estimate. In Exhibit 7.1 we show the conversion of the Sales of Smucker as reported in its financial statements for the years 1986 through 1992 to Sales figures expressed in 1992 dollars.

Exhibit 7.1

J. M. SMUCKER CO.
Adjusting Sales for Inflation

Fiscal year ending April 30	Sales ($M)	Average CPI	Constant-dollar sales
1986	262.80	108.57	333.07
1987	288.26	110.62	358.57
1988	314.25	115.18	375.41
1989	366.86	120.25	419.79
1990	422.36	126.12	460.80
1991	454.98	132.97	470.82
1992	483.47	137.60	483.47

Note: Smucker's fiscal year ends April 30. The consumer price index (CPI) in each row of the table is the average monthly CPI for the year ending April 30.

The adjustment of Sales for the inflation of a single year makes only a small difference. The cumulative effect of adjusting for inflation over many years, however, can be substantial. To illustrate this, in Figure 7.1 we plot the annual Sales figures as they were originally reported in the financial statements of 1986 through 1992, in *current dollars,* and adjusted for the different purchasing power of dollars in these years, in terms of *constant dollars* (specifically, 1992 dollars).[1]

[1]Since Smucker's fiscal year ends April 30, references to years refer to the fiscal year ending on April 30. Thus, for example, "1992" refers to Smucker's fiscal year ending April 30, 1992.

FIGURE 7.1   Smucker's Sales in current and constant dollars.

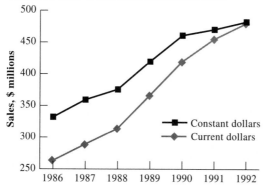

We can calculate compound growth rates of Sales for the 1986 through 1992 period by taking the

$$\text{Compound growth rate} = \left[\frac{1992 \text{ Sales}}{1986 \text{ Sales}} \right]^{1/6} - 1$$

There is a substantial difference between the inflation-unadjusted (i.e., nominal) annual Sales growth of 10.69 percent and the inflation-adjusted (i.e., real) growth of 6.41 percent. Although Sales growth driven by changes in the price level should be accounted for in valuations, it is not a growth that is due to the firm's efforts, and therefore should be considered separately from sales growth driven by further market penetration, market expansion, and the like. If inflation rates of the past are expected to prevail in the future, it will make no difference whether we analyze current-dollar or constant-dollar Sales figures. Typically, this is not the case, and thus it makes better economic sense to consider separately the growth in real Sales and the increase in Sales due to the adjustment of prices for changes in the purchasing power of money.

Smucker's products are consumer staples, that is, basic goods, of which the consumption varies only slightly with economic conditions. We don't expect, for example, people to say, "Since this year I earn less money than I usually do, I'll eat less" or, perhaps more importantly for predicting Smucker's sales, "I'll make my kids eat less this year." Thus, in the long run we expect Smucker's U.S. sales to grow with the growth of the U.S. population. This means that as a first pass at predicting Smucker's sales we should see how past sales in the United States are related to the size of the U.S. population. In Figure 7.2 we present Smucker's sales, restated to 1992 dollars, against the number of U.S. households.

As is evident from Figure 7.2, Smucker's sales are highly correlated with the size of the U.S. population. Calculating the ratio of sales to the number of households, we see that the average household consumed $4.47 of Smucker's products

FIGURE 7.2   Smucker's Sales versus the number of U.S. households, 1986–1992.

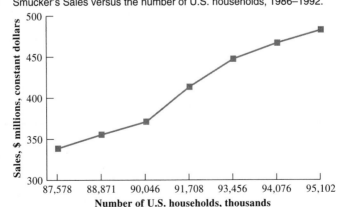

per annum. Regressing the percentage change in real sales on the percentage change in the number of households for the last 6 years gives

% change in real Sales

$$= -0.0087 + 5.1284 \cdot \% \text{ change in households}, \qquad R^2 = 0.5865$$

As might be expected, the y-intercept of -0.0087 is not statistically significantly different from zero, and the coefficient of the percent change in households is highly significant. Thus, extrapolating the trend from data for the last 6 years leads us to conclude that a 1 percent increase in the number of U.S. households will lead to an approximate 5 percent change in Smucker's real sales. We will use this 5 percent figure to estimate *short-term growth prospects for domestic Smucker's sales.* Estimating the growth in the number of U.S. households at 1.4 percent (its average growth over the preceding 5 years) gives 7 percent as the short-term real growth of Smucker's sales.[2]

What about the longer run? It is unreasonable to expect that in the long run Smucker's sales will continue to grow 5 times faster than the number of households. At this rate Smucker would soon capture the whole U.S. jam and jelly market! In the long run it is more reasonable to expect that the increase in Smucker's sales will roughly parallel the increase in U.S. household formation. Thus, we expect that *Smucker's long-run real sales growth will be 1.4 percent.*

In estimating the long-run growth rate of Smucker's sales on the basis of the growth in the population, we implicitly make two assumptions:

• Future per-capita consumption of jams and jellies will remain the same as it was in the past few years.
• Smucker's share of the jam and jelly market will remain the same as it was in the past few years.

These are assumptions that we should examine carefully. Specifically, to go beyond the basic projection of annual sales growth of 1.4 percent per year, we need to consider trends in food consumption and in the strengths and weaknesses of Smucker relative to its competitors as determinants of Smucker's market share. Probably the most noteworthy recent trend in food consumption is toward low-fat, low-sugar "healthier" foods and ingredients. On the one hand, this suggests a decline in the overall consumption of jams and jellies. On the other hand, Smucker's high-quality product probably makes Smucker more likely to benefit from this trend than low-cost competitors in the industry. The recent increase in Smucker's market share and the management discussion of this point in its 1992 financial statements suggest this is a change that is already taking place. Moreover, the emergence of the U.S. economy from a recession may further benefit Smucker as

---

[2]Students often feel that the R^2 of 58.65 percent of the regression is low; we, on the other hand, think this is a very reasonable number: It says that about 60 percent of Smucker's sales growth variability is attributable to household formation. The rest, presumably, has to do with factors that depend on the company and its competitors—advertising, product mix, and so on.

the high-quality, high-price producer of jellies and jams at the expense of the lower-quality, lower-cost producers. This is because as personal income growth returns to normal (i.e., nonrecession) levels, families that switched to low-cost substitutes will resume buying Smucker's more costly but higher-quality products. For this reason we expect Smucker's short-term Sales growth to be higher than its basic, longer-term Sales growth.

The upshot of these considerations is that we may expect Smucker's U.S. sales to grow at 7 percent in 1993 and 1994 and to revert to a long-term growth rate of 1.4 percent per year from, say, 1996. Interpolating the growth rates of 7 percent in 1994 and 1.4 percent in 1996, we arrive at a projected intermediate growth rate of 4 percent for 1995.

Smucker is attempting to penetrate international markets. Its international sales increased by more than 20 percent in 1990 but increased barely 3 percent in 1992. For illustration purposes we project that Smucker will be able to attain faster growth rates internationally than it has in 1992 but not as high a growth as that achieved in 1991. Specifically, we project a 10 percent annual growth in Smucker's international sales in the years 1993 through 1995. From 1997 onward we expect Smucker's international Sales to grow no faster than its domestic sales, that is, at the annual rate of 1.4 percent. In 1996 we interpolate the growth rate to 6 percent.[3]

Using the projected growth rates and levels of domestic and international sales in 1992, we can project Smucker's Sales in the fiscal years 1993 through 1997. Exhibit 7.2 provides the detailed calculation of the projected Sales.

[3]Obviously, a more realistic analysis of Smucker requires a more detailed analysis of its sales' prospects. Since our intention in this chapter is to illustrate the techniques with a *reasonable* number, we consider past values and gross trends in establishing the projected sales growth rates.

Exhibit 7.2

J. M. SMUCKER CO.
Projected Real Growth, 1993–1997

		Year			
	1992 (base)	1993	1994	1995	1996	1997
U.S. real growth rate		7%	7%	4%	1.4%	1.4%
U.S. Sales (in $ millions)	$442.88	$473.88	$507.05	$528.35	$535.75	$543.25
International real growth rate		10%	10%	10%	6%	1.4%
International Sales	$ 40.59	$ 44.65	$ 49.11	$ 54.03	$ 57.27	$ 58.07
Constant-dollar Sales	483.47	518.53	556.17	582.37	593.01	601.32
Projected real Sales growth		7.25%	7.26%	4.71%	1.83%	1.40%

The projected Sales in Exhibit 7.2 are in terms of *1992 dollars*. These projections will be enough if you plan to project *real* cash flows and discount them at a *real* discount rate. If, on the other hand, you prefer to do *nominal* projections, as we do here, *the constant-dollar projections should be converted to current-dollar projections by using the projected inflation rate*. Macroeconomists project that U.S. inflation will be moderate in 1993—roughly 3 percent. For future years it is not clear whether the picture is equally rosy on U.S. inflation prospects: The economies of many developed countries are likely to recover from the long-lasting downturn and with it inflation is more likely to increase. Thus, we use a rate of 4 percent inflation for the years 1994 and onward. By using these projected inflation rates, we can convert the constant-dollar Sales projections to current-dollar Sales projections. Exhibit 7.3 demonstrates how this is done.

Exhibit 7.3

J. M. SMUCKER CO.
Projected Nominal Sales, 1993–1997

	Year					
	1992	1993	1994	1995	1996	1997
Constant-dollar Sales	$483.47	$518.53	$556.17	$582.37	$593.01	$601.32
Annual inflation rate		3%	4%	4%	4%	4%
Cumulative adjustment factor	1.00	1.0300	1.0712	1.1140	1.1586	1.2050
Current-dollar (nominal) Sales	$483.47	$534.09	$595.77	$648.79	$687.07	$724.56
Projected nominal Sales growth		10.47%	11.55%	8.90%	5.90%	5.46%

Note: Sales in $ millions.

7.3 RATIO ANALYSIS

Given the projected Sales of Smucker in the next 5 years, we can turn to the estimation of Smucker's financial performance. Toward that end, we analyze the *past* performance of Smucker relative to past sales. The discussion in this section refers to the financial statements of Smucker in the years 1986 through 1992, which are given in Exhibit 7.4.

It is important to note that Smucker has gone through a rather rapid expansion during the period analyzed. Some of this expansion was achieved by acquiring firms with related business. A full ratio analysis should explicitly examine whether Smucker's ratios before and after the acquisitions remain the same. If the ratios prior to the acquisitions differ from the postacquisition ratios, only the postacquisition ratios should be used to predict the performance of Smucker in future years. Since ours is only an illustrative example, we don't perform a full analysis of this issue but, rather, consider it only when relevant.

Exhibit 7.4

J. M. SMUCKER CO.
Financial Statements, 1986–1992

				Year ending April 30*			
	1986	1987	1988	1989	1990	1991	1992
			Assets (in $ thousands)				
Cash and Cash Equivalents	$ 18,095	$ 25,227	$ 27,111	$ 36,652	$ 18,402	$ 24,513	$ 36,268
Trade Receivables, Net	21,096	26,192	24,799	29,640	35,591	42,328	41,565
Finished Goods	12,923	13,122	17,885	19,856	22,775	27,791	34,604
Raw Materials, Containers, and Supplies	25,683	29,824	29,115	27,324	38,720	38,740	43,173
Other Current Assets	2,125	2,096	2,937	4,657	4,459	7,664	5,961
Land and Land Improvements	4,569	4,802	5,190	7,095	9,475	10,473	11,985
Buildings and Fixtures	24,853	25,658	32,157	34,960	41,818	45,233	47,191
Machinery and Equipment	34,817	39,324	47,670	58,039	67,908	78,893	88,781
Construction in Progress	1,221	5,129	3,019	2,390	2,967	2,123	2,922
Accumulated Depreciation	(22,805)	(28,597)	(34,053)	(40,570)	(46,750)	(53,813)	(62,556)
Intangible Assets	8,533	8,145	11,594	14,011	23,459	22,460	20,961
Amounts Due from ESOP†	5,092	5,012	4,922	8,807	8,815	9,876	11,103
Other Assets	1,064	1,950	2,601	4,403	6,016	6,024	6,913
Total Assets	$137,266	$157,884	$174,947	$207,264	$233,655	$262,305	$288,871

*Smucker's fiscal year ends April 30. Thus, "1986" refers to figures for the fiscal year ending April 30, 1986, and so on.
†"Amounts Due from ESOP" refers to loans that Smucker makes to its employees to finance their purchase of equity as part of an employee stock ownership plan (ESOP). The ESOP purchases shares in Smucker, financing these purchases with loans it receives from the company itself (loans that subsequently appear on the Balance Sheet of Smucker as an asset). From the point of view of a financial analysis these loans are more properly subtracted from Smucker's Equity. In our projections (the pro-forma model at the end of this chapter), we will ignore these loans; we do this by subtracting the ESOP loans from the Assets and the Equity accounts.

Exhibit 7.4 continued

J. M. SMUCKER CO.
Financial Statements, 1986–1992

	Year ending April 30						
	1986	1987	1988	1989	1990	1991	1992
	Liabilities (in $ thousands)						
Accounts Payable	$ 19,145	$ 23,341	$ 23,517	$ 18,368	$ 21,992	$ 24,819	$ 28,363
Salaries, Wages, and Additional Compensation	4,418	4,808	5,239	5,922	6,741	7,405	7,934
Accrued Marketing and Merchandising	0	0	0	9,524	6,680	7,121	6,444
Income Taxes Payable	1,934	3,638	4,581	1,357	2,624	3,795	2,249
Dividends Payable	1,100	1,323	1,620	1,913	2,511	2,806	3,101
Current Portion of Long-Term Debt	1,666	2,503	667	0	0	0	0
Other Current Liabilities	0	0	0	4,772	5,194	4,083	5,469
Long-Term Debt	4,503	4,150	3,081	4,954	4,277	4,267	3,827
Deferred Federal Income Taxes	0	4,067	4,254	5,641	6,150	6,374	6,692
Other Liabilities	4,940	1,496	1,744	1,470	1,546	1,536	1,474
Class A Common	3,670	3,675	3,681	3,678	3,692	3,692	3,692
Class B Common	0	0	0	0	0	0	3,692
Additional Capital	3,385	4,408	5,746	7,733	10,158	10,544	7,034
Retained Income	93,340	105,946	122,797	143,383	165,436	186,919	209,586
Less: Deferred Compensation	(835)	(1,471)	(1,980)	(1,017)	(2,818)	(1,728)	(947)
Currency Translation Adjustment	0	0	0	(434)	(528)	672	261
Total Liabilities and Shareholder Equity	$137,266	$157,884	$174,947	$207,264	$233,655	$262,305	$288,871

Exhibit 7.4 *continuted*

J. M. SMUCKER CO.
Financial Statements, 1986–1992

	Year ending April 30						
	1986	1987	1988	1989	1990	1991	1992
Annual Income Statement (in $ thousands)							
Net Sales	$262,802	$288,263	$314,245	$366,855	$422,357	$454,976	$483,472
Cost of Goods Sold (COGS)	(175,735)	(192,169)	(206,144)	(240,227)	(281,450)	(295,681)	(314,133)
Gross Profit	87,067	96,094	108,101	126,628	140,907	159,295	169,339
Selling, General, and Administrative Expenses (SG&A)	(58,063)	(62,032)	(70,529)	(83,907)	(91,908)	(107,750)	(114,888)
Operating Income	29,004	34,062	37,572	42,721	48,999	51,545	54,451
Interest Income	1,729	993	1,360	2,048	1,969	1,280	1,510
Other Income, Net	574	273	85	234	62	544	568
Total	$ 31,307	$ 35,328	$ 39,017	$ 45,003	$ 51,030	$ 53,369	$ 56,529
Interest Expense	$ (1,238)	$ (598)	$ (425)	$ (421)	$ (1,086)	$ (788)	$ (446)
Income before Income Taxes	30,069	34,730	38,592	44,582	49,944	52,581	56,083
Federal Currently Payable	11,328	14,520	14,332	14,265	16,057	18,402	18,236
Federal Deferred Taxes	1,087	608	(918)	708	690	(692)	434
State and Local	1,794	1,923	2,308	2,054	3,020	3,127	3,295
Net Income	15,860	17,679	22,870	27,555	30,177	31,744	34,118
Dividend					(8,112)	(10,267)	(11,451)
Change in Retained Earnings	$ 15,860	$ 17,679	$ 22,870	$ 27,555	$ 22,065	$ 21,477	$ 22,667

Components of Smucker's Operating Costs

We begin the analysis of Smucker's past financial performance by estimating the fixed and variable components of its operating costs. The data for the analysis are provided in Exhibit 7.5.

Exhibit 7.5

J. M. SMUCKER CO.
Components of Operating Costs, 1987–1992 (in $ thousands)

	Year ending April 30					
	1987	1988	1989	1990	1991	1992
Net Sales	$288,263	$314,245	$366,855	$422,357	$454,976	$483,472
Cost of Goods Sold (COGS)	192,169	206,144	240,227	281,450	295,681	314,133
Selling, General, and Administrative Expenses (SG&A)	62,032	70,529	83,907	91,908	107,750	114,888
Depreciation	5,792	5,456	6,517	6,180	7,063	8,743
(COGS + SG&A − Depr.)/Sales	86.17%	86.31%	86.58%	86.94%	87.12%	86.93%

Smucker's financial statements lump depreciation expenses in with the Cost of Goods Sold (COGS) and Selling, General, and Administrative Expenses (SG&A). In a typical analysis of the relation between operating costs and Sales we attempt to consider costs net of noncash charges, primarily by adjusting for depreciation expenses since noncash charges represent accounting allocation decisions more than real expenses. In Smucker's example, however, we are not privy to information that will allow us to separate the Depreciation charges into their COGS and SG&A components. This means that we can make separate adjustments to the COGS and SG&A figures for Depreciation only if we make somewhat heroic assumptions. An alternative (which we choose here) is to project our pro formas for Smucker with one set of operating expenses (COGS + SG&A − Depreciation) as a ratio of Sales. Exhibit 7.5 shows that this ratio has remained roughly between 86 and 87 percent for the last few years; we will project future Smucker's performance assuming that it will be 86.5 percent.

Analysis of Smucker's Net Working Capital

First, we consider the components of working capital that are related to the operating activity of Smucker—Accounts Receivable, Accounts Payable, and Inventory. Exhibit 7.6 describes how these balance sheet items relate to Smucker's operations as proportions of Smucker's Sales.[4]

---

[4]We would have preferred to do an analysis of Smucker's Inventories and Accounts Payable as proportions of its COGS (as described in Chapter 6). However, because of the problems described previously in separating Depreciation from the COGS and the SG&A, in this case it makes more sense to work with percentages of Sales.

Exhibit 7.6

J. M. SMUCKER CO.
Analysis of Net Working Capital

	Year ending April 30					
	1987	1988	1989	1990	1991	1992
Accounts Receivable/Sales	9.09%	7.89%	8.08%	8.43%	9.30%	8.60%
Accounts Payable/Sales	9.77%	9.15%	9.22%	8.38%	8.65%	8.84%
Inventories (raw materials)/Sales	10.35%	9.27%	7.45%	9.17%	8.51%	8.93%
Inventories (finished)/Sales	4.55%	5.69%	5.41%	5.39%	6.11%	7.16%
Total inventories/Sales	14.90%	14.96%	12.86%	14.56%	14.62%	16.09%

Note: For purposes of this analysis the Accounts Payable/Sales ratio lumps together Accounts Payable; Salaries, Wages, and Additional Compensation; and Accrued Marketing and Merchandising Expenses from the Smucker balance sheet.

Although Smucker's Accounts Receivable and Accounts Payable ratios appear to be fairly stable, there has been a noticeable worsening in its Inventories as a percentage of Sales. This may be due to Smucker's expansion via the acquisition of related businesses that require larger inventory holdings; on the other hand, it may reflect a change in Smucker's inventory management policies.

For illustrative purposes we use the average ratios of the preceding years to project the following ratios for Smucker:

- Accounts Receivable/Sales = 8.6 percent.
- Accounts Payable/Sales = 9 percent.
- Inventories/Sales: 16% in the coming year, improving over a period of 2 years to 15 percent.

Estimating Smucker's Capital Expenditures

The projection of Smucker's capital expenditures, or equivalently, Smucker's future levels of Fixed Assets, is more problematic than the projection of the components of future working capital. This is because Fixed Assets are needed to provide the production capacity that is commensurate with the projected levels of Sales, and as already noted, Smucker has expanded its production capacity quite materially in the recent past. To see the recent expansion, we plot in Figure 7.3 the ratio of Sales to Fixed Assets where Fixed Assets are included in the computation of the ratio *at their original cost*. We use the *undepreciated* value of Smucker's Fixed Assets in the calculation of this ratio (rather than the depreciated value) because we consider it more reasonable that the productive capacity of Smucker's machinery and equipment doesn't materially deteriorate with their age. If we thought that the productive capacity deteriorated with age (so that a 5-year-old machine with 5

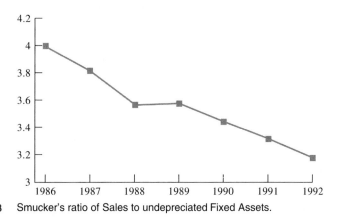

FIGURE 7.3   Smucker's ratio of Sales to undepreciated Fixed Assets.

more years of useful life could produce approximately half of what a similar new machine would produce), we would model the Fixed Assets of the company based on its *Net Fixed Assets* to Sales ratio.

The decline in the ratio of Sales to Fixed Assets, which reflects Smucker's recent expansion, means that as of 1992 *Smucker has a considerable excess production capacity.* Specifically, assuming that the ratio of Sales to Fixed Assets in 1986 of 4.01 leaves no excess production capacity, the fact that Sales are only 3.20 times Fixed Assets in 1992 suggests that Smucker can produce and sell 25 percent more than it did in 1992 using the same Fixed Assets. Therefore, Smucker can support the projected growth in Sales over the next 3 years without making any capital investments beyond the replacement of fixed assets that become obsolete. On the other hand, Smucker's stated intention of increasing market share and expanding internationally means that, despite the *existing* excess capacity, Smucker may continue to make capital investments. This is a question that is best explored with Smucker's management, for example, during shareholder meetings or presentations to analysts. Since in our case we are primarily interested in illustrating the techniques of pro-forma modeling, we make the simple assumption that Smucker will increase capacity at the rate of Sales growth.

In addition to expanding the capacity, Smucker has to replace existing equipment that reaches the end of its useful life. To estimate these needs, we calculate two ratios:

• The ratio of the cost of depreciable assets—the sum of Buildings, Fixtures, Machinery and Equipment—to the total of Fixed Assets
• The ratio of annual depreciation charges to the total cost of the depreciable assets.

Both of these ratios are given in Exhibit 7.7.

Exhibit 7.7

J. M. SMUCKER CO.
Analysis of Depreciation Charges, 1988–1992

	1988	1989	1990	1991	1992
Annual Depreciation Charges	$ 8,018	$ 9,679	$ 10,452	$ 10,772	$ 11,309
Depreciable Fixed Assets	82,846	95,389	112,693	126,249	138,894
Total Fixed Assets	$88,036	$102,484	$122,168	$136,722	$150,879
Depreciable versus Total Fixed Assets	94.1%	93.1%	92.2%	92.3%	92.1%
Annual Depreciation Rate	9.7%	10.1%	9.3%	8.5%	8.1%

Note: The Depreciation charges given in Smucker's financial statements reflect an adjustment for replaced assets (see discussion below). The Depreciation charges in this table have been calculated by adding each year's asset replacement back to the financial statement depreciation. This procedure assumes that all replaced assets were fully depreciated.

To project the capital expenditures that are needed to replace assets whose useful life reaches an end, note first that Land—Smucker's single nondepreciable asset—constitutes only a small and declining fraction of Fixed Assets. This reflects Smucker's recent capital investments, which modernized Smucker's equipment and increased its efficiency, as well as increased the cost of the machines in Smucker's factories. In light of Smucker's intention to keep modernizing its production facilities, we project that Land will remain the same fraction of total Fixed Assets—8 percent of them to be precise. This means that 92 percent of the projected level of fixed assets are assets that, at some point, will need replacement. As a second step we examine the rate at which the depreciable assets are depreciated. Again, by using 1992 figures, which reflect the more modernized pool of equipment, we see that the average life expectancy of Smucker's equipment is roughly 12 years (which is 100 percent divided by 8.1 percent). In order to use this average life to project the capital expenditures that are necessary to replace existing production capacity, we would need to trace back Smucker's acquisitions of fixed assets as far back as 12 years ago. Instead, we take a simpler modeling route:

• We start with Smucker's current annual level of asset retirement, $3.148 million in fiscal 1992 (this figure is taken from the notes to Smucker's 1992 annual report) and project it to grow at the rate of growth in Smucker's Sales.
• We assume that in the long run Fixed Assets (at cost) grow at the same rate as Sales.
• We assume that average depreciation is straight-line, both for tax and financial reporting purposes.[5]

With these assumptions we derive Exhibit 7.8, which gives Fixed Assets and the cost of new Property, Plant, and Equipment (PP&E).

---

[5]The Appendix to this chapter considers the case of straight-line depreciation for reporting purposes and accelerated depreciation for tax purposes and shows how to derive the resulting changes in Deferred Taxes.

Exhibit 7.8

J. M. SMUCKER CO.
Calculation of Fixed Asset Account

	1992	1993	1994	1995	1996	1997
			Year ending April 30			
Projected Sales growth		10.47%	11.55%	8.71%	5.90%	5.46%
Land	$ 11,985	$ 13,240	$ 14,769	$ 16,055	$ 17,003	$ 17,930
Property, Plant, and Equipment (PP&E)						
Depreciable Assets at cost	138,894	153,435	171,155	186,065	197,043	207,794
This year's Depreciation (8%)		(11,693)	(12,984)	(14,289)	(15,324)	(16,193)
Retirement of assets	3,148	3,478	3,879	4,217	4,466	4,710
Accumulated Depreciation	(62,556)	(70,772)	(79,876)	(89,948)	(100,806)	(112,290)
Net PP&E	$ 76,338	$ 82,664	$ 91,279	$ 96,117	$ 96,237	$ 95,504
			Calculation of New PP&E Purchased			
Increase in depreciable assets		$ 14,541	$ 17,720	$ 14,909	$ 10,979	$ 10,751
Replacement of retired assets		3,478	3,879	4,217	4,466	4,710
New PP&E purchased		$ 18,019	$ 21,599	$ 19,127	$ 15,445	$ 15,460

Note: Numbers may not add up precisely because of rounding errors.

7.4   PRO-FORMA PROJECTIONS

In the previous section we analyzed the financial statements of Smucker and examined various ratios and relations in order to determine the dependencies among the different items in Smucker's income statements and balance sheets. In this section we use the results of this analysis to build pro-forma statements that reflect our understanding of Smucker's business.

To complete the specification of the relation among the items in Smucker's financial statements, we have to consider Smucker's financing. This is necessary in order to close the pro-forma model: We use the financial policies to model the *uses* of the funds generated by Smucker's operation and to assure internal consistency of the model and its underlying assumptions. In general, the determination of the optimal financial policies of the firm is a difficult theoretical problem: Finance theory on this question is both complex and somewhat ambiguous. We don't get much practical help in determining the optimal financial decisions for a firm, and so we have little to rely on in projecting the financial policies that the firm's management will choose. (E.g., What is the optimal leverage for the firm? How much dividend should the managers pay? What should the managers do with the firm's excess cash?)[6]

---

[6]Some of these issues are covered in Chapter 8. Although financial theory doesn't help much in determining the optimal financing mix of the firm, it does help us to determine how the financing mix affects the discount rates. This is the primary topic of Chapter 8.

In Smucker's case, however, the projection of financial policies is a relatively simple step. This is because Smucker's management has demonstrated a clear preference for avoiding debt financing. For example, at the end of fiscal year 1992 less than 1 percent of Smucker's capital structure is in the form of long-term debt. Moreover, the only debt Smucker has is *subsidized* debt—Industrial Development Revenue Bonds that bear below-market interest rates.[7] Thus, it is reasonable to project that Smucker's management will not accrue additional debt in the future and will use its excess cash to pay back its loans. We use the maturity schedule of the existing debt, provided in the notes to Smucker's 1992 report and reproduced in the following table, to project the change in Smucker's outstanding long-term debt obligations.

J. M. SMUCKER CO.
Projection of Debt Balances

	Year ending April 30				
	1993	1994	1995	1996	1997
Maturing debt ($K)	440	440	430	430	27
Remaining balance of debt ($K)	3,387	2,947	2,517	2,087	2,060

As for dividend policy, Smucker's management has a fairly stable dividend policy of paying out about one-third of its annual profits as dividends. Thus, we project 1/3 to be the dividend payout ratio of Smucker in the future as well.

Both the long-term debt and the dividend policies of Smucker's management leave Smucker with excess cash. The practice of Smucker's management to date was to invest this excess cash in marketable securities. This means that Cash and Cash Equivalents are a natural choice to be a *plug* for a pro-forma model of Smucker. Recall that the choice of a plug is not merely a question of modeling, but it also reflects the financial policies of the firm. In this case the policies of Smucker's management lend themselves to an easy and natural plug.

The fact that cash and marketable securities are the plug for Smucker's projected financial policies and its pro-forma model means that we have to consider the effect that this financial policy will have on the financial statements and the value of Smucker. Again, given Smucker's financial policies, this is a rather simple exercise. Since Smucker invests in marketable securities about which its management has no special knowledge, the net present value (NPV) of these investments, by definition, is zero. Thus, the value of these investments is precisely the amount invested—the excess cash that we project for Smucker. In practical terms this means

---

[7]This subsidized financing is provided by local authorities that are interested in attracting corporations to their localities. In return for the low-interest financing the corporations provide employment to local residents and increased tax revenues.

that the value we estimate for Smucker doesn't depend on the rate of return that we project for Smucker's investment in cash and marketable securities. This is because the same rate that we project for the *generation* of interest income is the rate at which we *discount* this interest income to find its value. Since the value of Smucker doesn't depend on the expected return on its excess cash, we arbitrarily select 5 percent as the rate of return on these investments. This rate will allow us to close the pro-forma model of Smucker according to accepted accounting principles. When we get to the stage where it is necessary to value Smucker, we will value *separately* the operating side of Smucker (by discounting the FCFs at the risk-adjusted discount rate) and then *add* the market value of Smucker's short-term investments.

Building the Pro-Forma Model

The basis of our pro-forma model for Smucker is a set of ratios and values that serve as the parameters for the model (Exhibit 7.9). When applied in the method outlined in Chapter 4, these parameters give the Smucker pro-forma financial statements.

The projected income statements are given in Exhibit 7.10. The formulas underlying the projected income statements are

```
Sales(t) = Sales(t − 1) * (1 + growth rate(t))

COGS(t) = Sales(t) * COGS_Sales(t)

SG&A = Sales(t) * SG&A_Sales(t)

Interest_Income(t) = Cash(t − 1) * return_on_financial_investments(t)

Interest_Expense(t) = Long_Term_Debt(t) * interest_rate(t)

Income_Taxes(t) = Income_Before_Taxes(t) * effective_tax_rate(t)

Dividend(t) = Net_Income(t) * payout_ratio(t)
```

A few points are worth mentioning regarding the pro-forma Income Statements:

• The ratios are indexed by year. This is because we have projected different degrees of operating efficiency for different years. For example, we have projected ratios of Inventory to Sales as 16 percent in 1993, 15.5 percent in 1994, and 15 percent thereafter.

• The Interest Income and Interest Expense items tie balance sheet items with the income statement. We have done this by calculating the annual flows based on *last year's balances* of Cash and of Long-Term Debt outstanding. Implicitly, we assume that all financial transactions take place at year-end. An alternative approach is to use the *average* amount of debt outstanding or of cash balances to calculate interest expenses or income. In the case of interest income this would be done as

```
Interest_Income(t)
    = {[Cash(t − 1) + Cash(t)]/2} * return_on_financial_investments(t)
```

Exhibit 7.9

J. M. SMUCKER CO.
Financial Statement Model Parameters

				Year ending April 30			
	1992	1993	1994	1995	1996	1997	1998 +
Sales growth		10.47%	11.55%	8.71%	5.90%	5.46%	5.46%
(COGS + SG&A − Depreciation) to Sales		86.50%	86.50%	86.50%	86.50%	86.50%	86.50%
Accounts Receivable to Sales		8.60%	8.33%	8.33%	8.33%	8.33%	8.33%
Accounts Payable to Sales		9.00%	9.00%	9.00%	9.00%	9.00%	9.00%
Inventory to Sales		16.00%	15.50%	15.00%	15.00%	15.00%	15.00%
Fixed Asset growth, before Asset Retirement		10.47%	11.55%	8.71%	5.90%	5.46%	5.46%
Return on financial investments		5.00%	5.00%	5.00%	5.00%	5.00%	5.00%
Interest on Debt		8.00%	8.00%	8.00%	8.00%	8.00%	8.00%
Dividend payout		33.00%	33.00%	33.00%	33.00%	33.00%	33.00%
Income Tax Payable to Income Taxes		25.00%	25.00%	25.00%	25.00%	25.00%	25.00%
Dividends Payable to Dividends		25.00%	25.00%	25.00%	25.00%	25.00%	25.00%
Effective tax rate		40.00%	42.00%	42.00%	42.00%	42.00%	42.00%
Depreciable Fixed Assets as a percent of Total Fixed Assets		92.00%	92.00%	92.00%	92.00%	92.00%	92.00%
Depreciation rate		8.00%	8.00%	8.00%	8.00%	8.00%	8.00%
Asset retirement ($ thousands)	3,148	3,478	3,879	4,217	4,466	4,710	5.56%
Debt retirement ($ thousands)		440	440	430	430	27	20.00%

Note: "Income Tax Payable to Income Taxes" and "Dividends Payable to Dividends" represent the percentage of income tax and dividends (respectively) that are not paid by the end of the fiscal year, and thus appear on the Smucker's balance sheet as liabilities.

Exhibit 7.10

J. M. SMUCKER CO.

Financial Statement Model—Pro-Forma Income Statements

			Year ending April 30			
	1992	1993	1994	1995	1996	1997
Sales	$483,472	$534,089	$595,769	$647,666	$685,882	$723,304
COGS + SG&A (excluding Depreciation)		(461,987)	(515,340)	(560,231)	(593,288)	(625,658)
Gross Profit		72,102	80,429	87,435	92,594	97,646
Depreciation Expense		(11,693)	(12,984)	(14,289)	(15,324)	(16,193)
Operating Income		60,409	67,445	73,146	77,270	81,453
Interest Income		1,813	2,516	3,158	4,134	5,403
Interest Expense		(306)	(271)	(236)	(201)	(167)
Income before Taxes		61,916	69,691	76,069	81,203	86,688
Income Taxes		(24,766)	(29,270)	(31,949)	(34,105)	(36,409)
Net Income		37,150	40,421	44,120	47,098	50,279
Dividend		(12,259)	(13,339)	(14,560)	(15,542)	(16,592)
Increase in Retained Earnings		$ 24,890	$ 27,082	$ 29,560	$ 31,555	$ 33,687
Earnings per Share		1.26	1.37	1.50	1.60	1.70

- The projected earnings allow us to calculate Smucker's projected earnings per share (EPS) by dividing the projected profit by the number of shares outstanding—29.5 million at the end of fiscal year 1992. For example, this gives a projected 1993 EPS of $1.26. This is obviously a too-simplistic calculation: It ignores the million options that were granted to top management and their potential dilution of EPS. Another way of calculating EPS is on a fully diluted basis, which assumes that options meeting certain criteria will be exercised for sure. While neither EPS calculation is perfect, EPS often serves as a basis for valuation—projected EPS are multiplied by average earnings multiples in the industry to arrive at a ''fair value'' for the stock. We defer a more complete discussion of this point to Chapter 10.
- We do not project the income statements beyond fiscal 1997. This is because our analysis suggests that beyond this year Smucker will enter the phase of steady-state growth. Technically, this is modeled as a constant growth in all income statement and balance sheet items of 5.56 percent per year—the compound effect of long-run real sales growth (driven by the projected population growth) and the long-run projected annual change in the purchasing power of money (inflation). The value of Smucker's FCFs beyond fiscal 1997 is not ignored: It is included in Smucker's terminal value, which is discussed subsequently.

Simplifying the April 1992 Balance Sheet as a Basis for Projections

The projected income statement combined with Smucker's initial financial position—the balance sheet of the fiscal year ending April 1992—allow us to project future balance sheets. However, before starting, we want to make some simplifications of the 1992 balance sheets that make them more appropriate as a basis for our model. The main simplification has to do with the ESOP loans (see footnotes to Exhibit 7.4); we subtract these loans from the Assets and make a corresponding adjustment to Smucker's Equity accounts.

These and other adjustments are given in Exhibit 7.11.

Projecting the Pro-Forma Assets

The Assets side of the balance sheet (as shown in Exhibit 7.12) reflects the following relations:

- Accounts Receivable, Inventories, Land, and PP&E are related to projected Sales via the ratios projected for each year.
- Accumulated Depreciation, Land, and PP&E are taken from Exhibit 7.8.
- Other current and noncurrent assets, which are unrelated to the level of production and sales, are kept at their value on the last day of fiscal year 1992.

Exhibit 7.11

J. M. SMUCKER CO.
Adjustments to April 1992 Balance Sheet
To create basis for pro-forma model

	Fiscal year ending April 1992	Initial balances for pro forma	New name
		Assets	
Cash and Cash Equivalents	$ 36,268	$ 36,268	Cash and Short-Term Investments
Trade Receivables, Net	41,565	41,565	Accounts Receivable
Finished Goods	34,604	77,777	Inventories—the sum of Finished Goods
Raw Materials, Containers, and Supplies	43,173		and Raw Materials, and so on
Other Current Assets	5,961	5,961	
Land and Land Improvements	11,985	11,985	Land
Buildings and Fixtures	47,191	138,894	Depreciable Assets at Cost
Machinery and Equipment	88,781		
Construction in Progress	2,922		
Accumulated Depreciation	(62,556)	(62,556)	Accumulated Depreciation
Intangible Assets	20,961	27,874	Other noncurrent assets—the sum of
			Intangible Assets and Other Assets
Other Assets	6,913		
Amounts due from ESOP	11,103		Deducted here and from Equity
Total Assets	$288,871	$277,768	
		Liabilities	
Accounts Payable	$ 28,363	$ 42,741	Accounts Payable—the sum of A/P,
			Salaries, and Accrued Marketing
Salaries, Wages, and Additional Compensations	7,934		
Accrued Marketing and Merchandising	6,444		
Income Taxes	2,249	2,249	Income Taxes Payable
Dividends Payable	3,101	3,101	Dividends Payable
Other Current Liabilities	5,469	5,469	Other Current Liabilities
Long-Term Debt	3,827	3,827	Long-Term Debt
Deferred Federal Income Taxes	6,692	6,692	Deferred Income Taxes
Other Liabilities	1,474	1,474	Other Liabilities
Class A Common	3,692	7,384	Common Stock—the sum of Class A and
			Class B
Class B Common	3,692		
Additional Capital	7,034	7,034	Additional Capital
Retained Income	209,586	209,586	Retained Income
Less: Deferred Compensation	(947)	(11,789)	Miscellaneous Adjustments—the sum of
Currency Translation Adjustment	261		Deferred Compensation and Currency
			Translation, minus ESOP Loans
Total Liabilities and Shareholder Equity	$288,871	$277,768	

Exhibit 7.12

J. M. SMUCKER CO.
Financial Statement Model—Pro-Forma Balance Sheets

				Year ending April 30		
	1992	1993	1994	1995	1996	1997
Assets						
Cash and Short-Term Investments	$ 36,268	$ 50,327	$ 63,166	$ 82,687	$108,052	$136,992
Accounts Receivable	41,565	45,932	49,647	53,972	57,157	60,275
Inventories	77,777	85,454	92,344	97,150	102,882	108,496
Other Current Assets	5,961	5,961	5,961	5,961	5,961	5,961
Land	11,985	13,240	14,769	16,055	17,003	17,930
Property, Plant, and Equipment (PP&E)						
Depreciable Assets at cost	138,894	153,435	171,155	186,065	197,043	207,794
Accumulated Depreciation	(62,556)	(70,772)	(79,876)	(89,948)	(100,806)	(112,290)
Net PP&E	76,338	82,664	91,279	96,117	96,237	95,504
Other Noncurrent Assets	27,874	27,874	27,874	27,874	27,874	27,874
Total Assets	$277,768	$311,452	$345,040	$379,816	$415,166	$453,032
Liabilities and Equity						
Accounts Payable	$ 42,741	$ 48,068	$ 53,619	$ 58,290	$ 61,729	$ 65,097
Income Taxes Payable	2,249	6,192	7,318	7,987	8,526	9,102
Dividends Payable	3,101	3,065	3,335	3,640	3,886	4,148
Other Current Liabilities	5,469	5,469	5,469	5,469	5,469	5,469
Long-Term Debt	3,827	3,387	2,947	2,517	2,087	2,060
Deferred Income Taxes	6,692	6,692	6,692	6,692	6,692	6,692
Other Long-Term Liabilities	1,474	1,474	1,474	1,474	1,474	1,474
Common Stock	7,384	7,384	7,384	7,384	7,384	7,384
Additional Capital	7,034	7,034	7,034	7,034	7,034	7,034
Retained Income	209,586	234,476	261,558	291,118	322,674	356,361
Miscellaneous Adjustments	(11,789)	(11,789)	(11,789)	(11,789)	(11,789)	(11,789)
Total Liabilities and Equity	$277,768	$311,452	$345,040	$379,816	$415,166	$453,032

• Cash and Short-Term Investments is our plug: It is the residual balance sheet account that is necessary to make the pro-forma Assets equal to the pro-forma Liabilities.[8]

Projecting Pro-Forma Liabilities

In creating the Liabilities side of the balance sheet:

• We assume that the year-end balance of taxes payable and of dividends payable is 25 percent of the annual tax expense and the annual dividend payment, respectively, representing one quarter's payments.

• We hold Other Current Liabilities, Long-Term Liabilities, and Miscellaneous Adjustments constant since they are not directly related to the level of activity of Smucker. Deferred Income Taxes are also held constant; calculating these requires consideration of accelerated depreciation. We consider this issue in the Appendix to the chapter; the effect of performing these calculations on the Smucker valuation is not great.

• We calculate the year-end balance of Accounts Payable as

```
Accounts_Payable(t) = COGS(t) * Accounts_Payable_to_COGS(t)
```

• We reduce the amount outstanding of Long-Term Debt according to the maturity schedule provided in the notes to Smucker's 1992 financial statements (see details on page 214).

• We increase Retained Earnings by Net Income less distributed Dividends as projected in the Income Statement.

Projecting Pro-Forma Cash Flows

We begin the cash-flow projections by projecting a cash-flow statement according to accepted accounting principles (GAAP). That is, we calculate the cash flows from *the point of view of the existing shareholders of Smucker* [Exhibit 7.13(a)]. We proceed to convert these accounting cash flows to cash flows that conform with valuation principles: FCF and their uses [Exhibit 7.13(b)].

In the projection of the FCF we also include a check to show that our computations are internally consistent: We check that the cash distributed to the security holders and the increase in the cash holdings of Smucker add up to the total cash available for distribution to the security holders. We want to make sure in every

---

[8]As related below, we double-check this calculation by ascertaining that the Cash and Short-Term Investments account is the same as the increase in cash calculated from the FCF accounts, after taking into account cash flows paid to either the bondholders (interest and principal) or to the shareholders (dividends and shares repurchased). This double checking is one way of scrutinizing the internal consistency of our model.

Exhibit 7.13

J. M. SMUCKER CO.
Financial Statement Model
Pro-forma cash-flow statements
(a) GAAP cash flows

	Year ending April 30				
	1993	1994	1995	1996	1997
Operating Activities					
Net Income	$ 37,150	$ 40,421	$ 44,120	$ 47,098	$ 50,279
Depreciation	11,693	12,984	14,289	15,324	16,193
Increase in Accounts Receivable	(4,367)	(3,716)	(4,325)	(3,185)	(3,118)
Increase in Inventories	(7,677)	(6,890)	(4,806)	(5,732)	(5,613)
Increase in Accounts Payable	5,327	5,551	4,671	3,439	3,368
Increase in Taxes Payable	3,943	1,126	670	539	576
Cash Flow from Operations (CFO)	$ 46,069	$ 49,476	$ 54,619	$ 57,483	$ 61,685
Investing Activities					
Land	$ (1,255)	$ (1,529)	$ (1,287)	$ (947)	$ (928)
Property, Plant, and Equipment (PP&E)	(18,019)	(21,599)	(19,127)	(15,445)	(15,460)
Net Cash from Investing Activity	$(19,274)	$(23,128)	$(20,413)	$(16,392)	$(16,388)
Financing Activities					
Increase in Debt	$ (440)	$ (440)	$ (430)	$ (430)	$ (27)
Dividends Paid	(12,296)	(13,069)	(14,254)	(15,297)	(16,330)
Net Cash from Financing Activity	(12,736)	(13,509)	(14,684)	(15,727)	(16,357)
Net Increase in Cash	14,059	12,839	19,521	25,365	28,940
Cash at Beginning of Year	36,268	50,327	63,166	82,687	108,052
Cash at End of Year	$ 50,327	$ 63,166	$ 82,687	$108,052	$136,992

(b) Valuation cash flows
Free Cash Flow

	1993	1994	1995	1996	1997
CFO	$ 46,069	$ 49,476	$ 54,619	$ 57,483	$ 61,685
Net Cash from Investing Activity	(19,274)	(23,128)	(20,413)	(16,392)	(16,388)
Add back after-tax Interest Expense	184	157	137	117	97
Subtract after-tax Interest Income	(1,088)	(1,459)	(1,832)	(2,398)	(3,134)
Free Cash Flow	$ 25,890	$ 25,045	$ 32,510	$ 38,810	$ 42,260
Nonoperating Cash Inflow					
After-tax Interest Income	$ 1,088	$ 1,459	$ 1,832	$ 2,398	$ 3,134
Cash available to security holders	$ 26,979	$ 26,505	$ 34,342	$ 41,208	$ 45,394
Distribution of Cash Available to Security Holders					
Payment to bondholders	$ (624)	$ (597)	$ (567)	$ (547)	$ (124)
Payment to shareholders	(12,296)	(13,069)	(14,254)	(15,297)	(16,330)
Increase in Cash Balances	$ 14,059	$ 12,839	$ 19,521	$ 25,365	$ 28,940

possible way that our model is consistent because typical models are fairly complicated, often much more than the Smucker's model we built here.[9] In such models there are many formulas that depict economic relations and it is very easy to err in relating various variables. When building your model, you should, preferably, put in as many checks and flags as possible. Invariably you will find that you have put in one too few.

Now that we have projected the financial performance of Smucker for the next 5 years we are able to value Smucker. Toward that end, we need two more inputs—the terminal value of Smucker and the risk-adjusted discount rate (RADR) with which we convert the projected cash flows to values. In the following section we will see that these two inputs are not independent of each other.

7.5 TERMINAL VALUE PROJECTION

The terminal value is a value that we assign to Smucker at the end of the period for which we make specific financial projections. The idea is that up to the projection horizon we can make specific statements about Smucker's prospects, which are based on our analysis of Smucker's environment and operations. These statements are reflected in the projected Sales and projected ratios. Beyond a certain point, however, our analysis and information don't allow us to make specific statements about Smucker. At this point we stop making detailed projections, which formally means that we prepare no further pro-forma statements. But Smucker doesn't cease operations at this point and Smucker's operations beyond the projection period also have value. Thus, we have to assign a value to the cash flows that Smucker can generate beyond the period for which we prepared specific projections—the **terminal value.** Some of the most common methods for estimating terminal values are:

• *Book value.* We can estimate Smucker's terminal value by using the projected (pro-forma) book value of its financial assets. The objection to this method is that it equates accounting numbers with market values, something that we are usually reluctant to do in finance.
• *Multiples.* The value of Smucker's equity at the end of the projection period may be computed by *multiplying the last projected earnings by an "appropriate" price/earnings (P/E) ratio.* Alternative methods of valuation by multiples are less common: For instance, *multiplying the projected book value of Smucker's equity in the horizon year by a projected market/book ratio* to get the terminal value of Equity.
• *Gordon formula.* The value of the cash flows that Smucker can generate

---

[9]This is especially true of models generated internally, as part of strategic planning, business negotiations, and so on. This is because the firm's insiders are privy to much more information than the outside analysts and can build into their models much more detailed relations about items such as unit sales, unit price, raw material consumption, and wage structure.

beyond the last fiscal year for which we build pro-forma statements is computed as *the present value of a constant-growth flow at the risk-adjusted discount rate.*

To apply either of the last two methods, you must estimate an appropriate price: In the multiples method we look for the way that the market relates values to earnings, and in the method based on the Gordon formula we look for the price at which the market values cash flows. The ways that the methods are applied and the ways that these appropriate prices are estimated—how to compute the appropriate earnings multiples and how to estimate the RADR—are discussed in more detail in the following chapters. Since we prefer the use of cash flows and discount rates for valuation purposes, we illustrate at this point only the last method in which the terminal value of Smucker is calculated by using the Gordon formula.

Recall from Chapter 1 that the Gordon formula gives the value of a free cash flow that grows perpetually at a constant rate, g, under a risk-adjusted discount rate, r, as

$$\text{Value} = \frac{\text{FCF}_1}{r - g}$$

where FCF_1 is the cash flow to be received one period hence.[10] In Smucker's case so far we have only estimated its long-run growth prospects as the compound effect of long-run population growth and long-run inflation, 5.46 percent. We need estimates of FCF_1 and of r to apply the Gordon formula.

The last estimate of the cash-flow streams generated by Smucker's operations are the FCF projected for fiscal year 1997, $42.260 million. From 1998 onward, Smucker's FCFs are projected to grow at the steady-state rate of 5.46 percent per year. Thus, we project FCF_1 as

$$\text{FCF}_1 = 42.260 \cdot (1 + 5.46\%) = \$44.567 \text{ million}$$

We will estimate Smucker's RADR by using the Capital Asset Pricing Model (CAPM). Recall from Chapter 1 that in the CAPM, the RADR is given by the Security Market Line (SML):

$$\text{RADR} = r_f + \beta[E(r_m) - r_f]$$

To estimate the appropriate discount rate for Smucker's operating FCF, we should measure the after-tax risk-free rate, Smucker's β, and the expected return

---

[10]A fine but important point: If the projected cash flow is the expected dividend payout, the Gordon model values the *firm's equity*. If, as here, the projected cash flow is the firm's FCF 1 year hence, and if r is interpreted as the firm's weighted average cost of capital (WACC), then the Gordon model values the *firm as a whole*. Since this is the interpretation of FCF_1 that we will be using here, we will first derive the value of the firm as a whole, and then subsequently struggle with the problem of splitting this value among the firm's claimholders—in Smucker's case its bondholders, shareholders, and warrant holders.

on the market portfolio $E(r_M)$. We assume that the risk-free discount rate is 3%. We further assume that Smucker's beta (β) is 0.9, and that $E(r_M) = 12\%$. This means that the appropriate RADR for Smucker is 11.1 percent.

By using the Gordon formula, we derive the terminal value of the FCFs in our model of Smucker as the value of the FCFs that we expect Smucker to generate beyond the period for which we prepared pro-forma statements:[11]

$$\text{Terminal value of Smucker's FCFs} = \frac{44.567}{11.1\% - 5.46\%}$$

$$= \frac{44.567}{0.0564} = \$790.202 \text{ million}$$

7.6 ILLUSTRATIVE VALUATION

Once we estimate the FCF that Smucker will generate in the next 5 years, the value of the FCF that will be generated beyond that point, and the appropriate discount rate, we can convert all these numbers into a value for Smucker as a whole. This is done by discounting the projected FCF and terminal values, detailed in Exhibit 7.14, at the RADR.

[11]Smucker's terminal value in Exhibit 7.14 differs slightly from the 790.202 calculated here. The difference is attributable to rounding errors that don't appear in the spreadsheet.

Exhibit 7.14

J. M. SMUCKER CO.
Projected FCF and Terminal Value

Beta	0.9				
r_f	3%				
$E(r_M)$	12%				
Risk-Adjusted Discount Rate (RADR) for Free Cash Flow (FCF)	11.10%				
FCF Growth, after year 5	5.46%				
Terminal FCF	$ 42,260				
Terminal Value, Gordon Model	$789,616				

Valuation Based on FCF Discounting and Terminal Value

	1993	1994	1995	1996	1997
FCF	$ 25,890	$25,045	$32,510	$38,810	$ 42,260
Terminal Value					789,616
Total	$ 25,890	$25,045	$32,510	$38,810	$831,876
Value (year-end discounting)	584,236				
Value (midyear discounting)	615,808				
Add initial Cash and Marketable Securities	36,268				
Total Firm Value	$652,076				

Exhibit 7.14 illustrates two steps of discounting FCFs:

• Year-end discounting, which assumes that all cash flows occur at the end of the year, gives a value of $584.236 million for Smucker.
• Midyear discounting assumes that cash flows arrive, on average, at midyear. Since the operating cash flows that we project arrive at Smucker as a flow, we should discount these flows by using midyear discounting.[12] One way to do this is to discount the first year cash flows for half a year, the second year cash flows for a year and a half, and so on. A technically simpler way to do the same thing is to discount for full years and multiply the resulting value by $(1 + r)^{0.5}$. This yields a value of $615.808 million.

The value of $615.808 million is the value of Smucker's *operations.* To this value we should add the value of Smucker's *nonoperating assets,* that is, the value of Smucker's excess Cash and Marketable Securities. As of the financial year ending April 30, 1992, Smucker held $36.268 million in Cash and Marketable Securities. Adding together the value of Smucker's operations and nonoperating assets, we find that the total value of Smucker is $652.076 million. This value should be divided among the various holders of Smucker's securities.

The Importance of the Terminal Value

One aspect of Smucker's valuation is worth noting since it recurs in many valuations: Much of Smucker's value is derived from the terminal value that we estimate for the end of the projection period (in our case, the end of fiscal year 1997). The economic intuition for this phenomenon is simple: Smucker, the corporation—unlike its workers, managers, and shareholders—has indefinite life; thus, the value of the first 5 years (for which we make specific forecasts of financial performance) is only a small fraction of the value of the cash flows that it can generate. This may seem a troublesome aspect of valuation since most of the value is an amount about which we know the least. But this is not quite as troublesome as it seems because it is also the period for which we discount the most for uncertainty. When estimating the discount rate with which we calculate present values, we add a risk premium to the risk-free rate of interest. This risk premium is compounded as we compound the discount rate in the present value calculation. Thus, effectively, the first year's cash flows get one "dose" of risk premium, the second year's cash flows get two doses, and so on. This means that although the distant cash flows are indeed less certain than the immediate cash flows, they are discounted appropriately for their added uncertainty.

---

[12]More accurately, we should discount these cash flows from the point in time that corresponds (in present value terms) to a continuous discounting of a flow that is evenly spread throughout the year. Midyear discounting is only an approximation, although a good one in most cases.

Valuing Smucker's Securities

The calculation we performed earlier, which gave the value of all of Smucker's securities as $652.076 million, is only the first step. We must now value each of the securities of Smucker separately.

Valuing Smucker's Debt   The first security that we value based on the value of the firm as a whole is the debt of the firm. Typically, the debt is valued by discounting the promised cash flows to the debt holders—interest and principal repayment—at a discount rate that is appropriate for the debt of a similar risk. In Chapter 11 we discuss ways by which to estimate the appropriate discount rate to use in discounting the debt holders' cash flows. At this point we make some general comments about the value of Smucker's debt:

1 Smucker's debt is as close to being default-free as any corporate debt can be. This is because Smucker hardly has any debt in its capital structure—less than 1 percent to be exact. This means that if Smucker's debt were publicly traded, it would probably be rated at the highest risk rating for corporate bonds—AAA. It also means that the appropriate discount rate with which Smucker's debt should be valued is very close to the rate on an equal-maturity government bond.

2 Some of Smucker's debt cannot be valued by discounting its promised cash flows (interest and principal) at an appropriately chosen discount rate: Some of Smucker's debt is floating-rate debt—debt on which the interest is reset periodically according to market conditions. In Smucker's case the floating debt bears interest at the rate of 85 percent of prime, where we know that the prime rate fluctuates over time. Thus, we should value this part of the debt by using alternative methods.

3 Some of Smucker's debt was issued a long time ago at interest rates that were much higher than the rates prevailing at the time this book was written. As a result, some of Smucker's debt that bears interest at the rate of 8 percent has an economic value that exceeds its book value.

Overall, these points suggest that the valuation of Smucker's debt involves more than the discounting of the debt's expected payments. In Smucker's case, however, this hardly makes a difference: Since Smucker's debt is less than 1 percent of its total value, we can take its value to be 100 percent of par, 50 percent of par, or 150 percent of par with little effect on the value that we assign to Smucker's stock. We thus simplify things by taking the economic value of Smucker's debt as its book value, $3.8 million. This leaves $648.276 million to be divided among the holders of Smucker's stock and Smucker's options.

Valuing Smucker's Options and Stock   Smucker has about 1 million warrants outstanding with exercise prices ranging from $11 to $22 per share. Ways to value warrants granted by the corporation (to outside investors or to managers) are discussed in Chapter 12. It is difficult to discuss the assignment of value to these warrants at this stage, so we simply estimate this value by the difference between the average exercise price of $16 and the value of Smucker's stock. In notation, denote the value of a Smucker stock by S and the value of an "average" Smucker warrant by W. Then the total value of Smucker's 29.5 million shares and 1 million warrants is

$$\$648{,}276{,}000 = 29{,}500{,}000 \cdot S + 1{,}000{,}000 \cdot W$$

Since we estimate the value of a warrant W by the difference between the stock price S and the average warrant exercise price of $16, we have

$$W = S - 16$$

Substituting for W into the previous equation, we get

$$\$648{,}276{,}000 = 29{,}500{,}000 \cdot S + (S - 16) \cdot 1{,}000{,}000$$

Solving for the value of the Smucker's stock, we obtain a value of $21.78 for each of Smucker's stock and a value of $5.78 for each of Smucker's warrants. This value is lower than Smucker's market value in April 1992 of $25 per share.[13]

7.7 SENSITIVITY ANALYSIS

No valuation is complete without some sensitivity analysis. In this section we present two such analyses; the model offers room for a wide variety of sensitivity checks.

---

[13]We can improve our estimate of the warrant value somewhat by using the Black-Scholes pricing model (discussed in Chapter 12). By using this model, you will see that the warrant price for a deep-in-the-money warrant is very close to $S - Xe^{-rT}$, where T is the average maturity of the warrants (which, unfortunately, we don't know!). Assuming that $T = 2$ (i.e., the warrants mature in 2 years) and substituting this into our equation, we get $7.25 for the value of a warrant and $21.73 for the value of a share of Smucker.

FIGURE 7.4   Smucker's stock price sensitivity to growth parameters as predicted by the model.

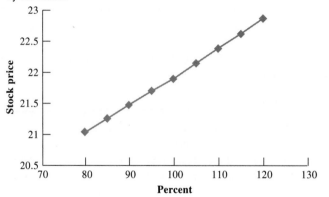

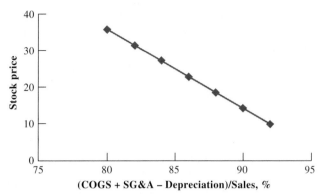

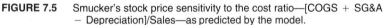

FIGURE 7.5   Smucker's stock price sensitivity to the cost ratio—[COGS + SG&A − Depreciation]/Sales—as predicted by the model.

Sensitivity to Sales Growth

One of the most obvious parameters for a sensitivity analysis is the sales growth of the company. Figure 7.4 shows what happens to Smucker's stock value estimated by the model when we vary the nominal sales growth. The numbers on the x-axis indicate percentages of the original nominal sales growth; that is, 90 percent indicates that all growth estimates have been scaled down by 10 percent.

Sensitivity to Cost Parameters

The second sensitivity analysis that we illustrate in Figure 7.5 involves a cost parameter. We vary the ratio of (COGS + SG&A − Depreciation)/Sales (recall that in our original analysis this ratio was kept at 86.5 percent). Not surprisingly, considering the fact that Smucker has a relatively low margin, this ratio has a much greater impact on cash flows (and hence the stock value) than the sales growth. There are big payoffs to greater operating efficiencies in Smucker!

SUMMARY

Valuing a company involves two major steps:

1 Build a pro-forma model that reflects the expected future performance of the company. This model incorporates a sales projection model, a ratio model of the firm, and a model of the firm's financing and dividend behavior.

2 Discount the FCFs predicted by the model at the company's WACC to arrive at the value of the company. This value is then split up among the holders of the firm's securities.

In this chapter we have illustrated this procedure for the J. M. Smucker Company. Our initial results seem to indicate that Smucker stock is somewhat overvalued. Sensitivity analysis on some of the major parameters indicates that this conclusion must be tempered: Smucker's current market value is approximately equal to that which we have calculated, and the value estimate is sensitive to some of the model's parameters.

Having estimated the value of the securities of Smucker, we should now make a recommendation: Buy, sell, or hold any of Smucker's securities if you are an analyst following the food industry; acquire, merge, or divest if you are considering Smucker as a candidate for a business combination; or lend or reject the loan request if you are Smucker's banker.

Finally, here are some caveats (doubtless there are more) about our valuation:

• Our estimate of Smucker's value is sensitive to the discount rate of 11.1 percent. If the discount rate were higher, the value of the shares would be lower, and vice versa. As we have shown you, it is also quite sensitive to operating efficiency parameters. Sensitivity analysis should indicate on which valuation parameters you should spend most of your research time. For example, given the high sensitivity of Smucker's stock value to the cost parameter, it is probably a good idea to try to get as much information as you can about the components of this parameter.

• Smucker has two classes of shares that differ by their voting rights. The two shares trade for different prices with the share with the preferred voting rights trading at a slight premium. We have not taken into account the differential voting rights in our valuation of Smucker's shares. Rather, we have taken into account only the rights of the shares to cash flows, which are identical for both share classes.

• Finally, we have not examined additional information that may indicate whether Smucker's management, which is privy to more information than we are, agrees with our conclusion that Smucker's shares are not a good buy. For example, it would be problematic to see Smucker's management acquiring shares of Smucker or repurchasing shares (as **treasury stock**) in the market as these actions would indicate that Smucker's management considers Smucker's shares a bargain.

APPENDIX: Modeling Accelerated Depreciation and Deferred Taxes

Some Theory and a Simple Example

In the model presented in the chapter we have assumed straight-line depreciation. In many cases firms report straight-line depreciation to their shareholders but pay taxes on the basis of accelerated depreciation. In this case there will be Deferred Taxes in the balance sheet.

This is illustrated in the following simple example (see Exhibit 7A.1). Consider a firm that has just started and that has the following balance sheet.

Exhibit 7A.1

NEW FIRM, INC.
Initial Balance Sheet, January 1, 1995

Cash	$ 100	Current Liabilities	$ 0
Fixed Assets at Cost	1,000	Deferred Taxes	0
Depreciation	0	Equity	1,100
Net Fixed Assets	1,000		
Total Assets	$1,100	Total Liabilities	$1,100

In its first year of operation the firm has Sales of $1,000 and COGS (excluding depreciation) of $500. It reports $200 of depreciation to its shareholders but pays its taxes on the basis of an accelerated depreciation of $300. This gives rise to *two* profit and loss statements (one to the shareholders and one to the IRS), which are presented in Exhibit 7A.2.

Exhibit 7A.2

NEW FIRM, INC. Shareholder Profit and Loss, December 31, 1995		NEW FIRM, INC. Profit and Loss Reported to IRS, December 31, 1995	
Sales	$1,000	Sales	$1,000
COGS	(500)	COGS	(500)
Depreciation	(200)	Depreciation	(300)
Profit before Taxes	$ 300	Profit before Taxes	$ 200
Taxes (40%)	(120)	Taxes (40%)	(80)
Profit after Taxes	$ 180	Profit after Taxes	$ 120

The profit and loss statement to the IRS determines the actual cash position of the firm. Assuming that New Firm pays no dividends and bought no new assets, its Free Cash Flow (FCF) can be derived from the profit and loss statement sent to the IRS:

NEW FIRM, INC.
1995 Free Cash Flow
Based on IRS Profit and Loss

Profit after Taxes	$120
Depreciation	300
Free Cash Flow	$420

Since New Firm pays no dividends, has bought no new assets, and has no Net Working Capital, the cash at the end of the year must be $1,000 (the initial cash balances) plus the $420 FCF. On the other hand, the Retained Earnings that shareholders and analysts see are based on the shareholders' profit and loss so that Accumulated Retained Earnings at the end of the year are $180, not $120 as reported to the IRS. This gives rise to the Deferred Taxes on the balance sheet in Exhibit 7A.3.

Exhibit 7A.3

NEW FIRM, INC.
Balance Sheets for Beginning and End of 1995

	January 1, 1995	December 31, 1995		January 1, 1995	December 31, 1995
Cash	$ 100	$ 520	Current Liabilities	$ 0	$ 0
Fixed Assets at Cost	$1,000	$1,000	Deferred Taxes	0	40
Depreciation	0	(200)	Equity	1,100	1,100
Net Fixed Assets	$1,000	$ 800	Accumulated Retained Earnings	0	180
Total Assets	$1,100	$1,320	Total Liabilities	$1,100	$1,320

Note that the change in Deferred Taxes is given by

$$\text{Change in Deferred Taxes} = t_c \cdot [\text{shareholder Depreciation} - \text{tax Depreciation}]$$
$$[\text{tax Depreciation} - \text{shareholder Depreciation}]$$

Once you understand the principles involved, you can, of course, also calculate the FCF from the *shareholders'* profit and loss, by properly including the change in Deferred Taxes:

NEW FIRM, INC.
1995 Free Cash Flow Based on
Shareholder Financial Statements

Profit after Taxes	$180
Depreciation	200
Increase in Deferred Taxes	40
Free Cash Flow	$420

Exhibit 7A.4

J. M. SMUCKER CO.
Calculating Deferred Taxes

ACRS depreciation rates	
Year	%
1	14.28
2	24.49
3	17.49
4	12.50
5	8.92
6	8.92
7	8.92
8	4.48

	Year					
	1992	1993	1994	1995	1996	1997
Land	$ 11,985	$ 13,240	$ 14,769	$ 16,335	$ 17,298	$ 18,242
Property, Plant, and Equipment (PP&E)						
Asset replacement		3,148	3,512	3,884	4,113	4,337
Depreciable Assets at cost (including above)	138,894	153,435	171,155	189,310	200,466	211,404
Accumulated Depreciation	(62,556)	(71,101)	(80,573)	(91,108)	(102,586)	(114,723)
Net PP&E	$ 76,338	$ 82,334	$ 90,582	$ 98,202	$ 97,880	$ 96,680

Actual Depreciation Using ACRS and Age of Assets

Age of Existing Assets, Beginning 1992	3

	New Assets	Depreciation				
		1993	1994	1995	1996	1997
Pre-1993 Existing PP&E	$138,894	$12,389	$12,389	$12,389	$12,389	$ 0
1993 New PP&E	17,689	2,526	4,332	3,094	2,211	1,578
1994 New PP&E	21,231	0	3,032	5,200	3,713	2,654
1995 New PP&E	22,039	0	0	3,147	5,397	3,855
1996 New PP&E	15,269	0	0	0	2,180	3,739
1997 New PP&E	15,275	0	0	0	0	2,181
Total ACRS Depreciation		$14,915	$19,753	$23,830	$25,892	$14,007
Depreciation reported		$ 8,545	$ 9,472	$10,535	$11,478	$12,137
Tax Depreciation (above)		$14,915	$19,753	$23,830	$25,892	$14,007
Tax Rate		40.00%	42.00%	42.00%	42.00%	42.00%
Increment to Deferred Taxes		$ 2,548	$ 4,318	$ 5,584	$ 6,054	$ 785

Note: Dollar amounts are in $ thousands.

Estimating Smucker's Deferred Taxes

We are now in a position to estimate Smucker's deferred taxes. We will assume that these taxes stem only from the difference between the 8 percent depreciation rate used for reporting to the firm's shareholders and the accelerated depreciation rates allowed by law. In order to project Deferred Taxes, we make two somewhat arbitrary assumptions:

• We assume that the 1992 existing PP&E is 3 years old. (If we had an aging schedule of fixed assets, we could alter this assumption.)
• We assume that all PP&E is depreciated on a 7-year ACRS schedule. Since ACRS works on a half-year convention, this means that the assets are depreciated over 8 years (see Exhibit 7A.4 for rates).

Given these assumptions, the ACRS depreciation schedule of PP&E, and the resulting Deferred Taxes, are given in Exhibit 7A.4. As might be expected, the new pro-forma model produces balance sheets for Smucker with somewhat higher cash balances. Since these cash balances earn interest, the income statements for Smucker show higher Net Income. (See Exhibit 7A.5).

In Exhibit 7A.6 we reproduce the calculations for the value of Smucker's shares and warrants. As you can see, the Accelerated Depreciation has the anticipated effect: It has increased Smucker's cash flows and made both the shares and the warrants more valuable. Given the margins for error, you will have to decide whether these differences are meaningful.

Exhibit 7A.5

J. M. SMUCKER CO.
Pro-Forma Model with Accelerated Depreciation and Deferred Taxes
(a) Income statements

	Year					
	1992	1993	1994	1995	1996	1997
Sales	$483,472	$534,089	$595,769	$647,666	$685,882	$723,304
COGS + SG&A (excluding Depreciation)		(461,987)	(515,340)	(560,231)	(593,288)	(625,658)
Gross Profit		72,102	80,429	87,435	92,594	97,646
Depreciation Expense		(11,693)	(12,984)	(14,289)	(15,324)	(16,193)
Operating Income		60,409	67,445	73,146	77,270	81,453
Interest Income		1,813	2,651	3,444	4,703	6,283
Interest Expense		(306)	(271)	(236)	(201)	(167)
Income before Taxes		61,916	69,826	76,354	81,771	87,568
Income Taxes		(24,766)	(29,327)	(32,069)	(34,344)	(36,779)
Net Income		37,150	40,499	44,285	47,427	50,790
Dividend		12,259	13,365	14,614	15,651	16,761
Increase in Retained Earnings		$ 24,890	$ 27,134	$ 29,671	$ 31,776	$ 34,029
Earnings per Share		1.26	1.37	1.50	1.61	1.72

Exhibit 7A.5 *continued*

J. M. SMUCKER CO.
Pro-Forma Model with Accelerated Depreciation and Deferred Taxes
(b) Balance sheets

	Year					
	1992	1993	1994	1995	1996	1997
Assets						
Cash and Short-Term						
Investments	$ 36,268	$ 53,026	$ 68,878	$ 94,060	$125,656	$155,793
Accounts Receivable	41,565	45,932	51,236	55,699	58,986	62,204
Inventories	77,777	85,454	92,344	97,150	102,882	108,496
Other Current Assets	5,961	5,961	5,961	5,961	5,961	5,961
Land	11,985	13,240	14,769	16,055	17,003	17,930
Property, Plant, and						
Equipment (PP&E)						
Net Depreciable Assets	138,894	153,435	171,155	186,065	197,043	207,794
Accumulated Depreciation	(62,556)	(70,772)	(79,876)	(89,948)	(100,806)	(112,290)
Net PP&E	76,338	82,664	91,279	96,117	96,237	95,504
Other Noncurrent Assets	27,874	27,874	27,874	27,874	27,874	27,874
Total Assets	$277,768	$314,150	$352,341	$392,916	$434,600	$473,762
Liabilities						
Accounts Payable	$ 42,741	$ 48,068	$ 53,619	$ 58,290	$ 61,729	$ 65,097
Income Taxes Payable	2,249	6,192	7,332	8,017	8,586	9,195
Dividends Payable	3,101	3,065	3,341	3,654	3,913	4,190
Other Current Liabilities	5,469	5,469	5,469	5,469	5,469	5,469
Long-Term Debt	3,827	3,387	2,947	2,517	2,087	2,060
Deferred Income Taxes	6,692	9,391	13,919	19,585	25,654	26,561
Other Long-Term Liabilities	1,474	1,474	1,474	1,474	1,474	1,474
Common Stock	7,384	7,384	7,384	7,384	7,384	7,384
Additional Capital	7,034	7,034	7,034	7,034	7,034	7,034
Retained Income	209,586	234,476	261,610	291,282	323,058	357,087
Miscellaneous Adjustments	(11,789)	(11,789)	(11,789)	(11,789)	(11,789)	(11,789)
Total Liabilities and Equity	$277,768	$314,150	$352,341	$392,916	$434,600	$473,762

Exhibit 7A.6

J. M. SMUCKER CO.
Pro-Forma Model with Accelerated Depreciation and Deferred Taxes
Share valuation

Beta	0.9
r_f	3%
$E(r_M)$	12%
Risk-adjusted discount rates (RADR) for free cash flow (FCF)	11.10%
FCF Growth, after year 5	5.46%
Terminal FCF	$ 43,100
Terminal Value, Gordon Model	$805,303

Valuation Based on FCF Discounting and Terminal Value

	Year				
	1993	1994	1995	1996	1997
FCF	$ 28,589	$27,999	$38,054	$44,807	$ 43,100
Terminal value					805,303
Total	$ 28,589	$27,999	$38,054	$44,807	$848,403
Value (year-end discounting)	606,800				
Value (midyear discounting)	639,591				
Add initial Cash and Marketable Securities	36,268				
Total firm value	$675,859				

Value of Securities

Value of firm	$675,859
Value of debt	(3,800)
Value of warrants and shares	$672,059
Value per share	$ 22.56
Value per warrant	$ 6.56

CAPITAL STRUCTURE AND THE COST OF CAPITAL

OVERVIEW

Who needs to know about capital structure? You do! That is, if you want to be able to make sensible decisions about how to estimate the risk-adjusted discount rates (RADR) for cash flows in your pro-forma models and how to take into account the effect that taxes may have on values of firms and their securities. Capital structure is a difficult topic, and in this chapter we will make no pretense of presenting a complete theoretical explanation of all its intricacies. Instead, we will focus on the minimal amount of theory needed (usually explained with examples) to enable us to understand the effects of capital structure on valuation and risk-adjusted discount rates (RADR).

Although the chapter includes a review of the theory of capital structure, the question of optimal capital structure is not the main purpose of this chapter. Our goal in this review is to understand *how capital structure affects the cost of capital of the firm's assets.* Such an understanding is required before we can discuss methods of estimating the cost of capital for firms and for projects. The application of these methods is the subject of the following chapter. Accordingly, throughout this chapter we will emphasize the implications of the theory of optimal capital structure for the estimation of the cost of capital.

Here is the outline of this chapter:

1 We start with a section entitled "Basic Insights—Rules of Thumb," which summarizes what we want you to learn from this chapter. In Chapter 9 we will convert these rules to practical ways of estimating costs of capital.
2 Section 8.2 discusses the principle of additivity, which is central to finance and certainly to any discussion of the effects of capital structure on valuation.

237

3 Section 8.3 presents a long example in which we assume that personal tax rates on debt and equity income are zero. If you had a previous finance course, you will recognize this example as an illustration of the Modigliani and Miller (M&M) theorem. The example in Section 8.3 has two important aims:

  a First, it illustrates the general method of analyzing the effect of capital structure on the value of the firm. Although we illustrate this method in Section 8.3 by using only corporate taxes, the same principles apply when, in Section 8.5, we analyze the Miller equilibrium, which includes personal taxes. We have found that the discussion of this issue in many introductory finance courses is often confused. We hope that this simple example, which contains all the elements of the standard introfinance discussion, will clear up some of this confusion.

  b Second, the discussion of the M&M equilibrium in Section 8.3 allows us to demonstrate the *incomplete nature of M&M's analysis* of taxes and capital structure choice.

4 Section 8.4 continues the discussion of the example in Section 8.3. This section will consider a number of technical issues: Why do only interest tax shields matter, and how do we deal with subsidized debt, as well as with infinitely lived debt. Finally, this section initiates our discussion of the problematics of the M&M approach for optimal capital structure.

5 Section 8.5 discusses why the analysis of M&M leads to conceptual problems and offers some answers found in the finance literature. The most important element of this section is the explicit analysis of the effect of *personal* income taxes on the relative values of debt and equity. Accounting for *all* taxes—corporate and personal—within what is known as a **Miller equilibrium** yields qualitatively different conclusions about the impact of taxes and capital structure upon the cost of capital from the conclusions of the M&M analysis of corporate income tax alone.

Keep in mind that although this chapter does discuss the theoretical relations between capital structure and cost of capital, it is not intended to cover all issues. Rather, in this chapter we emphasize how *tax effects of leverage* impact the process of estimating costs of capital. In particular, the choice of capital structure may have many nontax implications. If such effects exist, they affect how the firm operates and consequently should be reflected in the expected operating cash flows. The focus of this chapter is on how *taxes, leverage,* and the *cost of capital* interact.

8.1   BASIC INSIGHTS—RULES OF THUMB

Sometimes it helps to summarize a subject first before we offer any explanation of how we came to our conclusions. In the case of capital structure we feel that it is a good idea *to start with the rules of thumb.* You may (sensibly!) want to return to this section after you have read the rest of the chapter at least once.

1 The **value of a firm** is the value of its *equity* plus the value of the firm's *interest bearing debt.* Strictly speaking, we should define the value of the firm as the

value of its equity, its debt, *and all other non-working capital-type securities.* Although our analysis is generalizable to the case where the firm has many kinds of securities, in this chapter we will assume that a firm has only debt and equity in its capital structure. In particular, we will assume that the firm has issued *no convertible securities* (e.g., the firm has no convertible bonds outstanding, and no employee has been awarded stock options).

2 There are two equivalent ways to take into account the effect of taxes on the value of a levered firm:

   a Discount the firm's expected free cash flows (FCFs) (which is an *after-corporate-tax concept*) and the expected terminal value at the end of the projection horizon at the firm's weighted average cost of capital (WACC):

$$V(L) = \sum_{t=1}^{N} \frac{\text{FCF}_t}{(1 + \text{WACC})^t} + \frac{\text{terminal value at time } N}{(1 + \text{WACC})^N}$$

   b Discount the firm's expected FCFs and its terminal value at its cost of unlevered equity, denoted by $r(U)$, and add to this number the present value (PV) of the firm's *net (i.e., after-all-taxes) interest tax shields*:

$$V(L) = \sum_{t=1}^{N} \frac{\text{FCF}_t}{[1 + r(U)]^t} + \frac{\text{Terminal Value}}{[1 + r(U)]^N}$$
$$+ \sum_{t=1}^{\infty} \frac{[(1 - t_d) - (1 - t_e)(1 - t_c)] \cdot \text{interest}_t}{[1 + (1 - t_d)r_d]^t}$$

where t_c = corporate tax rate

   t_e = personal tax rate on equity income

   t_d = personal tax rate on interest income

   $r(U)$ = cost of equity when the firm is unlevered

   r_d = cost of the firm's debt

Note that $r(U)$ is the expected rate of return to a holder of unlevered equity, before paying personal taxes on this return. Similarly, r_d is the expected pre-personal-tax rate of return to a debt holder.

   The second method is an example of the **adjusted present value (APV)** method. To apply the APV method, compute the PV of an asset *under perfect market conditions* and add the PV of the *effects of market imperfections.* Under the APV method we take into account the effect of taxes on the value of the firm by first estimating the value of the firm by discounting the FCF by $r(U)$, the cost of unlevered equity, and then adjusting the "perfect market" value of the firm for the tax effects of leverage. Note that because $r(U)$ is the cost of equity capital when the firm is *unlevered,* it only reflects the *business risk* of the firm, not its *financial* risk. (Note that these formulas ignore midyear discounting. See the box "An Important Comment on the Discounting Formulas" on page 242.)

3 The WACC is given by

$$\text{WACC} = r_e(L)\frac{E}{V} + r_d(1 - t_c)\frac{D}{V}$$

where $r_e(L)$ = cost of the firm's equity given its current leverage
E = market value of the firm's equity
D = market value of the firm's debt
$V = E + D$ = market value of the firm

If the firm has more securities than just simple debt and equity, say, N different securities, the more general formula for the WACC is

$$\text{WACC} = \sum_{i=1}^{N} r_i^{AT} \cdot \frac{V_i}{V_{\text{firm}}}$$

where
r_i^{AT} = *after-corporate-tax* cost of security i
V_i = value of security i
$$V_{\text{firm}} = \sum_{i=1}^{N} V_i = \text{value of the whole firm}$$

4 To calculate the cost of unlevered equity, you have to *unlever the cost of equity*. In some cases you can do this by using the following formula:[1]

$$r(U) = \frac{r_e(L) + r_d(1 - t_c)\dfrac{D}{E}}{1 + (1 - T)\dfrac{D}{E}}$$

where
$$T = \frac{(1 - t_d) - (1 - t_c)(1 - t_e)}{(1 - t_d)}$$

T is the PV of the net-of-all-taxes benefit of debt financing. It takes into account the effects of both *corporate* and *personal* taxes on the cost of debt and equity.

There are sound economic reasons for believing that the *net* tax benefit of debt is small. In other words, in equilibrium, $T \approx 0$.[2] For the same reasons the

---

[1] In deriving this "unlevering" formula, we assume *very strong assumptions*: a *constant capital structure* comprised of *only perpetual debt and equity* and *no growth* of the business. When these assumptions don't hold, the formula is an approximation.
[2] "$\approx$" denotes "roughly equal."

WACC *is hardly affected by the firm's capital structure.* If you, like Merton Miller (and the authors of this book), choose to believe these reasons, then the WACC is roughly equal to the firm's *cost of unlevered equity, r(U).*

5 We prefer to value firms by using the APV method. Even though the APV method is theoretically equivalent to the first method (discounting FCF by WACC), it is "cleaner": The APV method separates the tax-related net present value (NPV) of the firm's debt from the value of the firm's operating assets, whereas the WACC-based method lumps both of them together. The APV method is also easier to apply when the capital structure of the firm includes more than just "plain vanilla" securities.

6 If you are using the capital asset pricing model (CAPM) to calculate the cost of capital, you should use an after-tax version of the CAPM. The after-tax version of the Security Market Line is

$$\text{WACC} = \left(\frac{1 - t_c}{1 - T}\right) \cdot \left(1 - \frac{DT}{V}\right) rf_{\text{debt}} + \beta_{\text{assets}} \left[E(r_m) - \left(\frac{1 - t_c}{1 - T}\right) rf_{\text{debt}}\right]$$

where rf_{debt} is the yield of a default-free corporate bond (which can be approximated by the yield of an AAA-rated corporate bond); β_{assets} is given by

$$\beta_{\text{assets}} = \left(\frac{E}{D + E}\right) \cdot \beta_{\text{equity}} + \left(\frac{D}{D + E}\right) \cdot \beta_{\text{debt}} \cdot (1 - t_c)$$

where β_{equity} and β_{debt} are the equity and the debt betas estimated relative to the *equity* market portfolio that we use as a proxy for *the* market portfolio (e.g., the S&P 500 index); and $E(r_m)$ is the expected return of the benchmark equity portfolio.

7 In the Appendix to this chapter we show that under the CAPM the cost of debt and cost of equity are given by:

$$E(r_{\text{equity}}) = rf_{\text{debt}}\left(\frac{1 - t_c}{1 - T}\right) + \beta_{\text{equity}}\left[E(r_m) - rf_{\text{debt}}\left(\frac{1 - t_c}{1 - T}\right)\right]$$

$$E(r_{\text{debt}}) = rf_{\text{debt}} + \beta_{\text{debt}}\left[E(r_m) - rf_{\text{debt}}\left(\frac{1 - t_c}{1 - T}\right)\right]$$

Here β_{equity} and β_{debt} are both calculated with respect to a market portfolio of equity securities. If you believe that $T \approx 0$, then the WACC equation in the CAPM simplifies to

$$\text{WACC} = rf_{\text{debt}}(1 - t_c) + \beta_{\text{assets}}[E(r_m) - rf_{\text{debt}}(1 - t_c)]$$

$$\text{where } \beta_{\text{assets}} = \left(\frac{E}{D + E}\right)\beta_{\text{equity}} + \left(\frac{D}{D + E}\right)(1 - t_c)\beta_{\text{debt}}$$

- There is no bankruptcy risk.
- The firm is financed exclusively with common stock and straight debt.

A Simple Replacement Example

We start our discussion by solving an example that appears in the capital budgeting section of almost every introductory finance course. This example, which in itself has nothing to do with capital structure, serves as a useful vehicle for illustrating the classic M&M capital structure propositions.

XYZ Corp. is considering the purchase of a new widget machine to replace an older, less efficient machine. Here are the relevant facts about the two machines.

New Machine

- The price is $200,000.
- The depreciable life is 10 years. Depreciation will be straight line, with an expected terminal salvage value of zero.
- The new machine will give XYZ expected annual pretax savings of $30,000 per year in materials and labor costs.

Old Machine

- It was bought 10 years ago for $100,000.
- Its economic life at purchase was 20 years. The old machine is being depreciated on a straight-line basis with an expected salvage value of zero.
- If XYZ purchases the new machine, XYZ can sell this old machine for $25,000, which is a half of its current book value of $50,000.

Company

- XYZ pays a 34 percent corporate tax rate.
- The relevant discount rate for *after-corporate-tax nonfinancial cash flows* is 12 percent. We ask you to regard this discount rate as *given*. It is the appropriate RADR for the risk of the machine cash flows in mind. The 12 percent rate may, perhaps, have been calculated by using the after-tax version of the CAPM:

$$12\% = rf_{\text{debt}}(1 - t_c) + [E(r_m) - rf_{\text{debt}}(1 - t_c)] \cdot \beta_{\text{machine}}$$

Should XYZ Replace the Machine?

To answer this question, we calculate the *incremental cash flows* from the replacement of the machine.

Year 0

- Spend $200,000 for the new machine.
- Realize $25,000 for the old machine.

• Since the old machine has a book value of $50,000, XYZ can claim a *loss over book value* of $25,000, and this loss will generate *corporate tax* savings of 34% · $25,000 = $8,500.[3]

Thus, for year 0 CF = −200,000 + 25,000 + 8,500 = −166,500.

Years 1–10

• XYZ has an additional pretax income of $30,000. Net of corporate taxes, this becomes (1 − 34%) · $30,000 = $19,800.

• XYZ's purchase of the new machine generates an annual *differential* depreciation deduction of $15,000: The new machine generates an annual depreciation deduction of $20,000, whereas the old machine had an annual depreciation of $5,000. This generates an annual *marginal* tax savings of 34% · $15,000 = $5,100.

Thus, the total marginal annual operating CFs = $19,800 + $5,100 = $24,900.

Discounting the cash flows at the RADR of 12 percent, we find that the NPV of the replacement cash flows is −$25,809. Thus, XYZ should *not* replace the old machine with the new machine.

Machine Replacement Problem
Cash Flows and NPV

Year	FCF
0	(166,500)
1	24,900
2	24,900
.	.
.	.
.	.
9	24,900
10	24,900

Machine NPV @ 12% = −$25,809

Adding in Financing

We now make this story slightly more complicated: The machine manufacturer offers XYZ financing to facilitate the purchase of the machine. The terms of the financial package are as follows:

• The machine manufacturer offers to give XYZ Corp. a loan of $150,000 if it buys the machine.

• The loan bears an annual interest rate of 10 percent, to be repayable over 10 years. In years 1–9 XYZ will pay only the interest on the loan ($15,000 annually),

---

[3]Using a privilege of textbook examples, we simplify our example by assuming that tax shields are realized immediately.

and in year 10 it will pay both the interest and the principal ($165,000). Of course, interest payments are an expense for tax purposes so that the after-tax cash outlay of XYZ will be less.

• For the moment we assume that the 10 percent interest on the loan is the *market rate of interest on similar loans.* Thus, the identity of the lender—the seller of the machine—is irrelevant: *Any* lender would lend $150,000 to XYZ for the same terms. (Later we will drop this assumption to examine *subsidized* debt.)

By the principle of additivity it follows that

$$NPV(machine + loan) = NPV(machine) + NPV(loan)$$

Since we have already calculated the NPV(machine) $= -\$25,809$, it follows that we only need to calculate the NPV of the loan. To do this, we build a **loan cash-flow table.**

Year 0 In this year XYZ gets the loan from the machine manufacturer. This is an *inflow* of $150,000.

Years 1–9 In each of these years, XYZ pays the lender interest of $15,000. This interest is an expense for tax purposes. Therefore, the *after-corporate-tax* cost of the loan is $(1 - 34\%) \cdot \$15,000 = \$9,900$.

Year 10 At the end of this year XYZ pays both the interest on the loan and the loan principal, leading to an *after-corporate-tax* outflow of $159,900.

To value the loan, we must discount the loan cash flows at the appropriate RADR. Since the market rate for similar loans is 10 percent, we use it to price the loan. This gives the following cash-flow table for the loan:

Loan Cash Flows and NPV

Year	CF
0	150,000
1	(9,900)
2	(9,900)
⋮	⋮
9	(9,900)
10	(159,900)

Loan NPV @ 10% = $31,337

We can now answer the question with which we started: *If the firm borrows in order to (partially) finance the machine, it should accept the project.* The NPV of the machine plus the loan package is

$$\text{NPV(machine + loan)} = \text{NPV(machine)} + \text{NPV(loan)}$$
$$= -\$25{,}809 + \$31{,}337 = \$5{,}528 > 0$$

Conclusion: Accept the project with the financing!

There are two important facts to note about this example:

• *The loan changed our capital budgeting decision.* Without the loan, XYZ would have rejected the machine replacement, but with the possibility of getting the loan, it should accept the machine replacement. Later we will ask whether this makes any sense. There is a quick fix for the problematic conclusion of the example: If financing is available elsewhere, XYZ should borrow as much as it can *independent of its decision whether or not to take the machine.*

• But, in fact, the **machine** + **loan** *problem is very similar to the problem of valuing a firm with or without leverage.* It is largely a question of semantics: If we asked whether we should buy a firm when the purchase of the firm is partially financed with debt, then we essentially have the machine + loan problem; it is just that "machine" has been replaced by "firm," and "loan to buy the machine" has been replaced by "firm's debt." Thus, the problem we have been discussing is completely general; all the conclusions we draw here will also apply if we discuss the effects of leverage on the valuation of firms.

8.4 WHAT CAN WE CONCLUDE FROM THE MACHINE EXAMPLE?

The machine + loan example is a very fruitful way to understand many of the issues related to the capital structure problem. In this section we explore five issues raised by this example. The issues are *not* presented in the order of importance: The most important issue—the implications of the example for the problem of optimal capital structure—is brought up last to lead us to a more complete discussion of taxes, capital structure, and cost of capital (Section 8.5). The first four issues are more technical in nature and we put them out of the way first.

Issue 1 *Why is the loan valuable?*

Let's write the NPV of the loan once more:

$$\text{NPV(loan)} = +150{,}000 - \sum_{i=1}^{10} \frac{(1 - 0.34) \cdot 15{,}000}{(1 + 0.10)^i} - \frac{150{,}000}{(1 + 0.10)^{10}}$$

$$= +150{,}000 - \sum_{i=1}^{10} \frac{15{,}000}{(1 + 0.10)^i} - \frac{150{,}000}{(1 + 0.10)^{10}}$$

$$+ \sum_{i=1}^{10} \frac{0.34 \cdot 15{,}000}{(1 + 0.10)^i}$$

The sum of the first three terms in this last expression is zero.[4] Thus, the NPV of $31,337 of the loan *derives solely from the last term*:

$$31,337 = \sum_{i=1}^{10} \frac{0.34 \cdot 15,000}{(1 + 0.10)^i}$$

Thus: NPV(loan) = PV(loan interest tax shield @ loan interest rate)

$$= \sum_{i=1}^{N} \frac{t_c \cdot \text{interest payment}}{(1 + r_d)^i}$$

In the next section you will see that even when we take into account personal taxes in determining the tax effects of debt, this principle remains valid.[5]

Issue 2   *What happens if the loan is infinitely lived?*

Suppose the loan terms were that the firm would never have to repay the principal of the loan; then each period the firm would pay the loan interest, and these payments would go on forever. We call such a loan an *infinitely lived loan.*[6] When the loan is *infinitely lived,* the NPV(loan) can be valued as a perpetuity:

$$NPV(\text{loan}) = \sum_{i=1}^{\infty} \frac{t_c \cdot \text{interest payment}}{(1 + \text{interest rate})^i}$$

$$= \frac{t_c \cdot \text{interest payment}}{\text{interest rate}}$$

$$= \frac{t_c \cdot \text{interest rate} \cdot \text{loan principal}}{\text{interest rate}}$$

$$= t_c \cdot \text{loan principal}$$

---

[4]Why? The PV of the stream of repayments on a loan, *when the discount rate is the loan interest rate,* is equal to the initial principal of the loan.

[5]Although the principle remains valid, we will see that when both personal and corporate taxes are taken into account, the NPV of a loan is calculated by

$$NPV(\text{loan}) = \sum_{i=1}^{N} \frac{[(1 - t_d) - (1 - t_c)(1 - t_e)] \cdot \text{interest}_i}{[1 + (1 - t_d) \cdot r_d]^i}$$

The term in the numerator represents the after-all-taxes advantage of debt over equity, and the denominator reflects the discount rate that is applicable to cash flows of the debt's risk, *i*.

[6]Students often assume that the assumption of an infinitely lived loan is a professor's trick to make calculations simpler. There is some truth in this, but if you consider that maturing loans are often *turned over,* the debt may effectively be infinitely lived even though each component loan has a finite maturity.

For this case

$$\text{NPV(machine + loan)} = \text{NPV(machine)} + t_c \cdot \text{loan principal}$$

If you studied the M&M capital structure propositions in an earlier course, you will recognize this last formula as just another version of "M&M with taxes":

$$V(L) = V(U) + t_c \cdot D$$

where $V(L)$ is like PV(machine + financing)
$\quad\quad V(U)$ is like PV(machine without financing)
$\quad\quad t_c \cdot D$ is like PV(loan)

Issue 3 *What if the loan interest rate is different from the market rate?*

Suppose, for example, the loan has an interest rate of 9 percent instead of 10 percent so that the loan is subsidized. The NPV of the loan is now given by

$$
\begin{aligned}
\text{NPV(loan)} &= +150,000 - \sum_{i=1}^{10} \frac{(1 - 0.34) \cdot 13,500}{(1 + 0.10)^i} - \frac{150,000}{(1 + 0.10)^{10}} \\
&= +150,000 - \sum_{i=1}^{10} \frac{13,500}{(1 + 0.10)^i} - \frac{150,000}{(1 + 0.10)^{10}} \\
&\quad + \sum_{i=1}^{10} \frac{0.34 \cdot 13,500}{(1 + 0.10)^i}
\end{aligned}
$$

Note:

• The numerators of the preceding expression contain the *actual payments on the loan* and the denominators contain the *market rate of interest,* which is the correct RADR for the loan.

• The first three terms no longer sum to zero:

$$150,000 - \sum_{i=1}^{10} \frac{13,500}{(1 + 0.10)^i} - \frac{150,000}{(1 + 0.10)^{10}} = 9,217$$

Thus, $9,217 is the *loan subsidy,* the discount given in the loan terms by the manufacturer of the machine.

• The interest tax shield, which is proportional to the coupon *actually paid,* is smaller than before:

$$\sum_{i=1}^{10} \frac{0.34 \cdot 15,000}{(1 + 0.10)^i} > \sum_{i=1}^{10} \frac{0.34 \cdot 13,500}{(1 + 0.10)^i} = 28,204$$

- The NPV(subsidized loan) = NPV(subsidy) + NPV(tax shield)

$$= \$9{,}217 + \$28{,}204 = \$37{,}420$$

$$> \text{NPV(unsubsidized loan)}[7]$$

Issue 4   *Can we analyze the total cash flows of the machine plus loan instead of analyzing the operating and the financial cash flows separately?*

The answer is "yes, but with great caution." If you are not careful, this approach will involve you in a common internal rates of return (IRR) conundrum. To illustrate, let's start by considering Exhibit 8.1, which gives the total cash flows.

Exhibit 8.1

Machine + Loan Example
Composition of Total CFs

Year	Operating CF	Loan CF	Total CF
0	(166,500)	150,000	(16,500)
1	24,900	(9,900)	15,000
2	24,900	(9,900)	15,000
3	24,900	(9,900)	15,000
4	24,900	(9,900)	15,000
5	24,900	(9,900)	15,000
6	24,900	(9,900)	15,000
7	24,900	(9,900)	15,000
8	24,900	(9,900)	15,000
9	24,900	(9,900)	15,000
10	24,900	(159,900)	(135,000)

Exhibit 8.1 deserves some considered attention:

- First, note that the last column contains the cash flows pertaining to the *equity investment* in the machine. To see this, we notice that $-\$16{,}500$ is the amount that the firm's owners (i.e., its equity holders) have to pay for the machine after they have financed $150,000 of the machine's net cost of $166,500 with the loan.[8]
- Since the cash flows of the *levered* equity holders are *riskier* than the cash flows of the project, the correct RADR for the last column of cash flows is larger

---

[7]If you think about this for a moment, you should find this very reassuring: It says that when comparing a subsidized loan to an unsubsidized loan, the *lowered tax advantage of the interest cannot be more valuable than the subsidy.* If this were not so, firms would request financial institutions to *raise* interest rates on their loans in order to get greater interest tax shields!

[8]We remind you of Chapter 3: One of the most important questions that you can ask about a cash flow is "Whose cash flow is this?" Having answered this question, you will find it easier to say what the appropriate RADR for the cash flow should be.

than the rate of return of the *unlevered* cash flows. We denote the cost of equity for a levered series of cash flows by $r_e(L)$ and denote the cost of equity for an unlevered series of cash flows by $r(U)$. Since $r_e(L) > r(U)$, it follows that $r_e(L) > 12\%$.

This last point brings up a thorny problem. If we accept that $r(U) = 12\%$, how should we determine $r_e(L)$? Later we will present a rule for determining $r_e(L)$ (*under some nontrivial assumptions*), but now let's pretend that we don't know this rule. One way out of this problem is to find the discount rate that will give us the NPV(machine + loan) that we have calculated from the *separate* cash flows— $5,528. We can use the graph (in Figure 8.1) of the NPV(machine + loan) for different discount rates to find the $r_e(L)$, which gives the levered cash flows of an NPV of $5,528. But here we run into another problem. There are *two* $r_e(L)$ values for the levered equity cash flows that give an NPV(machine + loan) of $5,528.[9]

We can also use the worksheet of cash flows to solve for each $r_e(L)$. Technically, this is like calculating the IRR with an *additional* investment of $5,528. Doing some spreadsheet manipulations, we can show that the cost of levered equity for the project is either 4.48 or 64.62 percent. Since the RADR of the *levered* cash flows, $r_e(L)$, cannot be less than the cost of the *unlevered* cash flows, $r(U)$, the cost of capital for the levered equity cannot be 4.48 percent. It must be that $r_e(L) = 64.62\%$. Thus, if we discount the levered-equity cash flows at 64.62 percent we will get the correct value for the project with the loan. This is, however, a tricky

[9]The graph in Figure 8.1 also makes clear, even if you want to use the IRR, why you should make a graph of the NPV. The IRR in such a graph is given by the points where it crosses the *x*-axis, but the NPV graph gives us much more information. For instance, in this example the NPV graph indicates whether the NPV is *positive* or *negative* between the two IRRs, which is extremely important information.

FIGURE 8.1   The graph of the NPV(machine + loan) for different discount rates to find $r_e(L)$.

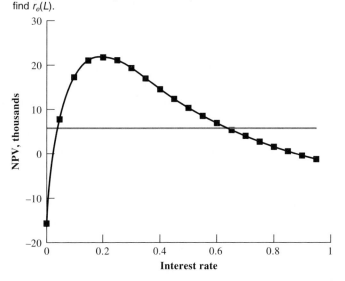

"if": To find the appropriate RADR for the levered-equity cash flows, *we need to know the NPV of the combined cash flows*. This is true of many formulas for $r_e(L)$ that you can find in textbooks. To find formulas for $r_e(L)$, we first find the NPV of the debt's tax savings by using the APV method (under some not-too-mild assumptions!) and then look for a discount rate that gives the same answer.

Our last issue is much more difficult and important than issues 1 through 4, which were largely technical in nature:

Issue 5 *There is a contradiction in assigning value to the loan in relation to the machine:*

• The loan is at market rates. Why should a *market-value loan* convince us (potentially) to undertake a *bad project*?
• If loans add value, how much should we borrow? Why don't we borrow more money and use it either to reduce the equity investment in the machine further or (when we have "milked' the machine for all its worth) to reduce the equity investment in the rest of the company?[10]

We devote the entire next section of this chapter to issue 5, the **optimal capital structure problem.**

8.5 POSSIBLE SOLUTIONS TO THE OPTIMAL CAPITAL STRUCTURE PROBLEM

We now turn our attention to the optimal capital structure problem. The problem is that the M&M analysis leads to the counterfactual prediction that:

If the NPV of debt is the PV of the corporate tax shield on the interest, then in order to maximize their value, *firms should rely almost exclusively on debt to finance their operations.*[11]

Yet, very few firms finance their operations by using mostly debt. In fact, the capital structure of most firms has a larger fraction of equity in it than debt.

The financial literature presents three major solutions to this problem. We think that each of these solutions has something to add to our understanding of capital structure, which is why we present all three solutions in this section. However, although the first two solutions provide valuable insights into the problem of optimal capital structure, we believe that the last solution (usually called "the Miller equilibrium") is the one that makes the most economic sense. Moreover,

---

[10]As you will see later in this chapter, we can reduce the equity investment in the company by issuing debt and using the proceeds to repurchase equity.

[11]The correct statement is: Firms should *issue debt to shield all current operating income*. This slight modification is relevant for firms whose income is expected to grow. Growth firms don't need *now* to issue debt that can shield the higher income expected in the *future*; it is enough to issue debt whose interest expense covers the *current* income and to issue more debt as the operating income rises.

since we are more interested in the effect of taxes and leverage on the *cost of capital* than in the question of optimal capital structure per se, the last solution is the most relevant. Thus, in the following section and in the next chapter we will discuss estimation methods for the cost of capital that are consistent with a Miller-type analysis.

Solution 1: Costs of financial distress

This is the earliest approach to solving the problem of optimal capital structure. Roughly speaking, it says, "Perhaps debt conveys some advantages and makes the firm's value larger, but greater debt also brings *larger potential costs of financial distress.*" The present value of these costs reduces the leverage-adjusted value of the firm. The universal colloquialism for "costs of financial distress" is "bankruptcy costs," and we shall follow the rest of the finance profession in denoting the costs of financial distress by PV(BC). In an equation

$$V(L) = V(U) + t_c \cdot D - \text{PV(BC)}$$

Among the reasons that economists like this theory is the fact that it has a very nice graphical representation, as seen in Figure 8.2. As the figure shows, when PV(BC) increases with leverage, there is an optimal capital structure for the firm.

What are these "potential costs of financial distress"? They can be classed into two types of costs:

• Legal and administrative costs that are tied to possible future bankruptcy proceedings. Extensive academic research appears to show that these costs, although large in some cases, are too small to counter the corporate tax benefits of debt predicted by the M&M theory.

• Costs related to the *disruption of the normal commercial activities of the firm* that are incurred because of the *possibility* of financial distress. To imagine these costs, ask yourself whether you would advise your company to make a long-term commitment to a supplier who was in financial trouble. Such losses go under the heading of "indirect costs of financial distress" and are clearly possible by-products

FIGURE 8.2 A schematic representation of debt's tax savings and the costs of financial distress.

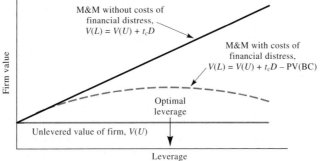

M&M without costs of financial distress, $V(L) = V(U) + t_c D$

M&M with costs of financial distress, $V(L) = V(U) + t_c D - \text{PV(BC)}$

Firm value

Optimal leverage

Unlevered value of firm, $V(U)$

Leverage

of over leverage. Again, although the indirect costs of financial distress can be larger than the direct costs of a financial distress, empirical research and theoretical arguments suggest that they too are relatively unimportant, given the M&M prediction that each dollar of additional debt adds t_c to the value of the firm.

Solution 2: Opportunities for shareholder misbehavior

This is another attractive and plausible theory. In effect, it says that shareholders in a levered firm will take greater risks because they have less to lose than shareholders in an unlevered firm. Loaning money to shareholders in a levered firm is somewhat like inviting them to raise the risk of the operating assets of the firm. Modern finance offers us an analytical tool, the option theory, which allows us to put a lot of structure on this problem. The logic of the argument is the following:

• We can view shareholders as owners of a call option on the assets of the firm: The shareholders pay their debts only if the value of the firm's assets justifies paying off the debt holders. If the value of the assets of the firm deteriorates enough, the shareholders can simply walk away from the firm, that is, declare bankruptcy. Clearly, the shareholders' right to own the firm's assets only when they are worth more than the firm's debt obligations is equivalent to a call option on the firm's assets.

• Since an option becomes *more valuable as the risk of the underlying asset increases,* and since the underlying asset for the shareholders' option is the firm's operating assets, shareholders of a levered firm—like any other option holder—have a reason to *increase the risk of the assets.*

• Knowing the preceding logic, lenders will build the *expected increase in the risk of the firm's operations* into their valuation of the debt. Thus, the *shareholders* will end up paying for their own misbehavior.

This is different from classical M&M, which assumes that *borrowing doesn't affect the risk of the underlying assets.* According to this explanation, the shareholders choose different investments when the firm is levered as compared to when it is not. Therefore, in choosing a capital structure, the shareholders trade off the corporate tax benefits of debt with the cost of suboptimal investments that are entailed by the use of debt.

The option approach to the capital structure problem presents some real insights into the nature of lending, but, like the cost of financial distress approach, it is not computationally implementable. More importantly, since debt holders typically write elaborate covenants that limit the shareholders' ability to misbehave, it is not clear to what extent such considerations affect the capital structure decision of firms or their values.

Solution 3: Personal taxes

The discussion of the effects of leverage in Sections 8.2 and 8.3, ignoring the effects of personal taxes, suggests that the *corporate tax shield on interest* makes it advantageous for shareholders to buy out equity and to replace it with debt. In 1977 Merton Miller published a famous paper in which he indicated that when personal taxes are incorporated into the analysis, trade-offs are created that may decrease and even completely eliminate the effect of leverage on the firm's value. Miller's approach, which is summarized in Exhibit 8.2 on page 258, suggests that debt has both tax advantages *and* tax disadvantages:

The *tax advantages of debt* derive from the tax deductibility of debt interest at the *corporate* level.

The *tax disadvantages of debt* come from the fact that the *personal taxes* levied on interest income are typically higher than those levied on income derived from equity.

Miller's argument is quite involved. Although we will not prove his results here, we will indicate the general lines of the argument.

Miller argues as follows. Suppose the corporate tax rate on profits before taxes is t_c and the shareholders' personal income from equity is taxed at t_e.[12] This means that *net of all taxes,* the shareholders receive $(1 - t_c) \cdot (1 - t_e)$ for each dollar paid to them. Furthermore, suppose interest income from corporate bonds is taxed at a personal tax rate of t_d. Since a dollar paid to the debt holders is recognized as an expense for the computation of taxable *corporate* income, a dollar paid as interest is not taxed at the corporate level. Hence, a dollar of pre-corporate-tax income paid (as interest) to the debt holders is worth $(1 - t_d)$ net of all taxes.

The *relative advantage (RA)* of paying a dollar to the debt holders instead of paying it to the shareholders is

$$\text{RA} = \frac{(1 - t_c) \cdot (1 - t_e)}{(1 - t_d)}$$

If $\text{RA} > 1$, the end recipients of the dollar will get more net-of-*all*-taxes cash if we call the dollar ''return to shareholders'' than if we call it ''return to bondholders.'' In other words, taxwise it is less costly to pay the dollar to the shareholders than to pay it to the debt holders. The reverse is true if $\text{RA} < 1$.

Miller suggests that we should weigh the *trade-off* between **net after-all-taxes income from equity** and **net after-all-taxes income from debt.** He shows that the PV of the net tax advantage of one dollar of perpetual debt when there are taxes on personal as well as corporate incomes is

$$T = 1 - \text{RA}$$

$$= 1 - \frac{(1 - t_c) \cdot (1 - t_e)}{(1 - t_d)} = \frac{(1 - t_d) - (1 - t_c) \cdot (1 - t_e)}{(1 - t_d)}$$

(The derivation of this formula is explained in Appendix A of this chapter.)

---

[12]Miller's paper assumed that the shareholders could avoid *all* taxation on equity income so that $t_e = 0$. We will generally take t_e to be some average between the rate of taxation on dividends and the effective rate of taxation on capital gains. Whereas the former is often the ordinary income tax rate, the capital gains rate is generally lower: Even if the statutory rate on *realized* capital gains is equal to the ordinary tax rate, the fact that realizations of capital gains *may be postponed* lowers the *effective* capital gains tax rate.

How Large Is the Net Tax Effect of Debt?

The Miller formula allows us to gauge the tax effect of leverage on the firm's value that incorporates both corporate and personal taxes. Here are some casual calculations. Let's start with approximate federal tax rates:

$t_c = 34\%$

$t_e = 28\%$ This assumes that equity income is *immediately* realized long-term capital gain. Postponement of capital gains will lower this rate.

$t_d = 39.5\%$

Then the *capitalized net tax advantage of one dollar of perpetual debt* is

$$T = 1 - \frac{(1 - t_c) \cdot (1 - t_e)}{(1 - t_d)} = 1 - \frac{(1 - 0.34) \cdot (1 - 0.28)}{(1 - 0.395)}$$

$$= 0.2145 = 21.45\%$$

This is much lower than the corporate tax rate of 34 percent!

Now suppose the shareholders can defer realizations of capital gains to lower the *effective* tax rate on equity income to 15% (i.e., $t_e = 0.15$). Then $T = 0.073$! In other words, suppose we are valuing a highly levered firm with a 50 percent debt, and suppose the relevant tax rates are as in the example—$t_c = 34\%$, $t_e = 15\%$, and $t_d = 39.5\%$. Then ignoring the leverage tax effects altogether amounts to an error of 3.65% ($= 7.3\% \cdot 50\%$) in the valuation of the firm. Given the uncertainties associated with most corporate valuations, this is an inconsequential error.

Finally, suppose there is a 20 percent chance of bad economic times in which the firm will lose money rather than make a profit. Further, assume that when the firm reports a loss, its tax rate is 0 percent.[13] The *expected* corporate tax rate of this firm is

$$t_c = 34\% \cdot 0.80 + 0\% \cdot 0.20 = 27.2\%$$

With $t_e = 15\%$ and $t_d = 39.5\%$, we get $T = -0.023$. This means that the replacement of a dollar of equity by a dollar of debt *reduces* the value of the firm by $.023.

Empirical evidence on the tax effects of debt, much like the calculations with which we started this subsection, suggests that *T is indeed much smaller than t_c.*

---

[13]This is a simplification of reality: The firm may be able to offset losses against past or future earnings, in which case the effective tax rate on losses is either 34 percent or the PV of 34 percent, respectively.

Moreover, casual empiricism indicates that the net tax effects of debt cannot be too important: If they were, we would not expect to observe such dissimilar capital structures as we do. Rather, a trade-off between the debt's tax savings and costs of financial distress should lead to much more homogeneous capital structures, especially *within industries,* than we actually observe. It seems that firms care about their capital structure much less than corporate tax considerations alone would indicate. We think that $T \approx 0$ *is an appropriate starting point for most corporate valuations.*

There is another, more theoretical, argument why T is likely to be very small. As noted previously, T—the capitalized tax advantage of debt—may take on any value, depending on the relative tax rates imposed on corporate and personal incomes. Simple equilibrium arguments indicate that T may well be zero: Economic reasoning suggests that the forces that create an equilibrium in the markets for corporate securities also tend to equalize the total tax burdens on financial assets. Suppose, for example, we find a company whose equity had zero risk. Payments on this company's equity would be taxed at a total rate of $(1 - t_c)(1 - t_e)$, whereas payments on the zero-risk debt would be taxed at $(1 - t_d)$. Now suppose these rates differ so that, for example, $(1 - t_c)(1 - t_e) > (1 - t_d)$. Then it would be advantageous for the investors to buy the equity instead of the zero-risk debt. This, the argument goes, would drive up the price of the equity, and hence drive down the return on the equity. In effect, this means that investors adjust their portfolios until, in equilibrium, the after-tax returns on all securities (independent of their names—equity or debt) are roughly the same:

$$(1 - t_c)(1 - t_e) \approx (1 - t_d)$$

If in equilibrium $(1 - t_c)(1 - t_e) \approx (1 - t_d)$, then $T \approx 0$. For this case there is *hardly any net tax advantage to debt financing*![14]

A Simple Comparison Table

Exhibit 8.2 summarizes the differences between the M&M analysis and Miller's equilibrium. Note that both models have essentially the same approach (although with very different conclusions!). Furthermore, the M&M model is a special case of the Miller model for the case when personal tax rates are equal ($t_e = t_d$).

---

[14]The actual mechanics of how tax burdens get equalized are complicated. On the one hand, they involve individuals who try to exploit differential personal tax burdens by shifting more of their portfolios into assets that have personal tax advantages. On the other hand, firms try to exploit cheaper after-corporate-tax ways of financing by issuing more of the corporate-tax-advantaged securities. In the process of issuing more tax-advantaged securities firms raise the tax rate of the marginal investor in these securities, thus narrowing their tax advantage. A complete description of this process is beyond the scope of this book, but an interested reader might start with Merton Miller's famous article, "Debt and Taxes," *Journal of Finance,* May 1977, pp. 261–275.

Exhibit 8.2

Classic M&M with corporate taxes	Miller equilibrium with personal and corporate taxes
Corporate income is taxed at t_c. There are no taxes on personal income.	Corporate income is taxed at t_c. Personal income is taxed at rates that depend on its source: t_e = personal tax rate on equity income t_d = personal tax rate on debt income
Replacing equity by debt unequivocally *adds value* to the company by reducing corporate tax payments.	Replacing equity by debt *trades*: • *Net after-all-taxes equity income* $$(1 - t_c) \cdot (1 - t_e)$$ • *Net after-all-taxes debt income* $$(1 - t_d)$$
The *capitalized tax advantage of one dollar of debt* is t_c.	The *capitalized advantage of one dollar of debt* is $$T = 1 - \frac{(1 - t_c) \cdot (1 - t_e)}{(1 - t_d)}$$
$$V(L) = V(U) + D \cdot t_c$$	$$V(L) = V(U) + D \cdot T$$

Note: The *classic M&M model is a special case of the Miller model*: If you let $t_e = t_d$ in the Miller model, you will get $T = t_c$ and the classic M&M model.

Using the CAPM: What Is the Appropriate RADR for FCFs?

For our purposes the most relevant implications of the discussion of taxes and capital structure are the implications for the estimation of the cost of capital. Suppose we wish to use the CAPM to estimate the RADR with which to discount FCFs. The differential taxation of the debt and the equity creates a problem in estimating the model's inputs: We use the market return, which is measured by an *equity* portfolio, to estimate betas and risk premiums of bonds and of stocks, *which are taxed differently*. In the Appendix we explain intuitively the way to take into account the differential taxation in computing the RADR for FCFs. The resulting equation is

$$\text{RADR} = \left(\frac{1 - t_c}{1 - T}\right) \cdot (1 - T \cdot x_d)\, rf_{\text{debt}} + \beta_{\text{assets}} \cdot \left[E(r_m) - \left(\frac{1 - t_c}{1 - T}\right) \cdot rf_{\text{debt}} \right]$$

where rf_{debt} is the yield of a default-free corporate bond (which can be approximated by the yield of an AAA-rated corporate bond). β_{assets} is given by

$$\beta_{\text{assets}} = \left(\frac{E}{D + E}\right) \cdot \beta_{\text{equity}} + \left(\frac{D}{D + E}\right) \cdot \beta_{\text{debt}} \cdot (1 - t_c)$$

β_{equity} and β_{debt} are the equity and the debt betas that are estimated relative to the *equity* market portfolio that we use as a proxy for *the* market portfolio (e.g., the S&P 500 index). $E(r_m)$ is the expected return of the benchmark equity portfolio. (The use of an *equity* market index assures that its returns are taxed at t_e.) Finally, x_d is the weight of debt in the firm's capital structure, measured by the ratio of the market value of the debt to the market value of the whole firm—*D/V*.

We believe that a good starting point for valuations is the assumption that the Miller equilibrium *roughly describes reality*. That is, we believe that $T \approx 0$ is a good starting point for valuations. In this case the preceding equation for the RADR simplifies to

$$\text{RADR} = (1 - t_c) \cdot rf_{\text{debt}} + \beta_{\text{assets}} \cdot [E(r_m) - (1 - t_c) \cdot rf_{\text{debt}}]$$

The RADR equation in the Miller equilibrium has a simple and intuitive interpretation:

• The RADR with which we discount *after-corporate-tax* FCFs is the sum of the *after-corporate-tax* risk-free rate and a risk premium.
• The risk premium is the expected return on the market portfolio (e.g., S&P 500) less the risk-free benchmark—the *after-corporate-tax* risk-free rate.
• β_{assets} is the weighted average of β_{equity} and β_{debt} (or, more generally, the weighted average of the betas of all the securities in the firm's capital structure) with the beta estimate of the debt adjusted downward to an after-corporate-tax basis.

If you believe that $T \approx 0$ doesn't describe market conditions well, yet you want to work with the simple structure entailed by assuming that $T \approx 0$, you can use the APV approach to adjust the value obtained under the "no-net-tax-gain-to-debt-financing" valuation by adding to this value the net tax benefits of debt. For the simple case of constant infinite debt level the PV of the debt's net tax benefits is $T \cdot D$. For less simple cases the PV of the net tax benefit of debt financing can be calculated by

$$\text{PV(net tax benefit)} = \sum_{i=1}^{\infty} \frac{[(1 - t_d) - (1 - t_e)(1 - t_c)] \cdot \text{interest}_i}{[1 + (1 - t_d)r_d]^i}$$

where interest$_i$ is the annual before-corporate-tax interest payments on the debt (according to the projected capital structure of the firm), and r_d is the before-corporate-tax RADR that is appropriate for the projected debt level.

8.6   ANOTHER TEXTBOOK EXAMPLE

We started this chapter with a textbook example, and conclude it with another example:

A company with FCFs of $10,000 per year, which is expected to continue forever, currently has no debt.[15] The company is planning to issue $40,000 of 5 percent infinitely lived debt and to use the proceeds to repurchase equity. The company's cost of equity is now (i.e., when the company is financed with equity only) 12.5 percent. The firm's marginal corporate tax rate (t_c) is 35 percent, the personal tax rate paid on income from shares (t_e) is 28 percent, and the personal tax rate paid on income from bonds (t_d) is 40 percent.

If this were an exam question, your assignment would be to analyze this problem thoroughly. In this case we will pose the questions and answer them:

- **What is the value of the company *before* the refinancing?**

Answer   The value of the firm before the refinancing is the value of a perpetuity of $10,000 discounted at 12.5 percent:

$$V(U) = \sum_{t=1}^{\infty} \frac{\text{FCF}_t}{(1 + r(U))^t} = \frac{\text{FCF}}{r(U)} = \frac{10,000}{12.5\%} = 80,000$$

- **What will be the value of the company *after* the refinancing?**

Answer   Applying the Miller model, we have

$$T = 1 - \frac{(1 - t_c) \cdot (1 - t_e)}{(1 - t_d)} = 1 - \frac{(1 - 35\%) \cdot (1 - 28\%)}{(1 - 40\%)} = 0.22 = 22\%$$

We can now adjust the value of the *unlevered* firm for the *net tax savings of debt* by using the formula given in Exhibit 8.2:

$$V(L) = V(U) + D \cdot T$$
$$= 80,000 + 40,000 \cdot 0.22 = 88,800$$

---

[15]Note that FCF is already an *after-corporate-tax concept*. Thus, there is no need to say "after-tax FCF." Some finance texts use (earnings before interest and taxes) EBIT $\cdot$ $(1 - t_c)$ instead of FCF, but this needlessly confuses accounting terminology with finance terminology.

- **What will be the value of the company's *equity* after the refinancing?**

Answer   Since the value of the firm ($88,800) is the sum of the value of the equity and the value of the debt ($40,000),

$$\text{Value of equity} = \$88,800 - \$40,000 = \$48,800$$

- **What will be the *cost of equity* $r_e(L)$ of the firm after the refinancing?**

Answer   The annual expected *equity holders'* cash flows (which can be distributed to them as dividends or as share repurchase) will be the *Free Cash Flows* less the *after-corporate-tax interest payments*:

$$\text{FCF} - (1 - t_c) \cdot \text{interest} = \$10,000 - (1 - 0.35) \cdot 5\% \cdot \$40,000$$

$$= \$8,700$$

We can use the Gordon formula with zero growth (i.e., $g = 0$) to solve for the cost of levered equity by using the expected annual cash flows and the *known* value:

$$r_e(L) = \frac{D_0 \cdot (1 + g)}{P_0} + g$$

$$= \frac{D_0}{P_0} = \frac{8,700}{48,800} = 17.83\%$$

For the case of no growth and perpetual debt we can derive a general formula that relates $r_e(L)$ to $r(U)$ and the tax rates on corporate and personal incomes. The formula is

$$r_e(L) = r(U) + [r(U) \cdot (1 - T) - r_d(1 - t_c)] \frac{D}{E}$$

Under the Miller equilibrium where $T \approx 0$ this simplifies to

$$r_e(L) = r(U) + [r(U) - r_d(1 - t_c)] \frac{D}{E}$$

Applying the formula to our example, we get

$$r_e(L) = 12.5\% + [12.5\%(1 - 0.22) - 5\%(1 - 0.35)] \frac{40,000}{48,800}$$

$$= 17.83\%$$

- **What will be the firm's *weighted average cost of capital (WACC)* after the recapitalization?**

(Of course, the firm's WACC *before* the recapitalization equals the cost of the unlevered equity—$r(U) = 12.5\%$.)

$$\text{WACC} = r_e(L) \cdot \frac{E}{E + D} + (1 - t_c) \cdot r_d \cdot \frac{D}{E + D}$$

$$= 17.83\% \cdot \frac{48,800}{88,800} + (1 - 0.35) \cdot 0.05 \cdot \frac{40,000}{88,800} = 11.26\%$$

An important fact to note is that for a no-growth firm we can always find the WACC by using

$$\text{WACC} = \frac{\text{FCF}}{E + D}$$

This reflects a general and very useful and important result:

The WACC is always the correct RADR for the firm's Free Cash Flows.

Two Methods of Discounting

We take a short break from our question and answer format to explore the implications of the information that we have discovered so far. The fact that the WACC is the correct RADR for the firm's FCF means that there are two correct ways to discount:

- We can discount *separately* the operating cash flows and the PV of the tax effects, *each discounted at its own RADR.*
- Alternatively we can discount the firm's FCFs at a *combined* cost of capital—the WACC. This will also give you the value of the firm's debt plus its equity.

The first way—the APV approach—is the basic method of finance. If you look carefully at the preceding examples, you will see that this is the method that we have used. When we considered replacing the machine, for example, we first valued the machine for replacement and then *added* the value of the financing for the machine. In our current example we discount the firm's FCF to get $V(U)$, and then add the net tax savings of debt, $D \cdot T$, to obtain the total value of the firm. Depending on which type of problem you face, one or the other of these methods will often prove to be more convenient. Here are two examples:

- In many capital budgeting situations we derive only the *operating* cash flows of the project. However, the firm that takes on the project may well be financed by a combination of debt and equity. If the project will not cause a significant change in the firm's financing mix, and if the business risk of the project is similar to the business risk of the rest of the firm's operations,[16] then you can value the project by discounting its free cash flows at the firm's WACC.

• In valuations, recapitalizations, and a host of other situations *when the capital structure of the firm is expected to change over time,* it is often more convenient to value cash flows separately. Whenever possible, we prefer, when valuing a firm, to discount its FCFs at an appropriate risk-adjusted (for business risk only!) discount rate. We can then consider separately the value, if any, of the firm's financing.

Let's go back to the example of the firm that replaces debt for equity.

• **Is the fact that the value of the equity of the levered firm is lower than the value of the equity prior to the recapitalization** *good* **or** *bad* **for the shareholders?** The only way to answer this question is to compute the *wealth effect* of the recapitalization—the total effect of the recapitalization on the shareholders' wealth.

To answer this question, assume that *before the refinancing* there were 1,000 shares in the firm. Since the total value of the firm was $80,000, each share was worth $80,000/1,000 = $80. The firm uses the debt proceeds of $40,000 to *repurchase shares.* How many shares does it repurchase? The most intuitive way to do this is to use two equations with two unknowns. Let x denote the number of shares repurchased, and let y denote the price at which the shares are repurchased. Note that the price at which the shares are repurchased (y) will no longer be $80: Once the refinancing of the firm is announced, the price of the shares will rise to reflect the effect of the announced recapitalization on the value of the firm. If this were not the case, no shareholder would tender her shares: Rather, she would hold on to them to reap the tax benefits of the refinancing. The two equations are that the total funds paid to redeeming shareholders are the $40,000 raised by issuing debt:

$$x \cdot y = \$40,000$$

and that the total value of the equity after the repurchase of x shares is $48,800:

$$(1,000 - x) \cdot y = \$48,800$$

Solving them gives the answer:

$$y = \text{price per share, after relevering} = \$88.80$$

$$x = \text{number of shares repurchased} = \frac{\$40,000}{\$88.80} = 450.45$$

---

[16]Be careful! These are two big "ifs"! However, they are often appropriate.

Why does the share price rise from \$80 to \$88.80? The answer is that the rise reflects each initial shareholder's portion of the value of the tax shield created by the new debt:

$$\frac{T \cdot \text{new debt}}{\text{initial number of shares}} = \frac{0.22 \cdot \$40,000}{1,000} = \$8.80$$

Once the firm announces the recapitalization, the total value of the shares rises to $V(L)$ (the sum of the value of the unlevered firm, $V(U)$, and the value of the net tax savings that the new financial structure will generate, $D \cdot T$). This means that there is a shorter way to determine the new share price: Simply divide $V(L)$ by the number of shares:

$$\text{New share price} = \frac{V(L)}{\text{initial number of shares}}$$

This indicates that we also can simply find the number of shares that will be bought back for the \$40,000 raised by floating-debt securities:

$$\text{Number of shares bought} = \frac{\$40,000}{\$88.80} = 450.45$$

SUMMARY

An understanding of the effects of capital structure choice is necessary to derive the RADRs that are appropriate to the cash flows that commonly arise in valuation problems. In this chapter we have attempted a simple discussion of this issue. Our main conclusions may be summarized as follows:

• We prefer a valuation in which the value of the firm without leverage, $V(U)$, is calculated *separately* from the value of the firm with leverage:

$$V(U) = \sum_{i=1}^{N} \frac{\text{FCF}_t}{(1 + r(U))^i} + \frac{\text{terminal value at time } N}{(1 + r(U))^N}$$

• Whether the firm's debt adds or subtracts value depends on both *personal* and *corporate* tax rates. The NPV of the firm's debt is given by

$$\text{NPV(debt)} = \sum_{i=1}^{N} \frac{[(1 - t_d) - (1 - t_e)(1 - t_c)] \cdot \text{interest}_i}{[1 + (1 - t_d) r_d]^i}$$

where t_c, t_d, and t_e are the corporate, debt, and equity income tax rates, respectively.

- If the firm's debt is kept at a fixed level and is infinitely lived, the previous formula becomes

$$NPV(debt) = T \cdot debt$$

where
$$T = 1 - \frac{(1 - t_e)(1 - t_c)}{(1 - t_d)}$$

- In either case (finitely lived or infinitely lived debt)

$$V(L) = V(U) + NPV(debt)$$

- To calculate the cost of unlevered equity $r(U)$, we must *unlever the market cost of equity* $r_e(L)$. For the case of infinitely lived debt and no growth in the FCFs, we may use the formula

$$r_e(L) = r(U) + [r(U) \cdot (1 - T) - r_d \cdot (1 - t_c)] \frac{D}{E}$$

You can use this formula as an approximation to the general case of finitely lived debt and growing FCFs.
- Strong economic arguments, first suggested by Merton Miller (who received the Nobel prize in Economics for his analysis of the question of capital structure), imply that it is reasonable to assume that $T \approx 0$ (so that $V(L) \approx V(U)$).

EXERCISES

8.1 In a given economy the corporate income tax is 30 percent, the personal equity income tax is 10 percent, and the personal debt income tax is 28 percent.
  a What is the effect of a replacement of $1 of equity by $1 of debt on *the value of a firm* in this economy?
  b What is the effect of this change on *the value of the firm's equity*?
  c What is the effect of this change on *the wealth of this firm's shareholders*?
8.2 In a given economy the following are the expected tax rates for personal income: the equity income tax is 10 percent, and the debt income tax is 19 percent. The statutory corporate tax rate is 35 percent. The TP Co. expects to be profitable in 4 out of 5 years. In this economy losses cannot be carried backward or forward. What happens to the value of TP when it replaces $1 of equity by $1 of debt? (*Hint:* Define T by using the *expected* corporate tax rate.)
8.3 Assume that in Utopia Land there are no taxes and financial distress is costless. The ABC Co., incorporated and operating in Utopia, currently uses no debt financing. The current beta of its equity is 0.5. The management of ABC proposed to its shareholders, all of whom are Utopia residents, that 50 percent of the firm's equity should be replaced by debt.

Assume that in Utopia the risk-free rate is 2 percent and that the risk premium for a beta of 1.0 is 8 percent. What is the rate of return that the *shareholders* should expect under the new capital structure?

8.4 Assume that there are no taxes and financial distress is costless. The BBC Co. currently uses 75 percent equity financing. The current beta of its equity (β_e) is 2.0 and the current beta of its debt (β_d) is 0.4. The management of BBC proposes to its debt holders that 100 percent of the firm's debt should be replaced by equity.

BBC hires you as a financial consultant. You find that the risk-free rate is 3 percent and that the risk premium for a beta of 1.0 is 8 percent.

a What rate of return should the bondholders expect upon becoming shareholders?

b Some of the debt holders of BBC refuse to go along with the plan. BBC decides to go along with the exchange of stock for bonds despite the fact that after the deal is consummated there will still be a 20 percent debt in its capital structure. What will be β_e after the limited reorganization is completed?

c Assume that all the preceding information (regarding rates of return and betas) is correct but that the income of all sources *is* taxed at the following rates: the corporate income tax is 20 percent, the personal equity income tax is 20 percent, and the personal interest (i.e., debt) income tax is 36 percent. How will your answers to parts **a** and **b** be affected by the new information?

8.5 You estimate the following information for the LVRD company:

Market value of debt	$25,000
Market value of equity	$50,000
After-corporate-tax cost of debt	6%
Weighted Average Cost of Capital (WACC)	12%
Expected growth rate of operations	3%

What is LVRD's cost of equity capital $r_e(L)$?

8.6 Suppose you estimate the following information for the ABC company:

Market value of debt	$50,000
Market value of equity	$50,000
Corporate tax rate t_c	40%
Cost of debt	6%
WACC	8%

a What would be ABC's cost of equity capital?

b Suppose we are in a Miller equilibrium (i.e., $T = 0$). If the yield to maturity of an AAA-rated corporate bond is 5.5 percent and the expected rate of return on the market portfolio is 10 percent, what will be the betas of the ABC's assets, debt, and equity in order to make the above rates of returns consistent? [Use equations (8.A4), (8.A6), and (8.A7) in Appendix B to answer this question.]

c Suppose ABC's equity was actually $25,000 common stock and $25,000 preferred stock. Would the estimated cost of the common stock be different from the cost of equity in part **a**? Why? Can you tell by how much?

APPENDIX A: Discounting Debt Tax Shields in the Miller Model

Why should *shareholders* care about *personal* taxes that are paid by debt holders? The answer is: because these tax rates are priced. What do we mean when we say that the tax rates are "priced"? We mean that the *relative* taxation of debt and equity income affects the *relative* prices of bonds and stock. Let's see how this works.

Consider a *riskless* bond and a *riskless* stock. Since holding both securities entails no risk, *both securities should earn the same rate of return* (otherwise arbitrage opportunities may exist!). We have to be careful about this statement: Since neither security holder cares about the money he or she doesn't see, the *after-tax* rates of return of the riskless bond and stock must be the same. However, the *before-tax* rates of return of the two securities may (and generally, will) differ!

Assume that investors demand 6 percent risk-free return net of taxes—6 percent is the net-of-tax time value of money. Further, assume that interest income is taxed at 40 percent; whereas equity income, comprised of capital gains and dividend, is taxed at an effective rate of 20 percent only. Because the tax rates on income from the two securities are different and investors demand equal returns *net of tax,* the *before-tax* returns of the two securities must be different! We can solve for the *before-tax* returns that will give an *after-tax* return of 6 percent.

- For the debt holders

$$rf_{\text{debt}} \cdot (1 - t_d) = rf_{\text{debt}} \cdot (1 - 40\%) = rf_{\text{debt}} \cdot 0.60 = 6\%$$

Solving for rf_{debt} gives $rf_{\text{debt}} = 10\%$. Thus, if debt holders earn 10 percent *before personal tax,* they will earn the required 6 percent *after* tax.
- For the shareholders

$$rf_{\text{equity}} \cdot (1 - t_e) = rf_{\text{equity}} \cdot (1 - 20\%) = rf_{\text{equity}} \cdot 0.80 = 6\%$$

Solving for rf_{equity} gives $rf_{\text{equity}} = 7.5\%$. Thus, if shareholders earn 7.5 percent *before personal tax,* they will also earn the required 6 percent *after* tax.

An important aspect of this example is that, even though both the equity and the debt of this firm are riskless, the managers of the firm, when choosing whether to finance their operations with debt or with equity, face different costs—10 percent for debt and only 7.5 percent for equity. This is because the *personal tax* disadvantage of debt income (relative to equity income) is *built into the relative yields demanded by investors in debt and equity!* On the other hand, the managers of the firm know that *at the corporate level* interest is tax deductible, whereas the return to the equity holders is not. If the tax on corporate income is 34 percent, the deductibility of interest at the corporate level makes the *after-corporate-tax* cost of debt

$$10\% \cdot (1 - t_c) = 10\% \cdot (1 - 34\%) = 6.6\%$$

This rate is lower than the cost of equity financing that the managers face (7.5 percent). Note, however, that the difference in the cost of the two capital sources is not merely the corporate tax. The difference between the costs of debt and equity faced by corporate managers also reflects the differential *personal* taxes of debt and equity. The Miller formula combines both effects for any combination of tax rates.

When a firm switches from equity financing to debt financing, it "redirects" part of its cash flows from equity holders to debt holders. Since a pre-all-taxes one dollar directed to equity holders is taxed twice, whereas the same dollar directed to debt holders is taxed only once, the net advantage of this redirection of cash flows is (for each dollar redirected)

$$(1 - t_d) - (1 - t_c)(1 - t_e)$$

In order to evaluate the advantage, if any, of debt over equity, we must *discount* the flow of this net advantage, over time. The Miller formula for the tax advantage of debt does this by making two assumptions:

• The net advantage of debt over equity is as risky as the debt itself.
• Since the net advantage is calculated after *all* personal and corporate taxes, it must be discounted at the after-all tax discount rate used by individuals to value debt. If the rate of interest on bonds is r_d, and if individuals pay a tax rate of t_d on interest payments, then the correct discount rate is $(1 - t_d)r_d$. This means that

$$\text{NPV(debt)} = \sum_{i=1}^{N} \frac{[(1 - t_d) - (1 - t_c)(1 - t_e)] \cdot \text{interest}_i}{[1 + (1 - t_d) \cdot r_d]^i}$$

When taxes on personal income are zero, $t_e = t_d = 0$, this expression is the same as the expression that we used in Section 8.3 for the M&M model. When the debt is infinitely lived, this expression becomes

$$\text{NPV(infinitely lived debt)} = \frac{[(1 - t_d) - (1 - t_c)(1 - t_e)] \cdot r_d \cdot D}{(1 - t_d)r_d}$$

$$= \frac{[(1 - t_d) - (1 - t_c)(1 - t_e)]D}{(1 - t_d)} = T \cdot D$$

APPENDIX B: CAPM and Tax-Adjusted RADRs

To derive the Weighted Average Cost of Capital (WACC)—the RADR for the firm's FCF—when there is differential taxation of personal debt and equity income, we begin with the benchmark—equilibrium *risk-free* returns on debt and equity. In equilibrium the *after-personal-tax returns* of any debt and equity securities that have the same risk must be the same.[17] Thus,

$$rf_{\text{debt}} \cdot (1 - t_d) = rf_{\text{equity}} \cdot (1 - t_e) = rf_0$$

---

[17]This is just another way of saying that the after-personal-tax return on a security depends only on the risk of the security, and not on its name. It doesn't matter whether you call it "debt" or "equity": If it has the same risk, then it should have the same after-personal-tax return.

where rf_0 denotes the equilibrium net-of-all-taxes risk-free return. rf_0 may be measured, for example, by the return on risk-free tax-exempt securities (e.g., AAA-rated municipal bonds).

As we have seen in Appendix A, this equation means that the *before-personal-tax* risk-free benchmarks for equity and debt are not the same: Since, in general, the personal tax rate on equity income (t_e) is lower than the tax rate on debt income (t_d), the *before-tax* risk-free benchmark for equity securities must be lower than the *before-tax* risk-free benchmark for debt securities. We can see this by manipulating the previous equation:

$$rf_{\text{debt}} = \frac{rf_0}{1 - t_d} > rf_{\text{equity}} = \frac{rf_0}{1 - t_e}$$

We can express rf_{equity} in terms of rf_{debt} and the relative personal taxation of equity and debt income:

$$rf_{\text{equity}} = rf_{\text{debt}} \left(\frac{1 - t_d}{1 - t_e} \right) \tag{8.A1}$$

We can use equation (8.A1) to convert observable risk-free rates—the yields on Treasury securities or default-free (e.g., AAA-rated) corporate bonds—to the appropriate risk-free benchmark for equity securities.

By using the definition of T, the net tax effect of debt,

$$T = 1 - \frac{(1 - t_c) \cdot (1 - t_e)}{(1 - t_d)} \quad \Rightarrow \quad \frac{1 - t_d}{1 - t_e} = \frac{1 - t_c}{1 - T}$$

we can rewrite equation (8.A1) to express the *before-personal-tax* risk-free benchmark for equity as

$$rf_{\text{equity}} = rf_{\text{debt}} \left(\frac{1 - t_c}{1 - T} \right) \tag{8.A2}$$

Now that we have the before-tax risk-free benchmark for equity returns, we can examine what happens when we add a risk premium to the risk-free benchmark. We assume that the CAPM describes risk premiums—that the risk premium of a security is proportional to its *beta*.

The beta of a security is estimated relative to a proxy for the market portfolio. Since stocks and bonds are taxed differently, it is important to specify the type of securities in the market index. We assume that betas for both debt and equity are estimated relative to a market index of *equity* securities (e.g., S&P 500). Under the CAPM the relation between the expected returns of equity securities and their betas is of the following type:

$$E(r_{\text{equity}}) = \alpha_{\text{equity}} + \beta_{\text{equity}} \cdot \Pi \tag{8.A3}$$

For a risk-free stock $\beta = 0$. This means [using equation (8.A2)] that

$$\alpha_{\text{equity}} = rf_{\text{debt}} \left(\frac{1 - t_c}{1 - T} \right)$$

Note that if there are no personal taxes (this is the assumption underlying the Modigliani-Miller perception of the world), then $T = t_c$, and the risk-free benchmark for equity securities will be the yield on a taxable risk-free bond. On the other hand, in a Miller equilibrium (i.e., $T = 0$), the risk-free benchmark for equity securities will be the *after-corporate-tax* yield on a taxable risk-free bond.

In the CAPM equation (8.A3) holds for all securities; in particular, it must be true for the *market portfolio* as well. Since β_m equals 1 by definition,

$$E(r_m) = \alpha_{\text{equity}} + 1 \cdot \Pi$$

which allows us to determine what the market price of risk, Π, must be:

$$\Pi = E(r_m) - \alpha_{\text{equity}} = E(r_m) - rf_{\text{debt}} \cdot \left(\frac{1 - t_c}{1 - T}\right)$$

Plugging the expressions for α_{equity} and for Π into the expression for RADRs [equation 8.A3)], we get the CAPM relation for the *before-personal-tax* returns of any equity security:

$$E(r_{\text{equity}}) = rf_{\text{debt}} \cdot \left(\frac{1 - t_c}{1 - T}\right) + \beta_{\text{equity}} \cdot \left[E(r_m) - rf_{\text{debt}} \cdot \left(\frac{1 - t_c}{1 - T}\right)\right] \qquad (8.\text{A}4)$$

In a Miller equilibrium ($T = 0$) this simplifies to

$$E(r_{\text{equity}}) = rf_{\text{debt}} \cdot (1 - t_c) + \beta_{\text{equity}}[E(r_m) - rf_{\text{debt}} \cdot (1 - t_c)]$$

We can also use equation (8.A4) to obtain an expression for the RADR of a debt security. One way of interpreting equation (8.A1) is that if r_{debt} is the return on a debt security, then

$$r_{\text{debt}}\left[\frac{1 - t_d}{1 - t_e}\right]$$

is the return on an equivalent-risk equity security. Furthermore, it follows from the definition of T that we can write

$$r_{\text{debt}}\left[\frac{1 - t_d}{1 - t_e}\right] = r_{\text{debt}}\left[\frac{1 - t_c}{1 - T}\right]$$

Since we already have the risk-return relation for equity securities (equation 8.A4), we can substitute to get

$$E(r_{\text{debt}}) \cdot \left(\frac{1 - t_c}{1 - T}\right) = rf_{\text{debt}} \cdot \left(\frac{1 - t_c}{1 - T}\right) \qquad (8.\text{A}5)$$

$$+ \frac{\text{Cov}\left[r_{\text{debt}}\left[\frac{1 - t_c}{1 - T}\right], r_m\right]}{\text{var}(r_m)} \cdot \left[E(r_m) - rf_{\text{debt}} \cdot \left(\frac{1 - t_c}{1 - T}\right)\right]$$

Look again at the covariance term in equation (8.A5):

$$\frac{\text{Cov}\left[r_{\text{debt}}\left[\dfrac{1 - t_c}{1 - T}\right], r_m\right]}{\text{var}(r_m)} = \left[\dfrac{1 - t_c}{1 - T}\right]\frac{\text{Cov}(r_{\text{debt}}, r_m)}{\text{var}(r_m)} = \left[\dfrac{1 - t_c}{1 - T}\right]\beta_{\text{debt}}$$

Using this equation to rewrite and simplify equation (8.A5) gives

$$E(r_{\text{debt}}) = rf_{\text{debt}} + \beta_{\text{debt}} \cdot \Pi = rf_{\text{debt}} + \beta_{\text{debt}} \cdot \left[E(r_m) - rf_{\text{debt}}\left(\dfrac{1 - t_c}{1 - T}\right)\right] \quad (8.\text{A6})$$

Thus, the before-personal-tax risk-adjusted return on a debt security is benchmarked at rf_{debt} and compensates for risk by the *equity* risk premium. Note that the betas of debt securities are also measured relative to the *equity* market index.[18]

Having calculated the RADR of equity and debt, we can calculate the WACC of a firm that finances a fraction of x_e of its operations by using equity and $x_d = 1 - x_e$ by using debt:

• First, write the WACC equation:

$$\text{WACC} = x_e \cdot E(r_{\text{equity}}) + x_d \cdot E(r_{\text{debt}}) \cdot (1 - t_c)$$

• Second, substitute in our expressions for $E(r_{\text{equity}})$ and $E(r_{\text{debt}})$:

$$\text{WACC} = x_e \left\{ rf_{\text{debt}}\left(\dfrac{1 - t_c}{1 - T}\right) + \beta_{\text{equity}}\left[E(r_m) - rf_{\text{debt}}\left(\dfrac{1 - t_c}{1 - T}\right)\right]\right\}$$

$$+ x_d \left\{ rf_{\text{debt}} + \beta_{\text{debt}}\left[E(r_m) - rf_{\text{debt}}\left(\dfrac{1 - t_c}{1 - T}\right)\right]\right\}(1 - t_c)$$

We can simplify this expression as follows:

$$\text{WACC} = rf_{\text{debt}}\left(\dfrac{1 - t_c}{1 - T}\right)(x_e + x_d(1 - T)) + \beta_{\text{assets}}\left[E(r_m) - rf_{\text{debt}}\left(\dfrac{1 - t_c}{1 - T}\right)\right]$$

$$= rf_{\text{debt}}\left(\dfrac{1 - t_c}{1 - T}\right)(1 - Tx_d) + \beta_{\text{assets}}\left[E(r_m) - rf_{\text{debt}}\left(\dfrac{1 - t_c}{1 - T}\right)\right] \quad (8.\text{A7})$$

where $\beta_{\text{assets}} = x_e\beta_{\text{equity}} + x_d\beta_{\text{debt}}(1 - t_c)$.

In a Miller equilibrium, when $T = 0$, the WACC becomes

$$\text{WACC} = rf_{\text{debt}}(1 - t_c) + \beta_{\text{assets}}[E(r_m) - rf_{\text{debt}}(1 - t_c)]$$

---

[18]Students familiar with the security market line (SML) of the traditional CAPM will note that our discussion shows that there are *two* SMLs, one for debt and one for equity securities. Both SMLs have the *same* market price of risk, and in both the asset's beta is measured with respect to the *equity* market index. However, the equity SML has a y-intercept of $rf_{\text{debt}}(1 - t_c)$, whereas the debt SML has an intercept of rf_{debt}.

Several points about the expression for the WACC in a Miller equilibrium deserve special mention:

- The WACC, which is the RADR for discounting Free Cash Flows, is the sum of the *after-corporate-tax* yield on *taxable* risk-free debt and a risk premium.
- The risk premium is the product of the asset beta (relative to the market portfolio of *equity* securities) and the market risk premium.
- The market risk premium is measured relative to the *after-corporate-tax* yield on *taxable* risk-free debt.

Last, but most importantly, when $T \approx 0$ (i.e., under a Miller-type equilibrium)

- *The WACC is independent of the capital structure of the firm!*

ESTIMATING DISCOUNT RATES

In this chapter we will implement the theoretical discussion of the preceding chapter by presenting practical methods to estimate the cost of capital. We will consider the estimation of both the cost of equity capital and the cost of total capital (i.e., capital provided by all security holders). In the notation of the preceding chapter we will discuss methods to estimate $r_e(L)$, $r(U)$, and the weighted average cost of capital (WACC). As you know by now, our preferred procedure is the following:

• Estimate the cost of capital for the firm as if it were unlevered, $r(U)$. As we explained in the previous chapter, we think it is likely that net asset taxation is such that $r(U)$ is close to the firm's WACC.
• Discount the projected free cash flows (FCF) to value the *firm as an unlevered entity,* which (using the notation of Chapter 8) is the estimated $V(U)$.
• Add in the value of any leverage effects to value the *firm as a levered entity,* $V(L)$. This is the adjusted present value (APV) method to take into account the effects of market imperfections—the net tax effects of debt financing.
• Derive the *equity* value by subtracting the value of more senior claims, such as debt, preferred stock, and warrants.

There are, of course, alternatives to this method. You can, for example, use the firm's equity cost of capital to estimate its equity value directly by discounting the equity holders' expected cash flows.[1]

---

[1]We think that our method, which we referred to in Chapter 3 as the "sequential" method of valuation, is simpler and theoretically sounder. After a few valuations our students usually agree with us. The direct valuation of equity cash flows is discussed in Chapter 13.

The role of leverage in estimating the cost of capital is very important. In Chapter 8 we examined how leverage affects the value of a firm and its cost of capital. We argued that the tax effect of leverage on the firm's WACC is, in most cases, small. In practice, the net effect of leverage depends on the combination of personal and corporate tax rates in the economy. By using the notation of Chapter 8, we argued that we can estimate the firm's cost of capital assuming that $T \approx 0$. If you think that a net tax benefit to debt financing exists, you can add an estimate of such net tax benefits to the unlevered value of the firm.

This two-step process, which is described in some detail in Chapter 8, is simple to implement, and as you will see in Chapters 11 and 12, can also accommodate nonstandard financing (e.g., with convertible securities or with floating-rate securities). As shown in Chapter 8, the value of leverage is the present value (PV) of the net tax shields on the firm's debt, discounted at the after-personal-tax debt interest rate:

$$\text{Value of leverage} = \sum_{t=1}^{N} \frac{[(1 - t_d) - (1 - t_c)(1 - t_e)] \text{ interest}_t}{(1 + (1 - t_d)r_d)^t}$$

There are two special cases of this formula that we discussed in Chapter 8:

- When the firm maintains a constant level of debt, the formula simplifies to

$$\text{Value of leverage} = T \cdot \text{Debt}, \qquad T = 1 - \frac{(1 - t_c)(1 - t_e)}{1 - t_d}$$

- When $T = 0$, the value of leverage $= 0$.

In this chapter we present three methods of estimating the cost of capital:

- In the first method we don't specify a relation between risk and return. Instead, the average of *past* realized returns of securities is taken to be representative of the *future* expected returns.
- In the second method we use current prices of traded securities (sometimes coupled with specific projections) to infer the required return on capital.
- In the third method we base the estimation of capital costs on a model of risk and return trade-off. We use the Capital Asset Pricing Model (CAPM), but other models, such as the Arbitrage Pricing Theory (APT), equally fit the approach: The model parameters are estimated and applied to the firm to estimate the firm's cost of capital.

In practice, all three methods are used. Since these methods involve some compromise entailed by such factors as data limitations and theoretical lacunas, we suggest that you employ more than one method to estimate the cost of capital. At the very least, the various methods will serve as "sanity" checks for the method with which you feel the most comfortable and the estimate that you trust the most.

Although these methods are different, here are some points that you should keep in mind when calculating discount rates:

1 *Calculate the firm's cost of capital and not the cost of equity.* The firm's cost of capital is the correct risk-adjusted discount rate (RADR) for FCFs. If you believe that the net tax effects of leverage are negligible, then $r(U) \approx$ WACC and you can estimate either $r(U)$ or the WACC.

2 *Be consistent in your treatment of inflation.* Most economists agree that the underlying process that moves the economy is the real process. This means that *real* cash flows and *real* discount rates should be estimated first, even if you are ultimately interested in nominal cash flows and discount rates.[2] In this chapter we will present two methods of calculating nominal discount rates:

   a The first method involves calculating the *real* discount rate first, and then "grossing up" this rate by the expected inflation rate to arrive at the estimated *nominal* discount rate.

   b The second method involves calculating the *risk premium* by subtracting the after-tax risk-free rate of interest from the nominal return. Adding this risk premium to the current nominal after-tax risk-free rate will give you the estimated nominal cost of capital.

3 *Use industry data to estimate the cost of capital for the firm that you value, not just the firm's own data.* This is because the cost of capital cannot be *calculated,* it can only be *estimated,* which means that the estimated cost of capital includes some estimation error. The use of data of comparable firms increases the accuracy of your estimate relative to estimating the cost of capital by using only the data for the firm that interests you the most. In this chapter the illustrations of the different estimation methods often use data about a single firm. In practice, as opposed to typical textbook illustrations, industry data of more than a single company should be used.

In our exposition of the three methods of estimating costs of capital we rely on materials that are covered in previous chapters. In particular, by now you should be comfortable with:

   • Inverting the Gordon formula to calculate the cost of capital implied by observed prices (Chapter 1)
   • Using the CAPM to calculate RADR by using estimated betas and risk premiums (Chapter 1)
   • Building pro-forma models and using them to predict FCFs (Chapters 4 through 7)

---

[2]A good example of this is our treatment of Smucker in Chapter 7: Even though our model ultimately projects nominal FCFs, the sales projections that underlie the model are in real terms. We go from real sales projections to nominal sales projections by superimposing an expected inflation rate on the real sales projections.

• Manipulating simple formulas relating leverage to discount rates (Chapter 8); in particular, you should be able to "unlever" the cost of equity in order to arrive at the discount rate for the firm's FCFs (Chapter 8).

Throughout the chapter we will focus on a particular example: We will try to estimate the cost of capital for Leggett & Platt, Inc. (LEG), a large manufacturer of furniture. Our method involves using data for both LEG and the rest of the firms in the industry.

9.1   USING HISTORIC RETURNS TO ESTIMATE THE COST OF CAPITAL

A Bit of Theory

One of the simplest ways to estimate the cost of capital is to average past returns and assume that investors expect to earn in the future the same returns they received, on average, in the past. Despite its almost counterintuitive simplicity, this method has a strong theoretical underpinning—the paradigm of "rational expectations." The rational expectations paradigm postulates that investors' expectations for returns that adequately compensate them for the risk they bear cannot be systematically off target. The intuition behind this theory is that investors cannot be systematically too optimistic or too pessimistic; rationality means that investors adjust their expectations when faced with repeated systematic errors. Therefore, although investors can (and do) make mistakes, *on average* they get the returns they expect to get. Under the rationality of expectations, it follows that the average of past returns is the return that investors are expected to receive: Sometimes the realized return is higher than expected and sometimes it is lower than expected, but the errors are not systematic.[3]

Applying the Concept

We use Leggett & Platt (LEG) and the other firms in the furniture industry to illustrate the application of historical returns:

• First we estimate the cost of equity for LEG.
• Next we estimate the WACC by calculating the average cost of debt (long- and short-term) and the weights of debt and equity in the capital structure of each of the firms.

[3]The statistically inclined reader will recognize that the "rationality" of expectations implies, among other things, that expectations are unbiased.

- Then we calculate the unlevered cost of equity, $r(U)$, by using the unlevering formula of Chapter 8 and compare it to the WACC for LEG.
- Finally, we compare our figures to the industry's averages.

Estimating the Return on Equity

The return of a stock over any period is given by

$$r = \frac{\Delta P_1 + \text{Div}_1}{P_0} = \frac{P_1 - P_0 + \text{Div}_1}{P_0} = \frac{P_1 + \text{Div}_1}{P_0} - 1 \qquad (9.1)$$

where $\Delta P_1 = P_1 - P_0 =$ price appreciation of the stock in the period
$\text{Div}_1 =$ dividend paid in the period
$P_0 =$ price of the stock at the beginning of the period—the initial investment

By using equation (9.1), we can decompose the total return on the stock into two components—capital gains yield and dividend yield:

$$r = \frac{\Delta P_1}{P_0} + \frac{\text{Div}_1}{P_0} \qquad (9.2)$$

Equation (9.1) is one case of a general formula to use in order to calculate the rates of return of securities: The rates of returns are the sum of the price appreciation of the security over the period and of the cash flows that the holders of the security received during the period divided by the initial value of the security. As another example, consider a firm that is financed by debt and equity. The rate of return on the *total* capital of the firm, debt *and* equity, is given by the ratio of the *total* price appreciation (i.e., of the equity and of the debt) plus the *total* periodic cash flows (i.e., dividends and interest) to the initial value of *total* capital:

$$r_{\text{firm}} = \frac{(E_1 - E_0) + \text{Dividends} + (D_1 - D_0) + \text{interest payments}}{E_0 + D_0}$$

where E_1 and D_1 are the equity and debt values at the end of the period and E_0 and D_0 are their respective values at the beginning of the period.

Exhibit 9.1 gives the price and dividend history of LEG's stock and computes the annual returns on LEG's stock. Note that in Exhibit 9.1 stock prices look odd. This is because the year-end LEG stock price was often in fractions of 64ths of a dollar. In subsequent tables we present the prices with two decimal places only.

Exhibit 9.1

LEGGETT & PLATT, INC.
Stock Prices, Dividends, and Nominal Stock Returns

Year	Year-end stock price	Dividend per share	Ex-post nominal return
1981	$3\frac{11}{16}$	0.20	
1982	$4\frac{17}{64}$	0.23	21.92%
1983	$6\frac{43}{64}$	0.25	62.27%
1984	$6\frac{19}{64}$	0.29	−1.27%
1985	$11\frac{5}{64}$	0.33	81.17%
1986	$12\frac{7}{8}$	0.40	19.83%
1987	11	0.56	−10.21%
1988	$11\frac{7}{8}$	0.64	13.77%
1989	15	0.74	32.55%
1990	$13\frac{3}{16}$	0.84	−6.48%
1991	$18\frac{15}{16}$	0.86	50.12%
1992	34	0.92	84.40%

Note: The *ex-post nominal return* is calculated from the year-end prices of the stock plus the dividend. Thus, for example,

$$r_{1982} = \frac{4\frac{17}{64} + 0.23}{3\frac{11}{16}} - 1 = 21.92\%$$

In subsequent tables, LEG's stock prices will be given in decimal form, rounded to two places.

Real Returns versus Nominal Returns?

In this and the next subsections we consider two important technical points. First, we have to take into account inflation in calculating the cost of capital. It is highly likely that you will ultimately project *nominal* cash flows and thus will want to use a *nominal discount rate*. But even if this is the case, you will still want to estimate average *real* returns separately from the expected inflation. The reason is that inflation rates vary over time. Let's assume that past *real* risks are the same as current *real* risks (which means that average past *real* expected returns equal current expected *real* returns). Then, in order to estimate a nominal (i.e., inflation-adjusted) discount rate for the firm, you should first estimate the firm's expected real return and then adjust this return for the *current* inflation rate by using the Fisher formula. The alternative, inferior, in our opinion, is to use historic nominal rates of return to predict a future nominal discount rate; this alternative mixes apples and oranges—past real rates of return and past inflation rates.

When we rely on historic returns, there are two ways of adjusting for inflation. The first way is to adjust each period's return by the inflation rate of the period in order to compute the *real* return of the period. The general relation is

$$1 + r_{\text{real}} = \frac{1 + r_{\text{nominal}}}{1 + \text{inflation}}$$

where the inflation rate can be measured by the change in the consumer price index (CPI). The adjustment is slightly more complicated when dividends are paid since dividends are typically paid *throughout* the year instead of at year-end. Exhibit 9.2 illustrates how to calculate annual real returns with a midyear inflation adjustment for dividends.

Exhibit 9.2

LEGGETT & PLATT, INC.
Ex-post Real Stock Returns

Year	Year-end stock price	Dividend per share	Ex-post nominal return	CPI	Ex-post real return
1981	3.69	0.20		90.9	
1982	4.27	0.23	21.92%	96.5	15.02%
1983	6.67	0.25	62.27%	99.6	57.31%
1984	6.30	0.29	−1.27%	103.9	−5.27%
1985	11.08	0.33	81.17%	107.6	75.03%
1986	12.88	0.40	19.83%	109.7	17.57%
1987	11.00	0.56	−10.21%	113.7	−13.30%
1988	11.88	0.64	13.77%	118.4	9.37%
1989	15.00	0.74	32.55%	124.1	26.60%
1990	13.19	0.84	−6.48%	130.7	−11.06%
1991	18.94	0.86	50.12%	136.3	44.09%

Note: Each year's ex-post nominal return was adjusted by that year's increase in the consumer price index (CPI). For example, for 1982 we have

$$1 + r_{\text{real}}^{1982} = \frac{4.27 + 0.23 \cdot \left[\dfrac{96.5/90.9 - 1}{2} + 1\right]}{3.69 \cdot \dfrac{96.5}{90.9}} = 1 + 15.02\%$$

This adjustment assumes that the firm's dividend was paid, on average, over the course of the year so that the dividend component is adjusted by *one-half the year's inflation rate*.

To convert the historic *real* returns into estimated current expected *nominal* returns, you should:

- First calculate the average historic real return.
- Adjust the estimated real rate for expected inflation:

$$(1 + \text{nominal discount rate})$$

$$= (1 + \text{real discount rate}) \cdot (1 + \text{expected inflation rate})$$

The second way of calculating nominal returns from average historical returns entails calculating the average *real risk premium* and adding the *current* nominal risk-free rate. This is done by:

• First, averaging the differences between the nominal rates of return and the nominal risk-free rates in each of the years of data to estimate the average *risk premium* earned on the asset in the past
  • Adding the *current* nominal rate to the average risk premium

The risk premium is defined as the difference between the expected nominal return and the after-tax risk-free rate:

Risk premium
    = expected nominal return − after-tax AAA corporate nominal rate

When using this method, we assume that the *risk premium* that investors expect to earn from the investment equals the risk premium that they expected to earn in the past. Since under the rationality of expectations the *average risk premium earned in the past* equals the *expected* risk premium, the expected return now is the sum of:

• The *historical average* risk premium
• The *current* risk-free rate (i.e., the current benchmark return)

Note that the same risk premium can be applied to estimate either the nominal or the real RADRs: Applying the average risk premium to the current *nominal* rate gives an estimate of the current *nominal* RADR, whereas applying the risk premium to the current *real* rate gives an estimate of the current *real* RADR.

Exhibit 9.3 presents these numbers for LEG's stock.

Exhibit 9.3

LEGGETT & PLATT, INC.
Calculating the Risk Premium on the Stock

Year	Ex-post nominal return	AAA bond yield	Marginal corporate tax rate	Stock risk premium
1982	21.92%	13.79%	51%	15.16%
1983	62.27%	12.04%	51%	56.37%
1984	−1.27%	12.71%	51%	−7.50%
1985	81.17%	11.37%	51%	75.60%
1986	19.83%	9.02%	51%	15.41%
1987	−10.21%	9.38%	40%	−15.84%
1988	13.77%	9.71%	40%	7.95%
1989	32.55%	9.26%	40%	26.99%
1990	−6.48%	9.32%	40%	−12.08%
1991	50.12%	8.77%	40%	44.86%

Note: The bond data are the average AAA corporate bond rate from *Moody's*; the corporate tax rates are the sum of the statutory federal corporate tax rate and a "guesstimate" of state and local corporate taxes.

Arithmetic Returns versus Geometric Returns?

Another point to consider is the way to calculate an average from the historical data. There are two ways to do this:

1 We can calculate the *arithmetic average* of the returns. If r_t is the return in year t, then the arithmetic average is defined as

$$\bar{r}_{\text{arithmetic}} = \frac{1}{10} \sum_{t=1982}^{1991} r_t$$

2 We can also calculate the *geometric average* of the returns:

$$\bar{r}_{\text{geometric}} = [(1 + r_{1982})(1 + r_{1983}) \cdots (1 + r_{1991})]^{1/10} - 1$$

When using historical data to predict future expected returns, we generally prefer the arithmetic average. This is because we are interested in the *expected annual* return and we view each year's actual return as a draw from the distribution of possible annual returns. The geometric average, although a good estimate of the *compound* rate of return, is a downward-biased estimate of the *average* annual return (i.e., of the *expected* annual return).[4] In the case of LEG we obtain the data presented in Exhibit 9.4.

Exhibit 9.4
LEGGETT & PLATT, INC.
Arithmetic versus Geometric Average Stock Returns[5]

Year	Nominal stock return	Real stock return	Stock risk premium
1981			
1982	21.92%	15.02%	15.16%
1983	62.27%	57.31%	56.37%
1984	−1.27%	−5.27%	−7.50%
1985	81.17%	75.03%	75.60%
1986	19.83%	17.57%	15.41%
1987	−10.21%	−13.30%	−15.84%
1988	13.77%	9.37%	7.95%
1989	32.55%	26.60%	26.99%
1990	−6.48%	−11.06%	−12.08%
1991	50.12%	44.09%	44.86%
Arithmetic average	26.37%	21.54%	20.69%
Geometric average	23.21%	18.43%	17.37%

[4]The bias is roughly one-half the variance of the return.
[5]We offer the geometric average only as an illustration. As explained earlier, we think that the correct average to use is the *arithmetic* average; it is the one that we will use in the remainder of this chapter.

Using the average historical returns, we can estimate current *expected* returns if we are willing to assume that past conditions and current conditions have not changed. Note that the different estimates of the cost of capital *require different assumptions about what has not changed*:

- Using average *nominal* returns implicitly assumes that past inflation and current inflation are the same. The use of average *real* returns is *not* predicated upon any property of inflation rates.
- Using average *total* returns assumes that the average historic risk-free rate is the same as the current risk-free rate. The use of the average *risk premium* is *not* predicated upon any property of risk-free rates.

Thus, to get the least restrictive estimate of the current nominal discount rate by using historical data:

- Average the historic risk premium;
- Add the current real risk-free rate to get the real RADR; or
- Add the current nominal risk-free rate to get the nominal RADR.

Using the numbers in the preceding exhibits, we obtain some initial estimates of LEG's cost of equity capital, as shown in Exhibit 9.5.

Exhibit 9.5

LEGGETT & PLATT, INC.
Some Initial Estimates of $r_e(L)$

Nominal $r_e(L)$ based on historic average	26.37%
Real $r_e(L)$ based on historic average	21.54%
Nominal $r_e(L)$ based on historic real stock premium, $t_c = 40\%$, and 1992 risk-free rate of 8.14 percent	$(1 - t_c) \cdot rf_{1992}$ + real risk premium = $(1 - 0.4) \cdot 8.14\%$ + 20.69% = 25.57%

Estimating the WACC

The numbers we have calculated in Exhibit 9.5 relate to LEG's stock returns. However, we know that these numbers *cannot* be used as the discount rate for the FCF since this discount rate requires that we estimate the WACC or, alternatively, unlever the cost of equity. Toward that end, we can calculate the average historical return on *total capital* by estimating the average realized return to all security holders, such as equity holders, debt holders, and preferred stockholders, over the sample period as we did for the equity holders. As in the estimation of the equity holders' returns, we can estimate average nominal or real returns and estimate either average total returns or average risk premiums. In fact, the assumption underlying the use of this method of estimating the cost of capital—that past risks and risk premiums equal current risks and current risk premiums—is more tenable for the firm as a whole than for its individual securities, since capital structures often don't remain stable over time. To illustrate this point, Exhibit 9.6 presents leverage figures for LEG for the period 1982–1991. LEG's leverage varied in this period from 21 to 48 percent of the firm's value. Thus, it is unreasonable to expect the risk of LEG's stock (and its equity RADR) to have been constant over this period.

Exhibit 9.6

LEGGETT & PLATT, INC.
Leverage History

No. of shares   17,649,272

Year	Stock price year-end	Equity value*	LT + ST debt*	Firm value*	Debt/assets
1982	4.27	75	34	109	30.92%
1983	6.67	118	54	172	31.52%
1984	6.30	111	67	178	37.65%
1985	11.08	196	51	247	20.82%
1986	12.88	227	88	316	27.98%
1987	11.00	194	84	278	30.10%
1988	11.88	210	107	316	33.76%
1989	15.00	265	148	412	35.78%
1990	13.19	233	213	446	47.76%
1991	18.94	334	179	514	34.93%

Note: This table involves a common compromise: We use the book value of debt (both long- and short-term) as a proxy for the market value of debt and the year-end value of LEG's shares to calculate the market value of its equity. (Stock prices and the number of shares have been adjusted for a 2-for-1 stock split in 1983 and 3-for-2 stock split in 1986.)
*In $ millions.

How do we apply this method of estimating expected returns to the *firm's* cost of capital? In principle we simply calculate the return on *all* the firm's securities. Often, however, this is easier said than done: Many of the firm's securities are not traded. It is difficult to compute the historic returns of nontraded securities. Fortunately, most of the nontraded securities that firms issue are securities of which the market value is close to their book value, such as bank loans and preferred stock. For such securities we can *approximate* the annual return by the ratio of the annual payments to their holders to the *book value* of the securities. For example, for the debt of the firm we estimate the rate of return by the ratio of annual interest expenses to the book value of debt (long-term and short-term);[6] for preferred stock we compute the ratio of the preferred dividend to the book value of the preferred stock. The returns of each of the securities in the capital structure of the firm are weighted by their weight in the capital structure in order to arrive at the return on the firm's *total* capital for that year. The calculation is repeated for each year (obviously with the securities' weights typically changing from one year to the

---

[6]In many financial statements interest income is lumped with interest expense. In these cases the estimated cost of debt is only the interest expense portion over the book value of the debt.

next) until we have a long enough sample to compute the firm's average WACC (see Exhibit 9.7).

Exhibit 9.7

LEGGETT & PLATT, INC.
Calculation of Ex-post Nominal WACC

Year	Equity value	Debt value	Ex-post nominal stock return	Interest expense	Marginal tax rate	After-tax interest rate	Ex-post nominal WACC
1982	75	34	21.92%	3.7	51%	5.38%	16.80%
1983	118	54	62.27%	4.6	51%	4.16%	43.95%
1984	111	67	−1.27%	5.5	51%	4.02%	0.72%
1985	196	51	81.17%	6.3	51%	6.01%	65.52%
1986	227	88	19.83%	6.4	51%	3.55%	15.28%
1987	194	84	−10.21%	6.5	40%	4.67%	−5.74%
1988	210	107	13.77%	7.4	40%	4.16%	10.53%
1989	265	148	32.55%	12.7	40%	5.17%	22.75%
1990	233	213	−6.48%	15.2	40%	4.29%	−1.34%
1991	334	179	50.12%	12.3	40%	4.11%	34.05%
					Average		20.25%

The average nominal return on LEG's *total* capital is 20.25 percent. As expected, this return is both lower and less volatile than the return on LEG's levered equity.

Having done this calculation, we still need to compensate for inflation. We do this in one of two ways: by either computing the real WACC or computing the risk premium.

Exhibit 9.8

LEGGETT & PLATT, INC.

Year	Ex-post nominal WACC	CPI	Ex-post real WACC	AAA bond yield	Marginal corporate tax rate	Ex-post business risk premium (WACC)
1981		90.9				
1982	16.80%	96.5	10.02%	13.79%	51%	10.05%
1983	43.95%	99.6	39.47%	12.04%	51%	38.05%
1984	0.72%	103.9	−3.45%	12.71%	51%	−5.51%
1985	65.52%	107.6	59.83%	11.37%	51%	59.95%
1986	15.28%	109.7	13.07%	9.02%	51%	10.86%
1987	−5.74%	113.7	−9.05%	9.38%	40%	−11.36%
1988	10.53%	118.4	6.14%	9.71%	40%	4.70%
1989	22.75%	124.1	17.11%	9.26%	40%	17.19%
1990	−1.34%	130.7	−6.32%	9.32%	40%	−6.93%
1991	34.05%	136.3	28.55%	8.77%	40%	28.79%
Average	20.25%		15.54%			14.58%

The fourth column in Exhibit 9.8 allows us to implement the first method. This column calculates the *real ex-post WACC* from the nominal WACC by taking into account actual inflation. Thus, for example, in 1982 we have

$$\text{WACC}_{1982}^{\text{real}} = \frac{1 + 16.80\%}{\dfrac{96.5}{90.9}} - 1 = 10.02\%$$

The average *real* WACC for LEG in the period is 15.54 percent. If we think that *expected* inflation for the *next* year is 4 percent, then we can use the *real* WACC and the *expected inflation* to calculate the nominal WACC:

$$\text{Nominal WACC} = (1 + \text{real WACC}) \cdot (1 + \text{expected inflation}) - 1$$

$$= 1.1554 \cdot 1.04 - 1 = 20.16\%$$

The last column of Exhibit 9.8 illustrates the second method of adjusting for inflation. Each row in this column calculates the *ex-post risk premium for the firm as a whole*. Thus, for example, in 1982

$$\text{Firm risk premium} = \text{nominal WACC} - (1 - t_c) \cdot \text{nominal risk-free}$$

$$10.05\% = 16.80\% - (1 - 51\%) \cdot 13.79\%$$

By adding the current risk-free rate (net of corporate taxes), we can estimate LEG's current WACC, a cost of capital that we use to discount projected LEG's FCFs. By using the historic risk premium of LEG's total capital and the *current* nominal risk-free rate, we find that the estimated nominal WACC for LEG in 1992 would be

$$\text{WACC}_{1992}^{\text{nominal}} = (1 - t_c) rf_{1992}^{\text{nominal}} + \text{LEG's risk premium}$$

$$= (1 - 0.4) \cdot 8.14\% + 14.58\% = 19.46\%$$

There is yet another way of calculating the WACC: As we saw in Chapter 8, when the net tax effects of leverage are approximately zero (i.e., $T \approx 0$), if the firm were unlevered, $r(U)$, the cost of capital of the firm is equal to the WACC:

$$r^{\text{nominal}}(U) = \text{WACC} = r_e^{\text{nominal}}(L) \cdot \frac{E}{D + E} + r_d^{\text{nominal}}(1 - t_c) \cdot \frac{D}{D + E}$$

For nonzero net tax effects of debt (i.e., when $T \neq 0$), we can unlever the cost of levered equity, $r_e(L)$, by using the formula given on page 240 of Chapter 8:[7]

---

[7]Remember the underlying assumptions of the formula—a flat term structure of interest rates, perpetual debt, no growth, and risk-free corporate debt.

$$r(U) = \frac{r_e(L) + r_d(1 - t_c)\dfrac{D}{E}}{1 + (1 - T)\dfrac{D}{E}}$$

Multiplying both numerator and denominator by E/V, this simplifies to:

$$r(U) = \frac{\text{WACC}}{1 - \dfrac{T \cdot D}{V}}$$

Suppose that $T = 10\%$, so that leverage affects the value of the firm. (As we argued in Chapter 8, given the differential between personal taxes on equity and debt income, $T = 10\%$ is a significant tax effect of debt.) By using the data from Exhibit 9.7 and the formula above, we obtain the data in Exhibit 9.9.

Exhibit 9.9

LEGGETT & PLATT, INC.
Unlevering $r_e(L)$

Year	Ex-post nominal $r_e(L)$	Debt/ asset ratio	After-tax interest rate	Ex-post nominal $r(U)$	CPI	Ex-post real $r(U)$
1981					90.9	
1982	21.92%	30.92%	5.38%	17.34%	96.5	10.53%
1983	62.27%	31.52%	4.16%	45.38%	99.6	40.86%
1984	−1.27%	37.65%	4.02%	0.75%	103.9	−3.42%
1985	81.17%	20.82%	6.01%	66.91%	107.6	61.18%
1986	19.83%	27.98%	3.55%	15.71%	109.7	13.50%
1987	−10.21%	30.10%	4.67%	−5.91%	113.7	−9.22%
1988	13.77%	33.76%	4.16%	10.89%	118.4	6.49%
1989	32.55%	35.78%	5.17%	23.60%	124.1	17.92%
1990	−6.48%	47.76%	4.29%	−1.40%	130.7	−6.38%
1991	50.12%	34.93%	4.11%	35.28%	136.3	29.72%
Average				20.86%		16.12%

As Exhibit 9.9 shows, even when debt confers considerable tax benefits, the $r(U)$ with which we discount the real FCFs is 16.12 percent, only slightly higher than the real WACC of 15.54 percent (for the case of $T = 0$) which we calculated in Exhibit 9.8.

Comparing LEG to Its Industry

Another issue that is relevant to this and the other methods of estimating the cost of capital is whether you should use a single company or the whole industry to estimate the cost of capital. If the company that we value is not publicly traded,

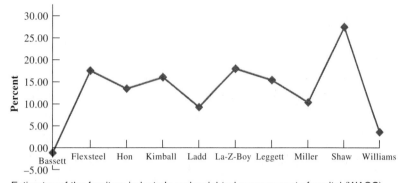

FIGURE 9.1   Estimates of the furniture industry's real weighted average cost of capital (WACC).

then we will have little choice: We will have to find a sample of comparable firms (i.e., firms in the same industry that appeal to the same clientele and use the same technology), estimate *their* cost of capital, and use the industry's average cost of capital as an estimate of the cost of capital for the nontraded firm that we value. On the other hand, if the company that we value is publicly traded, then we can either use the industry's average cost of capital or directly estimate the cost of capital (as illustrated earlier) for the firm that we value. *Generally speaking, even if the firm that we value is publicly traded, using more than one firm's data to estimate the cost of capital is preferable.* This is because each cost of capital estimate is only an *estimate* and as such it includes an *estimation error*. The overall estimation error can be made smaller by averaging several estimates, which is what we do when using industry data: The larger the sample of similar firms used in estimating the industry's cost of capital, the more likely the individual errors will cancel out each other. We can show how this works in the furniture industry by examining the *realized* real WACC's of firms in LEG's industry over the same period, 1982–1991.

As you can see in Figure 9.1, there are some extreme estimates of the industry's cost of capital (Bassett's *negative* realized WACC, Shaw's much higher WACC than the rest, and Williams's much lower WACC). But on the whole the estimated cost of capital for the industry's *assets* lie in a narrow range. This is indeed what we would expect from an industry: All firms in an industry should face similar demand risk, similar cost structure (i.e., fixed versus variable costs), similar raw material price risks, and so on. Accordingly, the *business* risk of all firms within an industry, as estimated, for example, by their beta of assets, should be similar and their cost of *total* capital, as estimated, for example, by the WACC, should be similar as well. This is precisely the logic underlying the use of *industry data* to estimate more accurately the cost of total capital of a typical firm in the industry.

A word of warning on the use of the industry's data to estimate costs of capital: In most industries the capital structure of the member firms of the industry are quite different. For example, in the sample of furniture producers that we use, Bassett uses no debt at all, whereas Shaw has 40 percent debt financing (measured in market values). This means that, even though the cost of *total* capital in an industry may well be similar, the cost of *equity* capital will typically be quite different. Thus it is important *before averaging across the industry* to unlever the cost of equity capital. In our previous example we first estimate each firm's WACC and then average across the industry. When using the CAPM, we first unlever each firm's equity beta (in a way detailed in Section 9.5 of the chapter) and average the *asset* betas across the industry.

One Final Issue: Selecting a Sample Period

The estimation of expected returns by using historical data raises the by now familiar issue of selecting a sample period. The same considerations that applied to selecting a sample period for computing representative financial ratios apply here as well: On the one hand, the longer the sample period is, the more reliable the average will be. On the other hand, the longer the sample period is, the less sure we are that conditions that prevailed in the past remain relevant for today's decisions. Clearly, each case should be decided separately depending on the circumstances of the firm being valued. For some firms stability over time is not an issue and a relatively long sample period is feasible. For other firms stability (or lack thereof) is a key issue and a short horizon is more representative of the current risk premium than a long-horizon risk premium.

9.2 USING MARKET PRICES TO ESTIMATE DISCOUNT RATES

The use of *historic* data that are manipulated and averaged in one way or another to estimate *current* discount rates is problematic whenever we suspect that *past* conditions differ from *current* conditions. In such cases we would like to use *current* information to estimate the currently relevant discount rates. In this section we will describe methods that allow us to use currently *observed prices* to *infer* the rates of returns that investors demand from assets.

Several aspects of the application of methods that we use to infer expected rates of return from observed prices are similar to the application of the historical average method. Therefore, we focus only on the features that are unique to this method. For the sake of completeness, however, here is a list of issues discussed in the preceding section that are relevant to this method as well:

- The method can be applied to both the estimation of the cost of equity and the estimation of the cost of total capital. The assumptions underlying the estimation of the cost of total capital (e.g., constant discount and growth rates in the application of the Gordon formula detailed below) are less restrictive and more tenable when applied to *total capital* than when applied to *equity* alone.
- When the firm is not publicly traded, estimate its cost of capital by the average cost of capital of similar firms, such as firms in the same industry that appeal to similar clienteles and employ similar technology.
- When the firm is publicly traded, while the cost of capital (equity or total) can be directly estimated by using the firm's data alone, a more reliable estimate is obtained by averaging the estimated costs of capital of similar firms.

Estimating the Required Rate of Return on Debt

Practitioners often use market prices to compute the expected returns of debt securities. The reason for the popularity of this method is its simplicity: Debt securities offer *fixed promised payments,* which makes the conversion of bond prices to bond returns a matter of solving an IRR equation.[8] To illustrate, consider a bond that matures in M years, promises to pay an annual coupon of C dollars, has a face value of F, and trades for P dollars. The **yield to maturity (YTM)** of this bond is the solution to the following equation:

$$P = \sum_{t=1}^{M} \frac{C}{(1 + \text{YTM})^t} + \frac{F}{(1 + \text{YTM})^M}$$

For low-risk debt the YTM is an acceptable substitute for the *before-tax cost of debt.* We warn you, however, that this statement is not generally true: As you will see in Chapter 11, when we discuss the use and interpretation of the YTM in the context of the valuation of debt securities, for risky debt the YTM of a bond is *not* the expected return of the bond. The YTM of a bond is the yield that the shareholders *promise* the debt holders; this promised yield, the YTM, will be the actual return *only if the shareholders don't default* on their debt service obligations. If default occurs, the debt holders will receive *less* than was promised to them. Therefore, bondholders' *expected* return is in general less than the bond's YTM. To convert YTMs to expected returns of bonds, we must consider the probability of default and what happens when the firm defaults. We postpone detailed examination of this issue until Chapter 11; in the meantime we can make the (not unrealistic) assumption that for many firms the YTM is close to the true cost of debt.

Using the Gordon Dividend Model to Calculate the Cost of Equity

The use of market prices to infer expected return is more challenging when we consider stocks or whole firms. The reason is that now the cash flows are not contractually specified. We present two ways of dealing with this—by using the Gordon model and the observed price earnings (P/E) ratios to estimate expected returns.

One of the simplest ways of calculating discount rates for stocks is to use the Gordon model. Recall that the Gordon formula assumes that the firm will pay out a stream of dividends that grow at an expected rate g. The formula further assumes that the term structure of the firm's RADR is flat (to infinity!). Under the assumptions of the Gordon formula (see Chapter 1) the cost of equity capital is given by

$$r_e(L) = \frac{\text{Div}_1}{P_0} + g = \frac{\text{Div}_0(1 + g)}{P_0} + g$$

[8]Since the equation typically cannot be solved analytically, it is often solved numerically.

where Div_1 is the firm's expected next period dividend, which under the assumptions of the Gordon model equals $Div_0(1 + g)$, and Div_0 is the firm's current dividend.

A key requisite in applying the Gordon formula to the estimation of costs of capital is a good estimate of the growth rate, g. This can be done by either considering historical average growth rates or by using current determinants of growth (and an additional assumption—that growth is financed by internally generated funds). We will illustrate the use of the Gordon formula by deriving the cost of equity for LEG. Before beginning, however, we must answer a few basic questions:

• *When relying on historical growth rates, should we use real dividends or nominal dividends as a basis for our calculations?* As indicated in Section 9.1, we do not recommend calculating the cost of equity by using the *nominal* growth rate. This is because the growth rates derived from the nominal numbers mix apples and oranges: They compound real changes in dividends with changes due to changes in the purchasing power of dollars. Since inflation rates change over time, *even when your eventual goal is to estimate the nominal RADR,* it is better to estimate the *real* historical growth rate and to add the *current* inflation expectations to the resulting estimated *real* RADR. (Remember, the use of a real dividend growth rate produces a *real* discount rate to be used with *real* cash flows—cash flows projected in terms of dollars of constant purchasing power. If your projections are of *nominal* cash flows, then you need the *nominal* growth rate to estimate the *nominal* discount rate. It is incorrect to discount *real* cash flows at a *nominal* discount rate or to discount a *nominal* cash flow at a *real* discount rate.)

• *Should we use geometric or arithmetic average growth rates?* This is another issue that we covered in Section 9.1. As we indicated there, the best extrapolation of annual growth rates from historic data is given by arithmetic average growth rates. Although the geometric average has an intuitive interpretation as the annually compounded growth rate, the arithmetic average is actually a better estimate of annual expected growth rates: Assuming that each year's growth rate is some realization from a *fixed* distribution of possible growth rates, the arithmetic average is an unbiased estimate of the average of the possible annual growth rates.

• *Should we use per-share dividends or total dividends to estimate growth rates?* Obviously, the question is relevant only when the number of shares has changed. When the change in the number of shares is due to stock splits or to stock dividends, we should restate all the numbers to an equal basis since such changes in the number of shares have no economic meaning. The answer is less obvious when the change in the number of shares is due to share repurchases or share issuances. In such cases, since we try to estimate *internally sustainable* growth rates, we should use per-share data: Using total firm data mixes internally generated growth with growth due to capital infusion.

• *What cash flow should we use to estimate growth rates for total firm capital?* The growth rate of dividends is the appropriate growth rate to use to estimate the cost of equity capital. It is inappropriate when we try to estimate the *assets'* cost of capital. To estimate the cost of the firm's *total* capital by using the market price of the whole firm, we should use the growth rate of all security holders' cash flows—the growth rate of the FCF: The FCF is the cash flow that can be distributed to *all* security holders of the firm, not just to shareholders.

• *What if we think that the current growth rate of the firm differs from its historic growth rate?* In such cases we have to find another way to estimate the current growth potential of the firm. One method that is often used to estimate current growth rates uses *the current rate of return that the firm earns on investments* and *the current rate of retention of profits.* Using this method, we obtain the following relations for equity and total firm growth rates:

$$g_{\text{equity}} = r_{\text{equity book value}} \cdot (1 - b_{\text{equity}})$$

$$g_{\text{FCF}} = r_{\text{asset book value}} \cdot (1 - b_{\text{FCF}})$$

where $r_{\text{equity book value}}$ = rate of return that the equity holders receive on their investments in the firm; it can be estimated as the net income over the book value of equity

$r_{\text{asset book value}}$ = rate of return that all the firm's security holders get on their investment; it can be estimated as the net income plus the after-tax interest over the book value of assets

b_{equity} = dividend payout ratio calculated as dividends over net earnings

b_{FCF} = FCF payout ratio calculated as an FCF over *after-tax* operating income, the net income plus the after-tax interest

The underlying assumption of these equations is that growth is generated by *retaining some of the profits and investing the retained profits* at rates of return that exceed the market's required return (i.e., by investing in positive NPV projects).

The Dividend History of Leggett & Platt

Exhibit 9.10 presents the dividend history of LEG.

Exhibit 9.10

LEGGETT & PLATT, INC.
Dividend History

Year	Dividend per share	Nominal dividend growth	CPI	Real dividend growth
1981	0.20		90.9	
1982	0.23	15.00%	96.5	8.33%
1983	0.25	8.70%	99.6	5.31%
1984	0.29	16.00%	103.9	11.20%
1985	0.33	13.79%	107.6	9.88%
1986	0.40	21.21%	109.7	18.89%
1987	0.56	40.00%	113.7	35.07%
1988	0.64	14.29%	118.4	9.75%
1989	0.74	15.63%	124.1	10.31%
1990	0.84	13.51%	130.7	7.78%
1991	0.86	2.38%	136.3	−1.83%
Mean growth		16.05%		11.47%

Note: As we repeatedly point out in this chapter, you should estimate *real returns* first and then use *current* inflation rates to estimate nominal expected returns. This says that the mean *nominal* growth is not a useful number. (This is the last time we will mention it.)

Let's assume that the mean real dividend growth of LEG is also the expected future real dividend growth rate. Based on LEG's dividend growth rate history, it follows that we predict the real annual future dividend growth rate of LEG to be 11.47 percent. Given that the current price of LEG's stock is $18.94, we can derive LEG's *real cost of equity by using the Gordon formula* as

$$r_e^{\text{real}}(L) = \frac{\text{Div}_{1991}(1 + g^{\text{real}})}{P_{1991}} + g^{\text{real}}$$

$$= \frac{0.86 \cdot \left[\left(\frac{136.3}{130.7} - 1\right)\bigg/ 2 + 1\right] \cdot 1.1147}{18.94} + 11.47\% = 16.64\%$$

(Note the adjustment that we have made for inflation in calculating Div_0—paid out, on average, in midyear—to convert it to *end-of-1991 dollars.*) We have written $r_e^{\text{real}}(L)$ to denote the fact that the real cost of equity calculated reflects the leverage of the firm. To calculate the corresponding *nominal cost of equity,* suppose we expect next year's inflation rate to be 4 percent. This gives

$$r_e^{\text{nominal}}(L) = [1 + r_e^{\text{real}}(L)] \cdot (1.04) - 1 = 21.3\%$$

Looking at the historical growth rates of dividends for LEG, we see that it is not clear what history is best representative of current conditions: LEG's dividend growth rate varies quite a bit and tapers off in the last few years so that the 10-year average of 11.5 percent is much higher than the average of the most recent 3 or 4 years—5.4 to 6.5 percent. One treatment of such cases is to use a *weighted average* of the historical growth rate, giving more weight to current growth rates than to "old" growth rates, instead of a simple average historic growth rate to predict future growth rates. An alternative approach is to *estimate the current growth rate from current returns on investments and from current reinvestment policies.* To provide some perspective on this issue, Exhibit 9.11 gives LEG's earnings per share (EPS) and dividend payment history.

Exhibit 9.11

Year	Dividends	EPS	Payout ratio, %
1981	0.20	1.05	19.05
1982	0.23	0.85	27.06
1983	0.25	1.26	19.84
1984	0.29	1.42	20.42
1985	0.33	1.76	18.75
1986	0.40	1.89	21.16
1987	0.56	2.22	25.23
1988	0.64	2.17	29.49
1989	0.74	2.58	28.68
1990	0.84	2.43	34.57
1991	0.86	2.18	39.45

As you can see in Exhibit 9.11, LEG's declining growth rate corresponds to larger dividend payout ratios or, equivalently, to lower retention ratios. This may reflect lower availability of attractive investment alternatives. By using LEG's most recent dividend payout ratio of roughly 40 percent and the most recent return on assets, we obtain a growth rate estimate that is lower than the historical average growth rate:

$$\text{Return on equity} = \frac{\text{EPS}}{\text{book value per share}} = \frac{\$2.18}{\$13.6} = 16\%$$

$$\text{Estimated } \textit{current} \text{ growth rate} = (1 - 40\%) \cdot 16\% = 9.6\%$$

The corresponding real cost of equity capital is 14.7 percent instead of the 16.6 percent obtained when we use the historical average growth rate to estimate the current growth rate.

Unlevering the Cost of Equity

The cost of equity calculated earlier is a *levered cost of equity.* We can use the current capital structure of LEG, 65 percent equity and 35 percent debt; the current cost of its debt, 8.77 percent before tax; and LEG's current corporate tax rate, 40 percent, to estimate the *nominal WACC:*

$$\text{WACC}^{\text{nominal}} = 21.3\% \cdot 0.65 + 8.77\% \cdot (1 - 0.4) \cdot 0.35 = 15.8\%$$

If the net tax benefit of debt is small, i.e., if $T \approx 0$, then this also corresponds to the firm's nominal $r(U)$.

Using P/E to Calculate the Cost of Equity

Using the Gordon model, we can also express the firm's cost of equity in terms of its *expected P/E ratio* and its *dividend payout ratio.* This is often a useful trick.

To see how to use the P/E in the Gordon model, recall that the Gordon formula states that the firm's cost of equity is given by

$$r_e(L) = \frac{\text{Div}_1}{P_0} + g$$

Now suppose we make the following assumptions:

• The firm pays out a *fixed proportion* of each period's earnings. We denote this proportion, the **payout ratio,** by b. Under this assumption the dividend at time t, denoted by Div_t, equals $b\text{EPS}_t$, where EPS_t denotes period t earnings per share.

• Earnings are expected to grow at a *fixed annual rate, g.* Since we are assuming a constant payout ratio, this means that dividends will also grow at rate g. With these two assumptions, we can rewrite the Gordon formula in terms of expected earnings instead of expected dividends.

$$r_e(L) = \frac{\text{Div}_1}{P_0} + g = \frac{b\text{EPS}_1}{P_0} + g$$

$$= \frac{b\text{EPS}_0(1 + g)}{P_0} + g$$

$$= \frac{b(1 + g)}{P_0/\text{EPS}_0} + g$$

Of course, P_0/EPS_0 is just the price/earnings ratio!

To use the preceding technique to calculate the cost of equity for LEG, we first calculate the payout ratio for the company over the past 10 years (see Exhibit 9.12).

Exhibit 9.12

LEGGETT & PLATT, INC.
Data for Calculating Cost of Equity from P/E Ratio

Year	Dividend per share	Real dividend growth	Earnings per share	Nominal earnings growth	CPI	Real earnings growth	Payout ratio
1981	0.20		1.05		90.9		19.05%
1982	0.23	8.33%	0.85	−19.05%	96.5	−23.75%	27.06%
1983	0.25	5.31%	1.26	48.24%	99.6	43.62%	19.84%
1984	0.29	11.20%	1.42	12.70%	103.9	8.03%	20.42%
1985	0.33	9.88%	1.76	23.94%	107.6	19.68%	18.75%
1986	0.40	18.89%	1.89	7.39%	109.7	5.33%	21.16%
1987	0.56	35.07%	2.22	17.46%	113.7	13.33%	25.23%
1988	0.64	9.75%	2.17	−2.25%	118.4	−6.13%	29.49%
1989	0.74	10.31%	2.58	18.89%	124.1	13.43%	28.68%
1990	0.84	7.78%	2.43	−5.81%	130.7	−10.57%	34.57%
1991	0.86	−1.83%	2.18	−10.29%	136.3	−13.97%	39.45%
Mean earnings growth						4.90%	
1991 ending share price			18.94				
1991 P/E ratio			8.69				

As we saw earlier, the dividend payout ratio of LEG has been steadily climbing throughout the decade. It is more reasonable, therefore, to use as a dividend payout ratio a number that is roughly representative of the end of the decade rather than some arithmetic average. Suppose we decide that the expected dividend payout of LEG is 40 percent. Then we can conclude from the P/E model that the real cost of equity for LEG is

$$r_e^{\text{real}}(L) = \frac{b(1 + g)}{P_0/EPS_0} + g = \frac{0.40(1 + 4.9\%)}{8.67} + 4.9\% = 9.74\%$$

Comparing the real cost of equity for LEG as calculated from the P/E ratio to that calculated directly from the dividend policy, we see that they are quite different. A comparison of the tables in Exhibits 9.11 and 9.12 shows why. Whereas LEG's real dividend growth during the last 10 years has slowed, the firm's real growth of earnings has slowed even further. (This is reflected in the increased dividend payout ratio of LEG over the period.)

Given all this hard won knowledge, we now must make some economic decisions: It is difficult to believe that the long-run dividend growth rate of LEG can be higher than the growth rate of its earnings. If shareholders recognize this, then we can conclude that the cost of equity as derived from the P/Es of the firm is more logical than that derived from the dividends.

Using the Gordon Model and the Market P/E Ratio to Estimate $E(r_m)$

The technique that we have just illustrated can also be used to estimate the *expected return on the market, $E(r_m)$*, which we can use with the CAPM to estimate costs of capital. Obviously, such estimates on the rate of return on the market, as in any other application of the Gordon formula, depend on the growth rate expectations used in the computation. Here is an example using Value Line estimates as of August 7, 1992:

Value Line Market Statistics, August 7, 1992

Median price/earnings (P/E) of all stocks with positive earnings	15.3
Estimated median dividend yield over next 12 months	2.8%
Five-year median appreciation potential	75%
Estimated payout ratio[9]	43%

We use these numbers to derive the *expected return on the market, $E(r_m)$*, which is used in the CAPM formula. We start by assuming that the 75 percent appreciation potential is to be equally realized over 5 years, which means that the *annual* expected growth rate is

$$(1 + g)^5 = 1 + 75\%$$

$$\implies g = (1 + 75\%)^{1/5} - 1 = 0.1184 = 11.84\%$$

By using this value for g and substituting in the formula we just derived, we obtain

$$E(r_m) = \frac{b \cdot (1 + g)}{P/E} + g = \frac{0.43 \cdot 1.1184}{15.3} + 0.1184 = 15.0\%$$

Thus, given the market's P/E ratio and its projected long-run growth rate, we estimate the market's expected return at 15.0 percent.

Note that since the projected market appreciation rate, g, is a *nominal* rate, the $E(r_m)$ that we have just calculated is a *nominal expected return on the market*. In

---

[9]Since the price/earnings ratio (*P/E*) is 15.3 and the dividend yield (*D/P*) is 2.8 percent, the implied payout ratio (*D/E*) is the product of the two: $D/E = 15.3 \cdot 2.8\% = 42.8\%$. This is consistent with the historic payout ratio of the market.

order to calculate the *real expected return,* we must know the *expected rate of inflation.* If we expect the rate of inflation for the coming years to be 4 percent, we may deflate our estimated nominal $E(r_m)$ by the expected inflation:

$$E(r_m^{\text{real}}) = \frac{1 + \text{nominal } E(r_m)}{1 + \text{expected inflation}} - 1 = \frac{1.15}{1.04} - 1 = 10.58\%$$

As explained in Chapter 8, the market risk premium is the difference between the expected return on the market and the *after-tax cost of high-grade corporate debt*:

$$\pi_m = E(r_m) - rf_{\text{debt}} \cdot (1 - t_c)$$

In August 1992 the AAA 5-year industrial bond nominal yield was 8.5 percent. Estimating the combined federal and state corporate tax rate as $t_c = 40\%$ gives the market risk premium as

$$\pi_m = E(r_m) - rf_{\text{debt}} \cdot (1 - t_c) = 15.0\% - 8.5\% \cdot (1 - 0.40) = 9.9\%$$

Comparing this premium to the historical long-run average risk premium of the market portfolio, roughly 8 percent, we see that this estimate is somewhat high.[10] We might suspect that the main reason that the estimated $E(r_m)$ is high is that Value Line's projection of the 5-year growth doesn't reflect the *sustainable long-term growth of the market.* In the long run it is hard to believe that the market will grow much faster than the economy, which means a long-term real growth rate of 2 to 3 percent. Adding to this long-run inflation rate of, say, 4 percent, we can expect that in the long run the market will grow at 6 to 7 percent. This is much lower than the Value Line's expectation of 11.8 percent market appreciation over the next 5 years. In the examples of the next section we use the long-run average market premium of 8 percent as our estimate of the market risk premium.

9.3   USING MODELS OF RISK/RETURN TRADE-OFF TO ESTIMATE THE COST OF CAPITAL

The methods of estimating the cost of capital described so far use market data, historical or current, to infer the market expectations about returns. Now we are ready to invoke *models* that *prescribe* both how to measure risk and how to compensate for this risk. The two primary models used in this task are the CAPM, which we described in Chapter 1, and the APT. We focus the discussion here on the application of the CAPM. This is the dominant model used in practice, and its

---

[10]See Roger G. Ibbotsen and Rex A. Sinquefield, *Stocks, Bonds, Bills, and Inflation: 1994 Yearbook,* Ibbotsen Associates, Chicago, Ill.

application is more understood than current applications of the APT. The way that the APT is applied, however, is very similar to the way that the CAPM is applied.

The main result of the CAPM model is that the risk-adjusted required rate of return for an asset is given by the **Security Market Line**:

$$\text{RADR}_{\text{security}} = rf_{\text{debt}} \cdot (1 - t_c) + \beta_{\text{security}} \, \pi_m$$

$$= rf_{\text{debt}} \cdot (1 - t_c) + \beta_{\text{security}}[E(r_m) - rf_{\text{debt}} \cdot (1 - t_c)]$$

where rf_{debt} = yield of taxable risk-free bonds

β (the **beta** of the security) = CAPM's measure of the asset risk

π_m = **the market risk premium** given by the difference between the market portfolio's expected return, $E(r_m)$, and the risk-free rate

Thus, to apply the CAPM formula to the estimation of the cost of capital of an asset, we need to estimate the beta of the asset and the market-risk premium (π_m).

The betas of traded stocks are routinely estimated by various services, such as Value Line, Merrill Lynch, and S&P. All of these services estimate the betas by regressing the returns of the stocks on a proxy for the returns of the market portfolio, usually the S&P 500 index. The sample period used in the estimations, the periodicity of the data—daily, weekly, or monthly returns—or the proxy for the market portfolio differ from one estimate to another. Accordingly, the estimated betas typically differ. (Afterall, these are only *estimates* and not the *true* betas, which we cannot observe.) Some services (e.g., Bloomberg) allow users to change these parameters and to estimate betas in any way that they choose. Unless the firm has gone through a major price change, however, various beta estimates are likely to be close to each other. Yet, since each individual estimate includes an estimation error, we repeat a point made early in the chapter: Use the industry's data to reduce the estimation error in your estimated beta and the corresponding cost of capital. We show how this is done below.

We illustrate the application of the CAPM formula by using it to estimate LEG's cost of capital. Value Line estimates the beta of LEG's stock as $\beta_{\text{LEG}} = 0.85$. Using this beta estimate and a market-risk premium (π_m) of 8 percent gives us

$$r_e^{\text{nominal}}(L) = 8.5\% \cdot (1 - 0.40) + 0.85 \cdot 8\% = 11.9\%$$

The rate of return on equity compensates the shareholders for both the *business risk* they are exposed to and the additional *financial risk* they bear when they lever their equity investment in the firm. To value the firm as a whole, however, we must estimate the cost of *total* capital—the cost of capital supplied by *all security holders*. This is because the value of the whole firm is estimated by discounting the FCFs that are cash flows that will be shared by all security holders, not just by the shareholders. To discount the FCF, we need an estimate of the beta of the *assets*. In the next section we will explain how the beta of the assets can be estimated.

9.4   UNLEVERING BETAS TO ESTIMATE THE FIRM'S COST OF CAPITAL

To discount FCFs, we need to estimate the cost of *total* capital. To base the estimated cost of total capital on the CAPM, we need an estimate of the beta of the assets. Unfortunately, the firm's total assets are not publicly traded, which means that we cannot estimate asset betas directly by regressing the returns of the assets on the market portfolio returns. Rather, asset betas are estimated indirectly. That is, we use the betas of the *securities* that the firm has issued—betas that *can* be estimated—to determine what the beta of the assets must be. In other words, we determine the beta of the *liabilities side* of the balance sheet (as the weighted average beta of the different securities) and equate it with the beta of the *asset side* of the balance sheet. Using the relative *market values* of the securities that the firm has issued, we weighted average the betas of the securities to estimate a leverage-free beta or an unlevered beta that reflects only the *business risk* of the firm. This is equivalent to unlevering the cost of these securities by weighted averaging their individual costs, which is effectively what we do when calculating the WACC.

To unlever the beta of the firm, we first observe that in the CAPM setting we can write the relation between the beta of the firm (i.e., the beta of the firm's assets, β_{assets}) and the betas of the individual securities in its capital structure as

$$\beta_{assets} = \frac{\text{market value of equity}}{\text{total firm value}} \cdot \beta_{equity}$$
$$+ \frac{\text{market value of debt}}{\text{total firm value}} \cdot \beta_{debt} \cdot (1 - t_c)$$

If there are additional securities, their beta estimates will also be added in proportion to their relative market value.

In practice, the preceding equation is often simplified by assuming that the beta of the fixed-income securities that the firm has issued, debt and preferred stock, is roughly zero. In this case the formula simplifies to

$$\beta_{assets} \approx \frac{\text{market value of equity}}{\text{total firm value}} \cdot \beta_{equity}$$

This relation allows us to estimate the *unobserved* beta of the assets from the *observed* beta of the stock and the *observed* leverage (measured by using market values!). Applying this to the furniture industry, we find the following pattern, as presented in Exhibit 9.13, for the equity and the asset betas.

Exhibit 9.13

FURNITURE INDUSTRY
Equity and Asset Betas

Company	Equity beta	No. of shares	Share price	Equity value	Debt value	Asset beta
				($ million)		
Bassett	0.80	11,535,893	19.47	225	0	0.80
Flexsteel	0.65	7,040,983	12.75	90	1	0.64
HON	0.75	32,208,685	19.25	620	42	0.70
Kimball	0.95	21,145,470	22.00	465	10	0.93
Ladd	1.10	18,984,452	7.50	142	138	0.56
La-Z-Boy	0.80	18,121,631	23.88	433	71	0.69
Leggett	0.85	17,659,272	18.94	334	179	0.55
Miller	0.85	25,164,759	17.63	444	76	0.73
Shaw	1.40	59,997,344	8.75	525	408	0.79
Williams	1.00	9,109,000	6.00	55	21	0.72
Average	0.92					0.71
Standard deviation	0.21					0.11

We observe in Exhibit 9.13 and in Figure 9.2 that the *equity* betas in the furniture industry are more widely dispersed than the *asset* betas in the industry. This makes sense; the asset betas reflect the industry's *business risk*, whereas the equity betas reflect the business risk augmented by the *financial risk*. The business risk of firms in the industry, while not identical, is similar and so are the asset betas. The leverage of firms in the furniture industry (as well as in other industries) can be quite different, which would lead to different equity betas. For example, while Shaw has the highest equity beta in the industry, 1.40, after unlevering Shaw's *asset* beta is similar to the industry's average (0.79 versus the industry's average of 0.71). This doesn't mean that all asset betas should be the same. First, even firms in the same industry may face different business risks that, for example, depend on their marketing policies. Second, we don't know what the *true* asset betas are; we only have *estimates* of these betas. And as any other estimate, estimated asset betas include an estimation error that is unique to each firm. The hope is that by averaging a few beta estimates, we can reduce the estimation error.

Note that we average the *unlevered* betas—the *asset* betas—not the *levered* betas—the *equity* betas. This is because, although we have reason to believe that the *business* risk in the furniture industry is similar for all competitors, we *know* that leverage in the industry is *not* similar. Thus, before averaging the betas to estimate the business risk of a typical firm in the furniture industry, we have to

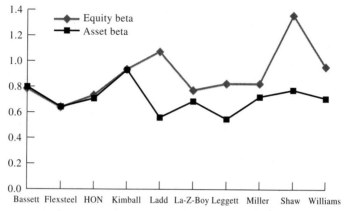

FIGURE 9.2 The graph shows the betas of the equities and of the assets in the furniture industry.

unlever the betas to offset the effect that leverage has on the equity betas. The estimated asset beta for a furniture producer, such as LEG, is the industry's average asset beta, 0.71. This means that the CAPM estimate for LEG's WACC is given by

$$\text{WACC} = rf_{\text{debt}} \cdot (1 - t_c) + \beta_{\text{assets}} \cdot \pi_m$$
$$= 8.5\% \cdot (1 - 0.40) + 0.71 \cdot 8\% = 10.78\%$$

This is considerably lower than the cost of capital calculated from the historical data.

A very important point should be made regarding the WACC equation and the equation for unlevering of the equity beta. Both equations are often taken to mean that the cost of the components of the capital structure such as equity, debt, and preferred stock *determine* the firm's cost of capital. This statement confuses the *economic* cause-and-effect relation with *statistical estimation procedures*. The true economic cause-and-effect relations are that the business risk of the firm (and so the return on its assets) determine the risk (and, accordingly, the returns) of the securities that the shareholders choose to have in the capital structure. The unlevering equations of the WACC and of the betas merely allow us to use the observed characteristics of the securities to *infer* the risk and return of the assets. The inference equations don't, however, change the causal relations: Business risk (and capital structure) determines the risk of the securities and not vice versa.

9.5 SO WHAT IS LEGGETT & PLATT'S COST OF CAPITAL?

In this chapter we have shown you several ways of estimating the cost of capital for LEG. The underlying assumptions of the various methods of estimating the cost of capital are different. Accordingly, the result is a variety of estimated costs of capital.

If the WACC is roughly independent of the firm's capital structure (i.e., if $T \approx 0$), then in principle we should have found that the WACC $\approx r(U)$, and that all the estimates for the WACC are similar. As you can see, it is difficult to claim that all these estimates of the cost of capital are consistent! The biggest inconsistencies seem to be between numbers based on *historic estimates* and those based on *current estimates of future parameters*. The latter category includes both the P/E model (remember how we speculated about LEG's ability to continue its high historic growth rate?) and the CAPM. Such a pattern is typical of situations where past performance is not indicative of future performance, when past performance is not expected to continue into the future. In these cases the *current* estimates are more indicative of the firm's risk and expected return. What do we recommend? If we had to make a choice, we would go for the market-based estimates: LEG's WACC is somewhere between 10 and 12 percent.

SUMMARY

In this chapter we have discussed three methods of estimating the cost of capital:

• *Using historic returns to estimate the cost of capital.* This method estimates discount rates to be used for future expected cash flows from past returns on the firm's assets.

• *Using market prices to estimate the discount rate.* We can estimate the required rate of return on bonds by calculating the yield to maturity from the bond's current market price and its promised future payments. In certain cases this YTM can serve as a proxy for the risk-adjusted rate of return on debt (we have postponed issues dealing with risky debt to Chapter 11).

When applied to shares, these methods are primarily based on versions of the Gordon dividend formula. We showed how this formula can be applied to calculate the cost of equity from the firm's dividend history; we also showed how the Gordon dividend formula can be applied to the firm's P/E ratio to estimate the cost of equity capital. It can even be applied to calculate $E(r_m)$, the expected rate of return on the market.

• *Using the CAPM to calculate the cost of capital.* By using this model, we can calculate the required rate of return for any asset based on the beta of the asset and the required rate of return on the market.

The various costs of capital for the furniture industry that we have presented in this chapter are close enough together for comfort. This coincidence of cost of capital estimates for different methods of calculation often doesn't hold. A careful perusal of our analysis shows some of the possible pitfalls:

• *Estimates of growth rates are critical.* If we were to cut our estimates of real growth, the cost of capital using the Gordon formula would fall. The cost of capital estimated by using other methods, such as the CAPM, would remain the same.

• *Historical data may be a poor proxy for expected future returns.* This is another version of the point made above. This means that besides using several methods to check your estimates, you should preferably rely on the most recent parameters in estimating costs of capital.

• *The risk and cost of equity capital typically varies,* both across an industry and over time. This often reflects changes in capital structures—again, both across an industry and over time. It is, therefore, safer and more accurate to estimate the more stable risks and costs—the risks and costs of total capital.

EXERCISES

9.1 Consider a firm that pays dividends regularly on December 31 of each year. The dividend history of this firm and the year-end consumer price index is:

Year	Dividend	CPI
1988	0.36	130
1989	0.42	132
1990	0.50	136
1991	0.55	140
1992	0.65	145
1993	0.73	149
1994	0.82	150

a What are the average nominal and real growth rates of the firm's dividends?

b If on December 31, 1994, the price of the firm's stock was $50 and the assumptions underlying the Gordon formula were valid, what would you estimate the real and nominal costs of equity to be if you believe that the expected inflation rate is 3 percent?

c If on December 31, 1994, the P/E ratio of the firm's stock was 20 and the assumptions underlying the Gordon formula were valid, what would you estimate the real and nominal costs of equity to be?

9.2 The LBO Corp. is financed with equity and debt only. LBO has 1 million traded shares, each priced at $6. You estimate the cost of LBO's equity capital to be 16 percent. LBO has also issued 30-year bonds with an aggregate face value of $1 million. The bonds trade for $1,300 per $1,000 face value and at a yield of 4.5 percent. Finally, LBO has borrowed $2,000,000 from banks at a floating rate that equals the yield on LBO traded bonds. LBO is very profitable. Consequently, LBO pays taxes at the (average and marginal) rate of 40 percent.

a Assuming that the term structure of interest rates is flat, what would be the weighted average cost of capital (WACC) of LBO?

b If the term structure of interest rates is not flat, can we tell what is the WACC of LBO? Why?

9.3 Consider the following data for XYZ International:

Year	Stock price year-end	Dividend per share	Consumer price index (CPI)	Value of debt ($ million)	Debt interest, %
1981	6.15	0.19	90.9		
1982	7.33	0.20	96.5	11.8	14.0
1983	8.45	0.24	99.6	13.2	11.0
1984	9.35	0.32	103.9	11.2	10.0
1985	11.00	0.35	107.6	24.5	8.0
1986	15.60	0.39	109.7	23.3	7.2
1987	18.35	0.40	113.7	76.2	6.9
1988	16.25	0.46	118.4	70.6	8.2
1989	20.10	0.54	124.1	69.1	8.0
1990	19.25	0.56	130.7	62.2	9.0
1991	22.35	0.59	136.3	55.0	12.0

Make the following assumptions: The historic returns are representative of future expected returns; XYZ pays dividends at year-end only; the end-of-year stock price is the *ex-dividend* stock price; XYZ has 5 million shares outstanding; and XYZ's corporate tax rate is 40 percent.

Calculate the following:

a XYZ's average real equity return.

b XYZ's nominal and real WACC, based on historic returns.

c XYZ's nominal WACC, assuming that the future expected inflation is 6 percent.

9.4 Consider the following information about ABC Corp.: The equity beta of ABC is 1.3, and the debt beta of ABC is 0.2; ABC's financing mix is 60 percent equity and 40 percent debt; the market risk-free interest rate, before taxes, is $rf_{debt} = 8\%$, and the expected return on the market portfolio is $E(r_m) = 15\%$; and the Miller equilibrium holds: $T = 0$. The corporate tax rate is $t_c = 35\%$.

Answer the following questions:

a What is ABC Corporation's WACC?

b What is the β_{assets} of ABC?

CHAPTER 10

VALUATION BY MULTIPLES

OVERVIEW

Although the bias of this book is very strongly tilted toward the use of discounted cash-flow (DCF) methods, it is impossible to ignore the fact that many analysts use other methods to value firms. The primary alternative valuation method is the use of multiples, in particular the Price/Earnings (P/E) ratio.

Valuation by multiples is quick and convenient. The simplicity and convenience of valuation by multiples constitute both the appeal of this valuation method and the problematics associated with its use: Simplicity means that too many facts are swept under the carpet and too many questions remain unasked. Multiples should never be your only valuation method and preferably not even your primary focus. When you have more than 5 minutes to value a firm, the DCF method, which *forces* you to consider the many aspects of an ongoing concern, is the preferred valuation method and the use of multiples should be secondary.

Having said this, multiple analysis can provide a valuable "sanity check." If we have done a thorough valuation, we can compare our predicted multiples, such as P/E and market to book (M/B), to representative multiples of similar firms. If our predicted multiples are comparable, we can, perhaps, feel more assured of the validity of our analysis. On the other hand, if our predicted multiples are out of line with the representative multiples of the market, then we have some explaining to do—first to ourselves, to convince us that our model is reasonable, and then to our clients and readers.

In valuation with multiples, we don't attempt to explain observed prices of firms. Instead, we use the *appropriately scaled average price of similar firms* to estimate values without specifying why prices are what they are. Hence, the trick in valuing with multiples is *selecting truly comparable firms* and *choosing the right scaling bases*—the right multiples.

We begin the discussion of valuation by multiples with a description of the method and some general principles and considerations in its application. We then focus on the P/E ratio. P/Es are the most useful and widely used of all valuation multiples. Nevertheless, the P/E ratio is often interpreted misleadingly and applied in a way which leads to ambiguous results. We will try to clear up some of these problems. We conclude the chapter with a discussion of other frequently used multiples.

10.1 PRINCIPLES OF VALUATION WITH MULTIPLES

To use the word ''multiples'' is to use a fancy name for market prices divided (or ''scaled'') by some measure of performance. In a typical valuation with multiples the average multiple—the average price scaled by some measure of performance—is applied to a performance measure of the firm that we value. For example, suppose we choose earnings as our scaling measure; that is, we choose earnings to be the performance measure by which prices of similar firms will be scaled. To scale the observed prices of firms by their earnings, we compute for each firm the ratio of its price to its earnings—its **P/E ratio** or its **earnings multiple.** We then average the individual P/E ratios to estimate a ''representative'' P/E ratio, or a representative earnings multiple. To value a firm, we multiply the projected profits of the firm that we value by the representative earnings multiple, the average P/E.

When we value with multiples, we are being agnostic about what determines prices. This means that we have no theory to guide us on how best to scale observed market prices: by Net Earnings, Earnings Before Interest and Taxes (EBIT), Sales, or Book Values. In practice, this means that valuation with multiples requires the use of *several scaling factors* or, in other words, several multiples. Often the best multiples for one industry may not be the preferred multiples in another industry. This implies, for example, that the practice of comparing P/E ratios of firms in different industries is problematic (and in many cases inappropriate altogether!). This further implies that when you do a multiple-based valuation, it is important first to find what the *industry* considers as the best measure of relative values: The square footage of the selling area may work with retail stores and the number of potential subscribers in the area may work for cellular telephone firms. These are often the best measures of relative values.

Although valuation by multiples differs from valuation by discounting cash flows, its application entails a similar procedure—first projecting performance, and then converting projected performance to values using market prices. This is done as follows:

• Project performance for the firm that you value, for example, by using pro-forma financial statements.

• Compute the average price per performance-measure dollar (i.e., the average multiple) by dividing observed prices of similar firms by the same performance measures you projected.

• Convert the projected performance to values by multiplying each projected performance measure by the relevant average multiple.

The detailed steps are described in the next subsection.

The Procedure of Valuation with Multiples

Valuation by multiples involves the following steps:

1 *Choose comparable firms.* Since we scale prices of *other* firms to value the firm being analyzed, we would like to use data of firms that are *as similar as possible to the firm that we value.* The flip side of this argument, however, is that by specifying too stringent criteria for similarity, we end up with too few firms to which we can compare. With a small sample of comparable firms, the idiosyncrasies of individual firms affect the average multiples too much so that the average multiple is no longer a representative multiple. In selecting the sample of comparable firms, you have to balance these two conflicting considerations. The idea is to obtain as large a sample as possible so that the idiosyncrasies of a single firm don't affect the valuation by much, yet not to choose so large a sample that the ''comparable firms'' are not comparable to the one that you value. (Some commonly used selection criteria are discussed in the following subsection.)

2 *Choose bases for multiples.* To convert market prices of comparable firms to a value for the firm being analyzed, you have to scale the valued firm relative to the comparable firms. This is typically done by using *several* bases of comparison. Some generic measures of relative size often used in multiple valuation are Sales, Gross Profits, Earnings, and Book Values. Often, however, industry-specific multiples are more suitable than generic multiples. Examples of industry-specific multiples are price per restaurant for fast-food chains and paid miles flown for airlines. In general, the higher-up that the scaling basis is in the income statement, the less it is subject to the vagaries of accounting principles. Thus, Sales is a scaling basis that is much less dependent on accounting methods than Earnings Per Share (EPS). Depreciation or treatment of convertible securities critically affect EPS calculations but hardly affect Sales. On the other hand, the higher-up that the scaling basis is in the income statement, the less it reflects differences in operating efficiency across firms—differences that critically affect the values of the comparable firms as well as the value of the firm being analyzed.

3 *Average across industry.* Once you have a sample of firms that you consider to be similar to the firm you value, you can average the prices that investors are willing to pay for *comparable* firms in order to obtain a price for your firm.

For example, after dividing each firm's share price by its EPS to get individual P/E ratios, you can average the P/E ratios of all comparable firms to estimate the earnings multiple that investors think is fair for firms with these characteristics. You do the same thing for *all* the scaling bases that you have chosen, calculating a "fair price" per dollar of Sales, per restaurant, per dollar of Book Value of Equity, and so on.

Note that we put "fair price" in quotation marks: Since there is no market for either EPS or Sales or any other scaling measure, the computation of average multiples is merely a scaling exercise and not an exercise in finding "how much the market is willing to pay for a dollar of earnings." Investors don't want to buy earnings; they only want cash flows (in the form of either dividends or capital gains). Earnings (or Sales) are paid for only to the extent that they generate cash. In computing average ratios for various bases, we implicitly assume that *the ability of firms to convert each basis (e.g., Sales, Book Value, and Earnings) to cash is the same.* Keep in mind that this assumption is more tenable in some cases than in others and for some scaling factors than for others.

4 *Project bases for the valued firm.* The average "prices per . . ." of comparable firms are applied to the projected performance of the firm being valued. Thus, we need to project the *same measures of the relative size* used in scaling the prices of the comparable firms for the firm being valued. For example:
   a To value a firm, we use Earnings as a scaling basis to determine the average earnings multiple (i.e., the average P/E ratio). Thus, we need to project the earnings of the firm being valued.
   b To use the average "price per restaurant" to value a fast-food chain, we need to project the number of restaurants the chain will have.
   c To use the average "price per dollar of book value" (the **market to book (M/B)** ratio), we need to project the Book Value of Equity.

The simplest application of valuation with multiples is by projecting the scaling bases 1 year forward and applying the average multiple of comparable firms to these projections. For example, we apply the comparable firms' average P/E ratio to the projected next year's earnings of the firm being valued. Clearly, by applying the average multiple to the next year's projections, we overemphasize the *immediate* prospects of the firm and *give no weight to more distant prospects.* To overcome this weakness of the one-step-ahead projections, we can use a more sophisticated approach, that is, apply the average multiples to "representative" projections—projections that better represent the long-term prospects of the firm. For example, instead of applying the average P/E ratio to *next year's* earnings, we can apply the comparable P/E ratio to the projected average EPS over the *next 5 years.* In this way the representative earnings' projections can also capture some of the long-term prospects of the firm, while next year's figures (with their idiosyncrasies) don't dominate valuations.

5 *Value the firm.* This is the final step—combining the average multiples of comparable firms to the projected parameters of the valued firm in order to obtain an estimated value. On the face of it, this is merely a simple technical step. Yet often it is not. The values that we obtain from various multiples (i.e., by using several scaling bases) are typically not the same; in fact, frequently they are quite different. This means that this step requires some analysis of its own— explaining why valuation by the average P/E ratio yields a lower value than the valuation by the Sales multiple (e.g., the valued firm has higher than normal Selling, General, and Administrative (SG&A) expenses) or why the M/B ratio yields a relatively low value.[1] The combination of several values into a final estimate of value, therefore, requires an economic analysis of both "appropriate" multiples and how multiple-based values should be adjusted to yield values that are economically reasonable. We consider these questions throughout the remainder of this chapter.

Selecting Comparable Firms to Estimate Average Multiples

Valuation with multiples doesn't begin with first principles. Rather, market prices of comparable firms are averaged under the assumption that they appropriately reflect all relevant determinants of value. Technically, we infer the value of the firm being analyzed by simply scaling the observed prices of similar firms to the size of the firm being valued. Thus, a crucial element in valuation with multiples is the exact definition of "similar" or, in other words, the criteria used in selecting a sample of comparable firms.

Selection criteria for comparable firms should give us tight enough restrictions so that firms whose market prices are averaged are indeed not too different from the firm being valued. On the other hand, since each firm has its own idiosyncrasies (which we don't want to take into account when valuing the firm analyzed), we need to obtain a large enough sample of comparable firms so that these idiosyncrasies are averaged out.

As an overall rule, we exclude "abnormal" firms—firms that experience unusual events such as business combinations or other major strategic alliances. There are two reasons for excluding such firms. First, the historic performance (measured by Sales, EPS, or any other potential scaling basis) of firms undergoing a strategic change is not indicative of future performance. However, the market prices of these firms reflect future performance, not historic performance. Second, firms in the midst of a strategic change are likely to undergo additional changes. Even if their current operations are comparable to those of the firm that we value, their future operations may be quite different. Thus, it is good practice to exclude such

---

[1]Here is a possible explanation. The firm being valued has issued equity long before the comparable firms have issued equity. Because accounting is in terms of historical costs, the valued firm's equity book value reflects "older" dollars than the book value of the comparable firms.

firms from the sample of comparable firms in order not to bias the computation of average multiples.

The following criteria are most often used for the selection of comparable firms:

• *Industry classification.* Include firms that produce or trade the same goods or services that the valued firm does. Preferably, although most often difficult to do, include only those firms with the same product characteristics. For example, although both weekly magazines and daily newspapers can be classified into a single "newspaper" industry, if it is possible to get separate multiples for weekly and daily publications, you would get more accurate valuation by separately averaging multiples than by pooling both industry segments together.

• *Technology.* When there are several possible ways of producing the same good or providing the same service, try to include only those firms that employ the same technology as the firm being valued. For example, although both railroad companies and trucking companies provide transportation services, it is difficult to compare the multiples of railroads to those of truckers because of differences in the cost structure.

• *Clientele.* Firms in the same industries may appeal to different clienteles. Clientele differences may be part of a deliberate strategic choice (e.g., the merchandise selection of a retailer depends on its positioning in the market), a matter of location (e.g., the location of a public utility), or any other physical constraint. Since different clienteles imply differences in product quality, markups, and so on, it is important to try to match clienteles in selecting comparable firms. For example, when you value public utilities, it makes sense to distinguish by geographical location since the price paid for a northeastern utility may be quite different (after scaling) from the price paid for a midwest utility.

• *Size.* Since there may be returns to scale in the production or in the marketing of the firm's product, it makes sense to try to select from the sample of comparable firms only those that sell about the same number of units. For example, when you value a hotel chain, it makes more sense to compare the Hilton to the Marriott, each of which has about 100,000 rooms, than to compare either company to La Quinta, which has fewer than 20,000 rooms.

• *Leverage.* In many valuations with multiples only the market price of the equity is included in the computation of average multiples. Yet leverage affects the risk of shareholders, and consequently the relation between market prices and the performance measure that is used for scaling these prices. For example, all other things being equal, the P/E ratio of a firm with high leverage should be lower (because its equity is riskier) than the P/E ratio of an otherwise similar firm with low leverage. Thus (unless you deal with leverage differences using whole-firm multiples, as described in the next subsection), match the leverage of the comparable firms to the leverage of the firm being valued.

Finally, keep in mind that there is no such thing as "a firm that is identical to the one that you value." Although the preceding selection criteria all make perfect sense, in practice you have to compromise or you will end up with no firm to which you can compare the firm of interest.

Valuation of Whole Firms versus Valuation of Shareholders' Equity

The most frequently used valuation multiple by far is the P/E ratio. In applying this ratio, we usually consider the EPS of comparable firms and the projected EPS of the firm being valued. It is possible that the leverage of the comparable firms and the leverage of the valued firm are quite different. Since leverage differences entail differences in the risk of the return to the shareholders, such leverage differences imply commensurate differences in multiples. We have suggested one way of dealing with leverage differences—selecting comparable firms with leverage similar to the leverage of the firm being valued. An alternative solution is to compute multiples for *whole firms* and, accordingly, to value the firm as a whole. The latter approach can also accommodate differential use of convertible securities, such as executive stock options or convertible bonds: Whenever convertible securities exist, their value is simply included in the total firm value. (To split the total value of the firm between the convertible and nonconvertible securities, we can use the Black and Scholes (B&S) or similar formulas. We discuss these issues in Chapter 12.)

Valuation of whole firms involves the same steps as the valuation of equities. The only difference is that both the values for the other firms and the bases for scaling these values are for the firm as a whole rather than for the shareholders' portion. For example, instead of using the P/E ratio, which is the ratio of the price of the *stock* and the earnings *per share,* we can compute the ratio of the *Total* Firm Value to *Operating Income*:

Total Value to Operating Income

$$= \frac{\text{value of Equity } + \text{ value of Debt } + \text{ value of all other Long-Term Securities}}{\text{Operating Income}}$$

In this multiple we scale the market value of *all* long-term securities by the *total* pre-tax income generated by *total* funds provided by *all* these securities. Similar multiples can be calculated by using Sales, FCF, or Total Assets as the scaling factors.

In estimating a total value multiple, we can easily find the market value of the firm's equity since it is mostly publicly traded. The market value of other long-term securities, such as debt, preferred stock, or convertible securities, however, may be harder to obtain if they are not traded. When we lack prices of fixed income securities, such as debt and preferred stock, it is common to calculate multiples using their book values, on the assumption (often correct) that for these securities book and market values are close. The problem is more severe when nontraded convertible securities exist. Here alternative proxies for nonexistent market values (based, for example, on the B&S formula and observed stock prices) can be used.

Beyond the effect that leverage may have on total firm value, total firm multiples are independent of the particular financing mix that the firm's management has chosen. Thus, using total firm multiples means that we don't have to be concerned about leverage differences among the comparable firms, or between the individual comparable firms and the firm being valued.

Total firm multiples allow us to value the firm as a whole. Often, however, we are interested only in the value of the equity of the firm. To get the equity value, we need to do an additional simple calculation—deducting the value of its debt obligations, the value of its preferred stock, or the value of its convertible securities from the total value of the firm. This is very similar to the procedure that we follow in estimating a value for the whole firm by discounting its Free Cash Flows (FCF) at a risk-adjusted weighted average cost of capital (WACC); only in the second stage do we divide this value among all its security holders.

10.2   EARNINGS MULTIPLES

The P/E ratio is one of the most widely used methods of valuation. Its simplicity—valuing a stock by multiplying its EPS by the industry's average earnings multiple—has made it an attractive method of valuing a company. This method of valuation has many obvious problems, however, which we discuss now.

There are two primary methods by which earnings multiples are calculated in practice: Either prices are normalized by *last year's* earnings or prices are normalizing by *next year's expected earnings.* The former are called **trailing earnings multiples** and the latter are called **leading earnings multiples.** Using "0" to denote last year's figures, "1" to denote this year's expected earnings, and P_0 to denote the current price of a stock, we express the formulas for these multiples as

$$\text{Trailing earnings multiple} = \text{AVG}\left[\frac{P_0}{E_0}\right]$$

$$\text{Leading earnings multiple} = \text{AVG}\left[\frac{P_0}{E_1}\right]$$

where the average is taken over all comparable firms. When earnings multiples are mentioned, the usual reference is to trailing multiples. However, since modern valuation techniques are applied to *future expected earnings,* leading multiples are more appropriate for valuation purposes.

The difficulty with leading earnings multiples is that to compute the average multiple, we need estimates of *all comparable firms' expected next year's earnings.* For an analyst following an industry this is no major problem: He or she routinely projects earnings for all the firms in the industry that they follow. Others who want to use leading earnings multiples but don't follow the whole industry can rely on commercially available services to obtain average analyst earnings projections for the comparable firms.

When using leading earnings multiples, you will find that the valuation of a firm based on the earnings you *project for next year* (e.g., the earnings' projections in the pro-forma statements of next year) is straightforward:

Estimated value = average [leading earnings multiples]

· projected earnings of the firm

$$= \text{AVG} \left[\frac{P_0}{E_1} \right] \cdot E_1^{\text{firm}}$$

Since both the earnings used to scale the prices of the comparable firm and the earnings used to value the firm are *next year's* earnings, E_1, the resulting value is indeed an appropriate estimate of the value of the firm *today*. This, however, is not the case when we use *trailing* earnings multiples to value the firm based on the *projected* earnings of the firm. Using the same notation, we have

$$\text{Estimated value} = \text{AVG} \left[\frac{P_0}{E_0} \right] \cdot E_1^{\text{firm}}$$

The equation shows that by using trailing earnings multiples, we would, for example, value a firm by multiplying the earnings projected for *1997* by employing the market's average multiple of *1996* earnings. An appropriate interpretation of the resulting value estimate is that this will be the value *next year,* the point in time when our *projected* earnings become *historical* earnings. In notation:

$$P_1^{\text{firm}} = \text{AVG} \left[\frac{P_0}{E_0} \right] \cdot E_1^{\text{firm}}$$

(Note the time subscripts!) To convert the projected P_1 to an equivalent price *today,* we need to discount P_1 for 1 year (at the equity RADR!):

$$P_0^{\text{firm}} = \frac{\text{AVG} \left[\frac{P_0}{E_0} \right] \cdot E_1^{\text{firm}}}{1 + \text{RADR}}$$

The application of a trailing earnings multiple in such a way, however, is problematic: When applying this method, we implicitly assume that the *current* earnings multiple will still apply 1 year from now.[2] The same problematic assumption underlies another use of multiples. Multiples are often used to estimate *terminal values* in valuations. For example, in a valuation of a leveraged buyout (LBO) it is common to assume that all the FCFs will be used to pay down the

---

[2]The use of multiples is often motivated by the analyst's desire to avoid the estimation of future cash flows and firm discount rates. Note that the use of trailing multiples implies the necessity of estimating such discount rates! As an alternative to the use of trailing multiples, you can use leading multiples, but in this case you have to estimate future earnings for all comparable firms.

debt issued at the time of the buyout. When debt reaches a "low enough" level, the LBO is expected to be sold back to the public. The selling price a few years down the road is often estimated by using earnings multiples for the projected earnings of the issue year. But is the implicit assumption—that the current multiples will still prevail in a few years when the issue is sold—in fact reasonable?

Valuation by earnings multiples has another major problem: It cannot be applied to firms with zero or negative current or expected earnings. This problem is not restricted only to firms with *current* negative earnings: A firm may well have projected earnings that are negative and positive projected FCFs (e.g., when projected depreciation charges greatly exceed projected capital investments). Such a firm should have a positive value, which cannot be computed by multiplying the projected negative earnings by the industry's average P/E ratio. One quick fix is to apply the average earnings multiple to the first year in which earnings are projected to be positive and to discount the resulting price back. Again, the implicit assumption underlying this solution is that current multiples will still prevail when the firm's earnings become positive, a nontrivial assumption.

The problem of negative earnings also plagues the calculation of *average* comparable earnings multiples. Since earnings multiples cannot be computed when earnings are negative, a common practice in calculating averages is to eliminate firms with negative earnings. This creates a subtle problem. We will use a simple example to illustrate how this practice affects valuations. Consider an industry with 10 firms. Each year each of the 10 firms has a 20 percent chance of losing $25,000 and an 80 percent chance of making a profit of $100,000. The expected earnings of a typical firm are

$$E(\text{earnings}) = 20\% \cdot \$(-25,000) + 80\% \cdot \$100,000 = \$75,000$$

We can consider the expected earnings as the "typical" earnings: Earnings fluctuate between $100,000 and $25,000, and on average are $75,000. Reflecting the possibility that earnings will be either negative or positive, we find that the price of each firm is $900,000. This implies an earnings multiple relative to the *representative* earnings of

$$P/E = \frac{\$900,000}{\$75,000} = 12$$

What would happen when only the *profitable* firms are included in the sample of comparable firms for the purpose of estimating the industry's earnings multiple? The prices in the numerator incorporate the possibility of a loss, but the earnings in the denominator are earnings of firms that are *selected because they had a profit.* This will create a *downward* bias in the calculated industry's average P/E ratio!

To see this, consider a typical year in which 8 out of the 10 firms had a profit of $100,000, whereas 2 firms lost $25,000. The P/E ratio calculated *by using only the prices and earnings of the profitable firms* will be

$$\text{AVG}\left[\frac{P}{E}\right] = \frac{1}{8}\sum_{i=1}^{8}\frac{\$900,000}{\$100,000} = 9$$

which is less than the true P/E ratio of 12.

The correct way to estimate the industry's earnings multiple in this case is to sum *separately* the values and earnings and to compute the ratio on the *aggregate* value and earnings:

$$\text{AVG}\left[\frac{P}{E}\right] = \frac{\displaystyle\sum_{i=1}^{10}\$900,000}{\displaystyle\sum_{i=1}^{8}\$100,000 + \sum_{i=1}^{2}\$(-25,000)} = \frac{\$9,000,000}{\$750,000} = 12$$

as it should be.

Last, but not least, there is our usual problem with earnings: Do earnings measure what they purport to measure? A wide body of evidence indicates that earnings—the denominator of the P/E ratio—are routinely manipulated.[3] Earnings reflect discretionary allocations of costs and revenues and are more easily manipulated than the firm's cash flows. Consequently, earnings-based valuations are unduly dependent on arbitrary accounting decisions. Although the use of several comparable firms reduces the impact of an individual firm's earnings manipulation on the estimated earnings multiple, remember to verify that the earnings that you use to scale the prices of the comparable firms don't include abnormal components.

Appropriate P/E Ratios

Despite the preceding qualifications and reservations about the use of P/E ratios as substitutes for full valuations of firms, P/E ratios are closely related to DCF-based values. In this section we will derive some simple relations, based on rather strong assumptions that buy us simplicity, between DCF-based values and P/E ratios. These relations help us to interpret some of the observed patterns in P/E ratios, such as why high-growth firms and industries have higher earnings multiples than stable firms and industries. By using these relations, we can also assess the validity of some interpretations and uses of P/E ratios and gain some theoretical foundation

[3]For example, there is an extensive accounting literature on the "smoothing" of earnings by firms and on the "management" of accruals (e.g., preceding initial public offerings or bankruptcies).

for estimating the appropriate P/E ratios from the fundamental determinants of value.

Our starting point is the Gordon formula that converts a constantly growing infinite stream of dividends to a price for the stock when the term structure of both interest rates and risk premiums is flat. We denote next year's expected dividend by Div_1 and the constant annual growth rate by g. The constant cost of equity capital, comprised of a constant risk-free rate and a constant risk premium, is denoted by r_e. Today's price of the stock, denoted by P_0, is given by

$$P_0 = \frac{\text{Div}_1}{r_e - g}$$

We can make a simple substitution into the Gordon model to find the P/E ratio. Assume that dividends are a fixed proportion b, the **payout ratio,** of EPS. Then next year's dividends are given by the relation

$$\text{Div}_1 = b \cdot \text{EPS}_1$$

Furthermore, next year's profits in the Gordon model are related to this year's earnings by the annual growth rate:

$$\text{EPS}_1 = \text{EPS}_0 \cdot (1 + g)$$

Thus, $$\text{Div}_1 = b \cdot \text{EPS}_0 \cdot (1 + g)$$

Substituting into the Gordon model, we get

$$P_0 = \frac{b \cdot \text{EPS}_0 \cdot (1 + g)}{r_e - g}$$

By dividing both sides of the equation by EPS_0, we get the current appropriate P/E ratio:

$$\frac{P_0}{E_0} = \frac{P_0}{\text{EPS}_0} = \frac{b \cdot (1 + g)}{r_e - g}$$

This formula shows that even under strong simplifying assumptions—constant income growth, constant discount rate, and constant payout ratio—the appropriate P/E ratio depends on:

• The firm's equity discount rate, which incorporates both its basic business risk and the additional risk incurred by leverage
• The growth rate of earnings
• The firm's payout ratio

Nonetheless, as we will see, the preceding formula may be useful.

Here are some examples that illustrate both the use of the formula and some important properties of P/E ratios. As our starting point, let's assume that our analysis indicates that the long-term growth potential of firm A is 4 percent per year, that its equity RADR is 8 percent, and that we expect the firm to pay 50 percent of its annual income as dividends. These projections imply that the firm's P/E ratio (using *trailing* earnings) should be

$$\frac{P_0}{E_0} = \frac{b \cdot (1 + g)}{r_e - g} = \frac{50\% \cdot (1 + 4\%)}{8\% - 4\%} = 13$$

Thus, assuming that these determinants of value are forever fixed, we can compute the benchmark earnings multiple. This P/E ratio can help us to determine if firm A is over- or underpriced. Suppose we observe that firm A's *actual* P/E ratio is only 11. This means that firm A's stock price *is too low*—its price should be $13/11 - 1 = 18.2\%$ higher than it actually is.

Suppose now another firm, firm B, in the same industry uses a higher leverage than firm A. Since higher leverage means higher risk, the RADR of firm B is higher, say, 12 percent. Firm B, being in the same industry, has a growth potential that is similar to firm A, 4 percent a year. Further, firm B's dividend payout ratio is also 50 percent. This means that the appropriate P/E ratio for firm B is

$$\frac{P_0}{E_0} = \frac{b \cdot (1 + g)}{r_e - g} = \frac{50\% \cdot (1 + 4\%)}{12\% - 4\%} = 6.5$$

which is *one-half* the appropriate P/E ratio of firm A.

Suppose now the *actual* P/E ratio of firm B is 8, higher than its fundamentals indicate it should be. This means that the price of firm B is *too high*—firm B's stock is overpriced. We can use the example of firms A and B to illustrate a problematic aspect of the common use of P/E ratios. Someone analyzing the industry of firms A and B may look at the earnings multiples of the A and B stocks and say, "Stock B is a better stock to buy in the XXX industry than stock A since stock A sells for 11 times its earnings, whereas stock B sells for only 8 times its earnings." In this example the conclusion is obviously false: The undervalued stock is stock A (which has a high multiple), whereas stock B (which has a low multiple) is the overvalued one. The erroneous conclusion occurs because stock B, being more risky than stock A, should have a low multiple, even lower than the one for which it sells.

The preceding example highlights the difficulty of interpreting P/E ratios: P/E ratios reflect—besides the relative pricing of stocks—differences in risk, growth, and financial policies. Therefore, a low P/E by itself *doesn't* indicate a low stock price: A low P/E ratio may well equally indicate high-risk or low-growth potential!

Estimating Growth

As discussed in Chapter 9, the growth rate, g, can be estimated from the history of dividend payments, by simply averaging prior years' dividend growth rates. The key assumption underlying this procedure is that prior growth rates are indicative of future growth rates. To apply this method, we need to have a series of historical dividend payments that is long enough to estimate reliably the growth rate.

In many cases it is not reasonable to assume that past growth rates are indicative of future growth rates. In such cases we can use nondividend information to estimate future growth rates. In particular, we can estimate the growth rate of dividends by the product of the retention ratio and the return on equity (ROE):

$$g = \text{retention ratio} \cdot \text{ROE} = (1 - \text{dividend payout ratio}) \cdot \text{ROE}$$

The underlying assumption of this estimate of growth potential is that *growth is financed exclusively from internally generated funds.* The reasoning is that earnings (which drive dividends in the Gordon formula) grow because the firm invests a fraction of the earnings—the retained earnings—and earns a rate of ROE on these additional investments. Obviously, if the assumption that growth is exclusively financed by retaining some earnings is wrong, this way of estimating growth will not work.

Application of this method of estimating growth rates requires an estimate of the firm's ROE. One method that is often employed relies on accounting for the numbers used in estimating ROE:

$$\text{ROE} = \frac{\text{Profit after Tax}}{\text{Book Value of Equity}}$$

The intuition behind this equation is that the Book Value measures the *cost* of the investments and that the Profit after Tax measures the *return* on the investment.

Here is an illustration. Suppose the per-share equity book value (BV) of firm C is $10 and its EPS (earnings per share) are $0.80. The firm's dividend payout ratio is 25 percent. The growth rate implied by these numbers *and the assumption that Retained Earnings is the only source of growth* is

$$g = (1 - b) \cdot \text{ROE} = (1 - b) \cdot \frac{\text{EPS}}{\text{BV per share}}$$

$$= (1 - 25\%) \cdot \frac{\$0.80}{\$10.00} = 0.75 \cdot 8\% = 6\%$$

Suppose we estimate that the RADR of the stock is 9 percent. By using the estimated growth rate of 6 percent and RADR of 9 percent, we can determine the appropriate P/E ratio of the firm by using the previous formula:

$$\frac{P_0}{E_0} = \frac{b \cdot (1 + g)}{r_e - g} = \frac{25\% \cdot (1 + 6\%)}{9\% - 6\%} = 8.83$$

This illustrates one more important point about growth that is often overlooked. Growth by itself *doesn't create value*. Look back at the last example: The firm is growing by investing in projects that earn a rate of return (ROE) of 8 percent. The firm keeps holding on to cash (by paying out only 25 percent of the earnings as dividends) and reinvesting the remaining funds. But the ROE that the firm earns on its investments *is lower than the rate of return that investors demand given the firm's risk*: Given the firm's risk, investors demand a return of 9 percent. Thus, in this example growth *destroys* value.

10.3 THE RETAIL STORE INDUSTRY

We illustrate the use of multiples in valuation with the retail store industry. Exhibit 10.1 gives some initial facts about a sample of retail store companies taken from Value Line.

Exhibit 10.1

Retail Store Industry
Value Line Data, May 29, 1992

Retail Store		Share price	Trailing P/E*	Beta[†]	Market/ book,[‡] equity	Price/CF[¶] per share
Dillard Dept.	DDS	41	22.28	1.20	2.89	3.55
Dayton Hudson	DH	65	17.47	1.45	2.41	20.31
Dollar General	DOLR	20	24.39	1.00	3.38	14.29
Family Dollar	FDO	17	23.29	1.25	4.17	14.17
Jacobson Stores	JCBS	16	21.92	1.30	1.07	3.60
J. C. Penney	JCP	67	16.75	1.20	2.23	23.10
Kmart Corp.	KM	23	11.39	1.20	1.57	2.71
L. Luria & Son	LUR	6.6	30.00	1.10	0.46	1.83
May Dept. Stores	MA	55	13.68	1.35	2.83	44.00
Fred Meyer	MEYR	24	13.26	1.10	1.05	3.20
Nordstrom, Inc.	NOBE	33	19.88	1.25	2.87	10.31
Pic 'N' Save	PICN	16	14.29	1.15	2.51	8.21
Sears, Roebuck	S	45	12.13	1.10	1.12	5.96
Service Merchandise	SME	11	14.47	1.70	10.38	6.29
Venture Stores	VEN	30	12.10	nmf	4.05	6.82
Wal-Mart Stores	WMT	53	37.86	1.25	8.72	23.56
Woolworth Corp.	Z	28	18.54	1.25	1.80	6.36

*P/E is defined as the recent share price divided by EPS_{1991}.
[†]Beta is the stock's beta against the NYSE Composite Index.
[‡]Market/Book (M/B) is the ratio of the recent share price to the 1991 year-end per-share book value of equity.
[¶]Price/CF per share is the ratio of the recent share price to the 1991 per-share Cash Flows from Operations, defined by Value Line as PAT + Depreciation.
Source: Based on data from *Value Line Investment Survey,* May 29, 1992.

P/Es in the Retail Store Industry

Suppose we want to value Dayton Hudson (DH) based on our prediction of the EPS of DH. Assume that we agree with Value Line's projection that in 1992 DH's EPS will be $4.85, up $1.13 from its 1991 EPS. Obviously, underlying this EPS prediction is a complete analysis of DH's store distribution, market share, product mix, general and specific price trends, and the like about which we have little information. To simplify our illustration of the use of P/E ratios, we start the valuation of DH almost at its end, assuming that the end product of the detailed analysis of Value Line's analysts is a valid EPS prediction of $4.85.

The next step is to select from all the potential firms in DH's industry those firms that are most similar to DH. In other words, we want to select the set of firms that we consider comparable to DH. The basic consideration is the similarity of business—products, clients, location, and so on. DH operates 770 upscale department stores throughout the continental United States. The firms that are the closest to DH in terms of the type of business are Dillard Department Stores, May Department Stores, and Nordstrom, Inc. Allowing for some location or clientele differences, we can expand the sample of comparable firms to include Jacobson Stores, J. C. Penney, L. Luria & Son, and Sears. Next we want to compare these firms on the basis of their size and leverage. Exhibit 10.2 provides data for this comparison. Clearly, the firms that we consider potential candidates for our sample of comparable firms are of different sizes and use debt financing to differing degrees.

Exhibit 10.2

Retail store	Debt	Preferred stock	Equity (market value)	Total value	Leverage	Stores	Sales	Sales per store
	Book value							
Dayton Hudson	4,227	377	4,630	9,234	49.86%	770	16,115	21
Dillard Dept.	1,038	0	4,572	5,611	18.51%	198	4,036	20
Jacobson Stores	98	0	92	190	51.33%	24	396	16
J. C. Penney	3,354	684	7,816	11,854	34.07%	1,813	16,201	9
L. Luria & Son	2	0	35	38	6.38%	53	208	4
May Dept. Stores	3,918	394	6,790	11,102	38.84%	3,613	10,615	3
Nordstrom, Inc.	482	0	2,701	3,183	15.15%	63	3,180	50
Sears, Roebuck	19,200	325	15,486	35,011	55.77%	1,800	57,242	32

A key question in deciding whether to include or exclude firms on the basis of size differences depends on whether size itself is a potential determinant of value. If larger retailers can manage inventories more efficiently, deal with suppliers more skillfully, or train and manage employees better, the retail store industry will exhibit **returns to scale** and we should restrict our sample of comparable firms to firms with similar scales—similar annual Sales or a similar number of stores. On the other hand, if there are no returns to scale in the industry that we are analyzing, excluding firms just because they have a different size from the firm being valued is not justified. (Remember that before we apply the prices of the comparable firms to the firm being valued, we *scale* these prices—by earnings, Sales, or any other economically meaningful scaling basis in the industry.) Since in the retail store industry Sales is a good proxy for the width of the geographical distribution of the stores of the chain, we drop from the sample of comparable firms Jacobson Stores and L. Luria because they are too small and geographically concentrated, and drop Sears, which is 4 times as large as DH. This leaves us with a sample of four comparable retailers: Dillard Department Stores, J. C. Penney, May Department Stores, and Nordstrom, Inc.

The next point to consider is leverage. Exhibit 10.2 also presents data on the leverage of the sample of retail store firms. To calculate leverage, we first calculate the total value of the firm: We add the year-end 1991 book value of the fixed income securities (Debt and Preferred Stock) to the market value of the Equity— the recent price of the shares times the number of shares outstanding. Leverage is then calculated as the fraction of this total value financed by fixed income securities.

Two things should be mentioned concerning the leverage of the sample firms. First, the extent of debt financing ranges from 6 percent of the firm's value to 55 percent. Such a large difference within a rather homogeneous group of firms is hardly consistent with a capital structure theory of a trade-off between tax benefits and costs of financial distress. Apparently, neither tax benefits nor costs of financial distress are important determinants of capital structure in the retail store industry. On the other hand, the range of observed leverage figures is consistent with a Miller-type equilibrium, where $T \approx 0$.

The second point that emerges from the leverage data is that DH is one of the most levered retailers: It has a leverage of 50%. This means that we have to take into account explicitly the leverage differences in our valuation of DH's equity! Suppose we ignored the leverage information in valuing the shares of DH. Then we would simply average the P/E ratios of the four closest competitors of DH. This would give us an average P/E of 18.15 relative to which DH's *actual* P/E of 17.5 is low, suggesting that DH is a (weak?) "buy" opportunity. Alternatively, we can use the average P/E to multiply the projected EPS of $4.85 to obtain an estimated year-end ("target") share price of $88, which is equivalent to a return of 35% [= ($88 − $65)/65] on an investment in DH equity. But the simple analysis of the attractiveness of investing in DH stock is misleading: DH is much more levered than the comparable retailers. Since DH stock is more risky than the comparable stocks, investors require *higher rates of return* for investing in DH stock, which means that DH's P/E should be *lower* than the P/E of the other, less levered retailers.

The dependence of P/E ratios on leverage is a general result. Low-leverage firms are less risky than similar highly levered firms. Thus, all other things being equal, shares of low-leverage firms trade for higher prices than shares of high-leverage firms. This means that, within industries, we expect to observe a negative correlation between leverage and P/E ratios. As an illustration, in Figure 10.1 we plot

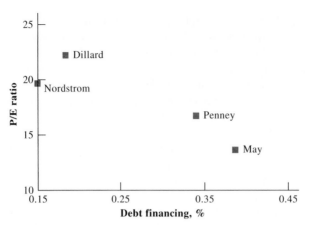

FIGURE 10.1   A plot of the Price/Earnings (P/E) ratios of four retailers in the retail store industry that are comparable to Dayton Hudson.

the P/E ratios of the four retailers that are comparable to DH. The negative correlation between leverage and P/E ratios is apparent.

Since we anticipate that the P/E ratios within the retail store industry will depend on leverage, our conclusion is that we cannot simply apply the average P/E ratio in the industry to DH's projected earnings because DH is more levered than comparable retailers. One quick fix for this problem is to value *whole firms* rather than just the equity of each firm. We can do this by computing ratios in which the total firm value is compared to some whole-firm scaling factor such as Operating Income or Sales. Exhibit 10.3 shows such ratios for the retailers that are comparable to DH.

Exhibit 10.3

Retail store	Total value	Leverage	EBIT	Value to EBIT	Sales	Value to sales
Dillard Dept. Stores	5,611	18.51%	412	13.625	4,184	1.341
J. C. Penney	11,854	34.07%	1050	11.285	17,295	0.685
May Dept. Stores	11,102	38.84%	1061	10.468	10,615	1.046
Nordstrom, Inc.	3,183	15.15%	263	12.086	3,170	1.004
Average				11.866		1.019

Note that the whole-firm multiples in Exhibit 10.3 show no leverage-related pattern: Neither Total Firm Value to EBIT nor Total Firm Value to Sales is related to leverage. Thus, whole-firm multiples appear to be, as they should if leverage doesn't affect the value of the firm, independent of the particular financing mix that the management of the comparable firms have chosen.

We can use the average whole-firm multiples to value DH. Suppose we follow Value Line in projecting that DH's 1992 Sales will be $18,000 million, up from its 1991 Sales of $16,115 million. If the EBIT/Sales ratio of DH stays at its current level of 4.78 percent, the expected Sales growth implies that DH's EBIT will grow from $770 million to $860 million. This means that based on the projected EBIT of DH and the average Value/EBIT ratio of the comparable firms, DH will be worth $860 · 11.866 = $10,210 million at the end of 1992. This value estimate of $10,210 million is based on the average *trailing* earnings multiple and DH's *leading* earnings. Hence, this is the value projected for DH *at the end of 1992*. To convert this value estimate to a value estimate in terms of *today's* dollars, we need to discount this value.

What is the appropriate discount rate? The value estimate is for the *whole firm*. Thus, the appropriate discount rate is the rate that reflects the risk of the whole firm, not just the risk of its equity. We can estimate this rate by estimating an industry's beta—the average asset beta of retail stores—and by using the CAPM. We can infer the beta of the asset of the industry from the beta estimates of the *equities* of the comparable firms and their leverage, using the following relation:

$$\beta_{assets} = \beta_{equity} \cdot \frac{E}{V} + \beta_{debt} \cdot (1 - t_c) \cdot \frac{D}{V}$$

where E = market value of the equity
D = market value of the fixed income securities
V = value of the whole firm—the sum of E and D

For low leverage levels $\beta_{debt} \approx 0$, so we can approximate the preceding relation by

$$\beta_{assets} \approx \beta_{equity} \cdot \frac{E}{V}$$

The following table is the basis for the estimation of the asset beta of retail stores that are similar to DH:

Retail store	E/V	β_{equity}	β_{debt}
Dillard	81.49%	1.20	0.98
Penney	65.93%	1.20	0.79
May	61.16%	1.35	0.83
Nordstrom	84.85%	1.25	1.06
Average			0.91

By using the average asset beta of comparable firms as our estimate of the asset beta of DH, we can estimate the RADR as

$$RADR = rf_{debt} \cdot (1 - t_c) + \beta_{asset} \cdot \pi_m$$

$$= 6\% \cdot (1 - 37\%) + 0.91 \cdot 8\% = 11.06\%$$

This estimate assumes a market-risk premium $\pi_m = 8\%$, the approximate value of the long-run historic average market-risk premium. By using the RADR of 11.48 percent, we can estimate the *current* value of DH as

$$DH, \text{ total value} = \frac{\$10,210 \text{ million}}{(1 + 11.06\%)} = \$9,193 \text{ million}$$

To obtain an estimate of DH's *equity* value, we have to subtract the value of DH's fixed income securities from the value of *all* of DH's long-term securities. Specifically, the estimated equity value of DH is

DAYTON-HUDSON INC.
Using EBIT projections and whole-firm
multiples to estimate firm and equity values
($ millions)

Estimated firm value	$9,193
Value of debt	(4,227)
Value of preferred stock	(377)
Estimated equity value	$4,589

Note that this estimated value for DH's equity, unlike those obtained by applying average P/E ratios, takes into account the *specific* leverage of DH, which is different from the leverage of the other retailers to which we compare DH. The current market value of DH equity, $4,630 million, is only slightly above the estimated value based on Value Line's EBIT projections and our Value/EBIT multiple. This leads us to conclude that DH's equity is fairly priced.

As an alternative to using the whole-firm Value/EBIT ratio, we might also consider using the whole-firm Value/Sales ratio. The average of this value for the firms that are comparable to DH is 1.019. Using this ratio for DH's projected 1992 Sales of $16,115 million gives a projected year-end 1992 value of $19,962 for the firm. This is almost *twice* as large as the total-firm-value estimate that we arrived at by using the projected EBIT of DH for 1992! Is something wrong here? Some thoughts come to mind: Another look at the numbers show that historically DH's Value/Sales ratio has been very different from the rest of the sample. This suggests that this particular ratio is not appropriate despite the fact that we have decided that these firms are similar in many other respects to DH. In one sense, our disbelief in the valuation produced by the Value/Sales ratio is not that surprising: As we mentioned in Section 10.1, the *higher up* that the scaling basis is in the income statement, the less it reflects differences in strategies and operating efficiencies across firms. For example, DH may deliberately choose lower-profit margins than its competitors (possibly expecting a higher volume in return). Since such differences are critical in valuation, it is not surprising that the Value/Sales ratio doesn't produce a reliable estimate.

10.4 SOME OTHER MULTIPLES

Many other multiples are used by financial analysts to compare asset prices. Any or all of these multiples may prove to be useful as appropriate ways of measuring relative sizes and relative values for some industries. In this section we will describe some commonly used multiples and will present an illustration of some industry-specific multiples.

In general, any number in the income statement can be used as a measure of relative size: Sales, Gross Profits, Operating Profits, or Net Income. The lower you go in the income statement, the more firm-specific information is contained in the scaling measure:

- Using Sales as a scaling measure, you don't incorporate any firm-specific information about pricing policies, efficiency of production, or efficiency of selling.
- Using Gross Profits as a scaling measure, you incorporate information about the firm's pricing policies (i.e., average margin) and production efficiency (i.e., the relation between the Cost of Goods Sold (COGS) to Sales), but no information about marketing efficiency (i.e., Selling, General, and Administrative (SG&A) costs).
- Using Operating Profits to scale prices incorporates all operating aspects of the firm but doesn't incorporate any information about the firm's financial policies.
- Finally, using Net Income to scale prices incorporates both operating aspects and financial aspects of the firm. As the example in the subsection "Estimating Growth" illustrates, this may be *too much* information: You may want to scale comparable firms only on the basis of their common *operating* characteristics abstracting from *financial* differences, such as different leverages used by firms in the same industry.

The use of these increasingly informative measures of relative size is not without a cost: The lower in the income statement we go with our search for an appropriate scaling measure, the more the number depends on the vagaries of the accounting principles used by comparable firms. These accounting principles of firms in any given industry are far from being unique. Since income recognition criteria within an industry are likely to be similar, Sales is a measure of relative size that is virtually free of accounting differences, whereas Net Income is most affected by the firms' accounting policies. One remedy for this problem is to use *cash-flow-based multiples,* such as Price divided by CF to equity holders, and Price to FCF.

These ratios have the benefit of reflecting the information incorporated in the corresponding earnings numbers while being less affected by accounting principles.

Price/Sales Multiples

Dividing the price per share of a company by its Sales per share (the **Sales multiple**) is a common way of comparing firms in the same industry. The intuition underlying this ratio is that *within an industry* the gross margins and the operating efficiency are typically similar. Thus, using Sales to measure relative sizes is close to measuring relative sizes by profits and is *free of the accounting idiosyncrasies of individual firms.* To the extent that pricing policies and operating technologies of the sample of comparable firms that you use to estimate the average multiple are similar to the firm that you value, the Price/Sales ratio will do a good job even though it doesn't reflect any of the information in the firms' income statements other than Sales.

Consider the graph in Figure 10.2, which shows this ratio for the firms in the retail store industry. As the graph illustrates, there is a considerable variation in the Price/Sales ratios in the retail store industry, which is a fairly homogeneous industry in terms of product and operating methods. There seem to be a number of reasons that the Price/Sales ratio may not be accurate in valuing a company:

- The Price/Sales ratio doesn't reflect differences in *efficiency* between firms.
- It doesn't reflect differences in *capital investments,* which we know are a major component of many firms' FCFs.
- It doesn't reflect differences in *growth prospects.*

The problems with the Price/Sales ratio stem from the fact that when using this multiple, we scale the prices of comparable firms by the top number in a cash-flow

FIGURE 10.2 A graph of the Price/Sales ratio for firms in the retail store industry. (*Source: Value Line,* May 29, 1992.)

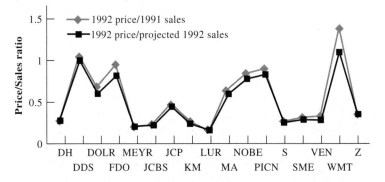

DDS = Dillard, DH = Dayton Hudson, DOLR = Dollar, FDO = Family Dollar, JCBS = Jacobson, JCP = Penney, KM = Kmart, LUR = Luria, MA = May, MEYR = Fred Meyer, NOBE = Nordstrom, S = Sears, SME = Service Merchandise, VEN = Venture, WMT = Wal-Mart, Z = Woolworth

statement. Such a scaling misses all the information contained in the numbers that follow Sales—COGS, SG&A, changes in working capital, and capital investments. By ignoring these numbers, we find that the Price/Sales ratio implicitly assumes that *within an industry all operating characteristics have the same relation to Sales for all firms.* If all the firms in an industry had the same operating efficiency and had no fixed costs, then their Price/Sales ratios would necessarily be equal. Under these assumptions earnings (and so EPS) would also be proportional to Sales, which means that

$$\frac{Price}{Earnings} = \frac{Price}{k \cdot Sales}$$

where k is a proportionality parameter that reflects the profit margins of the firm. This means that

$$\frac{Price}{Sales} = k \cdot \frac{Price}{Earnings}$$

Thus, if we think that the P/E ratio is meaningful, then the ratio of Price/Sales can be viewed as a backhanded way of getting at the firm's profit margin: Firms with a higher Price/Sales ratio can be taken, all other things being equal, to have a higher margin. We can check in our sample of retail stores if this is true.

As you can see in Figure 10.3, this premise appears to be largely true. The regression of Profit Margins on the Price/Sales ratio gives the following estimated relation for the department store industry:

$$\frac{Price}{Sales} = -0.0458 + 16.1622 \cdot \text{Profit Margin}, \qquad R^2 = 0.6074$$

This estimated relation can be used to value a retail store chain based on projected Sales and Gross Margins. If based on your analysis, you project 1992 Sales of

FIGURE 10.3   A comparison of the Price/Sales ratio with profit margin in the retail store industry. (*Source:* Based on *Value Line* predictions for 1992 Sales and profit margins, May 29, 1992.)

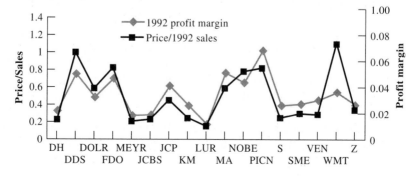

$250 million and a profit margin of 5 percent for the Goods "R" Us chain. First, by using the estimated relation between profit margins and Price/Sales ratios in the retail store industry, we can convert the projected profit margin of 5 percent to a projected Price/Sales multiple:

$$\frac{\text{Price}}{\text{Sales}} = -0.0458 + 16.1622 \cdot 0.05 = 0.762$$

Next the estimated "fair" Price/Sales ratio of 0.762 and the projected Sales of $250 million jointly imply a value of $250 million $\cdot$ 0.762 = $190 million.

Obviously, the simplicity of this valuation—all that it requires is the projection of Sales and Gross Margins—is both its advantage and a source of potential problems. The Sales-based valuation method will be valid only if Goods "R" Us is as efficient as the average (comparable) retailer: In applying the estimated relation, we implicitly assume that Goods "R" Us has similar SG&A and capital investments *per dollar of sales* as other retailers have. If this is a valid assumption, then the estimated value will be an accurate one. If Goods "R" Us is more efficient than its comparables, we will undervalue Goods "R" Us, whereas if Goods "R" Us is less efficient than its competitors, we will overvalue it.

Fixed Asset Multiples

There are many other multiples that are worth comparing for a given industry. In the next subsection we use data about the airline industry to examine some *fixed asset multiples*. In the airline industry the relevant fixed asset ratio is the ratio of **Market Value to Gross Equipment.** By *gross equipment* we mean the undepreciated equipment of each of the airlines. If the efficiency ratios, utilization rates, and growth prospects of any two airlines are roughly equal, then how much equipment an airline has will determine its *size* relative to other airlines in the industry as well as its *value* relative to the values of other airlines. This is also true of other industries: Fixed Assets at Cost will be a good measure of relative size if the industry's utilization rate is roughly the same; on the other hand, Fixed Assets will be a poor proxy for relative sizes if there are large intraindustry differences in efficiency and utilization.

A technical point discussed in relation to estimating capital expenditures of firms in Chapter 5 is worth repeating in the context of multiples valuation. When using Fixed Assets as a measure of relative size, you have to consider whether it is the *cost* of the fixed assets or the *net value*—cost less accumulated depreciation—that appropriately measures relative sizes. If production capacity deteriorates with the age of the fixed assets, *Net Fixed Assets* probably measures capacity better than Fixed Assets at Cost. If production capacity is little affected by the age of the machine (e.g., if an airplane can fly the same number of passengers for roughly the same cost in each year of its use until it is scrapped), capacity will be measured more accurately by the undepreciated cost of the Fixed Assets than by their net value. In our example we use the original cost of the airlines' equipment, implicitly assuming that airplanes' capacity to fly passengers doesn't deteriorate with age.

As with any fixed asset multiple, the use of the ratio of Value to Gross Equipment to compare airline values implicitly assumes that the *utilization rate* of the equipment is roughly the same across the industry. For airlines the actual utilization rate is called the **load factor**: An airline's *load factor* is the average percentage of occupied seats on its flights. Assuming that airlines don't own unused airplanes, the load factor can serve as a proxy for the *rate of utilization of fixed assets* of airlines. We use the load factor, which is reported by airlines, times the Gross Assets to measure the relative *effective* size of airlines. Figure 10.4 depicts both the ratios of **Market to Fixed Assets** and **Market to Load-Adjusted Fixed Assets.** The obvious pattern in the graph is that after adjusting the fixed assets by an estimate of their rate of utilization, the load factor, the cross-sectional dispersion of the ratio of market value to capacity is less widely spread than before the adjustment for the rate of utilization. This means that part of the intraindustry variation in the ratio of value to fixed assets is due to differences in the rate at which the fixed assets are utilized. Put differently, utilization-adjusted Fixed Assets is a better measure of relative size than Fixed Assets alone.

What does this result imply for the way that we use this ratio to value airlines? It means that to value an airline using Fixed Asset multiples, we need:

- To estimate the average ratio of Market to Fixed Assets adjusted by the utilization rate
- To project the Fixed Asset and the load factor for the airline being valued
- To apply the average utilization-adjusted Fixed Asset multiple to the projected Fixed Assets times the projected utilization rate of the airline that we want to value

These suggested steps are useful in other industries as well: It is better to compare firms on the basis of *utilization-adjusted* capacity than on the basis of *raw* capacity. The problem is that capacity utilization is not a readily available piece of data in most industries (the airline industry being a prominent exception). Nonetheless, if

FIGURE 10.4   The graph illustrates the Market to Fixed Asset ratios in the airline industry. (*Source: Value Line Investment Survey,* June 28, 1992.)

you want to use fixed asset multiples in valuation, you must get *some* estimate of the rate of capacity utilization.

SUMMARY

In this chapter we discussed the ''quick and dirty'' method of valuation—valuation with multiples. Valuation with multiples allows us to remain agnostic about the determinants of value. By using multiples, we *estimate values by appropriately scaling prices of similar firms.* Since the method is not based on an analysis of the determinants of value, it is important to select judiciously comparable firms and bases according to which the prices of these firms can be scaled to estimate values.

The process of valuation with multiples involves the following steps:

- Choosing comparable firms that are *as similar as possible to the firm that we value.*
- Choosing several bases to scale the prices of comparable firms, such as Sales, Gross Profits, Earnings, book values, and industry-specific measures.
- Averaging across industry the *scaled* prices of comparable firms—their prices divided by the various scales used to measure relative sizes
- Projecting bases for the valued firm to match the average ''prices per . . .'' of comparable firms
- Valuing the firm by multiplying the average multiples of comparable firms to the projected parameters of the valued firm

Since the values that we obtain from various multiples are typically different, the last step requires a careful examination of the differences in order to integrate them into a final value estimate. Since the selection of comparable firms has such a paramount role in valuation with multiples, special attention must be paid to selecting a true comparable sample of firms—firms that are in the same industry, employ the same technology, apply to similar clienteles, are of similar size, and so on. Inevitably, this selection will entail some compromises: Since there are no two identical firms, the selection of comparable firms should balance the desire to get as large a sample as possible so that idiosyncrasies of individual firms wash out against the desire to ensure a high degree of similarity of the sample to the firm being valued.

One potential source of cross-sectional differences is leverage: Even otherwise similar firms may choose quite different leverages. A possible solution is to use *whole-firm multiples*—multiples that compare total firm values to whole-firm measures of performance (Sales, EBIT, and the like)—rather than *equity multiples*—multiples that compare *equity* values to the measure of relative *equity* scale (most commonly, EPS). Whole-firm multiples can also be used when firms in the industry use a different mix of securities—some have issued preferred stocks, whereas others have not; some have given their employees stock options, whereas others have no warrants outstanding. When this is the case, simply add the value of all the securities of the firm to relate the value of the whole firm to the performance measure of the whole firm.

Finally, we return to the main message of this book: Athough we think that it is valuable to examine valuation ratios and multiples, we ultimately believe that you are better off concentrating your valuation efforts on a thorough analysis of the firm's cash flows. Valuation by multiples is subject to too many vagaries:

- It is too affected by transitory events.
- It hardly reflects future trends.
- It hardly reflects risk differences even when restricted to the same industry's comparisons.

EXERCISES

10.1 ABC Corp. has a Price/Earnings (P/E) ratio (defined as the ratio of the current price to last year's earnings, P_0/E_0) of 15. ABC's expected dividend payout ratio is 30 percent and its expected annual growth rate is 10 pecent.

   a What will be the cost of ABC's equity implied by its current P/E ratio if the assumptions of the Gordon formula are valid?

   b What would ABC's P/E ratio be if the cost of capital were 25 percent?

   c What would ABC's P/E ratio be if its cost of capital were 15 percent and its growth rate were 8 percent?

   d What do you learn from the relative P/E ratios about the appropriate use of P/E ratios?

10.2 The following 1994 information concerns the Grand-Widget industry's only two firms—LMN and QRS companies. The two companies face identical risks and are operated identically.

	LMN	QRS
Market value of debt	$200,000	$400,000
Market value of equity	$400,000	$100,000
Sales	$400,000	$200,000
Net income	$40,000	$12,000
After-tax interest expense	$10,000	$24,000

   a Based on their 1994 earnings, what are the *trailing earnings* multiples of LMN's and QRS's shares?

   b Based on their 1994 earnings and market prices, which of the two *firms* represents a better investment opportunity? Compare your answer in this part to your answer for part **a**. Is this reasonable? Given the relative *firm's* values, what would you expect the relative values of the stocks to be? Can you explain the difference?

   c If LMN's *total firm value* had the same relation to Sales as the relation of QRS's total value to Sales, what would be LMN's total firm value?

CHAPTER 11

VALUING THE FIRM'S DEBT

OVERVIEW

In the preceding chapters you learned:

- How to forecast the firm's financial performance
- How to convert these forecasts into a value for the firm, assuming that the firm is all-equity financed
- How to adjust the all-equity value of the firm for the effects that the actual capital structure may have on the value of the firm as a whole

Once you have estimated the value of the *whole* firm, you can turn to the question of how to divide this value among the various investors who have claims on the cash flows that the firm is expected to generate. *In this chapter we begin the discussion of how to value the securities that the firm has issued based on both the estimated value of the firm as a whole and the characteristics of the outstanding securities.*

Firms can issue various securities, each of which entitles its holders to a different type of claim on the firm's Free Cash Flows (FCFs). Although we cannot enumerate and value *all* these security types, we distinguish and discuss three broad classes of securities—debt, convertible securities, and stocks. In this chapter we will discuss the valuation of debt, and in Chapter 12 we will discuss the valuation of convertible securities. Since the value of the securities that the firm has issued adds up to the value of the firm's operations, the value of the firm's equity can be calculated as a *remainder*—the difference between the value of the firm and the value of the debt and the convertible securities that it has issued.

There are two primary reasons for beginning the valuation of specific-firm securities with the valuation of debt securities:

- Since debt holders' claim is the most senior claim on the firm's FCFs, it makes sense to determine first the cash flows that debt holders will receive before further dividing the remaining cash flows among the less senior claims.
- Debt holders' claims are typically tied to fixed periodical payments. The "fixed" nature of debt holders' cash flows makes the direct valuation of the debt the easiest and most accurate of all security valuations. If we were to value the debt after allocating part of the firm's FCF to securities that are less accurately valued, the same inaccuracy would be reflected in the valuation of the debt.

We begin by defining what we mean when we say "debt" and how, in principle, debt is valued. We then describe the cash flows to which debt holders are entitled, differentiating between the *promised* payments to debt holders and the *expected* payments. We proceed to dicuss how default risk is measured and estimated. Finally, we explain and demonstrate methods to translate debt holders' promised payments to values that take into account the assessed risks.

11.1 WHAT IS DEBT?

The term **debt** has several meanings, depending on the context in which it is used. In this chapter we refer to *debt* as any **fixed income security** that firms can issue, where the term *fixed income* means that *the income promised to the holders of debt is set by the terms of the contract.* We refer to this income as interest. Interest can be paid periodically ("coupon payment"), upon maturity, or in any other way. Our definition of the term *debt* includes bank loans; commercial paper (which are short-term IOUs issued by firms); corporate bonds; and even more esoteric securities such as variable-rate bonds, industrial revenue bonds (which in the United States is commonly used terminology for subsidized debt tied to certain investments), and bonds denominated in foreign currency or traded abroad (such as Eurobonds).[1]

Debt is distinguished from equitylike securities in that debt holders don't have a **residual claim** on the firm: They are not entitled to participation in the firm's success. Should the prospects of the issuing firm improve, debt holders will not participate in the improved fortune (beyond the higher safety of their fixed claims) since their payments are limited to those promised in the debt contract at the time that the debt was issued. On the other hand, if the firm's business should turn sour, the firm may default on its debt obligations, leaving debt holders with *less* than they were promised when the debt was issued. In other words, debt holders share the downside risk of the firm but don't enjoy the upside potential.

The common use of the term *fixed income securities* includes more securities than those we consider *debt*. Convertible bonds, for example, are often classed with straight debt as fixed income securities. These bonds, which can be converted to common stock at the option of their owners, clearly don't fall within the bounds of our definition of debt: If the firm's fortunes improve, holders of convertible bonds will convert their bonds to common stock and share some of this good

---

[1] An often used term is "straight debt."

fortune. We lump convertible bonds with other convertible securities and consider their valuation in Chapter 12.

Since our use of the term *debt* in this chapter is related to *the nature of the cash flows that bondholders are entitled to receive,* we include in the term *debt* securities that are "debtlike" but that have nondebt names. The primary example is straight preferred stock—securities that pay fixed periodic payments called "preferred dividend" (instead of "interest") that typically doesn't increase even if the firm begins to earn substantially more money.[2] Still it is worth noting some key differences between straight debt and preferred stock.

- Unlike straight debt, a preferred stock typically doesn't have a set maturity date. Although preferred stock may be redeemable, at a predetermined date or upon the issuing firm's choice, most preferred stocks can exist forever.
- Second, a firm's inability to pay preferred dividends doesn't trigger a default as would be the case for its inability to pay interest or principal of a regular debt security. Rather, the payment of the preferred dividend is simply omitted. Some preferred stocks entitle their holders to receive omitted dividends when sufficient funds are available.
- While interest payments on debt are tax deductible for corporate income taxes, preferred dividends are not deductible.

Although these differences make the analysis and valuation of preferred stock slightly different from that of a regular debt security, the principles of both analyses are so similar that we can safely lump them together in this chapter.

11.2 APPROACHES TO BOND VALUATION

In this section we briefly explain two methods of bond valuation:

- The first method involves discounting the *expected payments* of the debt at the *risk-adjusted discount rate (RADR).*
- The second method involves discounting the *promised payments* of the debt at the *risk-adjusted yield to maturity (RAYTM).*

If properly applied, the two methods will give the same valuations. The second method is used more commonly by analysts. It is this method that we describe and illustrate in the remainder of this chapter.

Discounting Expected Payments at the RADR

We can value bonds as we would any other security—by discounting the debt's *expected* payments at an *RADR.* Implementing this approach involves the following steps:

---

[2]Thus, we don't classify *participating* or *convertible* preferred stock as debt; the dividend on the former may increase if common stock dividends increase beyond a certain threshold, and the latter can be converted into shares of common stock.

1 Estimate the *expected debt payoffs,* based on
   a The *promised payments*
   b The *probability that this payment will be made* (or, equivalently, *the proba-bility of default*)
   c The *expected payment on the debt in case of default*
2 Calculate the *RADR* for the debt as the sum of
   a A *default-risk-free discount rate* such as the YTM of an *equal-maturity AAA-rated corporate bond*
   b A *risk premium* for the bond, which can be found, for example, by estimating the bond's beta and by using the Capital Asset Pricing Model (CAPM)

Discounting the Bond's Promised Payments at the RAYTM

Discounting expected cash flows at an RADR, although common in the valuation of whole firms or in the valuation of shares, is not the usual way of valuing debt securities. Instead, debt securities are typically valued by discounting the *promised bond payments.* Obviously, discounting *promised* payments at an RADR, which is an *expected* return, is inappropriate. Therefore, in this approach the promised payments are discounted at an RAYTM. Implementing this approach for a specific bond involves the following steps:

1 Find the bond's risk class. The default risk of bonds is routinely monitored by agencies that rate this risk. The published ratings can be used to classify the risk of the traded bond. Alternatively, appropriate ratings can be *estimated* for non-rated bonds, as described later in the chapter.
2 Calculate the RAYTM as the sum of
   a A *default-risk-free discount rate* equal to either the yield to maturity (YTM) of an *equal-maturity government bond* or the YTM of an *equal-maturity AAA-rated corporate bond.*
   b The average *yield spread* of traded bonds of the same rating, where the **yield spread** is the difference between the YTM of a corporate bond and the YTM of the risk-free benchmark bond.

The alternative to using the RAYTM is discussed in the Appendix to this chapter, which shows how to discount expected bond payments at the appropriate RADR. While correct in principle, this alternative is rarely used.

11.3   DEBT CASH FLOWS

The cash flows of debt securities are typically specified in the debt agreement, whether a bank loan contract or a bond indenture. These cash flows include two types of payments:

Principal or **par,** which is the **face value** of the loan
Coupons, which are the periodic payments of interest on the principal

A typical corporate bond pays interest semiannually until maturity and repays the principal (with the last interest payment) upon the debt's maturity. Other payment patterns are possible, however: Coupons can be paid annually; there may be no coupon (in which case the bond is called a **zero coupon bond** or a ''zero''), and the principal may be paid in several installments. Since the price of the bond reflects the pattern of the payments as set in the bond contract, chosen patterns merely reflect convention and convenience.

Figure 11.1 shows the cover page of the prospectus of the Chase Manhattan Corporation 6.25% Subordinated Notes Due 2006. It shows the terms—interest rate, date due, number of bonds offered, and so on—of the bonds.

The principal and the coupons are the payments that shareholders have *promised* to pay debt holders. If shareholders cannot pay either the promised coupon or the principal (or if they find it undesirable to do so), the firm will default on its debt obligations.[3] Upon default, the firm and its creditors begin negotiating the consequences of this default, such as resetting the terms of the debt and liquidating the firm. The actions that the firm and its creditors may take upon default are governed by the Bankruptcy Code and its various chapters. For example, Chapter 11 of the Bankruptcy Code defines the possible actions of a firm that seeks court protection of its ongoing business while renegotiating contractual obligations.

In any case, upon default debt holders receive less than they were promised. For example:

• In a liquidation debt holders receive whatever the firm's assets can be liquidated for
• In a Chapter 11 workout debt holders receive what bankruptcy courts decide is the value of their claims
• In voluntary renegotiations of debt terms debt holders receive what they agree to receive in lieu of their original claims

Thus, the *actual cash flows received by debt holders never exceed those they were promised and are sometimes less than the promised amounts.* This means that debt holders' *expected* cash flows are less than the *promised* cash flows.

The difference between the promised cash flows and those that are expected depends on:

• The probability of default
• The payment to debt holders *conditional* on default occurring

---

[3]Default may be entered even if the firm is *able* to pay the coupons and the principal as it promised to do. Such a default happens when other promises that were made upon issuance of the debt are not fulfilled. For example, in the indenture shareholders may promise to maintain a certain level of working capital. Failing to do so, the firm may be in a ''technical default.''

FIGURE 11.1   The cover page of a prospectus for $200 million of Chase Manhattan Corporation Subordinated Notes.

PROSPECTUS SUPPLEMENT
(To Prospectus dated November 23, 1994)

 **CHASE**

$200,000,000

The Chase Manhattan Corporation
6.25% Subordinated Notes Due 2006

Interest on the Notes is payable semi-annually on January 15 and July 15 of each year, beginning July 15, 1996. The Notes will mature on January 15, 2006. The Notes are not redeemable prior to maturity.

The Notes will be unsecured and will be subordinate to Senior Indebtedness of the Company as described under "DESCRIPTION OF NOTES—Subordination" in this Prospectus Supplement. At December 31, 1995, the outstanding Senior Indebtedness of the Company, exclusive of guarantees and other contingent obligations of the Company, was approximately $2.4 billion. Payment of principal of the Notes may be accelerated only in case of the bankruptcy, insolvency or reorganization of the Company. There is no right of acceleration upon a default in the payment of interest on the Notes or in the performance of any covenant of the Company. See "THE SUBORDINATED SECURITIES—Events of Default and Waiver Thereof" in the accompanying Prospectus.

The Notes will be issued in fully registered form only in denominations of $1,000 or integral multiples thereof. The Notes will be initially represented by one or more global Notes registered in the name of The Depository Trust Company, as Depository, or its nominee. Beneficial interests in Notes will be shown on, and transfers thereof will be effected only through, records maintained by the Depository and its participants. Owners of beneficial interests in Notes will be entitled to physical delivery of Notes in certificated form equal in principal amount to their respective beneficial interests only under the limited circumstances described herein. See "DESCRIPTION OF NOTES—Book-Entry Notes" in this Prospectus Supplement. Settlement for the Notes will be made in immediately available funds. The Notes will trade in the Depository's Same-Day Funds Settlement System until maturity, and secondary market trading activity for the Notes will therefore settle in immediately available funds. All payments of principal and interest will be made by the Company in immediately available funds. See "DESCRIPTION OF NOTES—Same-Day Settlement and Payment" in this Prospectus Supplement. Application will be made to list the Notes on the New York Stock Exchange. Listing will be subject to meeting the requirements of such Exchange, including those related to distribution.

THE NOTES ARE NOT SAVINGS ACCOUNTS, DEPOSITS OR OTHER OBLIGATIONS OF ANY BANK OR NON-BANK SUBSIDIARY OF THE COMPANY AND ARE NOT INSURED BY THE FEDERAL DEPOSIT INSURANCE CORPORATION, BANK INSURANCE FUND OR ANY OTHER GOVERNMENT AGENCY.

THESE SECURITIES HAVE NOT BEEN APPROVED OR DISAPPROVED BY THE SECURITIES AND EXCHANGE COMMISSION OR ANY STATE SECURITIES COMMISSION NOR HAS THE SECURITIES AND EXCHANGE COMMISSION OR ANY STATE SECURITIES COMMISSION PASSED UPON THE ACCURACY OR ADEQUACY OF THIS PROSPECTUS SUPPLEMENT OR THE PROSPECTUS TO WHICH IT RELATES. ANY REPRESENTATION TO THE CONTRARY IS A CRIMINAL OFFENSE.

	Price to Public(1)	Underwriting Discount(2)	Proceeds to Company(1)(3)
Per Note..	99.375%	0.550%	98.825%
Total	$198,750,000	$1,100,000	$197,650,000

(1) *Plus accrued interest, if any, from January 19, 1996.*
(2) *The Company has agreed to indemnify the Underwriters against certain liabilities, including liabilities under the Securities Act of 1933. See "UNDERWRITING" in this Prospectus Supplement.*
(3) *Before deducting expenses payable by the Company estimated to be $165,000.*

The Notes are offered by the Underwriters, subject to prior sale, when, as and if issued to and accepted by the Underwriters, subject to approval of certain legal matters by counsel for the Underwriters and certain other conditions. The Underwriters reserve the right to withdraw, cancel or modify such offer and to reject orders in whole or in part. It is expected that delivery of the Notes will be made in New York, New York on or about January 19, 1996.

This Prospectus Supplement and the accompanying Prospectus may be used by Chase Securities, Inc., a wholly-owned subsidiary of the Company, in connection with offers and sales related to market-making transactions in the Notes. Chase Securities, Inc. may act as principal or agent in such transactions. Such sales will be made at prices related to prevailing market prices at the time of sale.

Chase Securities, Inc.   **Chemical Securities Inc.**

Bear, Stearns & Co. Inc.

CS First Boston

Morgan Stanley & Co.
Incorporated

The date of this Prospectus Supplement is January 16, 1996.

Consider, for example, a firm that has issued debt that will mature in 1 year. We want to compute the expected cash flows of the bondholders. The indenture specifies a face value of *F* dollars and a coupon payment of *C* percent to the debt holder at the end of the year. The principal and the coupon will be paid only if the firm is solvent. On the other hand, if the firm defaults, we estimate that debt holders will not be able to collect the full promised amount. The process of settling when default occurs, the possible postdefault settlements, and the probabilities of various outcomes are summarized by a single variable, λ, the *expected value of debt holders' receipts when default occurs*. λ is expressed as a fraction of the face value of the bond. Finally, we denote the probability of default by *Pr*.

To compute the expected payment to debt holders, we have to weigh the promised payment, $F \cdot (1 + C)$, by the probability of receiving full payment, $1 - Pr$, and the payment upon default, $F \cdot \lambda$, by the probability of default, *Pr*. Therefore, debt holders' expected payment one year from now is

$$E(CF_1^{Debt}) = F \cdot (1 + C) \cdot (1 - Pr) + F \cdot \lambda \cdot Pr \tag{11.1}$$

A simple algebraic manipulation will show that the *promised* payment of $F \cdot (1 + C)$ exceeds the *expected* payment by

$$F \cdot (1 + C) - E(CF) = F \cdot [(1 + C) - \lambda] \cdot Pr \tag{11.2}$$

or as a fraction of the face value (equivalently, for $F = 1$):

$$[(1 + C) - \lambda] \cdot Pr \tag{11.3}$$

The difference between the cash flows that debt holders *expect* to receive and the cash flows they are *promised* increases when the probability of default increases. On the other hand, this difference is small if *upon default* debt holders can collect a large fraction of the promised payment.

Note that equations (11.1), (11.2), and (11.3) describe more than just 1-year bonds. Rather, these equations describe equally well the expected annual cash flows of multiyear debt securities. All that we have to do is to reinterpret the cash flows that bondholders receive when default doesn't occur: Under this interpretation the bondholders' end-of-period cash flow is the sum of the coupon and the end-of-period value of the bond. The only assumption, therefore, that we make in our analysis of a representative year in the life of a long-term bond is that the bond will trade at (approximately) par in one year. (Otherwise we have to use the expected price in one year instead of the face value of the bond in determining the expected cash flows.)

The probability of default, *Pr*, and the amount collected upon default, λ, are not independent of each other. Both depend on how much leverage the firm uses: The more debt the firm uses, the more likely it is that the firm will default on its debt service obligations and the less money debt holders should expect to collect upon default per dollar of face value. In a recent study Edward Altman estimated these values.[4] Although Altman's estimates reflect conditions at the time that his study was conducted, other studies have reached similar estimates so that Altman's estimates can be taken as representative figures. Debt risk is defined by Altman as the bond's rating on the day of issue. We discuss these ratings later in this chapter. For the moment it is enough to know that for the ratings in Exhibit 11.1 AAA is the *least risky* bond rating and CCC is the *most risky* rating.

Exhibit 11.1
Default Probabilities and Collection Percentages
for Various Risk Classes of Bonds

Rating of bonds on issue day	Risk	Annual probability of default (based on 5-year default rates)—*Pr*	Fraction of face value collected upon default—λ
AAA	Lowest	0.00%	78.67%
AA		0.47%	79.29%
A		0.14%	45.90%
BBB		0.18%	45.30%
BB		0.37%	35.71%
B		2.42%	42.56%
CCC	Highest	7.20%	41.15%

Source: E. I. Altman, "Measuring Corporate Bond Mortality and Performance," *Journal of Finance,* 44(4), 1989, pp. 909–922.

To see how the table in Exhibit 11.1 and equation (11.3) can be used to estimate the *expected* payment on a bond, consider a 1-year bond that pays a 10 percent annual coupon and is rated BB. In the absence of default, the bond will, 1 year from today, pay its bondholders $110 ($10 coupon plus $100 repayment of principal) for every $100 of face value. The probability of this happening is 100 percent less the probability that the bond will default:

$$100\% - 0.37\% = 99.63\%$$

On the other hand, if the firm defaults, bondholders will collect only $35.71. Default is highly unlikely, yet if it does occur, debt holders will collect materially less than if it doesn't occur. Consequently, the possibility of default reduces the *expected* payment to debt holders. The expected cash flow to debt holders is

$$110 \cdot 0.9963 + 35.71 \cdot 0.0037 = \$109.73$$

[4]E. I. Altman, "Measuring Corporate Bond Mortality and Performance," *Journal of Finance,* 44(4), 1989, pp. 909–922.

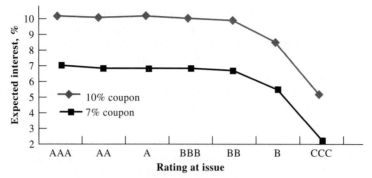

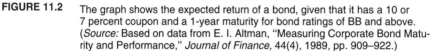

FIGURE 11.2   The graph shows the expected return of a bond, given that it has a 10 or 7 percent coupon and a 1-year maturity for bond ratings of BB and above. (*Source:* Based on data from E. I. Altman, "Measuring Corporate Bond Maturity and Performance," *Journal of Finance,* 44(4), 1989, pp. 909–922.)

Thus, the expected return on the bond is 9.73 percent, not the promised 10 percent.

Inspection of the graph in Figure 11.2 reveals that the difference between promised returns and expected returns is quite small for most bond-rating classes. Moreover, the difference between expected payments and promised payments is even smaller for maturities that are longer than the 1-year maturity on which the graph is based. Thus, the common practice of using promised payments and RAYTM to value debt may provide a close enough approximation to the value that we would obtain by discounting expected payments at an RADR.

11.4   BOND RATINGS

Bond ratings group bonds into risk classes. Ratings are given by rating agencies that are unrelated to the issuing firms and can be regarded as a substitute for some other risk measure, such as the bond's beta. Describing bond risk by broad categories is obviously somewhat misleading since a single rating group ignores differences between bonds *within* a rating category. Investors, however, don't ignore intrarating differences: Observed yield spreads within rating categories can be quite different, something we would not expect if rating classes were a sufficiently accurate way of measuring bond risks. Still bond ratings are extensively used for their simplicity.

The best-known rating agencies in the United States are Moody's Investors Service Inc. (Moody's) and Standard & Poors Corp. (S&P). There are also three other recognized rating agencies (Doff & Phelps; Fitch Investors Service; and McCarthy, Crisanti, & Maffei). Rating agencies are paid by the issuing firms and rate almost all bond issues. The incentive for issuers to be rated is that if the bond is unrated, it is considered an indication that the bond is very risky, which means that the buyers of unrated bonds demand high yields in order to compensate them for the high risk. The rating itself is done by committees, which reduces the possibility of one person unscrupulously biasing the rating of certain firms. In fact, rating agencies are held in such high regard that many regulations and firm charters are specified in terms of rating groups. For example, certain investors are prohibited from buying bonds rated below BBB, the lowest rating which is considered **investment grade.**

Many bond issues are rated by more than one rating agency. Over three-quarters of the bonds rated by more than one rating agency receive the same rating from both (or more) agencies. Approximately one-quarter of the rated bonds differ, mostly by one rating group. The rating groups of various agencies are similar. Exhibit 11.2 gives the rating categories used by S&P and Moody's:

Exhibit 11.2

S&P AND MOODY'S
Corporate Bond Ratings

S&P	Moody	
AAA	Aaa	Extremely strong capacity to pay the principal and interest
AA	Aa	Also high-quality debt—only a slightly diminished capacity to pay the principal and interest relative to the previous category
A	A	Strong capacity to pay the principal and interest but more suscepti-ble to adverse effects of changing circumstances and economic conditions
BBB	Baa	Adequate capacity to pay the principal and interest
BB, B CCC, CC	Ba, B, Caa, Ca	Predominantly speculative with respect to the issuer's capacity to pay the interest and principal in accordance with terms of obligation
C	C	Income bonds on which no interest is being paid
D	D	Bond in default

Note: S&P adds a plus ($+$) or a minus ($-$) to rating categories AA to B to indicate relative standing within the category. Moody's adds a 1, 2, or 3 subrating to the corresponding classes.
Source: Corporate and Municipal Bond Rating Definitions, Standard & Poors, 1989.

Bonds in rating categories of AAA through BBB are considered *investment grade,* whereas lower rating classes, because of their higher default risk, are often called **junk bonds** or, because of the associated higher required returns, are called **high-yield bonds.**[5] Many investors are restricted to investing only in investment-grade bonds. Consequently, the difference between a BBB rating and a BB rating may lead to a difference in the investor clientele that the issuer can attract.

The objective of rating agencies, as reflected in the description of the rating categories, is to rank the ability of issuers to meet their obligations to pay interest and principal. In terms of our notation and analysis rating agencies are mainly

---

[5]The terminology of bond traders is quite fancy. For example, bonds that were issued as investment-grade bonds and were subsequently down-rated are called *fallen angels.*

concerned with the probability that an issuer will default. The higher the probability of default is, the lower will be the rating assigned. Since a higher-default probability implies a higher yield spread, it follows that a lower rating implies a higher yield spread.

In his 1989 article in the *Journal of Finance,* Edward Altman also estimated the yield spread for various rating categories. Altman computed yield spreads for 1973 through 1987 relative to equal-maturity government bonds. His 1987 results, as shown in Exhibit 11.3, are typical.

Exhibit 11.3
Average Differences between YTM of Corporate Bonds and YTM of Equal-Maturity Government Bond Yields by Rating Categories in 1987

Rating	Yield spread
AAA	0.56%
AA	0.90%
A	1.16%
BBB	1.66%
BB	2.70%
B	4.20%
CCC	7.36%

Source: E. I. Altman, "Measuring Corporate Bond Mortality and Performance," *Journal of Finance,* 1989.

Because of their higher-default risk, the yield spreads of lower-rated bonds are, as expected, larger than the yield spreads of higher-rated bonds. Keep in mind, though, that yield spreads *exceed* the differences in the *expected* returns across the rating categories. This is because the YTM of a corporate bond, which is the *maximal* return on the bond, is higher than the bond's *expected* return, whereas the YTM of a government bond *equals* the expected return to its holder. For example, consider a B-rated bond with a 1-year maturity. The average yield spread in 1987 for B-rated bonds was 4.20 percent. But by using the estimated probability of default (*Pr*) and the estimated fractional loss upon default $(1 - \lambda)$ estimated by Altman, we find that the *expected* spread in returns is only

$$\Delta\text{RADR} = 4.20\% - (1 - \lambda) \cdot Pr$$
$$= 4.20\% - (100\% - 42.56\%) \cdot 2.42\%$$
$$= 2.81\%$$

The first term in the calculation is the yield spread and the second term is the expected loss in default times the probability of default. Thus, the difference in expected returns (2.81%) is smaller than the yield (4.20%). Nonetheless, the pattern of yields spreads is consistent with the pattern of expected returns of rating classes. This is because low-rated bonds have both a higher probability of default and a smaller fraction of their face value that is expected to be collected upon default than is the case for high-rated bonds.

11.5 ESTIMATING APPROPRIATE RATINGS

Since bond ratings play an important role in bond valuation and trading, much attention has been devoted to the question of what determines a bond's rating. Unfortunately, rating agencies don't disclose their rating guidelines because such a disclosure will allow manipulation, and because some of the considerations in determining a bond's rating are nonquantifiable. As substitutes, both researchers and practitioners build models that use observed characteristics of firms and bonds to explain observed ratings. These models are then used to predict likely ratings of bonds before they are issued and to estimate appropriate ratings and to predict rating changes for issued bonds. In this section we will discuss factors that are common to many of these models.

The principal aim of a bond-rating model is to assess the risk of default resulting from long-term instability and short-term liquidity problems. To assess long-term risks, analysts look at the firm's profitability, market significance, and leverage. To assess short-term liquidity, analysts look at the liquid assets and short-term liabilities of the firm. In general, the worse the firm appears in terms of both long-term stability and short-term liquidity, the lower the bond's predicted rating is or the more likely the bond will be down-rated by rating agencies.

The primary tools in gauging stability and liquidity are the financial ratios of the firm. If the objective of the analysis is to predict imminent rating changes or to judge whether current ratings properly reflect current risks (e.g., as part of the valuation of existing debt securities), then the financial ratios are computed on the basis of current financial statements. On the other hand, to predict likely ratings of debt securities that are considered for issuance or to choose among several proposed means of new financing, financial ratios are typically calculated by using *pro-forma* statements that reflect the firm's financial position subsequent to the security's flotation.

As with any other financial ratio analysis, ratios used in measuring stability and liquidity of firms are compared to standards—past ratios of the firm that we analyze or ratios of similar firms (i.e., firms in the same industry, with similar products and markets, etc.). There is an inherent problem in ratio comparison for rating assignment purposes that doesn't exist in the comparison of operating ratios as part of building pro-forma statements. When the operating ratios of a firm are compared to other firms in order to convert Sales projections to full pro-forma statements, it is done *within a single industry*. In this case it is reasonable to assume that firms in the same industry operate similarly. On the other hand, in comparing ratios of firms to determine bond risks, we often compare liquidity and leverage ratios of firms in *different* industries. For example, one of the ratios that is considered important in assessing firms' liquidity is the Quick ratio—the ratio of Current Liabilities to Current Assets less Inventories. If suppliers in the auto industry provide longer credit than suppliers in the food industry, then the Quick ratio of firms in the auto industry corresponds to liquidity needs that are of a longer term than the liquidity needs of the food industry. Yet the practice of comparing the ratios of a given firm to average ratios in a rating group underlies many methods of determining appropriate ratings. This means that you should never rely exclusively on mechanical rules and models of assigning ratings that ignore the specifics of the firms that are analyzed.[6]

Boeing Inc.

In the following subsections we describe ratios that are often used to assess the appropriate ratings of debt securities. We first discuss measures of long-term stability, profitability and leverage measures, and then measures of short-term liquidity. In our discussion of bond ratings and the ratios used in their estimation we illustrate the discussion by using Boeing's financial statements and Boeing's debt characteristics. To facilitate understanding the examples, Exhibit 11.4 presents the 1992 and 1993 financial statements of Boeing, which is a major aerospace firm producing commercial jets, military aircraft, and missiles.

Exhibit 11.4

BOEING INC.
Income Statements

	1992	1993
Net Sales	30,184	25,438
Expenses	(28,144)	(23,747)
Operating Income	2,040	1,691
Interest	(14)	(39)
Other Charges	(230)	(169)
Profit before Tax	1,796	1,483
Tax	(702)	(577)
Net Income	1,094	906
Additional Information		
Depreciation Charges	961	953
Other Noncash Charges	963	(465)

[6]As yield differentials within rating groups suggest, investors never do.

Exhibit 11.4 *continued*

BOEING INC.
Balance Sheets

	1992	1993
Cash and Marketable Securities	3,614	3,108
Accounts Receivable	1,428	1,615
Inventories	2,701	3,434
Other Current Assets	344	1,018
Total Current Assets	8,087	9,175
Long-Term Receivables	2,066	2,959
Depreciable Fixed Assets	10,277	11,786
Nondepreciable Fixed Assets	2,016	1,446
Accumulated Depreciation	(5,569)	(6,144)
Total Fixed Assets	6,724	10,047
Other Assets	1,270	1,228
Total Assets	18,147	20,450
Accounts Payable	2,869	5,854
Short-Term Liabilities	3,250	660
Short-Term Portion of Long-Term Liabilities	21	17
Current Liabilities	6,140	6,531
Long-Term Borrowing	1,772	2,613
Other Long-Term Liabilities	2,174	2,323
Total Liabilities	10,091	11,467
Common Stock	2,164	2,159
Retained Earnings	5,892	6,824
Total Liabilities and Equity	18,147	20,450

Profitability Ratios

Profitability is a key determinant of the firm's ability to pay its debt obligations. Thus, it is no wonder that the same ratios that equity investors rely on to forecast firm profitability are used by bond investors to judge the risk of the firm's debt securities. The most commonly used ratios for this purpose are those that can be called ''bottomline'' ratios—ratios that measure the net profitability of the firm and not the components of the profits.

Commonly used ratios include:

Pretax Return on Total Capital. The ratio of Operating Income before Interest Expenses to Total Assets
Operating Income to Sales. The ratio of Operating Income before Interest Expenses to Sales

These ratios are indicative of how profitable the firm is. Note that the profitability of the firm *as a whole* and not the after-tax *net* profit to which *shareholders* are entitled is relevant to debt holders. This is because debt holders have first priority on the cash flows of the firm, even before corporate taxes are levied. Thus, from the debt holder's point of view, the relevant ratios to measure profitability are the profitability of the *total assets* employed, as measured by the Pretax Return on Total Capital ratio, and the gross profitability of the firm's business, as measured by the ratio of Operating Income to Sales.

Using Boeing's financial statement data, we calculate its profitability ratios as shown in the following table:

	1992	1993
Net Sales ($ millions)	30,184	25,438
Operating Income ($ millions)	2,040	1,691
Total Assets ($ millions)	18,147	20,450
Pretax Return on Total Capital (%)	11.24	8.27
Operating Income to Sales (%)	6.76	6.65

Boeing's 1993 profitability ratios can be compared to previous years' ratios or to ratios of other firms. In the preceding table we can see that Boeing's profitability declined between 1992 and 1993, partially because its operating margin declined from 6.76 percent to 6.65 percent and partially because its asset base—the capital employed—increased from $18.1 billion to $20.5 billion. The substantial increase in assets used to generate Boeing's income raises another point regarding the way that the ratios are calculated.

Note that we calculate Boeing's return on capital by using the year-end value of total assets. In practice, it is also common to calculate this ratio by using the *average* assets employed—the average of the total assets at the beginning of the year and at the end of the year. For example, by employing the average assets that Boeing employed in 1993—$19.298 billion—the 1993 pretax return on total capital becomes 8.76 percent instead of the 8.27 percent that we calculated based on year-end total assets. The two calculation methods cause this large difference in ratios because Boeing increased its asset base in 1993 by more than 10 percent, or $2.3 billion. Unless the firm being analyzed is a high-growth firm, such large asset acquisitions, and the correspondingly large differences between ratios calculated by using the two methods, are not common. But when a firm does change its asset base materially during a fiscal year, the average asset base is more likely to reflect the correct asset base used to generate that year's income.

In a 1989 publication Standard and Poors (S&P) reported median ratios in the years 1986 through 1988 for industrial firms whose debt securities were rated.[7] S&P's median profitability ratios of different rating categories show that profitability is indeed closely related to bond ratings. (See Exhibit 11.5.)

---

[7]Standard and Poor's *Corporate and Municipal Bond Rating Definitions,* 1989.

Exhibit 11.5

Median Profitability Ratios in 1986–1988 for Various Bond Ratings

	AAA	AA	A	BBB	BB	B
Pretax Return on Total Capital (%)	24.2	22.1	17.1	14.4	12.8	9.9
Operating Income to Sales (%)	21.2	16.3	13.5	12.1	13.1	9.8

Source: Corporate and Municipal Bond Rating Definitions, Standard & Poors, 1989.

By using the 1989 median profitability ratios for comparison, we find that Boeing's profitability justifies a low-B rating. However, this cross-sectional comparison demonstrates a problem in comparing ratios across firms in the same rating group that we mentioned at the beginning of this section: Boeing's business is relatively capital intensive, making its return on capital low relative to firms that rely more on labor (such as textiles or computers). The fact that capital (rather than labor) is more intensively used by Boeing than by other firms doesn't necessarily make Boeing's business less desirable or more risky, and thus, by itself, should not indicate that Boeing's debt should have a low rating.

Besides these two profitability ratios, the economic prowess of a firm, and hence its economic stability, is often measured by the *size* of the firm. Size can be measured in several ways, but the most common one is Total Assets, which measures the total capital employed by the firm. S&P in the description of its rating process calls this factor **economic significance.** Empirically, it has been shown that, holding everything else equal, larger firms are rated higher than smaller firms. This partially has to do with the fact that larger firms have easier access to government aid when they fall on bad times. (Remember the U.S. government's guarantee of Chrysler's loans.) It may also reflect the fact that larger firms tend to encompass more lines of business so that their cash flows are more stable than those of smaller, more focused, firms. By using this criterion, Boeing as a multi-billion firm and a leader in its industry, definitely qualifies as having economic significance.

Leverage Ratios

Probably the most important determinant of default risk, and hence debt rating, is the leverage of the firm: The more debt that the firm employs in its capital structure, the less likely the firm will be able to meet its debt service obligations, or, in other words, the more likely that default will occur. Several ratios are used to measure leverage, some merely variants of each other. Popular leverage ratios are:

Long-Term Debt to Equity. The ratio of the book value of Long-Term Debt to the book value of Equity

Long-Term Debt to Capitalization. The ratio of the book value of Long-Term Debt to the sum of the book value of Equity and the book value of Long-Term Debt

Total Debt to Capitalization. The ratio of the book value of Long-Term Debt plus Short-Term Debt—Total Debt—to the sum of the book value of Equity and the book value of Total Debt

Several points are important to note regarding these ratios: First, these ratios exclusively use the book values of Debt and Equity. The market values of securities better reflect the events that took place from the time the securities were issued to the date of analysis. Thus, it is preferable to use market values in the calculation of such ratios. Unfortunately, market values for the firm's securities don't always exist. Moreover, since only book values are available for *all* firms, comparable ratios can be calculated by using only book values. In practice these ratios are largely calculated with book values rather than with market values.

A second point to remember is that the *economically relevant* leverage of the firm should have nonoperating liquid assets netted out. This is because liquid assets (often appearing as "Cash" or "Cash and Marketable Securities") can be used, if necessary, to repay some of the firm's debt. Suppose, for example, we want to calculate Boeing's ratio of Total Debt to Capitalization in 1993. The relevant numbers are presented in Exhibit 11.6.

Exhibit 11.6
BOEING INC.
Selected Balance Sheet Information, 1993

Cash and Marketable Securities	3,108
Short-Term Portion of Long-Term Liabilities	17
Long-Term Borrowing	2,613
Other Long-Term Liabilities	2,323
Total Assets	20,450

Assuming that Cash and Marketable Securities are essentially a *negative debt,* the ratio of Total Debt to Net Capitalization for Boeing is

$$\frac{\text{Net Total Debt}}{\text{Net Capitalization}} = \frac{-3,108 + 17 + 2,613 + 2,323}{20,450 - 3,108} = \frac{1,845}{17,342} = 10.64\%$$

Another point to remember is that accounting conventions often don't concur with economics. One particular case is the treatment of leases. Often firms lease assets in a way that doesn't fit the accounting classification as a capital lease. Nonetheless, the economic essence of many lease contracts is to combine an asset purchase with debt financing. In these cases we would like to convert annual lease payments into virtual debt. This is frequently done by assuming a discount rate and imputing an additional amount of debt equal to the present value (PV) of an infinite stream of annual lease payments. In equation terms, the calculation of the amount of virtual debt is

Leases and Lease Commitments

Total rental expense was $192 million in 1994, $177 million in 1993 and $166 million in 1992. Future minimum rental commitments under noncancelable leases for years ending December 31 are: 1995 $90 million; 1996 $63 million; 1997 $50 million; 1998 $40 million; and 1999 $35 million. For the ensuing three five-year periods, these commitments decrease from $39 million to $3 million. The minimum rentals over the remaining terms of the leases aggregate $9 million.

FIGURE 11.3   A note on leases and lease commitments. (*Source:* From Schlumberger's 1994 annual report.)

$$\text{Virtual debt} = \frac{\sum_t \text{annual uncapitalized lease payments}_t}{(1 + \text{discount rate})^t}$$

This virtual debt is added to the liabilities and to the assets side of the balance sheet before calculating the ratios involving Total Debt. This is because the vitual debt represents the unrecorded firm indebtedness resulting from lease commitments; on the other hand, it is the value of off-balance-sheets assets acquired through leases.

Information about such lease obligations appears in notes to financial statements. An example of a note on leases and lease commitments appears in Figure 11.3. As you can see, the information provided in financial statements about a firm's lease commitments is often very vague. Capitalizing lease obligations almost always requires ''guesstimates.''

Other nondebt obligations should also be included in the calculation of the leverage ratios, whether or not they are recorded as part of the firm's liabilities. For example:

• When a firm has both *funded* and *unfunded* employee-deferred compensation liabilities, only the unfunded portion appears in the balance sheet as a liability. In such cases it is common practice to add the funded liabilities (e.g., funded pension or health-care liabilities) to Total Debt and to add the earmarked assets to Total Assets.

• When firms have unconsolidated subsidiaries, it is common practice to add the debt of these subsidiaries to Total Debt. For example, a parent and a subsidiary in different lines of business (e.g., a finance subsidiary of a manufacturer) are often not consolidated even if the parent owns 100 percent of the subsidiary.[8] Economically, however, the liabilities of the subsidiary are not separate from those of the parent and should be reflected in the determination of the parent's rating.

---

[8] In such cases the net investments in subsidiaries are recorded as part of the parent's fixed assets.

Information about these liabilities doesn't always appear in the balance sheet as a formal liability. Although accepted current accounting practice (e.g., FASB statements 87 and 106) requires recording some of these liabilities as formal liabilities, more information about these liabilities can be found in footnotes to financial statements. An example of the information provided about pensions and other benefits for a company and its U.S. subsidiary (taken from Schlumberger's 1994 annual report) is shown in Figure 11.4. This information needs to be translated into virtual debt liabilities before leverage ratios are calculated.

FIGURE 11.4 This example gives information about pensions and other benefits for a company and its U.S. subsidiary. The analyst's job is to translate the information in these notes to debt liabilities. (*Source:* From Schlumberger's 1994 annual report.)

Pension and Other Benefit Plans

US Pension Plans

The Company and its US subsidiary sponsor several defined benefit pension plans that cover substantially all employees. The benefits are based on years of service and compensation on a career-average pay basis. These plans are substantially fully funded with a trustee in respect to past and current service. Charges to expense are based upon costs computed by independent actuaries. The funding policy is to contribute annually amounts that can be deducted for federal income tax purposes. These contributions are intended to provide for benefits earned to date and those expected to be earned in the future.

Net pension cost in the US for 1994, 1993 and 1992 included the following components:

	(Stated in millions)		
	1994	1993	1992
Service cost - benefits earned during the period	**$25**	$20	$16
Interest cost on projected benefit obligation	**44**	42	38
Expected return on plan assets (actual return: 1994 $3; 1993 $87; 1992 $44)	**(46)**	(42)	(41)
Amortization of transition asset	**(2)**	(2)	(2)
Amortization of prior service cost/other	**6**	3	5
Net pension cost	**$27**	$21	$16

The funded status of the plans at December 31, 1994 and 1993 was as follows:

	(Stated in millions)	
	1994	1993
Actuarial present value of obligations:		
Vested benefit obligation	**$577**	$567
Accumulated benefit obligation	**$579**	$570
Projected benefit obligation	**$645**	$643
Plan assets at market value	**584**	587
Excess of projected benefit obligation over assets	**(61)**	(56)
Unrecognized net loss (gain)	**9**	(3)
Unrecognized prior service cost	**28**	31
Unrecognized net asset at transition date	**(10)**	(12)
Pension liability	**$(34)**	$(40)

For 1994, assumed discount rate and rate of compensation increases used to determine the projected benefit obligation were 7.5% and 4.5%, respectively; the expected long-term rate of return on plan assets was 8.5%. For 1993, the rates were 7%, 4.5% and 9%, respectively. Plan assets at December 31, 1994 consist of common stocks ($367 million), cash or cash equivalents ($55 million), fixed income investments ($102 million) and other investments ($60 million). Less than 1% of the plan assets at December 31, 1994 represents Schlumberger Limited Common Stock.

Calculating the leverage ratios for Boeing, we get the following table:

	1992	1993
Long-Term Debt to Capitalization (%)	21.74	24.14
Total Debt to Capitalization (%)	55.61	56.07

The S&P estimates of the median leverage ratios in 1986 through 1989 are given in Exhibit 11.7.

Exhibit 11.7

Median Leverage Ratios in 1986–1988 for Various Bond Ratings

	AAA	AA	A	BBB	BB	B
Long-Term Debt to Capitalization (%)	12.4	18.8	30.1	37.7	50.5	66.1
Total Debt to Capitalization (%)	19.5	25.6	35.0	39.5	53.7	69.1
Total Debt + Leases (PV @ 8%) to Capitalization (%)	33.8	36.5	49.1	55.4	63.8	75.1

Source: Corporate and Municipal Bond Rating Definitions, Standard & Poors, 1989.

Compared to the median 1989 levels of the debt used by firms in the various rating groups, Boeing's long-term leverage ratio suggests that its debt is a weak AA, whereas because of high levels of short-term borrowing, Boeing's Total Debt ratio suggests only a weak BB rating. In deciding which debt ratio to weigh more heavily in estimating Boeing's appropriate rating, we should note that, unlike supplier credits, Boeing's traded debt is secured by Boeing's assets. This gives the holders of the traded debt priority in liquidation, which entails added security. Thus, the higher rating indicated by the long-term debt ratio is probably more important in the determination of the *traded* debt's appropriate rating.

All three ratios previously discussed as measures of leverage (or of long-term stability) are *balance sheet* ratios: They take their values from the latest balance sheet. As a result of the way that debt and equity are recorded in the books, changes in the values of debt and equity from the issue date are not recorded (until realized). One way to overcome this problem is to use **flow ratios**—ratios based on annual *flows* rather than on book values. These ratios are often called **coverage ratios** since they attempt to measure the extent to which the cash flows needed to serve debt holders are *covered* by the income of the firm.

A common coverage ratio used by analysts to determine the debt's risk is

$$\text{Pretax interest coverage} = \frac{\text{operating income}}{\text{interest charges}}$$

where operating income is Earnings before Interest and Tax (EBIT). A variant of this ratio computes a coverage ratio based on operating income before annual depreciation and amortization expenses (EBITDA). This is similar to computing coverage ratios based on cash flows, such as

$$\text{Pretax funds flow coverage} = \frac{\text{cash from operations}}{\text{interest charges}}$$

Often analysts add to the interest charges other fixed periodic payments that don't qualify as formal debt yet are virtually the same. For example, if the terms of a lease don't fall within the bounds of what qualifies as a capital lease, the lease will be recorded only as payments are made, even though from an economic point of view the lease payments may be fixed by a formal contract, like any other debt service obligation. In such cases the annual noncapitalized lease payments are added to the interest payments in the denominator of the ratios (as virtual interest).

Another variation of the preceding ratios is relevant when the firm has multiple debt securities of different seniority, such as senior and junior debt or straight debt and preferred stock. In such cases the coverage ratios of the *senior* debt securities compare the total income (e.g., EBIT) to the interest on the *senior* debt only, and the *junior* debt holders compute the coverage ratio *after deducting the senior debt's interest*:

$$\text{Junior interest coverage} = \frac{\text{operating income} - \text{senior interest expenses}}{\text{junior interest expenses}}$$

Some ratios are mixed—combining annual flows with balance sheet figures. For example,

$$\text{Pretax funds flow to debt} = \frac{\text{cash from operations}}{\text{total debt}}$$

or, taking into account the annual capital spending needs, the ratio

$$\text{Free funds flow to debt} = \frac{\text{cash from operations} - \text{net capital investments}}{\text{total debt}}$$

S&P median values for some of these ratios in 1989 are given in Exhibit 11.8.

Exhibit 11.8

Median Coverage Ratios in 1986–1989 for Various Bond Ratings

	AAA	AA	A	BBB	BB	B
Pretax interest coverage	13.5	9.0	5.3	3.7	2.4	1.3
Pretax interest coverage including rents	5.2	5.1	3.2	2.2	1.8	1.3
Pretax funds flow interest coverage	16.2	12.0	7.6	5.5	4.2	2.2
Funds from operations to total debt	109.5	83.9	47.7	37.1	23.4	9.5
Free operating cash flow to total debt	46.2	16.8	10.2	7.4	0.8	(4.2)

Source: Corporate and Municipal Bond Rating Definitions, Standard & Poors, 1989.

For Boeing the coverage ratios in 1992 and 1993 are presented in the following table:

	1992	1993
Pretax interest coverage	145.7	43.4
Pretax funds flow interest coverage	283.1	55.9

This means that, in terms of coverage, Boeing's debt should be rated AAA.

Liquidity Analysis

The objective of liquidity analysis is to determine whether the firm has enough liquid sources to meet its *immediate* cash needs and how liquid are the assets that may be necessary in case of a liquidity crunch. The liquidity needs of the firm are typically associated with the current liabilities of the firm. The underlying notion is a separation between long-run debt service obligations, which may be financed by cash from operations, and short-run cash needs, which the firm must meet with existing liquidity. The currently outstanding credit—both Accounts Payable and the current portion of the firm's debt obligations—constitutes the liquidity demand of the firm.[9]

In the short run only liquid assets can be used to meet the firm's short-term obligations. Two ratios are most frequently used to assess the firm's ability to meet its short-term obligations:

The **Current ratio.** The ratio of Current Assets to Current Liabilities

The **Quick ratio** *(or the **Acid ratio**).* The ratio of Current Assets exclusive of Inventory, Prepaid Expenses, and similar less liquid Current Assets to Current Liabilities

Both ratios compare the liquid assets that the firm has relative to the imminent payments it has to make. The difference is that in the Quick ratio we exclude inventory from the Current Assets since inventories may take a while to liquidate so that they represent funds that are less liquid than other current assets (such as Cash, Marketable Securities, and Accounts Receivable). Obviously, the higher either ratio is, the more liquid is the issuing firm and the lower is the risk of default due to unavailability of sufficient funds to meet short-term cash demands.

Boeing's Current and Quick ratios in 1992 and 1993 are given in Exhibit 11.9.

---

[9]Recall that current liabilities are liabilities to be paid within a year or within a business cycle.

Exhibit 11.9

	1992	1993
Cash and Marketable Securities	3,614	3,108
Accounts Receivable	1,428	1,615
Inventories	2,701	3,434
Other Current Assets	344	1,018
Total Current Assets	8,087	9,175
Current Liabilities	6,140	6,531
Current Ratio	1.32	1.40
Quick Ratio	0.82	0.72

Boeing's Current ratios show that Boeing had enough Current Assets to meet its short-term obligations and that its ability to meet short-term obligations, as measured by the Current ratio, improved slightly between 1992 and 1993. Since part of a firm's Current Assets, such as Inventory or Prepaid Expenses, are assets that can hardly be used to meet short-run cash needs, Current ratios are considered adequate when they are in excess of 2.0. Indeed, in Boeing's case the Quick ratio, which includes in its liquid assets only those assets that can be used to meet immediate cash needs, is less than 1.0, and had declined between 1992 and 1993. The discrepancy between the picture portrayed by the Current ratio and the one portrayed by the Quick ratio reflects Boeing's increase in Inventory and other Current Assets.

The Current and Quick ratios of one firm can be compared to the ratios of other firms in its same industry. This will indicate how liquid the firm is relative to comparable firms. The comparison of ratios for rating estimation purposes, however, is often not restricted to the same industry. The comparison of the Current and the Quick ratios across firms implicitly assumes that all firms' Current Assets are of the same quality. To check whether this implicit assumption is sensible, we may look at the quality of the Current Assets of firms. For example, we may use receivable days to learn how lax a firm's credit policy is and use inventory days to learn how liquid the firm's inventory is. This information may help to assess whether differences between the liquidity ratios of one firm and those of its industry's norm are perhaps justifiable, for example, by better than average current asset quality.

Converting Ratios to an Appropriate Rating

The profitability, leverage, and liquidity ratios just discussed are indicators of the extent to which the bondholders of the bond being valued are exposed to default risk. The next logical step is to convert these individual indicators of default risk to a single risk measure, such as a rating. By using this risk measure, we can estimate the appropriate (i.e., risk-adjusted) yield and value the bond.

Two primary approaches exist to assigning ratings to a bond—a qualitative approach and a quantitative approach. In the qualitative approach ratios are first evaluated individually and a final rating is assigned based on the overall picture that emerges. Initially, each ratio is compared to the average ratio of other issuers that are grouped by ratings. The rating whose average ratio is closest to the ratio of the issuer being analyzed is considered the best-fitting rating for the bond *based on this ratio.* For example, Boeing's Long-Term Debt to Capitalization ratio was 21.7 in 1992 and 24.1 in 1993. The average for this ratio over all AA-rated issuers (per S&P statistics reported earlier) is 18.8 and over all A-rated bonds is 30.1. Thus, Boeing's leverage ratio best fits an AA rating, although a weak one. Once the first step has been completed and several ratings have been assigned (each based on a different ratio comparison), it is hoped that a unified recommendation will emerge, that is, a single "best-fitting" ratio will emerge. This is hardly ever the case. For example, in Boeing's case a second leverage ratio—Total Debt to Capitalization, which also accounts for short-term borrowing, indicates only a BB rating. What ratings do we assign to Boeing in this case? When different ratios indicate several best-fitting ratings, a judgment call is required to assign an overall rating that reflects the individual ratings. Here the experience of the rater as well as other nonratio information determine which information to weigh more heavily in assigning a rating to a bond. In Boeing's case, probably because of Boeing's market significance, S&P rated the bond AA. On the other hand, Moody rated the bond A1 only. As we saw earlier, Boeing presents a tough call since different measures of the default risk provide widely differing indications, which entailed a discrepancy between Moody's and S&P's ratings.

The quantitative approach to converting individual ratios to a composite rating is more formal. In this approach we combine individual ratios into a composite score by using some sort of weighted average. The weights of individual ratios are estimated statistically by relating actual ratings of traded bonds to several ratios of the issuers of these bonds. An example of such models is the Z-score model of Altman,[10] which uses the following ratios and weights:

$$Z = 1.2 \cdot \text{Net Working Capital/Total Assets}$$
$$+ \ 1.4 \cdot \text{Retained Earnings/Total Assets}$$
$$+ \ 3.3 \cdot \text{Earnings before Interest and Tax/Total Assets}$$
$$+ \ 0.6 \cdot \text{Market value Equity/book value of Liabilities}$$
$$+ \ 1.0 \cdot \text{Sales/Total Assets}$$

In the formal method of assigning ratings, once the weights of the individual ratios are estimated, the combined score of an individual firm is computed by using the issuer's ratios and the estimated weights. The score of the issuer is then compared to the average scores of ratings groups, and the most fitting rating group is the

[10]E. I. Altman, "Financial Ratios, Discriminant Analysis and the Prediction of Corporate Bankruptcy," *Journal of Finance,* 23(4), 1968, pp. 589–609.

rating assigned to the bond. For example, Altman reported that a Z-score of less than 1.8 indicates a high probability of eventual default, whereas a Z-score above 3.0 indicates high safety.

Although the quantitative approach to assigning ratings may seem more objective than the qualitative approach, it is worth noting that formal rating systems, by their very nature, are rigid. Such systems don't use nonratio information, some of which may be very important in determining the default risk of a bond. The informal and qualitative approach allows for nonquantitative information to be incorporated into the rating process.

Here are some of the nonratio considerations that may affect rating assignments:

- **Seniority.** Firms often issue several bonds that are ranked by their seniority in default: holders of senior bonds are paid before holders of less senior bonds are paid. Since the higher the seniority of a bond the larger the payment will be to its holders in default, a higher seniority justifies a higher rating.

- **Collateral.** Often debt securities are collateralized by specific assets. In this case, upon default, the proceeds from the sale of such assets is first used to settle the claims of the holders of the collateralized bond. Clearly, the higher the value of the collateralized assets is and the more liquid their market is, the higher both the safety of the bond and the appropriate rating will be.

- **Sinking fund provisions.** Some bond indentures stipulate that the issuer should set aside funds (e.g., in an escrow account) according to a specific schedule whereby these funds will be used to pay back debt holders. Equivalently, indentures may require that the issuers redeem or repurchase in the market a predetermined fraction of the outstanding bonds prior to their maturity. Since setting money aside or redeeming bonds early reduces the bondholders' risk, bonds with sinking fund provisions deserve better ratings than bonds without such provisions.

These and other nonratio factors are typically part of the considerations of rating committees in rating agencies. On the other hand, quantitative models are typically the tools of analysts who try to capture the thinking process underlying rating committees' decisions by using a small number of ratios. Neither the quantitative nor the qualitative approach has a clear advantage over the other and the choice between them depends on the use. In general, it seems that a quantitative model is efficient in estimating appropriate ratings for many issues. On the other hand, when assigning ratings to only several bonds, the flexible (although inefficient) qualitative approach seems more suitable.

11.6 USING BOND RATINGS

Once the default risk of a firm's debt has been assessed and translated into a rating, we can estimate the appropriate (i.e., risk-adjusted) YTM with which to value the debt. The objective is either to judge the investment attractiveness of a debt security or to value the debt security. In the first case we compare the value of the bond that reflects our assessment of the bond's risk to its market price, and in the latter case we estimate a value for the bond that reflects our projections of the performance of the issuer (e.g., via the pro-forma statements generated for the firm).

Evaluating the Investment Attractiveness of a Bond

In practice, the investment attractiveness of a bond is evaluated by comparing the *actual yield spread* of the bond either to its *risk-adjusted yield spread* or to the yield spread justified by the assessed default risk of the bond. The process is as follows. We first estimate what we consider to be the *appropriate* rating for the bond. Then we compute the average yield spread of bonds in the same rating group. *The bond is regarded as a good investment opportunity (i.e., an investment offering a superior risk/return trade-off) if the actual yield spread of the bond exceeds the average yield spread of bonds in its rating.* Alternatively, the bond is considered a poor investment opportunity if the yield spread of the bond is less than the average yield spread of bonds in its rating.

To illustrate the idea, suppose we agree with the rating assigned by S&P to Boeing's bond—an AA rating. We can estimate the yield spread that is appropriate for Boeing's bond by averaging the yield spreads that investors demand of other AA-rated bonds of similar maturities. Exhibit 11.10 has such data for July 14, 1994: For each bond the table includes the YTM based on the average of the bond's bid and ask prices, the YTM of a government bond with a similar maturity date (denoted by r_f), and the difference between the YTMs—the yield spread.

Exhibit 11.10

Yield Spreads of AA-Rated Bonds on July 14, 1994

Firm	Coupon	Maturity	YTM	r_f	Spread
DuPont	9.150	15-Apr.-2000	7.33	6.60	0.73
Motorola	7.600	01-Jan.-2007	7.72	7.21	0.51
Wal-Mart	6.375	01-Mar.-2003	7.57	7.02	0.55
Mobil	8.375	12-Feb.-2001	7.36	6.74	0.62
Rockwell Int.	6.750	15-Sep.-2002	7.55	6.88	0.67
Upjohn	5.875	15-Apr.-2000	7.20	6.60	0.60
Gannett	5.850	01-May-2000	7.23	6.60	0.63
Coca Cola Co.	6.625	01-Oct.-2002	7.50	6.88	0.62

The average yield spread of 0.62 percent is our estimate of the market-required yield spread for AA-rated bonds. The YTM of Boeing's bond on that day was 7.85 percent and the YTM of a government bond maturing near the maturity date of Boeing's bond was 7.20 percent. Therefore, Boeing's bond yield spread of 0.65

percent was slightly above the average yield spread of other similarly rated bonds. This result may be interpreted in two ways. First, we can conclude that Boeing's debt is slightly more risky than the other AA-rated bonds, something that is consistent with the lower ratings assigned by Moody's (A1). As such, the higher than average return merely compensates for the higher than average risk within the rating class. Alternatively, if we are confident in our assessment of Boeing's bond risk, then the bond may be an attractive investment opportunity offering a better than average risk/return trade-off.

Note that by focusing on *yield spreads,* we effectively control for the two major risk sources for bonds:

* We control for the risk of changing interest rates by measuring yield spreads of an equal-maturity default-free bond.
* We control for the risk of default by comparing the spread to the average spread of equally rated bonds.

In comparing yield spreads across bonds in the same rating category, we implicitly assume that ratings are a *perfect measure of default risk.* But, of course, they are not. In fact, bond investors distinguish between ''strong'' and ''weak'' bonds within a rating class. A *strong* bond will offer a yield spread that is lower than the average bond in its rating category, whereas a *weak* bond will offer a yield spread that exceeds the average of the rating category. Thus, we should use our results regarding the relative strength of a rating assigned a bond in judging whether an above-average (or a below-average) yield spread indicates a good investment opportunity or properly reflects a differential default risk *within* a rating.

Using Bond Ratings in Valuation

An alternative use for bond ratings—a use that is most relevant in valuations—is estimating the value of a firm's debt by discounting its *promised* payments by the *appropriate YTM for its estimated rating*—the risk-adjusted YTM (RAYTM). As part of the sequential valuation process, we begin to split up the firm's value by estimating the value of its debt *given the estimated value of the firm and the characteristics of the debt.* To value the firm's debt:

* We use the current and pro-forma financial statements to compute the financial ratios used in the rating estimation, such as profitability, leverage, and liquidity ratios.
* We use the financial ratios to estimate the appropriate rating for the firm's debt either informally or by computing a combined rating score for the debt and comparing it to the scores of traded corporate bonds.
* We estimate the RAYTM by averaging the YTMs of traded bonds in the estimated rating group.
* We value the debt by discounting the *promised* cash flows at the RAYTM.

We can illustrate this use of the analysis of bond risk by using the example of the BB-rated bond. Recall that the bond's contract specified a coupon of 10 percent, a principal of $100, and maturity in 1 year. If our analysis concurs with the analysis of the rating agencies, we will accord the bond a BB rating. We can estimate the appropriate YTM of the bond, the RAYTM, by either averaging the YTMs of traded BB-rated bonds or using the current YTM of an equal-maturity government bond and an estimate of the long-run yield spread of BB-rated corporate bonds. To illustrate the latter method, we assume that the YTM of an equal-maturity government bond is 4 percent. We use Altman's estimated average yield spread for BB-rated bonds in 1987 of 2.7 percent as an estimate of the appropriate yield spread for BB-rated bonds. This means that the appropriate YTM for our bond is 6.7 percent.

By using this estimated *appropriate* YTM, we can value the bond by discounting the *promised* cash flows—the principal of $100 and the coupon of $10—in 1 year at this YTM:

$$\text{Bond value} = \frac{\$110}{1 + 6.7\%} = \$103.09$$

Similarly, we can value Boeing's debt by using the estimated RAYTM of the bond and the promised cash flows of the debt. The RAYTM is the sum of:

- The *average yield spread for bonds in its rating class,* estimated at 0.62 percent as of July 14, 1994
- The YTM of a government bond of the same maturity as the maturity of the debt that we value

For example, for the traded bond of Boeing we can use the government bond YTM of 7.20 percent to estimate a RAYTM of 7.82 percent. Suppose, for example, Boeing has another bond, say, a 3-year bond issued to pension funds. To value this bond, which doesn't need to be rated since it was privately placed and is not publicly traded, we would use the estimated yield spread of 0.62 percent and the YTM of a 3-year government bond, 6.17 percent on July 14, 1994, to estimate a RAYTM for this bond of 6.79 percent.

There are two caveats to the use of estimated RAYTMs and promised cash flows to value bonds. First, the estimated yield spreads are for *traded* debt securities. Applying them to *untraded* debt securities requires that we consider the effect of illiquidity on the required return on the debt. Specifically, since the value of illiquid debt is lower than the value of otherwise identical but liquid debt, the yield spreads of illiquid debt should be higher than average yield spreads of equally rated but traded debt. The second problem with the use of the YTM to value bonds is that yield spreads are anything but homogeneous. One reason for this is that bond-rating agencies are primarily concerned with *the probability of default.* Yet, as we have seen, the price of a bond also reflects the amount of money that is collectible when default happens. To an extent rating agencies also consider this factor in determining the appropriate rating for a bond: Rating agencies in determining a bond's rating consider the bond's seniority, the collaterability of the firm's assets, and other factors that relate to the amount of money that can be collected when the firm defaults. However, it is difficult to quantify the effect of such factors on the estimated RAYTM.

Empirical evidence suggests that yield spreads vary over time. This is to be expected, since, as economic conditions change, the probability of default as well as expectations about the amounts to be collected upon default change, the appropriate YTMs of bonds should change as well. Thus, we should be careful in using *historic* average yield spreads to estimate appropriate *current* YTMs: If economic conditions at the time that the averages were computed are not similar to current conditions, the historic yield spreads will differ from the yield spread that is relevant for today's default risks.

SUMMARY

In this chapter we discussed some of the basic issues of bond valuation. The practice of bond valuation is not to value debt securities, like any other security, by projecting *expected* cash flows and discounting them at an RADR. Instead, in practice, the *promised* cash flows of debt securities are discounted at the YTM of bonds of similar rating. The advantage of this method is its ease of implementation. To value debt securities in this method, you must:

• Estimate the appropriate rating of the debt by using financial ratios and non-financial information about the stability of the firm's cash flows.
• Estimate the yield spread by averaging the yield spreads of similarly rated bonds of similar lives.
• Discount the promised cash flows of the debt security being valued at an RAYTM—the YTM of a risk-free bond of a similar maturity plus the estimated yield spread.

The estimation of RAYTMs entails an assessment of the default risk of the bond expressed as a default-risk rating for the bond. Default risk of *traded* bonds is routinely monitored and rated by rating agencies. For untraded debt we assess the default risk by computing several financial ratios—profitability ratios, leverage ratios, and liquidity ratios—and convert these ratios into a representative rating class. The RAYTM of the debt is estimated as the average of the YTMs of *traded* bonds of the same rating or as the sum of the YTM of an equal-maturity government bond and the average yield spread of equally rated traded bonds.

Debt securities often include several options, such as callability and sinking funds requirements that can be satisfied in several ways at the issuer's option. Such features may affect the value of the debt security, and people who specialize in valuing and trading debt securities focus much more on these features than we have in this chapter. However, for the purposes of valuation this chapter will give you the basic necessary tools to value the bonds of a company—one important step in valuing the company's equity.

EXERCISES

11.1 The current date is January 1, 1996. The following table gives the term structure of interest rates—in terms of the pure discount rate—for risk-free government securities:

Year	Interest rate, %
1	6.03
2	6.17
3	6.31
4	6.45
5	6.60
6	6.74
7	6.88
8	7.02
9	7.16
10	7.18

You are trying to value a $1,000 face value bond about to be issued by Mort Corporation. The bond has a 10-year maturity and a coupon rate of 8 percent; in years 1 through 9 Mort Corporation will pay only interest (once a year, at the end of the year), and in year 10 it will pay interest and principal.

a If Mort Corporation's bond is free of default risk, how would you value it?

b What coupon rate would you assign to a similar bond, given that it is as riskless as a government bond, in order that the value today would be $1,000?

c If Mort Corporation's bond is rated A and the yield spreads required by investors on January 1, 1996, equal those given in Exhibit 11.3, what would be Mort Corporation's bond price?

11.2 Risky Company (RC) is about to issue a 1-year bond. The bond will bear a coupon of 12 percent (payable at the end of the year) and have a face value of $1,000. You estimate that the bond has a default probability of 10 percent and that RC will pay off 70 percent of face value if it defaults on the bond. If the bond is priced at par:

a What is the bond's expected return?

b What is the bond's yield to maturity (YTM)?

11.3 Reconsider problem 11.2. This time, however, assume that RC's bond has a 2-year maturity. Suppose in each of the 2 years the bond has a default probability of 10 percent and a payoff of 70 percent of face value in the case of default. Recalculate the expected return to a bondholder who plans to buy the bond (at par!) and to hold it for 2 years (unless it defaults at the end of the first year):

SP ratios	AAA	AA	A	BBB	BB	B
Pretax Return on Total Capital	24.2%	22.1%	17.1%	14.4%	12.8%	9.9%
Operating Income to Sales	21.2%	16.3%	13.5%	12.1%	13.1%	9.8%
Total Debt to Capitalization	19.5%	25.6%	35.0%	39.5%	53.7%	69.1%
Pretax Interest Coverage	13.5	9.0	5.3	3.7	2.4	1.3

11.4 You have constructed the following pro-forma model (see Exhibit 11.11) for the XYZ Corporation (the model is based on model 4 from Chapter 4).

a Based on the S&P bond-rating average ratios given above, what rating do you expect XYZ's debt will have in year 1?

b Do you expect an improvement in this debt rating? When? Explain.

Exhibit 11.11

XYZ CORPORATION
Pro-Forma Model 4

Sales growth	10%					
Initial Sales	1,000					
FA_Sales	95%					
CA_Sales	20%					
CL_Sales	7%					
COGS_Sales	75%					
Interest on Debt	10%					
Interest on Cash, Marketable Securities	9%					
Dividend Payout	50%					
Tax Rate	40%					
Depreciation rate	10%					
Year	0	1	2	3	4	5
		Profit and Loss				
Sales	1,000	1,100	1,210	1,331	1,464	1,611
Cost of Sales		825	908	998	1,098	1,208
Depreciation		102	110	121	133	146
Debt Interest		40	40	40	40	40
Interest on Cash, Marketable Securities		12	16	20	25	31
Profit before Tax		145	169	192	219	248
Taxes		58	68	77	87	99
Profits after Tax		87	101	115	131	149
Dividend		44	51	58	66	74
Retained Earnings		44	51	58	66	74
		Balance Sheet				
Cash and Marketable Securities	100	138	179	227	282	344
Current Assets	150	220	242	266	293	322
Fixed Assets						
At Cost	1,000	1,045	1,150	1,264	1,391	1,530
Accumulated Depreciation	300	402	512	633	765	911
Net Fixed Assets	700	643	638	632	625	619
Total Assets	950	1,001	1,059	1,125	1,200	1,285
Current Liabilities	70	77	85	93	102	113
Debt	400	400	400	400	400	400
Equity						
Stock	380	380	380	380	380	380
Accumulated Retained Earnings	100	144	194	252	318	392
Total Liabilities	950	1,001	1,059	1,125	1,200	1,285

APPENDIX: Valuing Bonds by Discounting Expected Cash Flows at RADR

The approach used to value bonds in the chapter (explained in Sections 11.2 and 11.3) is to value a bond by discounting its *promised payments* at its RAYTM. As mentioned in the chapter, there is another possible approach to valuing bonds, namely, discounting the bond's *expected cash flows* at its RADR. We will discuss this approach in this appendix.

The valuation of bonds by using expected cash flows and an RADR treats a bond as we would any other asset, that is, *by discounting the expected payoffs of the bond at an appropriate* RADR. Implementing this approach involves the following steps:

1 Estimate the *expected debt payoffs* based on an evaluation of the *probability of default* and the *expected payment on the debt in case of default*. Exhibit 11.1 gives some statistics from Altman (1989) that will help you estimate these parameters.
2 Estimate the RADR for the debt. We estimate the RADR by adding an appropriate risk premium to a base rate (the risk-free rate of interest). The RADR should be based on two factors:
   a The *basic risk-free discount rate* for the debt is the rate on an *appropriately equivalent government bond,* where the designation ''appropriately equivalent'' is based on a government bond having either:
     (i) The same *duration* as the corporate bond or
     (ii) The same *maturity* as the corporate bond
   b The *appropriate risk premium* for the bond is the second factor. We suggest that you base this risk premium on the CAPM, measuring a bond's beta as we would that of any other traded security.

Estimating a Bond's Expected Cash Flows

As discussed in Section 11.3, the expected cash flows of a bond reflect the *promised cash flows,* the *probability of default,* and the *amount collected by debt holders upon default.* Recall the notation of Section 11.3:

   F = face value of the bond
   C = annual coupon rate of the bond
  Pr = annual probability that the firm will default
   λ = fraction of the bond's face value that bondholders expect to collect upon default
r_{debt} = bond's expected annual return, which is commensurate with the bond's risk

Consider a bond maturing one year from now. With probability $(1 - Pr)$ the issuing firm doesn't default. In this case bondholders receive the full coupon, $F \cdot C$, plus the face value of the debt, F. With probability Pr the issuing firm defaults. In this case bondholders only receive $F \cdot \lambda$ dollars. The expected payoff to bondholders, which takes into account both the possibility that default occurs and the possibility that it doesn't occur, is

$$E(\text{CF}^{\text{debt}}) = (1 - Pr) \cdot (1 + C) \cdot F + Pr \cdot \lambda \cdot F$$

To illustrate, consider a 1-year bond with the following characteristics:

- The bond pays an annual coupon of 10 percent.
- The estimated annual probability of default is 0.4 percent.
- The fraction of the face value collected upon default is 36 percent.

(These are the average characteristics estimated by Altman for BB-rated bonds.) The year-end expected cash flow per $100 face value is

$$\$110 \cdot (1 - 0.4\%) + \$36 \cdot 0.4\% = \$109.704$$

Estimating a Bond's RADR

The most important risk to which debt holders are subject is that the firm will not be able to meet its debt service obligations; that is, the firm will be in default. Because of this risk, despite the fact that debt holders are promised ''secured'' cash flows, their cash receipts are actually not certain. The risk of default means that debt securities' values incorporate some default-risk premium.

To price default risk, we should first decide the extent to which default risk is *systematic*: Systematic default risk affects the RADR with which the expected payments to debt holders are discounted, whereas diversifiable default risk only affects the calculation of the debt holders' expected cash flows. But default risk is neither exclusively systematic nor exclusively diversifiable; it is a reflection of the firm's risk and as such it is partially systematic and partially diversifiable. To see this in the simplest way, note that default occurs when the firm encounters bad times because these are the times that shareholders are unable to meet their debt service obligations. On the other hand, in good times share-holders *can* service their debt and will not default. In other words, the payoff to debt holders is correlated with the payoff to equity holders: Equity holders, as residual claimants, are not paid until debt holders are paid in full, something that doesn't happen when the firm defaults.[11] Because the risk of default and the risk of the firm are correlated, the default risk is both systematic and diversifiable as much as the firm's risk is both systematic and diversifiable. Therefore, in valuing debt securities, we have to consider the effect of default risk on the discount rate as well as on the expected cash flows.

Since debt risk is almost always partially systematic, the estimation of the *expected* return on the debt requires that we estimate the sensitivity of the debt's payoff to macroeconomic risks. For example, to use the CAPM to determine the debt's expected return, we need to estimate the debt's beta, which we denote by β_{debt}. Once we have estimated β_{debt}, we can compute the expected return on the debt as the sum of the yield of an equal-maturity default-free bond and a risk premium that is proportional to the beta and to the price of a unit beta, which we denote by π_m, the risk premium on the market portfolio. To write this formally, we can estimate the expected return on the debt, which we denote by r_{debt}, by using the CAPM in the following relation:

$$r_{\text{debt}, t} = rf_t + \beta_{\text{debt}} \cdot \pi_m$$

---

[11]In practice, equity holders often get something even when their firm defaults on its debt obligations and debt holder's claims are not fully paid.

where the subscript t on the expected return of the debt and on the risk-free return reminds us that we have to match the maturities of the comparable government bond with the maturity of the debt that we value.

To illustrate this approach, suppose we estimate that the beta of a 10 percent 1-year corporate bond is 0.2. Additionally, we assume that the yield on a 1-year Treasury note is 4 percent and that the premium on the market portfolio equals 8 percent. To estimate the *expected* return on the corporate bond, we add to the risk-free yield of 4 percent a risk premium that reflects a β_{debt} of 0.2 and a market risk premium of 8 percent, or a premium of $0.2 \cdot 8\% = 1.6\%$. This gives us an estimated *expected* return on the debt (r_{debt}) of 4% + 1.6% = 5.6%.

It is important to remember that 5.6 percent is the *expected* return on the debt. The *actual* return on the debt, in general, will *not* equal the expected return: Sometimes the actual return will exceed the expected return and sometimes it will fall short of expectations. In particular, a firm that *may* default on its debt service obligations can either default, in which case the actual return to debt holders will fall short of the expected return, or fully repay its obligations, in which case the actual return will exceed the expected return. For most bonds the probability of no default far exceeds the probability of default (see, for example, Exhibit 11.1 earlier in this chapter). Thus, the probability of the actual return exceeding the expected return is much higher than the probability that the actual return falls short of the expected return. Yet the actual return *averages* to the expected return because when default does occur, the shortfall is much larger than the additional return earned when default doesn't occur.

How do we estimate β_{debt}? When the debt of the firm is publicly traded, we can simply estimate its beta in the same manner that we estimate betas of any other traded security. This is done by regressing the return on the traded debt with respect to the return of the market portfolio. Specifically, we estimate a regression equation of the form

$$r_{debt, t} = a + b \cdot r_{m, t} + \epsilon_t \tag{11A.1}$$

where a and b are the regression intercept and slope coefficients, respectively. The estimated slope coefficient, $\hat{b}$ in the regression equation, is the estimated β_{debt}.

To see how this is done, consider again the Boeing bond (8.1 percent of 2006) that we considered in the chapter. The weekly returns of this bond and of the S&P index in the period June 1993 through June 1994 are given in Exhibit 11A.1.

Exhibit 11A.1

Weekly Returns of Boeing Bond and S&P 500 Index

Week ended	S&P 500 return, %	Boeing bond return, %	Week ended	S&P 500 return, %	Boeing bond return, %
06/04/93			12/17/93	0.605	0.351
06/11/93	−0.545	1.248	12/24/93	0.291	1.169
06/18/93	−0.724	0.351	12/31/93	−0.122	1.264
06/25/93	0.960	1.169	01/07/94	0.817	1.294
07/02/93	−0.316	0.694	01/14/94	1.143	−0.428
07/09/93	0.586	0.194	01/21/94	0.037	0.455
07/16/93	−0.450	0.522	01/28/94	0.915	1.344
07/23/93	0.380	−1.845	02/04/94	−1.780	−1.865
07/30/93	0.307	0.413	02/11/94	0.156	0.122
08/06/93	0.200	0.627	02/18/94	−0.453	−1.551
08/13/93	0.402	1.169	02/25/94	−0.269	−0.700
08/20/93	1.414	0.972	03/04/94	−0.208	−1.284
08/27/93	1.037	1.148	03/11/94	0.443	−0.542
09/03/93	0.251	−2.398	03/18/94	1.067	−0.232
09/10/93	0.159	−1.186	03/25/94	−2.148	−0.937
09/17/93	−0.549	0.920	04/01/94	−3.141	−2.277
09/24/93	−0.185	−0.664	04/08/94	0.378	0.287
10/01/93	0.875	−1.275	04/15/94	−0.129	−0.078
10/08/93	−0.133	1.758	04/22/94	0.402	0.374
10/15/93	2.073	0.810	04/29/94	0.810	−0.797
10/22/93	−1.250	0.142	05/06/94	−0.608	−2.189
10/29/93	1.061	−0.915	05/13/94	−0.745	0.703
11/05/93	−1.689	1.330	05/20/94	2.504	2.187
11/12/93	1.343	−1.021	05/27/94	0.607	−0.581
11/19/93	−0.523	−0.526	06/03/94	0.689	1.138
11/26/93	0.176	−0.038	06/10/94	−0.240	−0.069
12/03/93	0.472	0.245	06/17/94	0.029	−0.069
12/10/93	−0.130	1.248	06/24/94	−3.337	−0.369

In Figure 11.5 we plot the returns to the holders of Boeing's bonds against the returns on the S&P. By using Figure 11.5, we can visually examine the relation among these returns.

Regressing the returns of the Boeing bond on the returns of the S&P index, we estimate the following regression parameters:

$$r_{debt}^{BA} = 0.02\% + 0.3 \cdot r_{S\&P} + \epsilon, \qquad R^2 = 0.0988$$

Thus, the beta of Boeing's 8.1 percent of the 2006 bond is estimated to be 0.3.[12]

---

[12]Although the R^2 of this regression may seem low, it is not unusual for CAPM regressions. Even though the beta is a significant risk factor for the bond, it explains only about 10 percent of the weekly variation in the bond's returns.

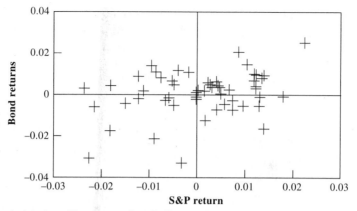

FIGURE 11.5   A plot of weekly returns to bondholders on Boeing's bond against the returns on the S&P 500 index, June 11, 1993, through June 24, 1994.

Combining the estimated beta of the bond with a risk premium (per unit beta) of 8 percent gives us an appropriate risk premium for this bond of 2.4% (= 8% · 0.3). At the end of June 1994, a government bond maturing in 2006 yielded 7.2 percent. Thus, we estimate that (at the end of June 1994) the RADR that is commensurate with Boeing's bond systematic risk is 9.6% = 7.2% + 2.4%. Remember, however, that this is only an *estimate* of the RADR. In particular, the RADR estimate is based on the beta estimate for the bond. The beta of Boeing's bond is clearly not zero as many of the often used formulas in corporate finance implicitly assume.[13]

Although the systematic risk of publicly traded debt is simple to estimate, most debt issued by corporations is not publicly traded. For example, the debt of most firms includes bank loans, privately placed debt, and letters of credit. For some of these firms, besides the nontraded debt, there exist debt securities that are traded. For these firms we can approximate the beta of the nontraded debt by the beta of the traded debt. This is a good approximation because debt holders' returns primarily depend on whether or not the firm defaults, and because when shareholders cannot service one debt security, it is unlikely that they can (for economic and legal reasons) continue serving other debt obligations.[14]

Thus, when one of the debt securities that the firm has issued is publicly traded, we can approximate the β_{debt} of *all* the debt securities issued by the same firm by the estimated beta of the *traded* debt security. For example, we can estimate that the beta of *all* the debt securities of Boeing, whether or not traded, is about 0.3 since we have estimated the beta of a traded debt security of Boeing to be 0.3.[15]

---

[13]The statistically inclined reader will recall that a formal test of whether Boeing's bond beta is zero is the *t*-test. The *t*-statistic of the equality of the beta of Boeing's debt to zero is 2.41.

[14]Almost all indentures include a cross-bankruptcy provision, specifying that default on one debt security automatically triggers default on all debt securities (or, at the very least, makes all other debt securities immediately payable).

[15]This approximation is not quite accurate. The beta of debt securities reflects (among other things) comovement of the market portfolio and of bond prices when interest rates change. This comovement is larger for long-maturity bonds than for short-maturity bonds. Thus, long-maturity bonds tend to have higher betas than short-maturity bonds.

Valuing a Bond Given Estimated Expected Cash Flows and RADR

To value the bond, as in the valuation of any other security, we discount the expected cash flows at the RADR:

$$\text{Price} = \sum_{i=1}^{M} \frac{E(CF_t)}{(1 + RADR)^i}$$

Returning to the example of a 1-year 10 percent bond, the expected cash flows of which are estimated as $109.704 and the RADR of which is estimated as 5.6 percent (4 percent risk-free rate and 1.6 percent risk premium), the value of the bond is

$$P = \frac{\$109.704}{1 + 5.6\%} = \$103.886$$

Note that this value for the bond reflects both the systematic risk of default, through the risk premium of 1.6 percent included in the expected return, and the diversifiable risk, through the computation of the expected cash flows.

What are the possible returns that debt holders can realize? In our example there are two possible outcomes: In a year the firm can either be in default or pay its debt holders. With 0.4 percent probability, default will occur and the debt holders will receive only $36. On the other hand, if default doesn't occur, the debt holders will receive the full promised payment of $110. In the first case the bondholders will lose a substantial portion of their investment. The bondholders' *realized* return in this case will be

$$R = \frac{CF_1 - P_0}{P_0}$$

$$= \frac{36 - 103.886}{103.886}$$

$$= -0.653 = -65.3\%$$

On the other hand, when default doesn't occur, the bondholders will receive payments in excess of the expected cash flow and their realized return will exceed the expected return:

$$R = \frac{110 - 103.886}{103.886}$$

$$= 0.0589 = 5.89\%$$

Since default, with the associated return of -65.3 percent, occurs with a very small probability (of 0.4 percent) it is still possible to expect an average rate of return of 5.6 percent, even though when default doesn't occur, the bondholders' actual return is merely 0.29 percent above the expected return.

The Relation between the RADR and RAYTM of Bonds

With the bond's price calculated, we can examine the relation between the YTM of a bond and its expected return. How do we calculate YTMs? To calculate a YTM, we determine the internal rates of return (IRR) of an investment in a bond for its market price relative to the *promised payments* as the cash inflows in the IRR equation. In our example of the 10 percent 1-year BB bond priced at $103.886, we solve the following equation:

$$103.886 = \frac{110}{(1 + \text{IRR})}$$

The solution of this equation is an IRR of 5.9 percent. This is the *maximal* return that bondholders can receive. But this is reasonable, since in calculating the YTM, we take the *promised* cash flows as if they are the *expected* cash flows. Thus, the YTM of a corporate bond is indeed the *maximal* return that bondholders can get: The firm will never pay bondholders more than it *promised* to pay. Yet, obviously, it may pay less if it encounters bad times causing the firm to default and the bondholders to realize a return that is lower than the bond's YTM.

The example shows us that we can decompose the YTM of a corporate bond into three parts:

- The risk-free rate (4 percent in our example)
- The premium for the systematic risk (1.6 percent in our example)
- The premium for the default risk (0.3 percent in our example)

This is true of bond YTMs in general. We can decompose the YTM, which is the *promised* rate of return to the time value of money, a premium for the systematic risk of the bond, and a premium for the possibility that what was promised will not be realized. Can we determine the appropriate promised return of a bond, that is, its appropriate YTM, from the estimated *expected* return, probability of default, and expected payment if default occurs? The relation was determined by Gordon Pye.[16] Using his reasoning, we assume that the following parameters have been estimated:

Pr = annual probability that the firm will default
λ = fraction of the bond's face value that bondholders will collect if the firm defaults
r_{debt} = bond's expected annual return, which is commensurate with the bond's risk

Now we want to know, given these estimates, what is the appropriate YTM on this bond. We can view this problem from a different angle: If the firm plans to issue new debt (with these parameters), what should be the coupon rate so that the bond can be sold at par? Denote the appropriate YTM by Y.

Let's normalize the face value of the bond to $1. By using the preceding estimates, we can see that if the firm doesn't default, something that happens with probability $(1 - Pr)$, bondholders will receive the full coupon, Y. In this case they also have the bond itself, which can be converted to one dollar in cash by either redeeming it (if this is the bond's maturity year) or selling it in the market.[17] Thus, absent default, bondholders will receive $(1 + Y)$. On the other hand, if default does occur, bondholders will receive only λ dollars. The expected payoff to bondholders, which takes into account both the possibility that default occurs and the possibility that it doesn't occur, is

$$E(\text{CF}^{\text{debt}}) = (1 - Pr) \cdot (1 + Y) + Pr \cdot \lambda$$

---

[16]Refer to Gordon Pye, "Gauging the Default Premium," *Financial Analyst Journal,* 1974, pp. 49–52.
[17]We ignore the price risk of the bond in this simple analysis. Formally, this analysis implicitly assumes that the *expectations theory* of the term structure of interest rates holds.

This expected cash flow when discounted at the bondholders' expected return, r_{debt}, should give us the value of the bond, which we normalized at one dollar. Thus, we obtain the following equation:

$$1 = \frac{(1 - Pr) \cdot (1 + Y) + Pr \cdot \lambda}{1 + r_{debt}}$$

Manipulating this expression to solve for Y, we get the promised yield that is commensurate with the default risk and the required return:

$$Y = \frac{r_{debt} + Pr \cdot (1 - \lambda)}{1 - Pr} \tag{11A.2}$$

The expression we obtained for the appropriate YTM is intuitive. First, note that when default is not expected (i.e., when $Pr = 0$), the appropriate YTM equals the expected return (i.e., $Y = r_{debt}$). This is reasonable since when default is not expected, the *promised* return is also the *expected* return. Thus, the expected return, r_{debt}, is the benchmark by which the YTM is determined. When default is possible, the expected return is converted into the YTM by two adjustments:

• We add $Pr \cdot (1 - \lambda)$ to r_{debt}.
• We divide the adjusted r_{debt} by $(1 - Pr)$.

The first adjustment is a compensation to debt holders for the loss that they incur when default happens. There is a Pr chance that debt holders pay one dollar but collect only λ. Hence, the promised return should exceed the expected return by the expected loss that debt holders sustain when default occurs.

The second adjustment is dividing the adjusted r_{debt} by $(1 - Pr)$. Intuitively, this adjustment is intended to capture the fact that the promised return, Y, is only earned with $(1 - Pr)$ probability. Thus, the promised return ''grosses up'' the expected return by the probability of its actually happening.

To see the equation in use, let's go back to the BB-rated bond that we considered earlier. Recall that this bond matures in 1 year, has a 0.4 percent probability of defaulting, will pay its holders 36 percent of face value if the firm defaults, and has an expected rate of return of 5.6 percent. The YTM of this bond that will make the expected return equal 5.6 percent is

$$Y = \frac{5.6\% + 0.4\% \cdot (1 - 36\%)}{1 - 0.4\%}$$

$$= 5.88\%$$

This is precisely the YTM that we obtained for the bond when we calculated it from the promised coupons and the price of the bond (which properly reflects the bond's default risk).

Equation (11A.2) tells us several things about the relation between the rate of return that the bondholders are *promised* and the rate of return that they *expect*. Specifically, the extent to which YTM exceeds r_{debt} increases when the probability of default increases and when the sums that debt holders can collect upon default declines. To illustrate this by using our fictitious BB-rate bond, suppose there is another firm of which the debt also has a β_{debt} of 0.2 and, commensurate with it, has an expected return of 5.6 percent. The only difference between the two firms (and their debt securities) is that the latter firm has a higher *diversifiable* risk of default. For example, let's assume that the new firm's annual default probability is 1 percent (instead of 0.4 percent as given for the first firm). What would be the appropriate YTM of this bond? Recalculating equation (11A.2) with the new default probability, we get

$$Y = \frac{5.6\% + 1.0\% \cdot (1 - 36\%)}{1 - 1.0\%}$$

$$= 6.30\%$$

Thus, a change in the default probability from 0.4 percent to 1.0 percent in our example means a change in the appropriate YTM from 5.88 percent to 6.30 percent. Remember that the difference in the YTM is exclusively related to differences in *diversifiable* default risk. Accordingly, despite the fact that the two bonds have different YTMs, *both bonds have the same expected return* (of 5.6 percent). This happens because the computation of YTMs compares *promised* payments to bond prices, whereas the computation of expected returns compares *expected* payments to bond prices. Still, because the expected payments depend on the promised payments (and on the probability of default), the two measures of bond returns are highly correlated.

It is common to measure the default premium of a bond by the difference between its YTM and the YTM of an equal-maturity government bond, which is also called the **yield spread** of the bond. From equation (11A.2) we can see that the yield spread indeed reflects default risk, systematic as well as diversifiable. We can also see that the yield spread reflects both default risk and the expected payment upon default. In fact, we can use equation (11A.2) to derive the *appropriate* yield spread:

$$\Delta Y = \frac{r_{\text{debt}} + Pr \cdot (1 - \lambda)}{1 - Pr} - Rf_t \qquad (11A.3)$$

where ΔY denotes the yield spread and Rf_t denotes the YTM of a government bond (i.e., a default-risk-free bond) with the same maturity date. For example, in our hypothetical BB-rated bond the yield spread is

$$\Delta Y = 5.88\% - 4.00\% = 1.88\%$$

For the second bond, the one with the higher probability of default, the yield spread is also larger:

$$\Delta Y = 6.30\% - 4.00\% = 2.30\%$$

If the bond that we value is publicly traded, we can compare the bond's *observed* yield spread to the spread that we consider appropriate given our estimated probability of default and the amount that we estimate can be collected upon default. For example, assume we observe that the hypothetical BB-rated bond that we consider has a YTM that is 2.70 percent above the YTM of an equal-maturity government bond. Since our estimates of the default probability and consequences of default (as detailed in the analysis of the example) justify a yield spread of only 1.88 percent, from our perspective, this bond presents an attractive buying opportunity. This is because our analysis suggests that the default risk of the bond is less severe than the market considers this risk to be.

CHAPTER 12

THE VALUATION OF CONVERTIBLE SECURITIES

OVERVIEW

In this chapter we discuss the valuation of corporate securities that incorporate optionlike features. These options typically allow security holders to convert securities into another security—thus their name, **convertible securities** or **convertibles.** Convertible securities can be of many types:

- **Warrants** are securities that entitle their holders to buy shares from the firm.
- **Convertible bonds** are bonds that entitle their holders to convert them into shares or, less often, into preferred stock, warrants, and so on.
- **Convertible preferred shares** are preferred stock that can be converted into common stock (or other securities).

In the process of valuing firms and their securities, which begins with a valuation of the whole firm and proceeds with the division of this value among the different securities, the valuation of convertible securities precedes the valuation of the stock of the firm. The value of the stock is then the residual value—the value of the whole firm less the value of the firm's debt and its convertible securities. In this chapter we discuss methods developed for the valuation of derivative securities to derive the value of convertible securities based on their contractual terms and the value of the whole firm.

The most commonly used convertible securities are warrants and convertible bonds. The prevalence of warrants is largely due to the proliferation of **employee stock option plans,** in which key employees are awarded options to buy their company's stock. Executive options, which are warrants, often comprise a significant fraction of the equity structure of the firm.

The way that convertible securities are valued follows from the nature of the contract: We first value the basic security and then add the value of the option to convert the basic security into another security. For example, to value a convertible bond:

- We value the straight debt part by discounting the promised cash flows at the yield to maturity (YTM) that is appropriate for the bond's risk (as explained in Chapter 11).
- We add to the straight-debt value the value of an option to buy shares from the firm according to the conversion terms.

Since there can be many types of convertible securities, we cannot discuss the valuation of *all* convertible securities in this chapter. Instead, we discuss the principles of the valuation of convertible securities. We show how to account for the effects of:

- Dilution of existing shareholders' claims
- Infusion of cash to the firm upon conversion
- Interim cash flows, such as dividends and interest

We consider the valuation of convertible securities in the context of warrants and convertible bonds. We begin with the valuation of warrants, which are the simplest convertibles to value. The valuation of a convertible bond, the other convertible security that we consider, is only slightly more complicated—besides the conversion option, we need only to value a straight bond, which we have already done in Chapter 11.

In the valuation of convertible securities we use the **Black and Scholes (B&S) formula** to value conversion options. We present in Section 12.1 a short review of option terminology, the logic underlying the derivation of the B&S formula, the formula itself, and its use. In Section 12.2 we discuss the valuation of warrants, which entails an adjustment of the B&S formula for the effects of dilution and cash infusion upon exercise. Section 12.3 applies the warrant valuation model to the Smucker warrants that were discussed in Chapter 7. In Section 12.4 we consider the valuation of convertible bonds. We illustrate the techniques of convertible security valuation in Section 12.5 by valuing a convertible bond of Home Depot.

12.1 A SHORT REVIEW OF OPTION THEORY

An *option* is a security that gives its owner the *right* to *purchase* or *sell* a given *asset,* on or before a given *date,* at a predetermined *price.* The key element in this definition is that the option holder has the *right* but not the obligation to a certain action.

The following terminology is standard:

- An option *to purchase* an asset is called a **call option,** whereas an option *to sell* is called a **put option.** Most convertible securities entitle their holders to *purchase* corporate securities (e.g., stocks), which means that the options embedded in convertible securities are typically *call* options.

- The asset that the option holder can buy (for a call option) or sell (for a put option) is called the **underlying asset.** In the convertible security contracts considered in this chapter the contract specifies the underlying asset as *shares of the issuer.*

- The last day on which the option can be exercised is called the **expiration date.** Options that can be exercised *on the expiration day only* are called **European options,** whereas options that can be exercised *on any day up to the expiration day* are called **American options.**

- The price at which an option can be exercised is called the **exercise price** or the **strike price** of the option.

- The price of the option, which the buyer pays for the right to buy or sell the underlying asset, is called the option's **premium.** The premium is paid to the seller of the option—in the jargon of option markets, the **writer** of the option.

- When an option is written by an investor, it is simply called an *option.* When the firm whose stock is the underlying asset writes the option, we call the option a *warrant.* Although warrants are basically call options, there is an important difference between a regular call option and a warrant: When a warrant is exercised, the number of shares in the firm increases. On the other hand, when a regular call option is exercised, there is no increase in the number of outstanding shares of the firm since at the exercise the writer of the option hands over shares that he or she holds to the owner of the option. In Section 12.2 we discuss how to incorporate this difference between regular options and warrants into the B&S option pricing framework.

As mentioned earlier, there are options on many underlying assets. In our review and illustrations we will implicitly assume that the underlying asset is a publicly traded stock. For example, in Exhibit 12.1 we give the prices of options on Intel stock. The options are exchange-traded standardized options: Their expiration days are the third Saturday of the expiration month, their exercise prices are in increments of $5, and each option is for 100 shares.[1] In Exhibit 12.1 you can see that:

1 The call option on Intel stock with an expiration date of May 20, 1994 and a strike price of $55 per share traded for $5\frac{5}{8} \cdot 100 = \$562.50$. This option gives its owner the right to buy 100 shares of Intel stock on or before May 20, 1994, for $55 per share. For this option:

   a $55 is the *exercise price* (or the *strike price*).

   b May 20, 1994, is the *expiration date.*

   c 100 Intel shares are the *underlying asset.*

2 The put option on Intel stock with an expiration date of May 20, 1994, and a strike price of $55 per share traded for $\$\frac{1}{4} \cdot 100 = \$25.00$. Similar to the call option, the put option's exercise price is $55, May 20, 1994, is its expiration date, and 100 shares of Intel are the underlying asset.

---

[1]The standard terms of traded options may vary depending on circumstances. The interested reader can consult CBOE publications for the exact terms of traded options.

The difference between the options is that the holder of the put option has the right *to sell* 100 shares of Intel for the price of $55 each, whereas the holder of the call option has the right *to purchase* 100 shares for the price of $55 each.

Exhibit 12.1

Options on Intel Stock

Intel's closing stock price on April 29, 1994: $61

Expiration dates of options: May 20, June 17, July 22

Expiration date	Strike price	Call price	Put price
May '94	55	$5\frac{5}{8}$	$\frac{1}{4}$
May '94	60	$2\frac{3}{8}$	$1\frac{7}{16}$
May '94	65	$\frac{7}{16}$	$4\frac{1}{2}$
May '94	70	$\frac{1}{8}$	$9\frac{1}{4}$
June '94	55	$5\frac{7}{8}$	$1\frac{5}{16}$
June '94	60	$3\frac{5}{8}$	$2\frac{1}{2}$
June '94	65	$1\frac{3}{8}$	$6\frac{1}{8}$
June '94	70	$\frac{7}{16}$	No trade
July '94	55	No trade	$1\frac{1}{4}$
July '94	60	$4\frac{1}{8}$	$2\frac{3}{4}$
July '94	65	$2\frac{1}{8}$	$5\frac{1}{2}$
July '94	70	$\frac{7}{8}$	$10\frac{1}{4}$

Source: Data are taken from *The New York Times* for Friday, April 29, 1994.

Option Payoff Patterns

On April 29, 1994—the quotation day of the Intel option table—Intel shares traded for $61. If this were the expiration day of the call option in the example—the call option with an exercise price of $55—its holders would have a valuable right: They could purchase Intel shares for $55 each, a bargain price compared to the prevailing market price of $61. In this case we say that the call option is **in the money,** that is, the market price of the underlying asset is above the exercise price of the call option. On the other hand, if this were the expiration day of a $55-exercise-price put option, its holders would have a worthless right: Rather than exercise the option and sell Intel shares for $55 each, they could sell these shares *in the market* for $61 each. We would then say that these put options are **out of the money.**

The payoff from an option on its expiration day depends on the relation between the option's exercise price and the stock's price on that day. Specifically, for a call option, if the stock price is above the exercise price, holders of the option will find it optimal to exercise the option since they can immediately sell the underlying stock for the *higher* market price. This means that when a call option is in the money on the expiration day, its value is the difference between the stock price and the exercise price. On the other hand, if it is cheaper to buy the stock in the market than to exercise the option, the option is worthless. In formula, the value of the option on the expiration day is

$$C = \text{Max}\{S_T - X, 0\}$$

where C = call option price
S_T = price of the stock on the expiration day, T
X = option's exercise price

Similarly, for a put option that gives its holder the right *to sell* the underlying asset, the value on the expiration day is

$$P = \text{Max}\{X - S_T, 0\}$$

Figure 12.1 gives the graph of the expiration-day payoff of a call option with an exercise price of $55.

Pricing Options—The Binomial Model

Option pricing models typically price an option by *finding a portfolio, comprised of the underlying asset and a risk-free investment, that replicates the payoffs of the option on its expiration day.* The **binomial option pricing model** is an effective illustration of this approach. Despite the apparent artificiality of its assumptions, this model can be extended to yield many powerful results, including the B&S

FIGURE 12.1   A graph of a call option value on the expiration day.

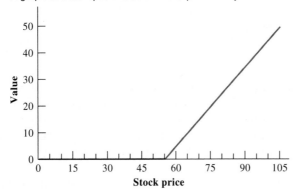

option pricing model. At the same time, despite its simplicity, the binomial model includes most of the intuition underlying more complicated option pricing models.

We illustrate the model with the following numerical example:

- The underlying asset—a share of the XYZ Co.—is currently selling for $60.
- One year from now the price of the XYZ stock will be either $75 or $55.
- The interest rate on risk-free bonds is 10 percent.

Now consider a call option on the XYZ stock, which has an exercise price of $65 and has 1 year to expiration. If the stock is worth $75 next year, the option will be worth

$$C = \text{Max}\{75 - 65, 0\} = \$10$$

On the other hand, if the stock is worth $55 next year, the option will be worth

$$C = \text{Max}\{55 - 65, 0\} = \$0$$

which means that the option will not be exercised and will expire worthless. Since the option value in 1 year will be either $10 or $0, its value today must be somewhere between these two extreme values. (See the box "The Binomial Option Pricing Model" on page 379.)

With a little high school algebra, we can construct a portfolio *whose returns replicate the options returns.* Suppose today we purchase A shares of stock and B bonds. One year from now:

- If the stock price is $75, our portfolio will be worth $75A + 1.10B$.
- If the stock price is $55, our portfolio will be worth $55A + 1.10B$.

We want to find an A and a B such that the portfolio's value in 1 year will be equal to the payoffs from the call option. Mathematically, A and B solve the following system of equations:

$$75A + 1.10B = 10$$

$$55A + 1.10B = 0$$

Solving these equations gives

$$A = 0.5, \qquad B = -25$$

This indicates that the portfolio which perfectly replicates the payoff of the call option entails the purchase of a one-half share, which costs $30 $(= \frac{1}{2} \cdot \$60)$, and *shorting* $25 of the risk-free asset. The short position in the risk-free asset is effectively a 1-year loan of $25. This loan partially finances the purchase of the one-half share. In 1 year the payment to the lender will be

$$\$25 \cdot 1.10 = \$27.50$$

independent of how well the stock investment performs. The value of the stock investment does depend on the stock price in 1 year.

- If the stock is worth \$75, the investment in the stock will be worth $\frac{1}{2} \cdot 75 =$ \$37.50. Upon repaying the loan, the holder of the replicating portfolio will be left with \$10.
- If the stock is worth \$55, the investment in the stock will be worth $\frac{1}{2} \cdot 55 =$ \$27.50. Upon repaying the loan, the holder of the replicating portfolio will be left with \$0.

Since the portfolio's payoff in 1 year replicates the option's payoff, to prevent arbitrage, *the call option's price should equal the cost of the replicating portfolio.* In the example the cost of the replicating portfolio is the cost of buying the stock less the fraction of the cost financed by the loan:

$$\tfrac{1}{2} \cdot \$60 - \$25 = \$5$$

This means that in order to prevent arbitrage the option's price must also be \$5!

Several salient features of options emerge from this example:

- *A call option is like a leveraged portfolio in which the purchase of a stock is partially financed with a risk-free loan.* In our example in order to replicate the option, we need to purchase a one-half share and partially finance this purchase with \$25 of debt. In more general option pricing models the proportions of the stock and the bond in the replicating portfolio are continuously adjusted over the life of the option. But always, the stock is held and the purchase is partially financed with a risk-free debt.
- The number of shares that are needed to replicate the option's payoff—one-half in our example—is called the **hedge ratio (HR)** of the option. The HR, customarily denoted by the Greek letter δ, indicates how many ''stock-equivalent'' units of risk the option holder bears. Thus, when the stock price changes by \$1, the price of a call option on the stock approximately changes by the HR. For a call option the HR is between 0.0 and 1.0. Keep in mind, though, that the investment in the option is much smaller than the investment in the stock so that, *per dollar invested,* the risk of the option is larger than the risk of the stock.[2]
- *The price of an option depends on the price of the stock, the exercise price, the rate of interest, and the return distribution of the stock.* One ostensibly missing potential determinant of the option price is the probability that the price of the stock will go up (to \$75 in our example): We computed the option price without even knowing the expected price of the stock! In other words, even though we don't know the expected return of the stock, we can compute the correct (i.e., arbitrage-free) value of the option. Intuitively, this happens because the price of the underlying stock already reflects the appropriate expected return: Since the

---

[2]In technical terms, the elasticity of the option price to the stock price is greater than 1: $(\partial c/c)/(\partial S/S) =$ HR $\cdot (S/c) > 1.0$, where HR denotes the hedge ratio.

THE BINOMIAL OPTION PRICING MODEL

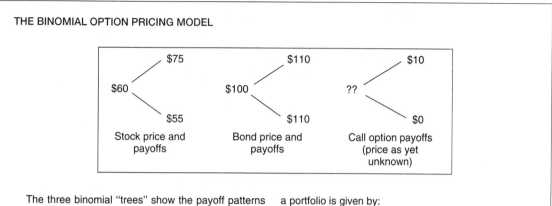

The three binomial "trees" show the payoff patterns of *a stock* (priced at $60), *a riskless bond* (yielding 10 percent per annum), and *a call option on the stock with an exercise price of $65,* the price of which is (as yet) unknown.

To calculate the price today of the option, we first find a portfolio of bonds and shares whose *year-end payoff replicates the option's payoff.* As shown in the text, such a portfolio is given by:

- The purchase of one-half share—the net cost today to the investor is $30.
- Borrowing $25 at the 10 percent interest rate—this reduces the net current cost to $5 to the investor.

This portfolio replicates the option payoffs:

$0.5 \cdot \$75 - \$25 \cdot 1.10 = \$10$

$\$30 - \$25 = \$5$

$0.5 \cdot \$55 - \$25 \cdot 1.10 = \$0$

computed value for the option reflects the current price of the stock, the computed option price implicitly reflects the expected return of the stock, although indirectly.

Extending the Binomial Model to Multiple Periods

At a first glance the binomial option pricing model may seem irrelevant in a world where stock prices may take many values. This first reaction, however, is misleading: If we allow more than one trading opportunity, we will be able to accommodate multiple possible stock prices. For example, by adding one more period of trading, we can allow three possible end-of-year stock prices. To illustrate, divide our 1-year horizon into two subperiods and assume that in each of these two subperiods the stock price can go up by 12 percent or down by 4 percent. Further, assume that the interest rate is 5 percent per one-half year. The diagram in the box "Two-Period Binomial Model" illustrates the resulting model.

The idea that the payoff of a call option can be replicated by buying the HR number of the underlying shares and borrowing is the basis for the celebrated B&S

TWO-PERIOD BINOMIAL MODEL

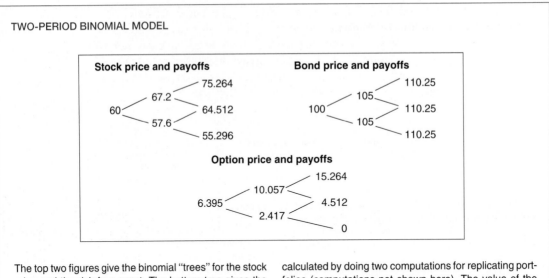

The top two figures give the binomial "trees" for the stock price and the risk-free asset. The bottom tree gives the payoffs for a call option on the stock with an exercise price of $60. The middle column of this figure gives the value of this option after one period. These values are calculated by doing two computations for replicating portfolios (computations not shown here). The value of the option today, $6.395, is also computed through a replicating portfolio.

formula. The formula is the solution to the problem of finding the value of a portfolio that is invested in the underlying stock and the risk-free asset, which is adjusted continuously and replicates the option's payoff on the expiration day. Thus, it is the continuous time equivalent of the binomial example that we have just analyzed.

The Black-Scholes Formula

The scope of this book doesn't permit us to give a formal proof of the B&S option pricing formula. We suggest that you consider the B&S formula to be a continuous version of the binomial model discussed in the previous section, with a number of additional assumptions:

- Markets are frictionless and operate continuously.
- Asset prices change continuously.
- The risk-free interest rate is constant.
- The natural logarithm of the stock return is normally distributed.
- The volatility of the instantaneous return of the stock is constant.
- The stock doesn't pay dividends.

In extensions of the model all of these assumptions can be relaxed, although often the cost of easing the assumptions is that options can no longer be priced by using a relatively clean analytical formula. (Even though it may not appear so to you, in modern financial theory the B&S formula is considered an elegant and simple solution to an extraordinarily complex valuation problem.) In surprisingly many cases it turns out that the B&S formula is an adequate *approximation* to a more complex option pricing relation based on relaxed assumptions.[3]

Given these assumptions, Black and Scholes showed that the value of a European call option is given by the following formula:

$$C = S \cdot N(d_1) - X \cdot e^{-rT} \cdot N(d_2)$$

where

$$d_1 = \frac{\ln\left(\dfrac{S}{X \cdot e^{-rT}}\right) + \dfrac{1}{2}\sigma^2 T}{\sigma\sqrt{T}} = \frac{\ln\left(\dfrac{S}{X}\right) + \left(r + \dfrac{1}{2}\sigma^2\right)T}{\sigma\sqrt{T}}$$

$$d_2 = d_1 - \sigma\sqrt{T}$$

and where S = current price of the stock

X = exercise price of the option

$\ln(\ )$ = natural logarithm function

T = time to maturity of the option, in years

r = *continuously compounded* risk-free interest rate: If R is the yield to maturity (YTM) of a government bond, then r = $\ln(1 + R)$

σ = *annualized* volatility of the stock's logarithmic return

$N(\ )$ = value of the standard normal distribution

The intuition behind this formula is not simple. One way to understand the B&S pricing formula is to assume that individuals are risk neutral. In this case the price of a call option should reflect the difference between the value of the underlying stock—S—and the exercise price—X. However, although the price of the underlying stock is *today's* price, the exercise price is to be paid upon expiration—at time T. Thus, the appropriate starting point for the valuation of a call option is the difference between the current stock price—S—and the *present value (PV)* of the exercise price—$X \cdot e^{-rT}$. The difference between the two, which is the payoff of the call option holder if the exercise of the option were certain, should be adjusted to reflect the possibility that the option will not be exercised. When investors are risk neutral, this adjustment is achieved by multiplying the value of the option *conditional on the exercise* (i.e., $S - X \cdot e^{-rT}$) by the probability of the exercise. Under the assumptions about the distribution of the stock price, $N(d_1)$ is the probability that the option will be exercised.

---

[3]There are many good textbooks on option pricing, all of which discuss these issues. See, for example, John Hull, *Introduction to Futures and Options Markets,* 2nd ed., Prentice-Hall, Englewood Cliffs, N.J., 1995.

Independent of our intuitive interpretation of the B&S formula (i.e., independent of whether investors are or are not risk neutral), $N(d_1)$ is the *hedge ratio (HR)* of a call option in the B&S formula. This means that a change of one dollar in the underlying stock price changes the option price by roughly $\$N(d_1)$. Since $N(d_1)$ is the cumulative normal probability of d_1, a dollar change in the value of the underlying asset is associated with a change in the value of a call option in the same direction but of a smaller magnitude. Knowing the B&S hedge ratios of derivative securities is useful in assessing the overall exposure of portfolios of derivative securities to the risk of the underlying asset by aggregating the HRs (or, the δs) of the individual securities into a portfolio HR (or portfolio δ).

There is also a B&S formula for pricing a European put option. By using the same notation as previously and the relation that must prevail between the prices of European put and call options on the same stock,[4] we can derive the following formula for pricing a European put option:

$$P = X \cdot e^{-rT} \cdot N(-d_2) - S \cdot N(-d_1)$$

Since most convertible securities issued by corporations are of the call type (for obvious incentive reasons), we focus the remaining discussion on the B&S formula for call options. However, the put–call parity relation implies that any statement about a call option has an immediate equivalent statement for a put option.

Using the Black-Scholes Model: A Simple Example

In this section we will show you how to calculate an option price directly from the B&S formula. Suppose we are trying to price one of the Intel options whose prices are given in Section 12.1. We price the July 1994 call option whose exercise price is $60. For this option we use the following parameters in the B&S call-pricing formula:

S = current (April 29, 1994) price of Intel stock is $61.

X = exercise price of the option is $60 (i.e., the call is virtually *at the money*).

T = time to maturity of the option is 84 days, which is the number of days between the current date (April 29, 1994) and the option's expiration date (July 22, 1994). In the B&S formula T, r, and σ are all in annual terms so that if the option has 84 days to maturity, we set $T = 84/365 = 0.2301$.

---

[4]The *put–call parity relation* states that the difference between the prices of European call and put options on the same stock, with the same exercise day and the same exercise price, equals the price of the stock less the PV of the common exercise price: $C - P = S - Xe^{-rT}$.

r = risk-free interest rate is 3 percent.

σ = volatility of the stock's logarithmic return is 29.5 percent; σ, the *annualized* standard deviation of the return on the stock, is a measure of the risk of the stock[5]

With these parameters, we can use the preceding formulas to calculate the spreadsheet implementation of the B&S option pricing formulas for a call and a put shown in Exhibit 12.2.

Exhibit 12.2

Black-Scholes Option Pricing in a Spreadsheet

S	61						
X	60						
r	3%						
T	0.2301	Uses formula (date(94,7,22) − date(94,4,29))/365					
sigma	29.50%						
d_1	0.2363	(ln(S/X) + (r + 0.5 * sigma^2) * T)/(sigma * SQRT(T))					
d_2	0.0948	d_1 − sigma * SQRT(T)					
N(d1)	0.5934	Uses formula NormSDist(d_1)					
N(d2)	0.5378	Uses formula NormSDist(d_2)					
Call price	4.15	S * N(d1) − X * exp(−r * T) * N(d2)					
Put price	2.74	− S * NormSDist(−d_1) + X * exp(−r * T) * NormSDist(−d_2)					

Early Exercise The B&S formula prices European options—options that can be exercised only on their expiration days. However, many options (and warrants, discussed in the next section) are of the American type—they can be exercised before maturity. The early exercise possibility, although not allowed for in the B&S option pricing formula, doesn't necessarily mean that the B&S formula cannot be used to value American-type options: It can be easily shown that *so long as the underlying stock doesn't pay dividends,* rational individuals will not want to utilize the early exercise possibility of American call options. This means that the value of an *American* option on a *nondividend-paying* stock is the same as the value of an equivalent *European* option on the stock. The result can be extended somewhat: If the dividends paid before the option's maturity are not too large, then early exercise of an American call is still not optimal.[6]

You should not be misled that early exercise is never important in pricing options. First, it is generally optimal to exercise a put option early if the stock price falls far below the exercise price. Second, it may be optimal to exercise a call early if the underlying stock pays dividends. (When it is optimal to exercise an American call option early, the optimal exercise time is just prior to the ex-dividend date.)

---

[5]This was the volatility of the stock price in the 30 days preceding the analysis date. In Section 12.3 we show how to estimate this volatility.

[6]What is ''not too large''? If the dividend is smaller than the interest that can be earned on the exercise price from the ex-dividend date to maturity, then early exercise will not be optimal.

In both cases the value of the American option may be larger than the value of an otherwise equivalent European option.

The pricing of American options usually requires more complicated computational techniques. The typical approach is to specify a binomial tree for the evolution of the stock price and to solve recursively for the value of the option taking into account optimal early exercise policies..

Dividends   As you have seen earlier, dividends can be important in driving a wedge between American and European option prices. In many cases an acceptable approximation for the price of a call option on a dividend-paying stock can be found by using the B&S formula on the *stock price minus the present value (PV) of the dividends expected to be paid until the expiration of the option*:

$$C = \hat{S} \cdot N(d_1) - X \cdot e^{-rT} \cdot N(d_2)$$

where

$$d_1 = \frac{\ln\left(\dfrac{\hat{S}}{X \cdot e^{-rT}}\right) + \dfrac{1}{2} \sigma^2 T}{\sigma\sqrt{T}}$$

$$d_2 = d_1 - \sigma\sqrt{T}$$

and where

$$\hat{S} = S - \text{PV(Div)}$$

is the adjusted stock price—the stock price less the PV of dividends to be paid until the option's expiration. Intuitively, this approximation works since holders of call options are not entitled to receive dividends prior to exercising their options. This means that a call option is effectively the right to buy the stock net of the dividends paid prior to the exercise. Accordingly, the current value of the underlying asset *from the option holders' perspective* is the current price of the stock less the value of the dividends to which they are not entitled.

12.2 WARRANT VALUATION

Warrants are options that are written by corporations on their own stock. When the warrants are exercised, the writing corporation issues new shares (or, *equivalently,* uses treasury stock) to deliver to the warrant holders. Since, *formally,* warrants are rights to buy shares, it may appear that we can value warrants by using the B&S formula in a straightforward manner as if they were options on the stock of the firm. The legal format of the warrant contract is, however, misleading. Recall that the B&S formula assumes a particular distribution for the stock price on the expiration day of the option. When the corporation itself writes the options, this can no longer be done: *The expiration-day value of the stock depends on whether or not the warrant holders decide to exercise their option.*

The dependence of the stock's expiration-day value on the decision of the warrant holders to exercise comes from two sources:

• First, when warrant holders exercise their rights, they pay the exercise price *to the issuing firm* rather than to a third-party writer as in the case of a regular option. Thus, upon the exercise of warrants, the value of the firm increases by the value of the exercise price times the number of options being exercised.

• Second, upon deciding to exercise, the holders of the warrants become regular shareholders with equal rights to the *existing* assets of the firm. This means that the exercise of warrants dilutes the claim of the *existing* shareholders.

Our approach to warrant valuation will be to adjust the B&S call pricing formula for these two effects. You should be aware, however, that there are additional issues in warrant valuation that we don't cover in this section. In particular, it is possible that a large warrant holder will find it optimal to exercise only *part* of the warrants; this may happen when the warrant-issuing firm pays dividends. When valuing warrants, we typically ignore this possibility by assuming that holders of warrants are competitive investors who don't coordinate their exercise policies. In this case, if it is optimal for one warrant holder to exercise, it will be optimal for all warrant holders to exercise. Thus, we ignore the *strategic aspects* of the warrant exercise.

To adjust the B&S formula for the two warrant effects noted earlier, we examine the *aggregate* effect of the warrant exercise on the equity of the firm. We employ the same notation that we used for the valuation of options, adding the following symbols:

m = number of shares outstanding

n = number of new shares created upon the warrant exercise

$\alpha = n/(n + m)$, the fraction of the firm that the warrant holders will own after they exercise their rights

If, for example, the XYZ Co. has 40 million shares and 5 million warrants outstanding, and if each warrant entitles its holder to buy two shares, then

$$m = 40\text{M}$$

$$n = 5\text{M} \cdot 2 = 10\text{M}$$

$$\alpha = 10/(40 + 10) = 20\%$$

Although, *formally,* warrant contracts specify a right to *buy shares,* we prefer to think of warrants as options to purchase an *α-fraction of the firm's assets.* By valuing warrants as options on an α-fraction of the firm's assets, we can take into account the dilution of the existing shareholders' claims in an intuitive and simple manner.

This way of thinking about warrants allows us to determine the parameters to put into the B&S formula when valuing the warrants. First, the current value of the underlying asset—S in the B&S formula—is $\alpha \cdot V$, where V is the *aggregate* value to be divided between stockholders and warrant holders.

Next we want to take into account the fact that the exercise price is *paid to the firm* rather than, as in the case of an option, to a third party. Again, we can use a simple and intuitive adjustment: Since subsequent to their warrant exercise the warrant holders will own α percent of the firm, the warrant holders are, in fact, paying an α percent of the exercise price *to themselves*! Thus, to use the B&S formula, we need to take into account *only the fraction of the exercise price paid to the existing shareholders*. In other words, only $(1 - \alpha)$ portion of the exercise price is considered to be the effective exercise price of the warrants in their valuation by the B&S formula.

Let's go back to the XYZ Co. example. Assume that the warrant contract specifies an exercise price of $10 *per share*. This means that in order to buy the 10M shares, the warrant holders have to pay $10M \cdot \$10 = \$100$ million. However, as soon as the warrant holders pay this sum, they become the owners of 20 percent of the firm. That is, 20 percent of the $100 million, or $20 million, is money that *the warrant holders effectively pay to themselves*. Hence, the warrant holders effectively pay the holders of the *existing* shares only $(1 - 20\%) \cdot \$100M$ or $80 million. This $80 million is the warrants' effective exercise price.

If we denote the value of a warrant to purchase a single share by W, then we can determine the value, $n \cdot W$, of *all* the warrants by using the B&S formula with the following parameters:

$$n \cdot W = \text{B\&S call option formula with:}$$

$$S = \alpha \cdot V$$

$$X = n \cdot X \cdot (1 - \alpha)$$

$$r = \text{interest rate}$$

$$T = \text{time to warrant expiration}$$

$$\sigma = \text{volatility of underlying assets}$$

Note that the warrant value in the preceding formula is the *aggregate* value of the warrants—the value of *all* the warrants, or nW—not the value W of an *individual* warrant. As mentioned at the beginning of this section, the trick to using the B&S formula in an intuitive way that correctly takes into account the differences between warrants and options is to value the warrants in aggregate—the aggregate underlying asset, the aggregate exercise price, and the aggregate value of the warrants.

The last three parameters that we need for the valuation of warrants are T, r, and σ. T is defined in the warrant contract by the warrant's expiration day. The B&S formula assumes that the option is European—that is, it cannot be exercised before the expiration day. Even if the warrant is of the American type, we may still use the B&S formula so long as the stock doesn't pay dividends. The payment of dividends creates special problems in warrant valuation—problems that we discuss later in the section and that cannot always be solved analytically. At this point we simply assume that the warrant is indeed European, as the B&S formula assumes, or that dividends are small enough so that early exercise will not be optimal.

The risk-free rate of interest, r, is directly observable. The only remaining variable of interest is σ, which in the B&S formula is the volatility of *the underlying asset*. Suppose the firm issuing the warrants has no debt. Since the underlying asset of warrants is an α-fraction of the firm, the σ in the B&S formula is *the standard deviation of the return on the firm's assets*. This standard deviation is *not* the standard deviation of the return of the stock! Intuitively, we can think of the volatility of the firm's assets as some average of the volatility of both the return on the warrants and the return of the stock. Moreover, since the volatility of the warrant as a levered claim is larger than the volatility of the stock,

$$\sigma_{\text{warrant}} > \sigma_{\text{assets}} > \sigma_{\text{stock}}$$

This makes sense: When the value of assets goes up, the value of the stock goes up as well but at a lower rate since the probability increases that warrants will be exercised and will dilute stockholders' claims. And the reverse is true when the value of the firm's assets goes down. This means that the volatility of the assets, which is the volatility that should be put in the B&S formula of warrants, is *larger* than the volatility of the stock.

How do we estimate σ_{assets}? We can estimate σ_{assets} very much like we estimate σ_{stock}: When the stock is publicly traded, we can estimate the variance of the return of the stock from a sample of actual stock returns. For a firm with traded warrants and traded shares, we can compute the value of the firm on any day t as the sum of the values of the warrants and the stock:

$$V_t = mS_t + nW_t$$

We can then compute a sample of returns of the *whole firm* as

$$r_t = \frac{V_t - V_{t-1}}{V_{t-1}}$$

and estimate the return's standard deviation from the sample. For most firms, however, this is impractical advice: The warrants of many firms are executive options that are not traded. Moreover, the terms of many of these executive options are often reported in the firm's financial statements only in averages—such as average time to expiration and average exercise price—which inhibits indirect estimation of volatilities. In many cases—as shown by Figure 12.2, which gives an example from Schlumberger's 1994 annual report—not even average exercise prices and warrant maturities are reported. Thus, in practice, we often estimate only the stock volatility and hope that the volatility of the assets differs only slightly from the stock volatility. This is usually not a bad assumption since for many

Reporting of Warrants in Annual Reports

In 1994, the Company adopted the Schlumberger 1994 Stock Option Plan, under which stock options may be granted until January 26, 2004. The number of shares that may be issued under this plan cannot exceed 10,000,000 shares.

Options to purchase shares of the Company's Common Stock have been granted under various incentive plans to officers and key employees at prices equal to 100% of the fair market value at the date of grant.

Transactions under stock incentive plans were as follows:

	Number of Shares	Option Price Per Share
Outstanding		
Jan. 1, 1993	10,097,828	$29.25-67.00
Granted	848,250	$59.81-64.81
Exercised	(966,402)	$29.25-67.00
Lapsed or cancelled	(387,680)	$29.25-67.00
Outstanding		
Dec. 31, 1993	9,591,996	$29.25-67.00
Granted	3,178,150	$53.25-57.94
Exercised	(728,637)	$29.25-44.63
Lapsed or cancelled	(480,660)	$33.13-67.00
Outstanding		
Dec. 31, 1994	11,560,849	$29.25-67.00
Exercisable at		
Dec. 31, 1994	5,389,722	$29.25-67.00
Available for grant		
Dec. 31, 1993	2,557,070	
Dec. 31, 1994	9,853,745	

FIGURE 12.2 An example of the reporting of executive warrants outstanding. (*Source:* From Schlumberger's annual report for 1994.)

companies the value of the warrants is much smaller than the value of the stock.

Continuing with the example of the XYZ warrants, assume that we have estimated that the standard deviation of the return on the assets of XYZ is 25 percent. We further find that the warrants have 2 years to expiration and that the continuously compounded risk-free interest rate is 8 percent. Our analysis of XYZ's environment and future (expressed in elaborate and artfully constructed pro-forma statements) suggests that XYZ's total value is $450 million. The aggregate value of XYZ's warrants is

$$n \cdot W = \text{B\&S call formula}[0.20 \cdot 450M, (1 - 0.20) \cdot 100M, 2, 8\%, 25\%]$$
$$= \text{B\&S}(90M, 80M, 2, 8\%, 25\%)$$
$$= 90M \cdot N(d_1) - 80M \cdot e^{-8\% \cdot 2} \cdot N(d_2)$$

By using our option pricing worksheet, we can calculate the value of the warrants shown in Exhibit 12.3. The exhibit shows that the *total value of the warrants,* as given by the B&S formula, is $25.21 million. Since there are 5 million warrants giving the right to purchase 10 million shares, the value of the right to purchase a share is $2.52 and the value per warrant is $5.04.

Exhibit 12.3

Calculating the Warrant Value—Adjustments to the Black-Scholes Formula

m	40	Number of shares outstanding	
n	10	New shares if warrants exercised	
alpha	0.2	Fractional ownership upon warrant exercise	
Exercise price	10	Per-share exercise price of warrants	
Total exercise price	100	m * per-warrant exercise price	
Total firm value	450	Derived from analysis of firm	
	Inputs to Black-Scholes Call Option Pricing Formula		
S	90	alpha * total firm value, in $ millions	
X	80	Total exercise price * (1 − alpha), in $ millions	
r	8%	Interest rate	
T	2	Time to maturity of warrants, in years	
sigma	25%	Asset volatility	
d_1	0.9625	(ln(S/X) + (r + 0.5 * sigma^2) * T)/(sigma * SQRT(T))	
d_2	0.6089	d_1 − sigma * SQRT(T)	
N(d1)	0.8321	Uses formula NormSDist(d_1)	
N(d2)	0.7287	Uses formula NormSDist(d_2)	
Total warrant value	25.21	S * N(d1) − X * exp(−r * T) * N(d2), in $ millions	
Per share value of warrants	2.52	Previous number divided by n	
Value of warrant	5.04	Two shares per warrant	

Note that $N(d_1)$ is 0.8321, which is close to 1.0. This is because:

- The warrants in our example are deep in the money: The exercise price is $80 million (which is even smaller in PV terms), whereas the current value of the underlying asset is $90 million.
- There are still 2 years to the warrants' expiration day.

Both factors mean that the option is very likely to be exercised, which indicates that its value today moves almost one-for-one with movements in the value of the underlying asset—20 percent of the value of the firm. By using the HR of 0.8321 calculated earlier (recall that in the B&S formula, $N(d_1)$ is the HR), we can do the following calculation:

• If the value of the *whole firm* changes by $10 million, the value of the underlying asset of the warrants—20 percent of the firm—will change by $2 million;
• If the value of the underlying asset of the warrants changes by $2 million, the *total value* of the warrants will *roughly* change by $2 \cdot 0.8321 = \$1.6642$ million.

This means that the HR of the value of the warrants with respect to the *total* value of the firm is $20\% \cdot 0.8321$ or 0.16642. Note that since one dollar change in the value of the whole firm goes to either warrant holders or shareholders, we can compute the HR of the shares as

$$\text{HR}_{\text{shares}} = 1.0 - 0.16642 = 0.83358$$

Therefore, a $10 million change in the value of the firm will change the value of the shares by approximately $8.3358 million.

Once we have the value of the warrants, it is fairly simple to determine the value of the stock: Since the value of the whole firm is $450 million and the value of the warrants is $25.2 million, the value of the stock is the residual—$424.8 million. By dividing the total value of the shares by the number of shares outstanding—40 million—we get a share value of $10.62.

Doing Some Sensitivity Analysis

We can use the spreadsheet to do a number of sensitivity analyses. For example, what would happen to the value of the warrants if the value of the firm changes? The graph in Figure 12.3 (based on a sensitivity table from our spreadsheet) gives a visual answer. For example, if the value of the firm goes up from $450 million to $460 million, the per-share value of the warrants goes from $2.52 to $2.69. Thus, a 2.2 percent increase in the value of the firm causes a 6.6 percent increase in the per-share value of the warrants. Warrants are highly levered!

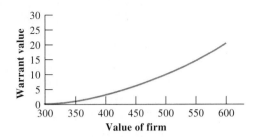

FIGURE 12.3   The graph shows how the value of the firm affects the warrant value.

Note the relative changes in value: Following a 2.22 percent change in the value of the assets, the value of the warrants rises by 6.66 percent, whereas the value of the stock rises by only 1.96 percent. This is in accord with the observation that we made earlier: The volatility of the stock price is lower than the volatility of the assets, which is lower than the volatility of the warrants. In fact, by using the B&S formula, we can calculate the volatility of the stock as a function of the volatility of the assets and the HR of the stock:

$$\sigma_{stock} = HR_{stock} \cdot \frac{\text{value of assets}}{\text{value of stock}} \cdot \sigma_{assets}$$

$$= 0.83358 \cdot \frac{\$450.0M}{\$424.8M} \cdot 25\% = 22.1\%$$

which is lower than the volatility of the returns of the assets.

Suppose we value the warrants as if they were options on the stock. To be specific, suppose the market price of the shares equals the value that we calculated for the shares—$10.62 per share—and the estimated volatility of the stock return equals the computed return volatility—22.1 percent. What would be the warrant value? As Exhibit 12.4 shows, the difference between the two valuation methods, for this example, is negligible.

Exhibit 12.4

Valuing the Warrants as If They Are Regular Call Options

S	10.62	Market value of share		
X	10	Warrant exercise price, per share		
r	8%	Risk-free rate of interest		
T	2	Time to maturity of warrants, in years		
sigma	22.10%	Stock volatility		
d_1	0.8607	(ln(S/X) + (r + 0.5 * sigma ^ 2) * T)/(sigma * SQRT(T))		
d_2	0.5481	d_1 – sigma * SQRT(T)		
N(d1)	0.8053	Uses formula NormSDist(d_1)		
N(d2)	0.7082	Uses formula NormSDist(d_2)		
Option value (per share)	2.52	S * N(d1) – X * exp(–r * T) * N(d2)		
Warrant value	5.03	Two shares per warrant		

There are two reasons that, in many cases, valuing a warrant as if it were a straight call option gives a good approximation to the actual warrant value. First, in many instances warrants, such as executive stock options, are only a small fraction of the total value of the firm, which means that the effects of dilution and cash infusion slightly affect the value of the warrants. Second, whereas the dilution caused by the warrant exercise *decreases* the value of the assets being valued, this same dilution *increases* the volatility used in the option valuation, which indicates that these two effects tend to offset out each other. This conclusion is supported by much empirical research.

Thus, have we been wasting our time in this section? We don't think so: In many if not in most valuations of the type discussed in this book, we actually *don't know the value of the stock* (since this is precisely what we are trying to estimate). In these cases the *only* way to determine the warrant value and the stock value is the one that we have just illustrated.

The Black-Scholes Formula: Some Caveats

The B&S formula may be misleading in its accuracy: The fact that we can get exact values for warrants doesn't mean that these values are what we will observe in the market! Empirically, it has been found that the B&S formula works fairly well only for options that are roughly at the money and short lived. The formula tends to overvalue long-term options and to undervalue options deep in or deep out of the money, which are precisely the characteristics of warrants. Unfortunately, we have no quick fixes for these problems. Just be aware of these biases in the B&S formula relative to observed prices. To try to gauge the severity of the bias, whenever possible compare the values that you obtain for warrants to traded option prices, especially if long-term options are traded on the stock of the firm that you value.

Another issue that we should consider in using the B&S formula to value warrants is dividends. The B&S formula asumes that the firm doesn't pay dividends. The difficulty with firms that do pay dividends is that although shareholders are entitled to receive dividends, warrant holders are not entitled to receive dividends until they exercise their warrants and become shareholders. If the warrants are European, we can take into account the dividend payments prior to the warrants' expiration by *deducting the present value of these dividends from the value of the firm.* This is, in fact, a general principle in dividing the value of the firm between convertible security holders and shareholders: *Before determining the relative values of the securities, deduct from the value of the firm the value of the cash flows that are exclusive rights of one class of security holders.* For short-lived warrants it is relatively simple to adjust for the shareholders' exclusive right to dividends since firms change their dividends only infrequently. For long-term warrants, however, this may be more difficult: Dividend payments in the long run are less stable than short-run dividend payments, yet since there are more of them, their present value is an important determinant of the value of the warrants. We can use our pro-forma model and the firm's observed dividend policy to project the firm's dividend payments until the warrants' expiration day and to compute the present value of the projected dividends (to which only the existing shareholders are entitled.)

When the warrants are not European, the adjustment for dividends is more complicated. In fact, it is so complicated that in order to deal with the adjustment, finance researchers have made assumptions that literally "throw the baby out with the bath water." The problem is that the exercise of warrants may affect the dividend policy of the firm, which may in turn affect the desirability of the exercise—partial or complete. In the true spirit of corporate finance our best advice here is, If you cannot deal with it, ignore it: Simply assume that the effect of the dividend payment on the value of the American warrants is approximately the effect of the same dividends on European options and deduct the PV of the projected dividends from the value of the underlying asset.

12.3 VALUING SMUCKER'S WARRANTS AND STOCK

In Chapter 7 we built a model for the J. M. Smucker Co. and used this model to value Smucker's stock. Since Smucker has warrants outstanding, and since in Chapter 7 we did not as yet have a warrant pricing model, we were forced to use a very simple model to value the warrant. In this section we return to this problem and apply the B&S warrant pricing techniques of this chapter to Smucker.

You will recall the following facts:

• After subtracting the value of Smucker's debt, we found that the value of Smucker's shares plus warrants was $648.276 million.

• Smucker has 29.5 million shares outstanding and has 1 million warrants. We assume that the warrants have an exercise price of 16 and a time to maturity of 2 years. Since there are several types of warrants, all with different exercise prices and different times to maturities, and since we don't have a detailed breakdown of either the time to maturity or the exercise prices of the various types of warrants, both of these numbers are to be interpreted as averages. After doing a basic valuation of the warrants, we do a sensitivity analysis to determine the impact of changing the estimated time to maturity.

• The annual riskless interest rate is 5 percent. Since this is a discrete interest rate, the equivalent continuously compounded rate, needed to implement the B&S model, is given by

$$r = \ln(1.05) = 4.88\%$$

We don't know the volatility (σ) of Smucker. We will derive an estimate for this volatility from information about Smucker's stock price. Since even after doing this calculation there is some uncertainty about the correct value of σ, we can also do a sensitivity analysis on σ.

Once we estimate σ, we will have enough information to value the warrants. The dilution caused by the warrants is

$$\alpha = \frac{\text{new shares created by warrants}}{\text{new plus old shares}} = \frac{n}{m + n}$$

$$= \frac{1,000,000}{29,500,000 + 1,000,000} = 3.28\%$$

As explained in the previous section, this means that the warrant holders, when exercising their warrants, will purchase 3.28 percent of a block of equity that today is worth \$648,276,000 for $(1 - 3.28\%) \cdot \$16,000,000 = \$15,475,410$.

Estimating the Volatility of Smucker's Assets

To implement the B&S formula, we need to estimate the volatility of Smucker's assets that are worth \$648,276,000.[7] Since the inflow from the warrant exercise is small, it is not unreasonable to assume that the volatility (σ) of this block is very close to the volatility of Smucker's equity. Thus, we use this stock price volatility as a proxy for the σ for which we are looking.

The calculation of the stock volatility involves two steps:

• Calculate the standard deviation of the logarithmic stock returns.
• Normalize this standard deviation to *annualize* the standard deviation.

Suppose, for example, we have price data $P_0, P_1, P_2, \ldots, P_N$ for Smucker's stock. Then the logarithmic return in period t (i.e., the continuously compounded return over the period) is defined as

$$r_t = \ln\left[\frac{P_t}{P_{t-1}}\right]$$

Here r_t is the continuously compounded return from the stock over the period. The annualized standard deviation σ is defined as

$$\text{Standard deviation } \{r_1, r_2, \ldots, r_n\} \cdot \sqrt{\text{number of periods per year}}$$

The term in the square root sign is the *normalization factor* that annualizes the standard deviation. If our data are monthly price data, this term will be $\sqrt{12}$; if the data are weekly price data, this term will be $\sqrt{52}$; and for daily data it is common to use $\sqrt{250}$ since there are approximately 250 business days per year.

The spreadsheet in Exhibit 12.5 shows price data for Smucker (in this case closing monthly price) and some calculations for the volatility.

---

[7]You might question why we have not added the warrant exercise price to the \$648,276,000 value derived for Smucker. This issue is discussed in the last subsection of this section.

Exhibit 12.5

Closing Monthly Prices of Smucker's "A" Stock

	Price	Monthly return			Price	Monthly return
Feb-88	12.9375			Jul-90	22.375	0.075398
Mar-88	12.3125	−0.04952		Aug-90	19.8125	−0.12163
Apr-88	12.625	0.025064		Sep-90	19.125	−0.03532
May-88	12.5625	−0.00496		Oct-90	19.5625	0.022618
Jun-88	13.8125	0.094858		Nov-90	19.8125	0.012699
Jul-88	13.53125	−0.02057		Dec-90	23.1875	0.1573
Aug-88	14.125	0.042944		Jan-91	21.5	−0.07556
Sep-88	14.46875	0.024045		Feb-91	22.5	0.045462
Oct-88	15.3125	0.056678		Mar-91	22.25	−0.01117
Nov-88	14.5	−0.05452		Apr-91	22.5	0.011173
Dec-88	14.9375	0.029726		May-91	22.3125	−0.00837
Jan-89	15.125	0.012474		Jun-91	24.25	0.08327
Feb-89	14.8125	−0.02088		Jul-91	25.1875	0.037931
Mar-89	14.6875	−0.00847		Aug-91	29.5	0.158042
Apr-89	14.9375	0.016878		Sep-91	28	−0.05219
May-89	15	0.004175		Oct-91	35	0.223144
Jun-89	15.59375	0.03882		Nov-91	35	0
Jul-89	17.25	0.100942		Dec-91	37.5	0.068993
Aug-89	17.71875	0.026811		Jan-92	34	−0.09798
Sep-89	17.75	0.001762		Feb-92	31.5	−0.07637
Oct-89	18.34375	0.032903		Mar-92	29	−0.08269
Nov-89	18.4375	0.005098		Apr-92	29.875	0.029726
Dec-89	18.21875	−0.01194		May-92	27.5	−0.08284
Jan-90	16.4375	−0.10289		Jun-92	25.875	−0.06091
Feb-90	16.1875	−0.01533		Jul-92	27.75	0.069959
Mar-90	16.1875	0		Aug-92	29.25	0.052644
Apr-90	18.21875	0.118212		Sep-92	29.5	0.008511
May-90	19.75	0.080702		Oct-92	27.25	−0.07934
Jun-90	20.75	0.049393		Nov-92	27.625	0.013668
				Dec-92	32.875	0.173991
	Estimates of Stock Volatility					
	Feb-88–Dec-92	24.26%				
	Dec-90–Dec-92	30.94%				
	Dec-91–Dec-92	28.75%				

Depending on the period taken, the volatility of Smucker's stock varies between 24 percent and 31 percent: We will take 28 percent as a representative estimate.[8]

[8]The data problem here is similar to problems encountered in the cost of capital calculations in Chapter 9: For a given period there is much, but relatively noisy, daily data; on the other hand, getting enough points to use monthly data involves going back to time periods that may no longer be relevant. A common compromise is to use weekly data. At the end of this section we will do a sensitivity analysis on the volatility to see its impact.

will be converted into 40 ($= 1,000/25$) shares. The conversion terms may change (in a predetermined manner) over the life of the bond. For example, debentures often specify conversion prices that gradually rise over the life of the convertible bond. In such cases we should explicitly consider prematurity conversion even when the firm doesn't pay dividends to avoid the rise in the conversion price. The technical aspects of how this is done (typically, with numerical analysis techniques) are beyond the scope of this chapter, and the interested reader should consult specialized books on the valuation of derivative securities.[9] Here we discuss the valuation of convertible bonds with a single (predetermined) conversion price.

The contractual terms of convertible bonds, besides specifying the conversion terms, specify the terms of the basic security—the bond. The basic bond may be of many types, such as a "plain-vanilla" fixed coupon bond, a zero coupon ("pure discount") bond, and a variable-rate bond. *The valuation of the bond component of a convertible bond is like the valuation of any other bond.* It essentially follows these steps:

* Assess the default risk of the bond. This gives the appropriate rating and lets you estimate the appropriate risk-adjusted yield to maturity (RAYTM).
* Discount the promised payments of the coupon and the principal at the estimated RAYTM.

The value of the straight-bond component is often referred to as the **straight-bond floor.** The idea is that even if the value of the conversion option falls to zero, the value of the convertible bond cannot fall below the PV of the bond part. The term, however, is somewhat of a misnomer: The value of the conversion option tends to approach zero when the value of the firm's assets falls well below the face value of the bond. In this case, however, the probability of default *on the bond principal* is nonnegligible, which causes the value of the bond part to fall as well. So the "floor" may fall from under the feet of the holders of the convertible bonds.

The valuation of the bond component of convertible bonds has been described in detail in Chapter 11, and therefore will not be discussed here again. Instead, we let PV(B) denote the PV of the bond part and focus on the conversion option, which is what distinguishes a convertible bond from an otherwise equivalent straight bond.

The *conversion option* embedded in convertible bonds is similar in many ways to a warrant—it is an option that is written by the corporation allowing bondholders to buy from the issuing firm shares for a prespecified price during a prespecified period. The main difference between a warrant and this conversion option is that *upon the exercise of the conversion options convertible bondholders don't pay cash to the corporation.* Rather, holders of convertible bonds give up their right to have their bond principal repaid in return for shares in the issuing company. Thus, in the valuation of convertible bonds:

---

[9]A good starting place is the discussion in John C. Cox and Mark Rubinstein, *Options Markets,* Prentice-Hall, Englewood Cliffs, N.J., 1985.

- As in the valuation of warrants, we need to take into account the dilution of existing shareholders' claims on the value of the conversion option.
- Unlike the valuation of warrants, however, we don't adjust the value of the firm for infusion of cash.

Technically, this means that we value the conversion option as an option on a fraction of the total value of the firm, while we keep the exercise price at the full value given up upon the conversion—the full face value of the converted bonds.

In our valuation illustration we keep the assumptions that the conversion option is European and that no dividends are expected until the bond's maturity. We keep the notation used in the valuation of warrants, modified appropriately:

V = *total* value to be divided between convertible bondholders and shareholders

m = number of shares outstanding

n = number of shares into which the bonds can be converted

$\alpha = n/(n + m)$, the fraction of the firm that convertible bondholders will own if they convert their bonds

The parameters n and α reflect the contractual terms of the convertible bond. Specifically, denote the number of convertible bonds outstanding by k, the face value of each bond by F, and the conversion ratio by c—the number of shares that each bondholder receives upon conversion. (Note that by using these definitions, we find that the *conversion price* equals F/c). The number of new shares to be issued upon conversion—n—is simply the product of the number of shares into which each bondholder can convert by the number of bonds outstanding:

$$n = c \cdot k$$

We can rewrite α as

$$\alpha = \frac{c \cdot k}{c \cdot k + m}$$

The cost of conversion is the face value of the bond since this represents the cash flow that bondholders will not receive if they choose to convert—$k \cdot F$. Note that since V—the value of the whole firm—already includes the value of the convertible bonds, there will be no cash infusion upon conversion so that we don't have to adjust the exercise price as we did in the case of options. By using the B&S formula, we can value the conversion option, denoted by CO, as

$$k \cdot CO = B\&S[\alpha \cdot V, k \cdot F, r, t, \sigma_V]$$
$$= \alpha \cdot V \cdot N(d_1) - k \cdot F \cdot e^{-rT} \cdot N(d_2)$$

where σ_V is the standard deviation of the return on V (defined and discussed below) and d_1 and d_2 are given by

$$d_1 = \frac{\ln\left(\dfrac{\alpha V}{kF}\right) + \left(r + \dfrac{1}{2}\sigma_V^2\right)T}{\sigma_V\sqrt{T}}$$

$$d_2 = d_1 - \sigma_V\sqrt{T}$$

Note that CO is the value of the conversion option *per bond*. To get the *per-share* value of the conversion option, we divide CO by c—the number of shares into which each bond can be converted.

The same problems that we pointed out regarding the use of the B&S formula in the valuation of warrants apply here:

• The B&S formula is less accurate in valuing long-term options than in valuing short-term options, which means that the accuracy of the B&S pricing of the conversion option becomes less accurate as the time to maturity of the bond increases.

• The B&S formula is less accurate in valuing deep-out-of-the-money options relative to its accuracy in pricing at-the-money options. Unfortunately, most convertible bonds are issued with conversion terms that, at issuance, are deep out of the money.

• To apply the B&S formula, we need an estimate of the volatility of the return on the *whole* firm—σ_V. These return volatilities are often harder to estimate than the return volatilities of stocks since the assets often include nontraded securities, such as bank loans and privately placed preferred stock.

A further point, which is an expansion of a fact made concerning the valuation of warrants, has to do with the question: "What is V?" The generic answer is that V is the *common* value to be shared by convertible bondholders and shareholders. Specifically, *V doesn't include the value of any cash flow that accrues exclusively to one party*. In particular, we should deduct from V the PVs of:

• *Dividend payments* expected until the conversion day since they are paid exclusively to the *existing* shareholders

• *Interest payments* until the conversion day since they are paid exclusively to convertible bondholders.

Once the value of the conversion option is estimated, the value of the convertible bonds is simply the sum of the value of its two components—the straight-bond component, which we denote by PV(B), and the conversion option, which we denote by CO:

$$CB = CO + PV(B)$$

Many convertible bonds are also callable: The issuing firm may call the bonds at a predetermined price during a predetermined period. The ability of issuers to call bonds makes the maturity day of such bonds uncertain and dependent on the issuers' decisions. Issuers benefit by calling outstanding debt when interest rates are lower than they were at the issue time. If the bond is also convertible, issuers benefit by calling outstanding bonds when such a call can force conversion of the bond, which happens when the conversion option is in the money: Calling a convertible bond effectively eliminates the remaining life of the conversion option. Since calls benefit issuers when they take place, callable bonds are worth less than otherwise identical noncallable bonds; the difference in value between a callable bond and an otherwise identical noncallable bond is the value of the call option. Valuing these call options, the exercise of which may depend on the level of interest rates, is beyond the scope of this book.

12.5   AN ILLUSTRATION OF A CONVERTIBLE BOND VALUATION

We illustrate the valuation of convertible bonds by using data about the convertible bond of Home Depot (HD). We construct this as an exercise, which means that many of the real-world complications in this case are assumed away. In particular, the capital structure of HD includes more than just the stock and the convertible bond that we value. To simplify, we assume that the convertible bond and the shares are the only two securities that HD has issued.

In a typical valuation we would start by valuing the whole company and proceed by dividing this value among the different security classes. Since in this chapter we focus on the division-of-value part, we take the market value of the outstanding securities *as if it were our estimate of the total firm value* and proceed to examine how this value should be divided. An alternative interpretation of what we do in this example is to say that we agree with both the market's assessment of the total value of the firm and the market's assessment of the value of the claims that are senior to the convertible bond and the shares. Thus, all that has to be done is to allocate the remaining value (whose stochastic properties we assume satisfy the assumptions of the B&S formula) between the shareholders and the convertible bondholders.

On February 16, 1994—the date of our valuation—the prices and quantities outstanding of the stock and the convertible bond of HD were:

Security	Number outstanding	Unit price	Market value, $ million
Shares	451.93 million	$39.875	$18,021 (95.0%)
Convertible bonds	805.0 million	$ 1.183	$ 952 (5.0%)
Total value			$18,973

Thus, in our example there is $18,973 million to be divided between the convertible bondholders and the shareholders; we refer to this as the *combined value* to be shared between bondholders and shareholders. The division of this combined value begins with the valuation of the convertible bonds; the value of the shares is then derived as the residual value.

The terms of HD's convertible bond are:

- $1,000 face value
- Maturity on February 15, 1997
- 4.5 percent semiannual coupon rate
- Convertible into 25.8067 shares

The conversion ratio, which implies a conversion price of $1,000/25.8067 = $38.75, is the result of the initial conversion ratio and the stock dividends and adjustments that followed stock splits that HD has gone through since the bond's issuance. This is a common feature of convertible securities: Their terms specify conversion ratios that adjust when a stock split or a stock dividend occurs. If this were not the case, shareholders could make the conversion option worthless by repeatedly splitting the stock, thus making the price of the stock as low as they wish and always below the conversion price.

The HD bond that we value is callable. The bond can be first called on February 15, 1995, at a price of $101\frac{1}{8}$ percent of par. How likely is it that the bond will be called? Since the price of HD's stock today is higher than the conversion price of $38.75, we conclude that a call on February 15, 1995, is highly probable.[10] This simplifies our example: Although a full analysis of the joint options—to convert and call—is beyond the scope of this section, current prices make the latter option virtually certain. Assuming that *it is certain* that the bond will be called (which will force bondholders to convert their bonds to stock), it is possible to value the HD bond as if it matures on February 15, 1995, instead of the latter maturity date specified in the indenture.

As with the valuation of any convertible security, we begin with a valuation of the basic security: First we value the bond component of the convertible bond by discounting the coupons par value at a YTM that is appropriately adjusted for the default risk of the HD bond. HD's bond is rated A− by S&P and A1 by Moody's. By using the tools described in Chapter 11, we might take the route of analyzing the risk of the HD bond and assign our own rating to the bond. In this example we take the easier route—assuming that this rating appropriately reflects the default risk of the HD bond. By using the table of yield spreads (relative to the YTM of treasury securities) and the rating category given in Chapter 11, we estimate that the appropriate (i.e., rating-adjusted) spread for HD is 1.2 percent. The YTM of the Treasury note with 1 year to maturity on February 16, 1994, was 3.9 percent.

---

[10]It appears that firms are slower to call than theory suggests: Theoretically, convertible bonds should be called as soon as the conversion option becomes in the money; firms, however, call convertible debt when the stock price is as high as 40 percent above the conversion price. Thus, although a forced conversion of HD's bond in 1995 is likely, it is not certain.

This gives us an RAYTM for HD's bond of

$$\text{RAYTM}_{\text{HD}} = 3.9\% + 1.2\% = 5.1\%$$

By using this rate, we can discount HD bond's promised payments—a coupon of 2.5 percent of par in one-half year and par plus the last coupon in a year. The promised payments and their PVs, expressed in percent of par, are shown in the following table:

Date	Aug. 15, 1994	Feb. 15, 1995	Total
Payment	2.250	102.250	
Discount factor	0.975	0.951	
Present value	2.194	97.288	99.483

Thus, the value of the bond part of the convertible bond is 99.483 percent of par. For the aggregate amount of convertibles outstanding—$805 million—the value of the bond part is $800.838 million.

Next we value the conversion option. Since each $1,000 bond can be converted to 25.8067 shares, the $805 million convertible bonds outstanding can be converted to 20.77 million shares. Upon conversion, these 20.77 million new shares will be

$$\alpha = \frac{20.77}{20.77 + 451.93} = 4.39\%$$

of HD's equity. Thus, upon conversion the convertible bondholders become entitled to 4.39 percent of the *combined* value.

What is the combined value shared by stockholders and convertible bondholders? To determine this value, we start with the *total current value* of the outstanding securities—$18,973 million. From this value we deduct the value of the *exclusive* cash flows: the interest that only bondholders receive and the dividends that only shareholders receive. In our example the exclusive cash flows are the 4.5 percent interest on the bond; one-half this interest is to be paid in 6 months and the other half will be paid in 1 year.

The present value of the dividends that shareholders of HD will receive prior to the bonds' conversion is slightly more problematic to determine: The dividend policy of firms depends on the success of the firm, and when convertible securities exist, the dividend policy may also depend on the conversion policies of the convertible security holders. Again, HD is a rather simple case to consider: The last dividend paid by HD before February 16, 1994—the day on which the analysis is done—was $.03 a share. This is a very small dividend payment relative to the value of the stock, so even if HD *doubles* its dividend payment in the next year (a rare event in dividend policies of firms), the effect on the combined value is small. In our valuation we assume that HD will raise its dividend to $.04 per share per quarter, and we discount the four dividend payments until the bond's expected call is at the bond's discount rate—5.1 percent. This gives us the following combined value (in million dollars):

Total value of assets	$18,973
Present value of interest	(43)
Present value of dividend	(70)
Shared value	$18,859

Now we can determine the value of the parameters of the B&S formula for the value of the conversion option. First, the value of the underlying asset for the conversion option (CO) is an α-fraction of the shared value:

$$\alpha \cdot \text{shared value} = 4.39\% \cdot 18,859 = \$828 \text{ million}$$

The exercise price is the aggregate face value that the convertible bondholders will give up if they convert—$805 million. The volatility needed to value the conversion option is the volatility of the return on the shared value (currently $18,859). In our example, since both claims against this value—shares and convertible bonds—are publicly traded, we can calculate the historical returns on the shared value by

$$r_t^{\text{value}} = \left(\frac{N \cdot P_{t+1}^{\text{shares}} + F \cdot P_{t+1}^{\text{c. bonds}}}{N \cdot P_t^{\text{shares}} + F \cdot P_t^{\text{c. bonds}}} \right) - 1$$

for each period (denoted by "t"). We then estimate the volatility of the return on the shared value by the standard deviation of these return series. For HD the annual volatility of the return on the shared value estimated from the return history in the month preceding February 16, 1994, is 36 percent. Finally, the continuously compounded 1-year risk-free rate is 3.9 percent.

We now calculate the total value of the conversion option on the k convertible bonds:

$$k \cdot \text{CO} = \text{B\&S}[S = 828, X = 805, r = 3.9\%, T = 1, \sigma_V = 36\%]$$

$$= 828 \cdot N(d_1) - 805 \cdot e^{-0.039 \cdot 1} \cdot N(d_2)$$

The value we obtain for the conversion option is

$$k \cdot \text{CO} = 828 \cdot 0.6441 - 805 \cdot e^{-0.039 \cdot 1} \cdot 0.5037 = \$143.82 \text{ million}$$

This is the value of the conversion option *in aggregate*—for all the convertible bonds. This sum represents 17.9% ($= 143.82/805$) of the face value of the bonds. The *total* value of the convertible bonds ($k \cdot \text{CB}$) is the sum of the value of the bond part ($k \cdot \text{PV}(B)$) derived above and the conversion option ($k \cdot \text{CO}$) derived from the B&S formula:

$$k \cdot \text{CB} = k \cdot \text{PV}(B) + k \cdot \text{CO} = \$800.84 + \$143.82 = \$944.66 \text{ million}$$

Dividing by the face value of the bonds outstanding—$805 million—we get a price of 117.35 percent. This is somewhat lower than the market price of the bond—118.3 percent.

Having estimated the value of the convertible bond, we can get the value of the stock by deducting the value of the convertible bonds—$944.66 million—from the total value of the firm—$18,973 million—and by dividing the residual value by the number of shares outstanding—451.93 million:

$$P_{stock} = \frac{18,973 - 944.66}{451.93} = \$39.891$$

which, not surprisingly, is also close to the market price of the stock ($39.875).

Recall that in our analysis we assumed that it is virtually certain that the bond will be called in February 1995. How does this assumption affect our valuation of the convertible bonds? The assumed certainty of the call means, in our context, that we assign a zero probability that the conversion option will remain alive after February 15, 1995. In fact, there is some chance (although small) that the holders of the convertible bonds will be able to hold on to the conversion option beyond February 15, 1995. Thus, the correct value for the convertible bond is slightly higher, and accordingly the correct value of the stock is slightly lower than the values that we determined.

SUMMARY

In this chapter we discussed the valuation of convertible securities. Having valued the firm as a whole and deducted from it the value of the firm's debt securities (as the most senior claims), we proceed to divide the remaining value between convertible security holders and equity holders. We do so by valuing the convertible securities using tools of valuation of derivative securities and by valuing the equity holders' claim as a residual.

Ordinary options such as calls or puts on stocks priced by the B&S formula are contracts between investors who are *unrelated to the corporation whose stocks are the underlying assets* of the options. Accordingly, the B&S formula assumes a *given stochastic process* for the price of the underlying stock, a process that is independent of the exercise decisions of the option holders. This is not the case with convertible securities: Convertible securities are issued by the firms whose stock is the underlying asset of the convertibles. Thus, with convertible securities we have to adjust the B&S for the potential effects entailed by the involvement of the issuing firm in the transaction. Specifically, we need to consider:

- Possible infusion of cash to the firm upon conversion
- Potential dilution of existing claims upon conversion
- Interim cash flows such as dividends and interest payments paid before conversion

We have suggested a trick to make the adjustment of the B&S formula for these potential effects intuitive: Work in aggregate. For example, under the aggregate approach to the adjustment:

• We value convertible securities as *options on the firm's assets* rather than as options on shares.

• We consider the *total* exercise price (to be paid by *all* convertible security holders) rather than the exercise price per security.

• We derive the *total value* of the convertible securities rather than the value per security.

We have illustrated the adjustment of the B&S formula to price two kinds of commonly issued corporate securities—warrants and convertible bonds. In the case of a warrant there is no basic security to value so that the value of warrants (such as executive stock options) equals the value of the option to buy *from the issuing firm* a predetermined number of shares, during a predetermined period, for a pre-determined price. Under the aggregate valuation approach we view warrants as rights to buy an α-fraction of the firm's assets. The value of the underlying security is, therefore, $\alpha \cdot V$, where V is the current value of *all* the firm's assets and the volatility is the volatility of the return on the assets (not on the stock!), which we denote by σ_V. Finally, since the exercise price of warrants is *paid to the issuing firm,* the exercise price paid to the nonwarrant-holder shareholders is only $(1 - \alpha) \cdot E$, where E denotes the *aggregate* exercise price of the warrants.

In the case of convertible bonds the basic security—a bond—is valued like any other bond by discounting the promised coupon and face value payments at a risk-adjusted yield to maturity (RAYTM). The conversion option, as in the case of a warrant, is also viewed as an option on an α-percent of the firm's assets (with the same current price of the underlying asset and volatility). Unlike warrants, however, since there is no money paid to the firm, the exercise price is the full face value given up by convertible bondholders upon conversion.

EXERCISES

12.1 Using the Black and Scholes (B&S) formula, determine the value of an option to buy one share of Intel in 3 months for a price of $60 if Intel's current stock price is $55, the volatility of the return of Intel's stock price is 40 percent, and the risk-free rate for 3 months is 8 percent (annualized). What is the hedge ratio (HR) of this option? To what will the option value change if Intel's stock rises by $1? Answer the last question in two ways—once by using the HR of the option and again by recalculating the B&S formula.

12.2 The ABC Co. has 100 shares and 40 warrants outstanding. Today is the expiration day of the warrants. On this day each warrant holder may buy one share for an exercise price of $5. The value of the firm prior to the exercise of the warrants is $1,000. Suppose all the warrants are exercised.

    a What is the value of the warrants?

    b What is the value of the shares?

    c What would happen to the price of the shares from the day just prior to the warrants' exercise to the following day?

12.3 Consider two bonds that are issued by the same firm, having the same seniority, the same maturity day, and the same coupon rate. Both bonds are convertible to the same number of shares but one of them is callable at par 2 years prior to maturity, whereas the second bond is not. Which bond is more valuable to investors? Why?

12.4 The CVB and the SB companies are identical in all respects except for their capital structures. SB has a capital structure comprised of common stock and a 5-year straight bond. CVB has a capital structure comprised of common stock and a 5-year convertible bond. The market values of the securities of the two companies on May 7, 1995, were

SB	Equity	$100,000	*CVB*	Equity	$100,000
	Debt	$150,000		Convertible	$150,000

On May 8, 1995, the *aggregate* value of the securities of *both* companies rose from $250,000 to $275,000.

a What do you expect has happened to the price of CVB's convertible bonds? Why?

b In percentage terms, which equity price changed by more? Why?

CHAPTER 13

VALUING EQUITY CASH FLOWS DIRECTLY

OVERVIEW

Throughout this book we have derived the value of all the firm's securities by using a sequential valuation method. As far back as Chapter 3, we noted that there is an alternative method of valuation: If we are primarily interested in estimating the value of the firm's shares, we could discount the equity cash flows directly. We believe (and we will restate our reasons for this below) that this direct valuation of equity is in most cases inferior to the seemingly more roundabout sequential method of valuation. Nevertheless, this method has its advocates. In this chapter we discuss the implementation of direct valuation of equity.

First we remind you of the essentials of the sequential valuation technique, which we prefer:

• We discount the firm's projected Free Cash Flows (FCFs) at their weighted average cost of capital (WACC) to get the *aggregate* value of all the firm's securities—debt, equity, and any other financial assets.

• We then divide this total value among the various security holders by valuing each of the firm's securities according to its contractual rights. At the bottom of the list there is the residual security, the firm's equity.

In the direct valuation of equity we discount the firm's equity cash flows at their risk-adjusted discount rate (RADR)—the *cost of equity*—to arrive directly at a value estimate for the equity. The basic steps in this valuation method are the following:

• Project the future performance of the firm by building a pro-forma model. Use this model to project the *future expected equity cash flows*. (The definition of these cash flows is somewhat different from the expected dividend stream. This topic is discussed in the next section.)

• Discount the future expected equity cash flows and the terminal value of equity at the appropriate RADR—the cost of equity.

13.1 WHAT ARE EQUITY CASH FLOWS?

Throughout this chapter we assume that the firm has only debt and equity as long-term securities. Adjustments for preferred stock are obvious. If, on the other hand, the firm has convertible securities, the direct equity valuation method is inapplicable and so we have to use a sequential valuation instead. We start with a basic definition: *The equity cash flow is the firm's FCF minus all the cash needed to service Debt*:

Definition of Equity Cash Flow

Free Cash Flow

− Net repayment of Debt principal

− After-tax interest payments on Debt

Returning to our definition of Free Cash Flow (see Chapter 2), we see that this is equivalent to:

Definition of Equity Cash Flow

Profit after Taxes

+ Depreciation

− Changes in Net Working Capital

− Changes in Fixed Assets at Cost

− Net repayments of Debt principal

By "net repayments of Debt principal" we mean the net decrease of Debt: If the firm repays $100 of bonds but issues $300 of new Debt, then the net repayment of Debt is −$200.

Equity cash flows are not just the expected dividend stream of the firm. They include *all* the cash available for equity holders. This means that our valuation of equity is *independent of the dividend stream.* This is a well-known proposition in finance, first expounded by Miller and Modigliani (M&M). In their 1961 *Journal of Business* article M&M show that, under certain conditions, the payment of dividends merely reduces by an equal amount the value of the remaining equity claim.[1] In other words, an extra dollar of dividends is one less dollar of capital

---

[1]Merton H. Miller and Franco Modigliani, "Dividend Policy, Growth and the Valuation of Shares," *Journal of Business,* October 1961.

gains for the shareholders, which indicates that shareholders neither gain nor lose from the payment of dividends. Essentially, our definition of equity cash flows follows this article by valuing the equity of the firm independently of its dividend payout policy (as long as changes in dividend policy don't affect the firm's investment and other financial policies).

A word of warning: You have to be very careful how you interpret the M&M "dividend irrelevance" theorem. The M&M theorem shows that the firm's dividend policy doesn't affect the value of the firm or the value of its securities if the following conditions hold:

- Taxation of dividends and capital gains is the same. If the taxation on capital gains is lower than the taxation on dividends, shareholders should prefer lower dividends and greater capital gains. In the United States the effective taxation on capital gains is, in fact, lower than the tax imposed on dividends; nevertheless, American companies pay impressive amounts of dividends.[2] Much academic energy has been devoted to trying to resolve this apparent paradox.

- The firm's investment policy doesn't depend on the firm's dividend policy. All the pro-forma models in this book implicitly make this assumption by modeling the assets needed to produce the firm's sales *independent of the firm's financial policies.*

- The dividend payout policy doesn't affect the firm's debt financing mix, or, if dividends do affect the firm's financing, then the Debt has no effect on firm valuation. In the language of this book, if

$$T = 1 - \frac{(1 - t_e) \cdot (1 - t_c)}{1 - t_d}$$

is the net effect of all taxes on the value of the firm (see Chapter 8), then if dividends affect the firm's leverage, they will also affect the firm's value unless $T = 0$.

- All investors are equally well informed about the prospects of firms. If this is not so, then some investors may use the firm's dividend policy to deduce information about the firm's prospects.[3]

These are important "ifs," and they are not always present in every case. M&M argue that, in perfect capital markets, the payment of dividends merely means that money moves from one pocket ("value of the firm's stock") to another pocket ("dividend checks"). In frictionless capital markets this movement of potential dividend money from one pocket to another will have no effect on the valuation of a share.

---

[2]This is not always true in other countries. Germany and Canada, to name just two countries, give the recipient of a corporate dividend a tax credit for the corporate taxes paid on dividends. This lowers the effective personal tax rate on dividends, and in many cases nullifies it altogether.

[3]There is an extensive literature on the information content of dividends; this literature is summarized in Laurie S. Bagwell and John B. Shoven, "Cash Distributions to Shareholders," *Journal of Economic Perspectives,* 1989, vol. 3, pp. 129–140.

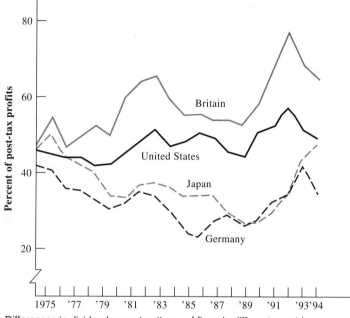

FIGURE 13.1   Differences in dividend payout patterns of firms in different countries. (*Source:* Datastream; *The Economist,* June 4, 1994, p. 114.)

Clearly the M&M theory is not the whole story. For example, M&M cannot explain the differences in the dividend payout patterns of firms in different countries, as illustrated in Figure 13.1. In 1993 British firms paid shareholders, on average, 69 percent of their post-tax profits. American firms paid out 51 percent, whereas German and Japanese companies paid only just over 40 percent of their profits.

Newer theories in finance suggest that dividend policy is determined by differences in the relative taxation of dividends and capital gains, differences in the way information is communicated to investors, and differences in contractual arrangements among the various suppliers of capital to the firm.

13.2 EQUITY CASH FLOWS: SOME EXAMPLES

If a firm follows a specific financing policy, we can be more specific about what goes into the Equity Cash Flow. In this section we discuss some important cases.

Debt Is a Plug

Consider a firm whose incremental financing in a particular period is done with Debt. This means that in this period the firm neither issues equity nor buys back equity. It also means that if the firm has excess cash flows, it uses these flows to pay down debt, and if it has additional financing needs, it floats new debt to meet these needs. In the modeling language of Chapter 4, we model the firm's balance sheet by assuming that Debt is the "plug." *If Debt is a plug, then the equity cash flow equals the dividend paid out by the firm.* Since for any firm the change in Assets equals the change in Liabilities, we obtain:

$$\Delta \text{Liabilities} = \Delta \text{Assets}$$

A little simple substitution gives the following equation:

$$\Delta \text{Current Assets} + \Delta \text{Fixed Assets at Cost} - \Delta \text{Accumulated Depreciation}$$

$$= \Delta \text{Current Liabilities} + \Delta \text{Debt} + \Delta \text{Stock} + \Delta \text{Accumulated Retained Earnings}$$

Since Δ Accumulated Retained Earnings equals Profits after Tax (PAT) less Dividends (Div) and since the change in Accumulated Depreciation equals the annual Depreciation charge in the income statement, Δ Accumulated Retained Earnings = PAT − Div. Thus we can write the preceding equation as:

$$- \Delta \text{NWC} - \Delta \text{Fixed Assets at Cost} + \text{Depreciation} + \Delta \text{Debt} + \text{PAT} - \text{Div} = 0$$

The Equity Cash Flow equation thus becomes:

Equity Cash Flow

$$= \text{PAT} + \text{Depreciation} - \Delta \text{NWC} - \Delta \text{Fixed Assets at Cost} + \Delta \text{Debt} = \text{Div}$$

This result involves a very simple intuition: When Debt is the plug (i.e., the firm neither issues new equity nor repurchases equity), the Equity Cash Flow is the dividend payment. You have to be careful in interpreting this scenario. A firm which has excess cash flows, and which consistently applies these flows to paying down debt, may ultimately pay off all its debt and begin to accumulate cash reserves. Although firms can build up considerable balances of Cash and Marketable Securities, these balances belong to the shareholders. If you expect that these cash balances will eventually be distributed to the shareholders, in the form of either dividends or share repurchases, you will want to add incremental cash balances to the dividends. Dividends are the equity holders' cash flows only if there are no share repurchases and the firm does not accumulate cash (or marketable securities) for possible *future* share repurchases.

Equity Is the Plug

Consider the case of a firm whose incremental financing is made with the following financing pattern:

• Debt is kept at a constant level—Δ Debt = 0. This means that whenever debt matures, it is refinanced with a new debt of identical value.

- All incremental financing comes from issuing new Stock and all incremental excess cash is used either to buy back shares or to pay dividends: That is, Stock is the balance sheet "plug."
- The firm's balances of Cash and Marketable Securities don't change over time.[4]

For this case, which we will call the case where "Equity is the plug," *the Equity Cash Flow equals the firm's FCF minus the after-tax interest payments.* This follows directly from our definition of the Equity Cash Flow when we substitute ΔDebt = 0:

$$\text{Equity Cash Flow} = \text{FCF} - \Delta\text{Debt} - (1 - t_c) \cdot \text{interest}$$

$$= \text{FCF} - (1 - t_c) \cdot \text{interest}$$

For this case the M&M dividend theorem means that a change in the dividend is exactly counterbalanced by a change in the Stock issued or repurchased:

- If the firm pays relatively small dividends, leaving it with excess equity cash flows, it will also repurchase stock. These Stock repurchases are part of the Equity Cash Flow.
- If the firm pays larger dividends than the Equity Cash Flow, it will need to issue new stock.

In both cases *the sum of the dividends plus the Stock issued (or repurchased) will be constant and equal to the Equity Cash Flow.* Miller and Modigliani originally focused on this case, showing that unless differential taxation of dividends and capital gains is an issue, shareholders should be indifferent to the split-up of the equity cash flow.

No New Stock Issued

This is the most common financial modeling scenario: Some of the firm's Cash is used to pay down Debt and the remainder is used to pay dividends or is retained as Cash and Marketable Securities. For this case the Equity Cash Flow is defined by

$$\text{Equity Cash Flow} = \text{Dividend} + \Delta\text{Cash} - \Delta\text{Debt}$$

For this case note that the M&M dividend theorem means that a change in the dividend is exactly counterbalanced by a change in the firm's Cash balances or a change in the firm's net issuance of Debt. We leave the proof of this case to you. (Note that it is a slight generalization of the case where Debt is the plug.)

---

[4]We remind you that from the point of view of the firm Cash is just "negative Debt." Therefore, requiring a firm to have no changes in Debt means that ΔDebt $- \Delta$Cash = 0.

13.3   VALUING THE EQUITY CASH-FLOW STREAMS—TWO EXAMPLES

Now that the concept of the Equity Cash Flow is clear, we use a simple pro-forma model to illustrate the method of direct equity valuation. In this particular model the firm sets a *target Debt/Equity (D/E) ratio* of 30 percent in terms of book value (see Exhibit 13.1, which is based on Model 3 in Chapter 4).

Exhibit 13.1

Initial Sales	2,500					
Annual Sales growth	6%					
Current Assets to Sales	25%					
Current Liabilities to Sales	8%					
Net Fixed Assets to Sales	70%					
Cost of Goods Sold (COGS) to Sales	55%					
Interest rate	7%					
Dividend payout ratio	85%					
Depreciation rate	10%					
Corporate tax rate	40%					
r(U)	20%					
Year	0	1	2	3	4	5
		Profit and Loss				
Sales	2,500	2,650	2,809	2,978	3,156	3,346
COGS		(1,458)	(1,545)	(1,638)	(1,736)	(1840)
Interest		(37)	(39)	(42)	(44)	(47)
Depreciation		(239)	(278)	(322)	(372)	(428)
Profit before Taxes		916	946	976	1,004	1,030
Taxes		(366)	(378)	(390)	(401)	(412)
Profit after Taxes		549	568	585	602	618
Dividend		(467)	(483)	(498)	(512)	(525)
Retained Earnings		82	85	88	90	93
		Assets				
Current Assets	625	663	702	744	789	836
Fixed Assets						
At cost	2,050	2,394	2,784	3,225	3,722	4,283
Accumulated Depreciation	(300)	(539)	(818)	(1,140)	(1,513)	(1,941)
Net Fixed Assets	1,750	1,855	1,966	2,084	2,209	2,342
Total Assets	2,375	2,518	2,669	2,829	2,998	3,178
		Liabilities and Equity				
Current Liabilities	200	212	225	238	252	268
Debt	502	532	564	598	634	672
Equity						
Stock	1,541	1,559	1,580	1,605	1,635	1,669
Accumulated Retained Earnings	132	214	300	387	478	570
Total Liabilities and Equity	2,375	2,518	2,669	2,829	2,998	3,178
Target Debt/Equity ratio	30%	30%	30%	30%	30%	30%

The next extract from our spreadsheet model (see Exhibit 13.2) derives the Free Cash Flow (FCF) and the Equity Cash Flow for the firm on a year-by-year basis.

Exhibit 13.2

Year	0	1	2	3	4	5
		Free Cash Flow				
Profit after Taxes		549	568	585	602	618
+ Interest after taxes		22	24	25	27	28
+ Depreciation		239	278	322	372	428
− Change in Net Working Capital		(26)	(27)	(29)	(30)	(32)
− Change in Fixed Assets at Cost		(344)	(390)	(440)	(497)	(561)
Free Cash Flow (FCF)		441	453	464	473	482
		Equity Cash Flow				
FCF		441	453	464	473	482
− Interest after taxes		(22)	(24)	(25)	(27)	(28)
+ Change in Debt		30	32	34	36	38
Equity Cash Flow		449	461	473	483	491

In order to determine the value of the firm through direct valuation of the equity cash flows, we have to determine the RADR for the equity cash flows. In doing this, we make a number of assumptions:

• We assume that the correct RADR for levered equity cash flows is given by the Chapter 8 formula when $T = 0$:

$$r_e(L) = r(U) + [r(U) - r_f \cdot (1 - t_c)] \frac{D}{E}$$

The cost of equity is constant since the D/E ratio is constant. Note, however, that this formula was derived for the case of no growth in FCFs, and is being used here as an approximation.

• We assume that at each date the book value of the Equity and Debt are close enough to their market values so that we can use them in the D/E portion of the preceding formula. This heroic assumption is necessary to be able to value Equity directly in this case. Whereas for Debt this is a rather trivial assumption, this is almost surely *not* the case for the value of the firm's Equity.[5] However, any other procedure for determining the market value of equity on a year-by-year basis is impossibly complicated (this is another good reason to prefer sequential valuations, in which this problem doesn't arise).

• We assume that $r(U) = 20\%$.

• We assume that the terminal value of Equity is determined by

---

[5]The equity value in any year should be the discounted value of all the equity cash flows from that year forward. Implementing this circular relation between the equity discount rate and the equity value in a pro-forma model is almost impossible.

Terminal Equity value =

$$\frac{\text{year 5 Equity CF} \cdot (1 + \text{long-run Equity CF growth})}{\text{year 5 } r_e(L) - \text{long-run Equity CF growth}}$$

We assume that the long-run Equity Cash Flow growth rate is the average of the annual growth rates in the model—2.28% per year.

Given this battery of assumptions, and by using midyear discounting, we can do our direct valuation of Equity (see Exhibit 13.3).

Exhibit 13.3

Valuing the Equity Directly

Year		1	2	3	4	5
Equity Cash Flow		449	461	473	483	491
Long-run growth rate	2.28%					
Risk-adjusted discount rate (RADR) for Equity		24.74%	24.74%	24.74%	24.74%	24.74%
Terminal value of Equity						2,237
Equity Cash Flow + Terminal value		449	461	473	483	2,729
Discounted at Equity RADR		402	331	272	223	1,009
Equity Value	2,237					

We can even run a check on this valuation by comparing it to the results of a sequential valuation (see Exhibit 13.4).

Exhibit 13.4

Year	0	1	2	3	4	5	
Free Cash Flow (FCF)		441	453	464	473	482	
Growth rate	2.21%						
Terminal value	2,824	= Year 5 FCF * (1 + average FCF growth) / (r(U) − FCF growth)					
PV of FCFs at r(U) = Value of Firm	1,373						
PV of Terminal Value	1,135						
Total Value of firm	2,747						
Equity = Firm value − year 0 Debt	2,245						

As you can see, the results of the two valuations are very close. The differences are caused by the fact that we have used cost of capital formulas from no-growth, infinitely lived models to do the valuation job in our pro-forma framework, in which cash flows are projected to grow.

Cash as a Plug

To see some of the complications that might arise in reality even for this simple case, we redo the example with some minor parameter changes and one major change in assumptions:

- We assume that both Stock and Debt are fixed, and that any cash generated by the firm goes into a Cash and Marketable Securities account. As explained in Chapter 4, this means that the *net Debt* of the firm is balance sheet Debt *minus* the Cash and Marketable Securities account. In economic terms we are saying that since the Cash could be used to repay Debt, the effective Debt of the firm is less than what appears on the balance sheet.
- The dividend payout ratio has been reduced to 75 percent and we differentiate between the interest paid on Cash and Marketable Securities balances (7 percent) and that paid on Debt (8 percent).

This model results in the set of pro-forma financial statements presented in Exhibit 13.5.

Exhibit 13.5

Initial Sales	2,500					
Annual Sales growth	6%					
Current Assets to Sales	25%					
Current Liabilities to Sales	8%					
Net Fixed Assets to Sales	70%					
Cost of Goods Sold (COGS) to Sales	55%					
Interest rate on Debt	8%					
Interest rate on Cash	7%					
Dividend payout ratio	75%					
Depreciation rate	10%					
Corporate tax rate	40%					
r(U)	20%					
Year	0	1	2	3	4	5
		Profit and Loss				
Sales	2,500	2,650	2,809	2,978	3,156	3,346
COGS		(1,458)	(1,545)	(1,638)	(1,736)	(1,840)
Interest on Debt		(56)	(56)	(56)	(56)	(56)
Interest on Cash		11	12	12	11	11
Depreciation		(239)	(278)	(322)	(372)	(428)
Profit before Taxes		908	941	973	1,003	1,032
Taxes		(363)	(376)	(389)	(401)	(413)
Profit after Taxes		545	565	584	602	619
Dividend		(409)	(424)	(438)	(451)	(464)
Retained Earnings		136	141	146	150	155

Exhibit 13.5 *continued*

Assets						
Cash and Marketable Securities	157	163	166	165	160	150
Current Assets	625	663	702	744	789	836
Fixed Assets						
At cost	2,050	2,394	2,784	3,225	3,722	4,283
Accumulated Depreciation	(300)	(539)	(818)	(1,140)	(1,513)	(1,941)
Net Fixed Assets	1,750	1,855	1,966	2,084	2,209	2,342
Total Assets	2,532	2,680	2,834	2,994	3,158	3,328
Liabilities and Equity						
Current Liabilities	200	212	225	238	252	268
Debt	700	700	700	700	700	700
Equity						
Stock	1,500	1,500	1,500	1,500	1,500	1,500
Accumulated Retained Earnings	132	268	409	555	706	861
Total Liabilities and Equity	2,532	2,680	2,834	2,994	3,158	3,328

Even if we are willing to make the assumption that balance sheet numbers reflect market values, calculating the cost of equity involves using the *effective* Debt/Equity (D/E) ratio:

$$\text{Effective D/E ratio} = \frac{\text{Debt} - \text{Cash and Marketable Securities}}{\text{Stock} + \text{Accumulated Retained Earnings}}$$

We employ the effective D/E ratio in the same formula for $r_e(L)$ that is used in the previous example. The cash flows and Equity valuation are given in Exhibit 13.6.[6]

Exhibit 13.6

Year	0	1	2	3	4	5
Free Cash Flow (FCF)						
Profit after Taxes		545	565	584	602	619
+ Net Interest after taxes		27	27	27	27	27
+ Depreciation		239	278	322	372	428
− Change in Net Working Capital		(26)	(27)	(29)	(30)	(32)
− Change in Fixed Assets at Cost		(344)	(390)	(440)	(497)	(561)
Free Cash Flow		441	453	464	473	481
Equity Cash Flow						
FCF		441	453	464	473	481
− Interest after taxes		(27)	(27)	(27)	(27)	(27)
+ Change in Debt		0	0	0	0	0
Equity Cash Flow		415	426	437	447	454

[6]A careful reader might ask, "If we assume that $T = 0$, why is the Equity value different when Debt is the plug from its value when Equity is the plug?" As we proved in Chapter 8, this shouldn't be the case. The reason this happens is that the formulas for the equity RADR are valid when the firm employs *constant* leverage and can only serve as *approximations* for cases where leverage changes over time. Alas, this is the best we can do with existing finance theory.

Exhibit 13.6 *continued*

Valuing the Equity Directly						
Year		1	2	3	4	5
Equity Cash Flow		415	426	437	447	454
Average growth rate	2.31%					
Effective Debt/Equity ratio		30.38%	27.99%	26.03%	24.48%	23.30%
Risk-adjusted discount rate (RADR) for Equity		24.62%	24.25%	23.96%	23.72%	23.54%
Terminal Value of Equity						2,190
Equity Cash Flow + Terminal Value		415	426	437	447	2,644
Discounted at Equity RADR		371	308	256	212	1,021
Equity Value	2,168					

Note that there is a consistency problem that is evident in the ratios: The effective D/E ratio is declining over time; given the same ratios and enough time, it will ultimately turn negative.[7] Although negative effective D/E ratios are not uncommon (meaning simply that the firm has more Cash and Marketable Securities than it has Debt), it would appear that ultimately a firm in this position would rethink its financing policies.

13.4   WHY NOT USE A DIRECT VALUATION?

Although from the preceding example it seems that we can do a workable direct valuation of equity, we believe that there are a number of reasons to prefer the sequential valuation procedure:

• In many cases the cash flows to the equity holders are difficult to predict. This is especially true when the more senior claim holders have *contingent* rights to cash flows. For example, debt holders may have floating interest cash flows [e.g., floating-rate debt with interest pegged to the London Inter-Bank Offer Rate (LIBOR)]. Another example: Convertible bondholders may receive interest payments, or they may not, if they convert their bonds to stock. Besides making the interest payments uncertain, this also dilutes the existing shareholders' claims to future cash flows. In many of these cases the *value* of senior securities can be determined even though their expected cash flows are difficult to estimate.

• In many valuations the discount rate with which to discount the equity holders' cash flows cannot be determined until the value of the firm is estimated. To see how this may happen, consider a privately held firm that we want to value. We can estimate the competitors' weighted average cost of capital (WACC) and use the average industry's WACC as the estimated WACC of the firm that we want to value. Suppose now we want to discount the equity holders' cash flows at the equity holders' RADR. We need to convert the estimated WACC to an estimated

---

[7] Our cost of equity formula implies that the cost of equity for a firm with a *negative* leverage ratio will be *less* than $r(U)$!

cost of *equity* capital. To do that, however, we need to know the *leverage* of the firm, but the leverage depends on the as yet unknown values of the equity and debt (or, alternatively, the values of the firm and the debt).

• If the firm has convertible securities, we cannot determine the relative value of the equity and convertible securities without knowing the *total value to be shared* by convertible holders and stockholders: To value derivative securities, we begin with the total value and calculate the value of the conversion option based on the conversion terms of the security. The value of the equity claim is the *residual value.* Thus, when the firm has convertible securities, the value of the equity altogether *cannot* be directly estimated by discounting the expected equity cash flows at an equity RADR.

Thus, the seemingly long way of sequential valuation is often actually the simplest and fastest way (or even the only way) to estimate equity values. Nevertheless, you can use the direct valuation technique for equity, if you feel comfortable with the additional assumptions that are necessary to make it work. The table in Exhibit 13.7 makes explicit the similarities and differences between the two methods:

Exhibit 13.7

A Comparison of Sequential Valuation of Equity to Direct Valuation of Equity

Sequential valuation of equity	Direct valuation of equity
Analyze the economy and the industry to project Sales.	Same
Analyze the firm's operating aspects by using financial ratios. Project costs and investments commensurate with the projected Sales. The end result is pro-forma statements that emphasize the operating aspects of the firm. The cash flows estimated are Free Cash Flows (FCFs)—cash flows that belong to *all* security holders of the firm.	Besides projecting the operating aspects of the firm, *project the financial aspects of the firm,* such as capital structure, dividend policy, and use of excess cash. Pro formas emphasize both the operating and financial aspects of the firm. The cash flows estimated are the *equity holders'* cash flows.
Estimate the firm's risk and weighted average cost of capital (WACC). Since the cash flows discounted in this approach are the FCFs, the discount rate should reflect the risk of capital of *all* sources.	In accordance with the difference in the projected cash flows—CF^{equity} instead of FCF— the appropriate discount rate is the *equity* risk-adjusted discount rate (RADR).
To check the discounted cash flow (DCF) valuation of the firm, use multiples as an alternative valuation method. In selecting matching firms, match the *operating* aspects of the industry's firms to those of the firm being valued. In estimating average multiples, use *whole-firm* multiples [such as Total Value to earnings before interest and taxes (EBIT)].	Use *equity* multiples to check the *equity* value arrived by discounting the equity's CFs. In selecting matching firms, besides matching operating aspects, *you need to match leverage.* In estimating average multiples, use *equity* multiples, such as Price to earnings per share (EPS)—P/E.
Analyze the risk of the firm's debt securities to value the Debt and divide the remaining value between the convertible security holders and the stockholders as residual claimants.	These steps are not needed in this approach.

SUMMARY

In this chapter we have shown how to calculate the value of the firm's equity by the direct discounting of the equity cash flows, defined as the difference between the FCF and all the payments to debt holders. The equity cash flow is equivalent to the dividend stream only for the case where the firm uses Debt financing as a plug. When the firm follows other financing policies, the equity cash flow includes both the dividend and the financing components.

The formula given in Chapter 8 for calculating the leverage-adjusted cost of equity can be used in a direct valuation of the equity cash flows. Provided you carefully follow the steps in valuing the equity directly [you should take into account the effect of (possibly changing over time) capital structure on the equity cash flows and on the equity RADR], you should obtain the same value for the equity of the firm by using either method. It is important to remember, however, that there are strong arguments as to why the long way to valuing equity may actually be the simpler, shorter, and more accurate way.

EXERCISES

13.1 In this exercise you are asked to construct the model in Exhibits 13.1 through 13.3. Having done this, do the following sensitivity analysis of changing the target Debt/Equity ratio to 10, 20, and 50 percent. For each Debt/Equity ratio calculate

  a the equity value.

  b the cost of equity.

  c the average growth rate of the equity cash flows.

  (Before you do this exercise on a spreadsheet, ask yourself the following questions: When does the Debt/Equity ratio increase? What do you *expect* will happen to the equity value, the cost of equity, and the average growth rate of the equity cash flows? Can you explain your qualitative results by reference to the theory presented in Chapter 8?

13.2 Take the model you developed in problem 13.1, but with one variation: Let Stock be the plug and assume that Debt is constant at its year 0 level of 502. Do a sensitivity analysis of the equity value on the growth rate of Sales.

  a Why does the year 0 equity cash flow *decrease* as the growth rate of Sales increases?

  b What happens to the value of the equity when the Sales growth increases?

  c For any given Sales growth, why does the cost of equity decrease between years 1 and 5?

13.3 Go back to problem 13.1, and make the following changes: Assume that the firm sets a *dividend growth rate* instead of a *dividend payout ratio*. Initially you can assume that this growth rate is 3 percent. Assume that the year 1 dividend is 472. Does a change in the dividend growth rate affect the equity cash flows or the equity valuation? Explain.

13.4 Repeat problem 13.3, assuming this time that Debt is the plug and that Stock is fixed. Assume that the year 0 levels of Debt, Stock, and Accumulated Retained Earnings are 500, 1543, and 132, respectively.

  a Does a change in the dividend growth rate affect the equity cash flows?

  b Does a change in the dividend growth rate affect the valuation of equity? Can you explain your result in terms of the analysis of Chapter 8?

14

FINAL REMARKS

OVERVIEW

In this chapter we summarize the process of estimating the value of a firm and its securities and reflect on some general principles.

Throughout this book we have set forth an approach to valuation that is *integrated, consistent,* and *implementable*:

• *Integrated* means that at every stage in the valuation we have considered the whole firm. No matter which firm security we are valuing, we remain aware of the interactions between the operating and the financing aspects of the firm. Integrated financial modeling necessitates an understanding of the interactions between the firm's sales and the efficiency (in terms of asset use) with which these sales are produced. It also requires us to understand the interactions between the operating and the financing sides of the firm.

• The valuation of the firm must not only be internally consistent (in the integrated sense of the previous paragraph), but it must also be *consistent with financial theory.* Our understanding of financial theory, although far from complete, has made enormous leaps forward in the past two decades. We understand much more today about the determination of the cost of capital, the interactions between leverage and the cost of capital, and the valuation of risky securities than we did in the 1960s. A consistent valuation approach must incorporate this theoretical financial framework, insofar as the theory has computational implications for valuation.

• We have insisted throughout this book that our recommendations for valuation should be *implementable*: We have tried to recommend only valuation methods that can be effected by a professional who has access to information about both the firm and financial markets. This means that we have excluded those parts of financial theory that cannot be translated into numbers and values.

In this way we have put forward a valuation approach that is understandable to both the finance professional and the finance academic.

14.1 HOW TO VALUE A FIRM?

From the valuation point of view a firm is a "black box" into which we put cash ("investments") in the hope of receiving even more cash in the future. The value of a firm, therefore, is the price that we are willing to pay *today* for the *expected cash flows* to be received in the future. The key elements in valuing firms (as well as their securities or any other asset) are:

• Estimating the expected future cash flows by using pro-forma financial statements
• Assessing the risk of the expected cash flows and matching them to an appropriate risk-adjusted discount rate (RADR).

Our basic prejudice is that the best way to value a firm is to discount Free Cash Flows (FCFs), which are the business cash flows that can be distributed to *all* suppliers of capital, at the weighted average cost of capital (WACC), the average cost of total capital—capital obtained from *all* sources. This procedure will give you the current value of the *whole* firm, which then has to be split up among all the security holders of the firm: Debt, Preferred Stock, Convertible Securities, and Equity.

Although we think that discounting FCFs is the most general valuation method that has the strongest theoretical foundations, a frequently used alternative valuation method uses prices of similar firms; this is valuation with **multiples.** Multiple-based valuations, instead of trying to determine the appropriate price of the stock from first principles that relate risk and return, use observed prices (properly scaled) to value similar firms. We believe that multiples have much to recommend them. However, the indiscriminate use of multiples as a substitute for the difficult task of building pro formas, projecting cash flows, and discounting these cash flows is inappropriate: It simply leaves too many questions about the way that the firm operates and finances itself unasked. Multiple-based valuations are best viewed as sanity checks on the discounted cash-flow (DCF) value estimate.

In the preceding chapters we discussed the steps taken in a typical valuation. To value a firm, you need to take the following steps:

1 *Analyze the firm and its environment.* Information about the firm's environment and its operations is necessary to assess the prospects of the firm. We need information to form expectations about the firm's marketing prospects, which are eventually expressed as sales projections—quantities and prices—and that reflect the strategic decisions of the firm and its competitors. The Sales projec-

tions are matched with projections of costs and investments that are required to achieve the projected Sales. The conversion of Sales projections to projected costs and investments is often achieved with the help of financial ratios.

2 *Build a pro-forma model.* The expectations about the firm's marketing, production, and investment aspects are expressed in the form of a coherent set of projected financial statements—pro-forma statements. The pro-forma financial statements tie together the income statements, consecutive balance sheets, and cash-flow statements to the projected Sales, costs, and investments that reflect your view of the firm and its industry. Pro formas, by tying together all the facets of a firm into one integrated, recognized framework, impose a discipline on the evaluator and ensure that the projected parameters of the firm's future financial performance are internally consistent.

3 *Use your pro forma to derive the cash flows you are interested in discounting.* Of course, pro-forma models have many other interesting uses—sensitivity analyses and cash budgeting, for example. For valuation purposes, however, the bottom line of the pro-forma statements is the projection of the firm's Free Cash Flows. The pro formas ensure that the projected FCFs correctly and consistently reflect your views of the firm.

One important use of the pro formas is to estimate the firm's *terminal value.* The terminal value is often the largest single cash flow of the projection. It also, paradoxically, has the most uncertainty in it! We have shown you several ways to estimate terminal values. They are all highly imperfect, but this seems to be the nature of the valuation process:

a Estimate the terminal value of the firm by discounting all future expected FCFs. For a firm we can use the Gordon formula to discount an infinite stream of FCFs that are expected to grow in the long run at a constant rate:

Terminal value of whole firm $=$

$$\frac{\text{last projected FCF} \cdot (1 + \text{expected growth of FCFs})}{r(U) - \text{expected growth rate of FCFs}}$$

(For a project with a finite horizon you can use the finite horizon equivalent of the Gordon formula.) This is the method that most closely corresponds to our preferred method of valuation. Note that in order to use the Gordon formula, we need to estimate the *long-run* growth rate of FCF; this, typically, is not the same as the growth rate of the FCFs in the short run.

b Use average multiples for the firm's industry. For example, by using the industry average Price/Earnings (P/E) ratio, we can estimate the value of the firm's Equity as

Terminal value $=$ last projected earnings $\cdot$ industry average P/E

Similarly, other multiples (e.g., Market to Book (M/B), Market to Sales) can be used with the projected pro formas to estimate terminal values.

4 *Analyze the risk of the firm to estimate the RADR of the FCF.* The FCF and the terminal value have to be discounted at a discount rate that reflects the risk of the discounted cash flows—the risk of the expected FCF. This point is often forgotten: The discount rate reflects *the risk of the cash flows being discounted.* If, for example, as the chief financial officer of firm A you value firm B as part of a planned acquisition of B, the cost of capital with which you should discount firm B's FCFs is firm *B's* cost of capital, not the cost of capital of firm A.

We discussed several methods of estimating RADRs—from historical returns, market prices, and models of risk return trade-offs. All of these methods involve statistical assumptions that relate to the inference of the current expected return from past data. Therefore, we recommend the following:

a Use more than one method to estimate the cost of capital.

b Use data of several similar firms to avoid overreliance on one firm's data.

When discounting FCF, we must keep in mind that FCFs are *operating* cash flows, which means that they flow throughout the year. Therefore, you should use *midyear* discounting (not *end-of-year* discounting).

5 *Adjust the value of the all-equity firm for the effects of the firm's actual capital structure on the value of the* whole *firm.* We recommend using the adjusted present value (APV) approach in valuing firms. Under this approach we first value the *operating side* of the firm as if the firm were all equity financed. In the second phase the effects of leverage on the value of the firm is added to the "all-equity" value, denoted by V_U. To take into account *the effect of differential taxation of the Debt and Equity,* a firm using a *constant amount* of D dollars of debt financing is valued as

$$V_L = V_U + T \cdot D$$

where
$$T = \frac{(1 - t_d) - (1 - t_e) \cdot (1 - t_c)}{1 - t_d}$$

is the *net* tax effect of debt financing. T can be either positive, negative, or zero, depending on the interaction of the corporate income tax rate, personal debt income tax rate, and personal equity income tax rates. Strong economic arguments suggest that T in equilibrium is roughly zero. If $T \approx 0$, the value of the firm is roughly independent of its capital structure.

6 *Use the scaled prices of similar firms to assess the reasonableness of the value estimate.* The alternative to discounting expected cash flows is to value firms by comparing them to similar firms. This method of valuation avoids the painful task of analyzing the long-run prospects of firms. Since similar firms are often of different sizes from the firm being valued, the prices of the similar firms are scaled. No theory exists for the appropriate scale to use so that several scales are often employed in this method—Earnings, Sales, Earnings before Interest and Taxes (EBIT), book values, and so on, which yield matching price multiples, such as Earnings multiples, Sales multiples, and EBIT multiples.

A very important aspect of valuation with multiples is the selection of a sample of comparable firms from which average multiples are estimated. Two conflicting objectives should guide you in selecting this sample:

a Select as large a sample as possible to minimize the effect that idiosyncratic aspects of the sample firms have on the average multiples and on the resulting value estimates.

b Select as small a sample as possible to maximize homogeneity of the sample firms and similarity to the firm being valued.

Clearly, if the firm that you value is unique (or is in a unique phase, is going through a unique transition, or so on), no sample of comparable firms may be found and the multiples method is inappropriate.

When you have followed the preceding steps, you will have derived the *value of the whole firm.* The next step in any valuation is to split the firm's value among the various claimants—debt holders, owners of convertible securities, and equity holders.

Valuing Equity Directly Rather than Sequentially

Throughout this book we have derived the value of all the firm's securities by using a sequential method of valuation, in which we first value the whole firm and then divide this value among the firm's securities. In Chapter 13 we have shown that there is an alternative to this seemingly roundabout procedure: We could discount the *expected stream of payments to equity holders* at the *equity holders' cost of capital* to value the firm's Equity *directly.* By using this direct valuation:

• We employ the pro-forma model to project the firm's *Equity Cash Flows* and terminal value of Equity.

• We discount these Equity Cash Flows at an appropriate *RADR for Equity.*

In Chapter 13 we have outlined a number of reasons that a sequential valuation process is preferred, *even if your ultimate goal is to value Equity.* Chief among these reasons is the fact that the sequential approach is actually simpler. However, if you employ a consistent approach to Equity valuation, the direct valuation approach will give you the same answer as the sequential valuation.

14.2 QUESTIONS WE ARE OFTEN ASKED

Q: How should we deal with nonoperating assets, such as excess Cash and Marketable Securities, in a valuation?

A: Our valuation method entails discounting FCFs at appropriate RADRs. Because FCFs are *operating* cash flows, this method yields a value estimate for the firm's *business*—the value of the assets in place plus the net present value (NPV) of expected investments employed in the firm's business. If the firm has nonoperating assets (besides its operating assets), *the value of the nonoperating assets should be added to the value of the business to obtain an estimate of the value of the whole firm*—operating and nonoperating assets together.

How do we value the nonoperating assets? One way would be to project the cash flows of the assets and to discount the expected cash flows at the RADR of the *assets.* Typically, that is not necessary! The reason we project and discount FCFs is that the business side of the firm is where value is created—the firm generates positive NPV in its line of business, the value of which we want to estimate. On the other hand, *nonoperating assets are effectively liquidity reserves that don't generate any positive NPV.* Hence, all we have to do is *to value such nonoperating assets at their current market price.*[1] Since generally accepted accounting principles prescribe recording such assets in the balance sheet at their current market value, we may find the value of assets that are held as liquidity reserves in the balance sheet of the firm.

Q: How far out do you go to predict pro-forma statements and cash flows?

A: The trivial answer is until the firm or the project that you are valuing ceases to generate cash flows. For some corporate finance problems, such as whether to purchase a new type of machine, or buy versus lease decisions, this may even be a practical answer. For most valuation problems, however, this is an impractical answer since firms have very long lives. (This is also true of many corporate decisions: Should we enter a new line of business? Should we abandon an existing line? Should we buy different machines from those bought to date?) In these cases, at some point, you stop making *specific annual projections* and represent the value of the remaining cash flows by a *terminal value.* In estimating terminal values, with either the Gordon formula or a multiple—of Earnings, cash flows, Sales, and so on—we implicitly assume that the long-run growth rate of FCF is constant. The assumption makes sense only when the firm is in a *steady state,* that is, when the fundamental characteristics of the industry and the firm are expected to remain constant. Therefore, the appropriate time to stop making specific projections of financial performance (i.e., pro-forma financial and cash-flow statements) is when you think it is reasonable to assume that the firm is in a steady state: At this point you may reasonably represent all remaining cash flows by a terminal value. To summarize: *Build specific pro-forma projections so long as you can say something* unique *about each year; when you expect the firm to enter a steady state, capture the value of the remaining FCF by a terminal value.*

Q: How do you estimate the terminal value for a high-tech company?

A: High-tech companies are especially difficult to value: The use of their products or services is frequently not as yet well defined (let alone understood), and the composition of their industry is often rapidly changing, with new suppliers entering the industry. This makes it difficult to project Sales and margins. Furthermore, their technologies are often not as yet fully developed, making it hard to project operating financial ratios. To compound these problems, many high-tech companies have very high growth rates, implying that the majority of their value is captured in the terminal value, about which we have the least knowledge.

---

[1]This procedure is also in conformity with the GAAP (generally accepted accounting principles), which prescribe writing the value of assets that are held as liquidity storage at their current market price.

We suggest that when valuing high-tech companies you should explicitly take into account the expected increase in competition in determining terminal values. One way to do this is to use a variant of the Gordon formula; two possible variations are:

• Calculate the terminal value by using a *negative* rate of growth for a one-product, high-tech firm. This procedure assumes that the product will eventually be superseded by better competitive products.
• Alternatively, calculate the terminal value of a high-tech firm by using a *positive* long-run growth rate of an *established* firm in an *established* industry. This assumes that the rate of growth in the high-tech industry will *eventually* stabilize at some slower, steady-state growth rate; it also assumes that the firm that you are valuing will find a way to keep its products competitive.

Instead of using the Gordon formula, you can estimate the terminal value based on an average multiple (of Earnings, Sales, or book value) of an established firm in an established industry and the last projected pro-forma financial statements.

Q: If you are calculating the WACC, how should you deal with convertible bonds, warrants, and other contingent liabilities?

A: When calculating the WACC, we average the after-corporate-tax expected returns of all the securities that the firm has issued, using as weights their relative market values:

$$\text{WACC} = \sum_{i=1}^{N} w_i \cdot r_i^{\text{after tax}}$$

where N = number of security types in the capital structure
w_i = weight of each security—its market value relative to the total market value of the firm
$r_i^{\text{after tax}}$ = *after-corporate-tax* expected return of security i.

The computation of the WACC is equivalent to the conversion of the risk estimates of individual securities under the capital asset pricing model (CAPM) to an estimate of the risk of the assets:

$$\beta_{\text{assets}} = \sum_{i=1}^{N} w_i \cdot \beta_i$$

where β_i is the after-corporate-tax beta estimate of each security.

If the firm has only Debt and Equity in its capital structure and the fraction of Debt in the capital structure (i.e., w_{debt}) remains fairly constant over time, the procedure is fairly simple: You can estimate from past returns either the average return of each security or the risk of the securities and average them into an estimate of the firm's WACC. This is not the case when convertible securities (such as convertible bonds and warrants) exist: By the very nature of these securities, their values, risks, and relative weights change continuously so that it is difficult to estimate their risk or expected returns from past data. This means that if we want to use statistical methods to estimate risks or expected returns, methods that implicitly assume that the parameters you estimate are *constant* over the estimation period, we should use a fairly short time interval from which to draw the data. Intuitively, for the statistical estimation to work *approximately,* we need an estimation period that is short enough so that we can comfortably assume that the risks of the firm's securities have not changed.

The estimation problem is often compounded by the fact that many convertible securities that firms issue are not publicly traded or are traded only infrequently. This means that we cannot apply statistical methods to all securities. In other cases, even if the convertible securities are publicly traded, it is not reasonable to assume that their risks are relatively stable, such as when a warrant is deep out of the money (see the discussion in Chapter 12). Yet in some of these cases we may reasonably expect that the risk of the *stock* is fairly stable (e.g., because the value of the convertibles is small relative to the value of the common stock).

It turns out that we can *approximately* convert the estimated risk of the common stock into estimates of the risk of the convertible securities. To discuss this approximation fully, we need some of the material covered in Chapter 12, but here is a brief nontechnical discussion of what can be done. Suppose we have just two securities in the capital structure, say, common stock and warrants (such as executive stock options). First we estimate the beta of the stock. (For the same reasons discussed earlier we may want to restrict our data to the most recent history of the stock price.) We then convert the stock's estimated beta into a beta estimate for the convertible security by using the relation

$$\beta_{\text{warrant}} = \frac{S}{W} \cdot \text{HR}_{\text{w/s}} \cdot \beta_{\text{stock}}$$

where S = price of the stock
        W = price of the warrant
        $\text{HR}_{\text{w/s}}$ = hedge ratio (HR) of the warrant price with respect to the stock price

The HR is a measure of relative risk: It measures how much the value of the warrant changes when the price of the stock changes by a dollar. (We discussed the HR in Chapter 12.)

Here is an example. Suppose the XYZ Corporation has 500,000 shares and 250,000 warrants outstanding. The shares trade for $25 each and the warrants trade for $4 each. You estimate that the beta of the stock is 0.8. By using the B&S formula discussed in Chapter 12, you can estimate the HR of the warrants with respect to the stock price to be 0.4. (An HR of 0.4 means that when the stock price rises by one dollar, the warrant price rises by approximately $0.4 \cdot \$1 = \$.40$.) By using these data, we can estimate the beta of the warrant to be

$$\beta_{warrant} = \frac{S}{W} \cdot HR_{w/s} \cdot \beta_{stock} = \frac{25}{4} \cdot 0.4 \cdot 0.8 = 2.0$$

The estimated beta of the *assets* of XYZ is the weighted average of the beta of the stock and the warrant:

$$\text{Value of firm (\$ thousands)} = \$25 \cdot 500 + \$4 \cdot 250 = 13,500$$

$$w_{warrant} = \frac{1,000}{13,500} = 0.0741$$

$$w_{stock} = 1 - 0.0741 = 0.9259$$

$$\beta_{assets} = 0.9259 \cdot 0.8 + 0.0741 \cdot 2.0 = 0.89$$

Undoubtedly, you will encounter many more problems in applying the principles of valuation discussed in the preceding chapters. For some of these questions you will find answers or approximate answers as you gain experience; and some questions are probably still unanswerable given the current knowledge and methods of finance and will have to await further developments.

SUMMARY

In this chapter we reviewed the process that we follow in valuing a firm and its securities. Our overall approach is:

- To examine the firm's environment—economywide and industrywide—in order to project the future sales of the firm
- To examine the way that the firm is operated to translate the marketing view of the firm (i.e., the sales projections) into full projections of financial performance expressed as pro-forma financial statements and to extract the firm's FCFs
- To analyze the risk of the firm's cash flows in order to estimate the RADR that is appropriate to discount the operating cash flows of the firm (FCF)
- To compare the value estimated by using the discounted cash-flow (DCF) approach to prices of similar firms that are publicly traded by using price multiples
- To divide the value of the whole firm among the security holders according to their contractual rights

An alternative to this sequential valuation approach is to value the firm's Equity directly by predicting the Equity Cash Flows and discounting them at an appropriate risk-adjusted equity discount rate. If you succeed in doing this while correctly taking into account the effects of firm leverage, the value estimate obtained from a direct valuation will be similar to that which you get from a sequential valuation.

INDEX